Beyond **Piggly Wiggly**

The University of Georgia Press   Athens

# Beyond Piggly Wiggly

## Inventing the American Self-Service Store

Lisa C. Tolbert

Some content was originally published by Lisa C. Tolbert in
"The Aristocracy of the Market Basket: Self-Service Food Shopping
in the New South," in *Food Chains: From Farmyard to Shopping Cart*,
edited by Warren Belasco and Roger Horowitz, 179–95. Philadelphia:
University of Pennsylvania Press, 2009.

Most University of Georgia Press titles are
available from popular e-book vendors.

Printed digitally

Library of Congress Cataloging-in-Publication Data

Names: Tolbert, Lisa C., author.
Title: Beyond Piggly Wiggly : inventing the American self-service store
    / Lisa C. Tolbert.
Description: Athens, Georgia : The University of Georgia Press, [2023] |
    Includes bibliographical references and index.
Identifiers: LCCN 2023006214 (print) | LCCN 2023006215 (ebook)
    | ISBN 9780820364421 (hardcover) | ISBN 9780820364414
    (paperback) | ISBN 9780820364438 (epub) | ISBN 9780820364445
    (pdf)
Subjects: LCSH: Self-service stores—United States—History.
Classification: LLC HF5429 .T64 2023 (print) | LCC HF5429 (ebook) |
    DDC 658.8/7—dc23/eng/20230412
LC record available at https://lccn.loc.gov/2023006214
LC ebook record available at https://lccn.loc.gov/2023006215

Lynn and David Holdzkom

# Contents

# Piggly Wiggly Timeline

| | |
|---|---|
| 1913 | Working as a wholesale salesman, Clarence Saunders persuaded twenty-one of his retail customers in Memphis, Tennessee, to form a cooperative chain called the United Stores. Each owner remained an independent operator. Saunders handled purchasing and advertising for the United Stores chain. |
| June 1913 | Saunders opened his flagship United Store in downtown Memphis on Jefferson Street between Front and Main. This operated as a cash and carry store based on traditional counter service. |
| September 1916 | Saunders redesigned his flagship United Store and reopened it as the first Piggly Wiggly. He called it "King Piggly Wiggly." |
| October 1916 | Saunders's second store, "Prince Piggly Wiggly," opened at the corner of Poplar and Dunlap in Memphis. |
| April 1917 | The first franchise outside of Memphis opened in Houston's City Market. |
| September 1917 | By the first anniversary of King Piggly Wiggly there were nine Piggly Wiggly stores in Memphis. |
| October 1917 | Saunders received his first patent for the Piggly Wiggly store interior. He began building store interiors in a warehouse at 461 South Front Street that also served as company headquarters. |
| April 1918 | *The Turnstile*, the Piggly Wiggly magazine for license holders, was inaugurated. |

| May 1918 | The first national Piggly Wiggly ad appeared, in *Collier's*. |
|---|---|
| August 1918 | Clarence Saunders, Leslie Stratton, and investors founded the Piggly Wiggly Corporation. The Piggly Wiggly Corporation board appointed Saunders president. |
| Summer 1918 | Piggly Wiggly franchises existed in forty cities. The Piggly Wiggly factory moved to Jackson, Tennessee. |
| 1919 | Saunders formed Piggly Wiggly Stores, Inc., issuing 150,000 shares of common stock that raised nearly $6 million, with the intention of buying up independently owned Piggly Wiggly franchise stores. Independently owned Piggly Wiggly franchise stores would always outnumber stores owned by Piggly Wiggly Stores, Inc. |
| November 1921 | Saunders opened self-service Piggly Wiggly Variety Store in old café of Peabody Hotel on Main and Monroe in Memphis. Piggly Wiggly Variety Stores opened in Nashville and Chicago, but the effort to expand self-service beyond grocery stores failed. Piggly Wiggly Variety Stores closed within a year. |
| February 1923 | Over twelve hundred Piggly Wiggly Stores were operating in forty-one states and two Canadian provinces. |
| August 1923 | Saunders was forced out of Piggly Wiggly in a stock scandal. |
| 1925 | Independent Piggly Wiggly franchisees and representatives of Piggly Wiggly Stores, Inc., formed the Piggly Wiggly Operators Association; 1,850 stores were operating in sixteen states (only 490 were owned by Piggly Wiggly Stores, Inc.). |
| 1926 | The Piggly Wiggly Operators Association began to raise money for a national advertising campaign that would appear in *Ladies' Home Journal*, *Saturday Evening Post*, and *Good Housekeeping* from 1927 through early 1933. |
| 1928 | Kroger bought Piggly Wiggly Stores, Inc., including the factory operation in Jackson, Tennessee. |
| 1929 | Safeway bought the 183 Piggly Wiggly stores in Los Angeles and expanded into other western markets as Safeway–Piggly Wiggly. |

| 1930 | Thirty-two hundred Piggly Wiggly stores were operating in over one thousand cities and towns. National Tea Company bought Piggly Wiggly stores in Chicago and integrated Piggly Wiggly as a specialized store format alongside its traditional counter-service outlets. |
| --- | --- |
| 1930s | Pigs wearing butcher hats replaced the turnstile as the chain's iconic symbol as Piggly Wiggly began to experiment with strategies for integrating fresh meat into the self-service store format. |
| 1937 | Safeway began closing Piggly Wiggly stores and smaller counter-service stores as the chain shifted to larger self-service supermarkets. |
| 1939 | Kroger sold its interest in Piggly Wiggly Stores, Inc., to Jacksonville, Florida, financier William R. Lovett. Lovett operated the parent company until his death in 1978. |
| 1982 | The Piggly Wiggly factory in Jackson, Tennessee, closed. |

# Preface

Piggly Wiggly 2.0

I finished writing this book during a global pandemic that upended retailing and consumer shopping habits. Reporters wrote about grocery stores as essential services during the time of crisis.[1] While journalists focused on new trends in shopping and wondered about stores of the future, what has resonated for me in these reports is their uncanny similarities to the past. Self-service stores first appeared and spread rapidly during the labor shortages created by World War I and a global flu pandemic. Optimism about technological solutions for improving the distribution system and reducing the cost of living fueled experimentation with new store designs in the 1920s. During the Great Depression, independent store owners transformed self-service stores into huge "super markets" that caught the most successful chain stores of the day by surprise. The economic dislocations that have accelerated disorienting changes in stores and shopping habits during the 2020 pandemic bring into sharper focus the pressures that produced the first self-service stores during the economic crises of the early twentieth century.

A look back at the roots of Piggly Wiggly is especially timely now, as retailers are using digital technology to experiment with store design to fundamentally change how shopping works. At first glance, our digital world controlled by mega corporations seems light years away from the world of small neighborhood grocery stores that shaped consumer experience a century ago. Yet our contemporary forecasts about stores of the future echo the kinds of conversations Americans were having in the early 1900s. Then, people concerned about inefficiencies in the food distribution system wondered, "Are there too many stores?" Now, with the expansion of online shopping, we question whether physical stores are necessary anymore. If they are, what purposes should they be designed to serve? Online retailing has also generated a return to in-store clerk service and to delivery, with expensive labor costs that chain stores worked hard to eliminate in the early twentieth century. Now clerks push hand trucks through supermarket aisles assembling the orders of online customers. They are sometimes called "pickers" to distinguish their work from shoppers selecting their own merchandise from the same grocery shelves. Warehouse fulfillment centers (sometimes ominously called "dark stores"), designed solely for servicing online orders, promise fast delivery or short-notice pickup times in densely populated areas. Some speculate that grocery chains may move toward a type of hybrid store in which shoppers submit most of their order online but shop in person for fresh produce or deli meats. One retail expert has suggested that robotics may become part of the "theater of the shopping experience" in which shoppers can watch machines that can fill fifteen thousand orders a day working behind the glassed-in center of the store space.[2]

Self-checkout machines have long been replacing supermarket clerks in the checkout line, but in 2017, almost exactly one hundred years after Clarence Saunders opened the first Piggly Wiggly store in Memphis, Tennessee, Amazon began to open a new kind of clerk-less store they called Amazon Go. Other experimenters soon followed Amazon's lead. In San Francisco the Standard Market opened, a nineteen-hundred-square-foot store with no cashiers but with twenty-seven cameras in the ceiling.[3] News coverage focused on the cutting-edge twenty-first-century innovations in artificial intelligence that made the automated systems work and presented the stores as radically new shopping experiences. But these efforts to change how stores work actually have deeper roots. Although the current generation of clerk-less stores may operate with more sophisticated robotic technologies, they are more or less just Piggly Wiggly 2.0. Here are some of the most striking similarities:

- *Small size and controlled entry.* The first Piggly Wiggly (1,125 sq. ft.) and Amazon Go (1,800 sq. ft.) stores were small, contained spaces, enclosed behind turnstile entrances, with a limited assortment of prepackaged goods.

- *Coordinated patented systems.* Like the patented Piggly Wiggly system, Amazon Go automated self-service with coordinated store fixtures. Patenting the technology was part of a larger plan to franchise the system.

- *Surveillance features.* Piggly Wiggly and other first-generation self-service stores engineered sight lines and included other surveillance features for monitoring customers. In Amazon stores, banks of cameras installed in the ceiling created a surveillance net to track customers as they move through the store. A smartphone app kept track of consumer purchases and charged accounts when customers waved their phones over the exit turnstile.

- *Clerk-less stores as oddities.* Like Piggly Wiggly, the first Amazon Go stores were tourist attractions, with customers lined up around the block for an opportunity to shop on opening day. They generated curiosity but also confusion. For customers trained from birth to circumnavigate regimented shopping aisles and line up to check out at the end of the trip, shopping in a cashier-less store is disorienting. One reporter said she felt "crippling indecision" in her first experience of shopping in a store with no cashiers.[4] Another observed, "At Amazon Go, checking out feels like—there's no other way to put it—shoplifting."[5] Such responses echo the reactions of the first generation of self-service shoppers who found self-service to be a discombobulating experience and worried they might be accused of stealing.

- *Capital intensive experimentation.* Self-service inventors promised to reduce store operating costs, but Piggly Wiggly grocery store interiors were among the most expensive to install in the early twentieth century. Today the patented technology for modern cashier-less stores costs an average of one million dollars for a store of less than two thousand square feet.[6]

- *Store spaces as laboratories for studying how customers use the system.* Just as Piggly Wiggly used franchised store spaces as laboratories for testing new retailing technologies, Amazon developed their tracking technology by franchising it to other retailers. Amazon studied customers using the stores to improve how their technology worked in different retail environments.[7] Amazon's vice president of physical retail and technology explained, "We observed areas that caused friction for customers, and we diligently worked backward to figure out ways to alleviate that friction."[8] He sounded very much like the original self-service store inventors who worked to eliminate what they called "congestion" points for customers in their store installations.

- *The checkout process.* Checkout has always been the biggest challenge for self-service store design. The first Piggly Wiggly patent was a failure because the design created huge bottlenecks in the checkout line. Amazon's technology is designed to eliminate the checkout line altogether. In the spring of 2022, Amazon extended its cashier-less store design to a twenty-one-thousand-square-foot Whole Foods supermarket in Washington, D.C. Now customers can sign in by scanning their palm instead of a smartphone. Hundreds of cameras track their route through the store while deep-learning software analyzes their shopping activity to ensure accurate charges. Electronic sensors embedded in the displays detect when shoppers lift an item from a shelf, freezer case, or produce bin. Amazon calls it a "Just Walk Out" store because you can skip a cash register and exit the store with another wave of your palm over the exit turnstile. The bill is automatically added to your Amazon account. Like the first generation of self-service stores, the checkout process is integral to the overall store design.

While the cutting-edge artificial intelligence technology has dominated news coverage as a driving force for change in retailing, the technological context obscures as much as it reveals. Surveillance may be pervasive and invasive in our digital world, but it was hardwired into the DNA of the original self-service stores. From the start they were, by definition, designed to automate control of workers and shoppers. The examples of the first generation of self-service stores you encounter in this book may look quaint compared to today's high-tech cameras and digital store systems, but in the early twentieth century they represented a visionary ideal of how shopping might someday work. They initiated the retail revolution on which Amazon's twenty-first-century clerk-less stores are built.

Beyond **Piggly Wiggly**

# Introduction

*Looking Backward*, Dreaming a Store of the Future

In Edward Bellamy's utopian novel *Looking Backward*, Bostonian Julian West falls asleep in 1887 and awakens in the year 2000 to find a city full of new technological wonders, including a new kind of clerk-less store where shoppers serve themselves.[1] It was more than a time traveler's tourist attraction. The self-service store had dramatically reduced the cost of living and resolved the inefficiencies of the distribution system in an industrial society. When Bellamy wrote the book at the end of the nineteenth century, no one had ever heard of a supermarket. The self-service store was a futuristic idea—a store for a new millennium.

Time traveler Julian West is astonished by the new methods of shopping he encounters in his first trip to the clerk-less store. In his Victorian world, city dwellers shopped for food daily, travelling to multiple stores—bakeries, butchers and fish mongers, the city market, and the grocery store to collect the ingredients for a day's meals. West is amazed to discover that the millennial store shoppers could find whatever they wanted under one roof. The store was a physical spectacle to behold and an engineering feat—a vast light-filled hall ringed by large glass windows, with an impressive dome rising a hundred feet above the open store floor. The furnishings and finishes were opulent. Frescoed walls decorated the space, and shoppers gathered on comfortable sofas and chairs to converse in the cooling mist of a huge fountain at the center of the hall. West is impressed but confused. He doesn't know how to find what he is looking for. In place of the forceful selling or product expertise of the human clerk, he has to follow signs around the space to identify the right counter to find what he needs. There are no aisles of open shelving. Customers inspect samples and read product descriptions, available at a counter, to make their shopping choices. Only then does a clerk appear at the counter to finalize the transaction.[2]

Bellamy's model for this store of the future was actually the most important retailing innovation of the nineteenth century. The lavish store interior he depicted resembled the extravagant department stores of the Victorian era.[3] Evoking their origins in the Industrial Revolution, department stores were the first retail spaces to be described as machines for selling. They were called department stores because the selling floor was organized into separate product divisions operated by clerks who served thousands of customers daily but had limited discretion in pricing or arranging goods. In 1876, department store entrepreneur A. T. Stewart reportedly described the workers in his huge Astor Place store in New York as "machines working in a system that determines all their actions."[4] While Stewart viewed the machinery of the department store as a personal achievement, Emile Zola's novelistic exposé of department store life in Paris decried the ways that the new retailing system converted workers into cogs in a machine.[5] But for all the rhetoric about department stores as machines for selling, human selling ability was nevertheless considered indispensable to store profits.

Even small stores needed sizeable teams of clerks to fill orders, wait on customers, and make deliveries. A study of the food-buying choices of thirty thousand shoppers by the *Chicago Tribune* in 1913 revealed that 55 percent of consumers were influenced by retailers, while only 36 percent were persuaded by advertising in making their purchases. "It is clear, therefore," economist Paul Nystrom concluded as a result of the *Tribune* investigation, "that the suggestion and salesmanship of the retailer was a powerful factor in introducing new articles to the customer."[6] Although clerk wages were typically one of the largest overhead expenses for store owners, it was hard to imagine being able to sell enough to make a profit if you hired fewer salesclerks. Somehow the store itself had to be designed in a new way to sell products automatically.

It didn't take a hundred years to invent a clerk-less store after all. In 1921 a group of students in a Chicago elementary school class built one out of fruit crates and construction paper for a social studies lesson about community life.[7] It was a very different kind of store compared to the cavernous, opulent millennial store Julian West had dreamed. The class was working on a lesson about how communities were organized, and their teacher began by asking them to identify the different kinds of buildings a town should have. The children listed a fire station, a church, a bank, and a grocery store. Once their list was complete, the teacher set the young students to work, instructing them to craft their structures and organize them along a residential street and a business street. Without apparent prompting, the children made their

FIG. 1. Teacher Isabel Robinson's innovative social studies lesson in 1921 used free experimentation and dramatization to help her kindergarten students build a miniature town at the University Elementary School of the University of Chicago. The structures were made of fruit crates covered with craft paper. Their Piggly Wiggly store included self-service shelves, a window display of packaged products, and entry and exit turnstiles. *Source:* Parker and Temple, *Unified Kindergarten and First-Grade Teaching*, 148.

grocery a Piggly Wiggly store. Piggly Wiggly had been open in Chicago for about two years by the time these kindergarten architects crafted their version. Significantly, it was the only store the children identified by proper name. The new self-service chain used advertising in unprecedented ways to build a national brand identity, promoting its unfamiliar self-service shopping experience as a distinctive selling point. The students recognized that Piggly Wiggly was not like other stores. They blocked the front door with a homemade turnstile—the gear that turned the self-service machine.

It is fitting that Piggly Wiggly should emerge in a social studies lesson about community organization. The students located it right next to the fashionable department store on the business street rather than on the residential street where their neighborhood grocery would typically be found. In a food retailing landscape dominated by hundreds of thousands of neighborhood grocery stores on residential streets, self-service stores carved out a distinctive place in communities across the United States. The children revealed more than they realized about relationships between consumption and social formation. Ultimately, self-service was more than a business decision; it was a fundamentally new social practice.

Though self-service stores stood out as unusual when they first appeared, they are not well represented in retailing history. Godfrey M. Lebhar, editor in chief of *Chain Store Age*, wrote that self-service was a "revolutionary idea in food retailing" that predated the advent of the supermarket. Nevertheless, he devoted only a footnote to the topic in his 1952 history of chain stores, focusing exclusively on Piggly Wiggly innovations.[8] In many ways, self-service stores are still invisible in the history of American commercial architecture, submerged in the histories of chain stores and supermarkets.[9]

*Beyond Piggly Wiggly* reveals the importance of Piggly Wiggly as the most influential self-service store of the early twentieth century and goes beyond the history of a single firm to explore the role of small-business entrepreneurs who invented the first self-service stores. When Piggly Wiggly began selling franchises in 1918, *The World's Work* magazine described it as "an interesting and hopeful experiment," worth watching because it offered promising potential for reducing the high cost of living.[10] Franchisees built Piggly Wiggly into the only self-service chain with a national distribution network before 1940, and the company's prolific use of advertising made it the most famous self-service store of the day. As the best documented self-service store, Piggly Wiggly has eclipsed the variety of experiments in self-service store design during the interwar years. Besides Piggly Wiggly there were small chains with names like Nifty Jiffy, Jitney Jungle, and Helpy Selfy that signaled the efficiency and novelty of the "serve yourself" practices customers would find inside the doors. The "M System Stores" got their name from the shape of the shelf arrangement that formed the self-service pathway. Self-service was not just a chain store invention. Independent entrepreneurs nationwide, like Robertson's Self-Serving Grocery in Dallas, linked their names to the modern retail systems they created inside their stores.[11]

Looking backward from our twenty-first century vantage point, self-service seems natural. From rolling a cart through the supermarket to buying clothes off the rack or filling your own gas tank, we simply take it for granted that self-service constitutes "shopping." But inventing the first self-service stores was a feat of imagination that required grocers to develop a completely new vision for how their stores might operate and convince their customers to cooperate in doing new kinds of unpaid labor. For centuries grocery stores were organized around counters where clerks, not customers, assembled merchandise, weighed or sliced bulk products, took payment, and wrapped items for customers to take home. The importance of counter service continued long after manufacturers started canning fruit and packaging cereal in standardized, branded containers.[12] In their efforts to automate various retailing processes, local grocers used trial-and-error methods of store arrangement. Their spatial experiments engineered new social relationships among workers, customers, and products. These inventors generated a wide variety of approaches to different kinds of challenges for implementing self-service, and their experiments represent an integral developmental stage in the invention of self-service retailing.

The dizzying variety of experiments is a testament to how hard it was to invent a self-service store that worked consistently everywhere. These diverse store arrangements nonetheless were all identified as self-service stores. Thus, before 1940 self-service stores represented a distinctive store type. The American self-service store was created in a local vernacular social process that fundamentally reconstituted how American consumption worked. The supermarket became the post–World War II model of American prosperity, an international emblem of the success of American capitalism, but it was not an inevitable outcome of self-service experimentation. *Beyond Piggly Wiggly* disentangles the origins of the self-service store from the histories of chain stores and supermarkets to recover its significance in the development of a mass consumer society. The first step is making the self-service store visible again.

## Learning to See the Self-Service Store

The invention of self-service retailing required widespread changes that involved multiple industries—from product manufacturers to store equipment suppliers. Historians of technology have studied a variety of specific artifacts in the complex history of automated selling. Victorian inventors tinkered with vending machines that automatically dispensed products with a coin dropped into a slot.[13] Cash registers automated accounting controls in small businesses in the late nineteenth century.[14] Consumer historians have documented the role of advertisers and brand name product manufacturers who promoted self-service as a strategy for direct appeal to customers that did not depend on the sales skills of retail merchants in neighborhood stores. Chain stores ultimately took advantage of mass-produced canned goods to systematize and standardize store displays, but a technological determinism infuses arguments that product packaging "made possible the self-service store, where customers could roam aisles, read labels, and choose items on their own."[15] Much as they might have liked, product manufacturers did not design the paths customers followed once they entered the store.

Scholars have primarily looked to chain store innovations to explain the origins of self-service practices inside stores. Woolworth is widely recognized as a pioneer of self-service innovation because by the turn of the twentieth century the variety chain used open display tables where customers could directly handle merchandise.[16] The open counter displays, however, were arranged around clerk service aisles where the staff monitored shoppers and collected payment in decentralized locations throughout the space. Woolworth was not a self-service store before World War II. When the company announced the first store conversion to a self-service format at its flagship store in New York in 1952, a worried company official reported, "We are trying it out to see how it works and how the public will respond."[17] Lawrence R. Robinson and Eleanor G. May, who studied self-service in variety stores during the 1950s, noted that self-service was not, in fact, a general practice in variety chains. Woolworth's tentative experiment with self-service in 1952 made it "the first store to be operated on a checkout basis by one of the major variety chains since the W. T. Grant Company had resorted to the use of that system during World War II."[18] By January 1956, only 435 of Woolworth's 2,065 stores had been converted to a self-service format.[19] In the early twentieth century, stores increasingly included open displays to encourage customers to serve themselves, but, like Woolworth, they were not understood as self-service stores. "Cash and carry" grocery stores cut overhead costs by eliminating delivery and credit services, required customers to come to the store to do their own shopping, and created product displays that encouraged customers to serve themselves. Business historians tend to present cash and carry stores as tantamount to self-service, but their daily operation methods still depended on clerks to assemble customer orders.[20] So what exactly was a self-service store?

In January 1916 *Illustrated World* offered a view inside one of the first self-service stores ever to be photographed—a small grocery store that had opened in Pomona, California, in 1915 (a full year before the first Piggly Wiggly store opened in Memphis).[21] It was a strange-looking place. You couldn't just walk right in. A turnstile controlled the separate entrance and

FIG. 2. One of the earliest photographs taken inside a self-service store. The Triangle Grocerteria opened on July 24, 1915, in Pomona, California, almost two years before the first Piggly Wiggly store opened in Memphis. The turnstile at the center foreground controlled entry and exit to the space. Though it was possible to see the entire interior in a glance, large handwritten signs directed customers to products they might be looking for around the store. *Source:* Cramer, *The Alpha Beta Story*, 9. Originally published in *Illustrated World*, January 1916.

exit. Big handwritten signs cluttered the space to help customers locate products and identify prices without asking a clerk. Albert Gerrard, inspired by the new "'wait-on-yourself' plan of [the] cafeteria," called his store the Triangle Grocerteria.[22] In his first arrangement, customers had so much trouble finding what they were looking for that the employees did not have time to stock shelves or check out customers, so he reorganized everything in alphabetical order—the "S" section included sardines, salmon, soups, and soap. A photograph of the unusual store accompanied an article explaining how it worked in *Illustrated World*, a science magazine that covered mechanical innovations for a popular audience. Though only a handful of shoppers appeared in the image, reporter Lee McCrae explained that "its turnstile had registered over five thousand in its first week." Remarkably, these five thousand customers were served by only three store clerks. At the exit, two women worked a checkout counter, where one rapidly sorted and listed the customer's packages and the other made change at the cash register.[23] *Illustrated World* covered the Triangle Grocerteria in its series on "oddities of life."

The first self-service stores worked as specialized retail systems that went far beyond displaying products on open shelving to offer unique physical and psychological advantages for automated sales. Arguing that his invention was a new apparatus for selling, Piggly Wiggly inventor Clarence Saunders became the first person to convince the U.S. Patent Office to approve a patent for a self-service store design in 1917.[24] The Patent Office went on to issue dozens of patents for self-service store designs over the next two decades. All modernizing grocers invested in new technologies with an emphasis on sanitation, electrification, and creating visually appealing displays to attract discerning customers newly alert to the role of germs and the dangers of adulterated food products. Self-service store inventors went beyond such cosmetic upgrades to profoundly change the way stores worked by organizing store spaces into systems for automatic selling. Their resulting configurations were ultimately patentable because they spatially systematized the management of store inventory, the surveillance of workers and customers, and the point of purchase at the checkout counter. Inventors used turnstiles, conveyor belts, turntables, monorails, market baskets suspended from cables, and other methods to move customers and products as efficiently as possible through the store. Only a few self-service stores were ever patented, but every self-service store embodied the idea of the store as a machine for automatic selling.

The self-service store was a machine that manufactured money. In his patent application, Saunders detailed the results of the same store space before and after it was converted to self-service as the most persuasive evidence that he had invented a new machine for selling. When the store was organized for counter service with clerks filling customer orders it sold $35,000 worth of goods in six months—a respectable performance for the time, comparable to a well-managed chain store. When Saunders eliminated counter service and organized the same store space for customers to serve themselves it produced $115,000 in sales in the equivalent six-month period. It also slashed operating expenses. The traditional counter-service operation had cost $5,800, while operating costs for the self-service store conversion totaled $3,400 over six months. With its increased sales and reduced overhead, the self-service store conversion nearly quadrupled store profits.[25] These results, Saunders reasoned, could never be achieved in a traditional counter-service store. It simply was not possible to serve enough customers under the same spatial and time conditions using counter-service methods. Meanwhile, on the busiest days in his self-service store five clerks could process the sales for twenty-five hundred customers. Given that sales over the six-month period averaged about $640 per day, the average sale per customer was less than fifty cents. Self-service store inventors were the alchemists of the machine age. Their machines turned pennies into gold.

Learning to see the self-service store requires connecting different kinds of sources. Store patents include floor plans that map customer pathways using arrows to indicate the direction of traffic through the space. Sometimes the stores they describe can seem whimsical and raise questions about whether the space was strictly conceptual or whether it was actually built. Meanwhile, there are myriad photographs of actual store interiors, but they do not always show a full view of the space, and it can be easy to overlook self-service systems in plain sight. L. E. Woods's IGA store in Lexington, Kentucky, looked the same as any other storefront from the street, and with a quick glance inside you might first think it was a small, old-fashioned mom-and-pop store. The local newspaper described L. E. Woods as an "experienced food merchant and one of the originators of the groceteria."[26] He did not patent his store arrangement, but it demonstrates the same principles of automating shopping documented by store patents.

Analyzing the store arrangement reveals how Woods organized his store fixtures to create a systematic customer pathway like the customer pathways marked by so many arrows on patented floor plans. He fenced in the selling space and instructed customers to pick up a basket from the bin before they entered the gate, just out of sight in the right corner of the picture. As visible in figure 3, he used display cabinets to restrict shoppers to a one-way path down an aisle running the length of the store. They had no choice but to follow the path all the way to the back of the space. Price tags were hung from the shelves so customers could easily find what things cost. At the back of the store the aisle opened up in front of the butcher counter where customers could gather to wait for service. The cash register at the front of the store defined the last point in the pathway where customers paid before exiting the retail space. The back of the store was screened by a lattice wall, beyond which may have been storage or office space out of view of customers. Patent rationales suggest that Woods and his clerks may have used the screened space as a vantage point for surveying customers on the retail floor.[27] Four years later Woods moved his store to a new location a few blocks away, and there is no

FIG. 3. L. E. Woods's Grocerteria, member IGA Stores, Lexington, Kentucky, on opening day, September 20, 1930. The sign in front instructs customers: "Our open shelves permit you to compare prices and make your own selections. Use our baskets." Customers could reach over and grab a basket as they entered the store. The fixture arrangement channeled shoppers down a long narrow aisle along the righthand wall. Low display shelving put products within arm's reach and enabled the clerk at the checkout counter across the room to monitor shoppers as they made their way down the aisle. Their pathway opened up onto a butcher concession at the rear left corner. The cash register on the front counter at the left marked the end of the self-service pathway. Customers exited the retail space through the swinging gate just past the cash register. *Source:* Lafayette Studios Photographs, Audio-Visual Archives, University of Kentucky Libraries, Lexington.

record of it after that.[28] Woods's Groceteria represents the grassroots origins of American self-service stores in the precarious small-business context of the early twentieth century. As many as half of the self-service stores built before 1940 were created by independent store owners like L. E. Woods.

Distinguishing specialized self-service stores from typical chain store operations is an essential step for building a more accurate understanding of the history of self-service retailing as a revolution in consumer capitalism. An emphasis on the role of chains and product manufacturers has left the impression that self-service retailing was a diffuse sales practice primarily generated through a top-down process of corporate innovation.[29] That perception is reinforced by the fact that the vast majority of scholarship about self-service has focused especially on mid-twentieth-century supermarket innovations.[30] Without a clear understanding of how store installations evolved, the self-service supermarket appears to be an inevitable outcome of chain store innovations that improved store efficiency and reduced overhead costs. The social history of inventing and implementing self-service is obscured.

Paul du Gay, who studied the impact of self-service in British retailing from the 1940s through the 1960s, argues that though scholars have made dramatic claims for self-service as a retailing revolution, few studies back these claims with empirical evidence of store operations. Instead, he argues, "the dominance of self-service is taken as a given because its innate economic logics are bound to make it the most efficient and effective system for maximizing the speed up of all retail operations and thus the turn over time of retail capital." On the consumption side, "an equally teleological set of arguments" explains the success of self-service in terms of consumer desire for autonomy and choice. "Either way, the question of how, practically, self-service changed the conduct of retail work and consumption remains unanswered."[31] Du Gay's argument that claims about self-service are both teleological and ahistorical also applies to scholarship about the history of self-service in the United States.

Piggly Wiggly routinely appears in scholarly accounts as a starting point for telling the history of the supermarket, but its small size and quirky features make it hard to connect to the large self-service stores of the mid-twentieth century. In his history of American grocery stores, James Mayo asserts that the Piggly Wiggly chain introduced a "radical store plan" that "revolutionized how stores were managed" but goes on to argue that "the coming of the supermarket was not so much a physical design revolution as it was an economic evolution shaped by business management, urban growth, and technological innovations."[32] Rachel Bowlby considers the significance of Piggly Wiggly in the invention of modern shopping but presents it as an alternative path—"a sort of Platonic idea of the supermarket that never was to be."[33] The revolutionary impact of the self-service store quickly dissolves into the functional inevitability of the supermarket without an empirical understanding of how stores actually worked. Scholars have not recognized the consequential distinction between the widespread use of open display techniques and the systemized arrangement of store fixtures that compelled customers to serve themselves.[34] Piggly Wiggly was not just another chain store, and it was not simply a small version of a supermarket.

## Evaluating Self-Service as a New Social Practice

*Beyond Piggly Wiggly* connects the first generation of self-service stores to the history of the supermarket through an empirical analysis of the distinctive physical store arrangements that automated self-service. I analyze how store designs were shaped by business principles of scientific retailing, the social politics and class dynamics of the retail space, and the race and gender systems of a culture of segregation. Empirical analysis of store arrangements demonstrates how small stores that have previously been overlooked or undervalued as quaint anomalies were integral to the creation of supermarkets.

Given the widespread renovation of obsolete store interiors on Main Street, it is no longer possible to analyze surviving store installations. The store patents included in this book all contain floor plans of store interiors as well as rationales for self-service design and, along with period photographs of store interiors, represent the best surviving evidence for studying the origins of self-service store design as the stores appeared to customers in their local contexts. Though store patents document a small fraction of the experiments in self-service grocery stores in the period, they offer important evidence of their inventors' design logic and the variety of problems they worked to address.

Physical description of store interiors alone is not sufficient to understand how they constituted a dramatically new social practice. My approach to studying these store spaces synthesizes methods of cultural history, geography, and the history of technology to evaluate self-service stores as a new spatial practice. Historians of technology have de-emphasized the role of the heroic inventor to evaluate the ways that inventions are socially produced.

As historian Thomas Hughes argues, technological systems are "both socially constructed and society shaping."[35] Scholarship in the history of technology focuses on how new technologies become integrated into the mainstream, including the importance of consumers in the sociological process of invention.[36] Because self-service depended so fundamentally on the cooperation of customers, the spatial challenges of store design document the social politics of consumption as well as entrepreneurs' business concerns. Self-service stores profoundly depersonalized the shopping experience compared to traditional counter-service stores. Their designers reconstructed power relationships between merchant and customer and between employer and employees. The space itself operated as an agent of change, transforming how consumers understood their role in the marketplace. It is crucial to consider not only how grocers experimented with different technologies and strategies for physically organizing store spaces, but also how self-service stores were symbolically represented and socially experienced by the first generation of self-service shoppers.[37] The cardboard Piggly Wiggly constructed by those Chicago kindergarteners is as important as Clarence Saunders's patent for evaluating the self-service store as a new social practice.

Automating shopping and store work processes was difficult, and the solutions were not obvious. There were a host of pragmatic and cultural challenges. Store inventors invested tremendous time and resources to make self-service retailing work from a practical point of view in daily operation with diverse customers. Shoppers understood the assembly of grocery orders as work that store clerks did for wages, not something they should do for free. Customers often found serving themselves to be more disorienting than liberating. Replacing human salesclerks with store fixtures and product packaging turned out to be a capital-intensive proposition. Coordinated self-service systems were often more expensive to install than traditional counter-service fixtures.[38] Though these machines for automatic selling promised greater profits over time, that investment did not appear to be worth it to the majority of grocers, including the most successful chains, who feared they would lose more customers than they could attract in the process of convincing them to serve themselves. Self-service stores had limited applicability in the grocery business throughout the interwar years.

*Beyond Piggly Wiggly* offers the first national perspective on the origins of self-service as a large-scale process with multiple regional clusters of experimentation. Because there was so much regional variation in the popularity of self-service, a singular focus on a local case study of stores in a particular town or city can offer misleading evidence about the origins of self-service. National patterns of store distribution show that self-service was simultaneously produced in urban and rural areas, complicating our understanding of the origins of mass retailing.[39] Evaluating the national scope of self-service experimentation, however, offers limited understanding of the social process of invention without a closer consideration of particular cultural contexts. An analysis of store interiors in the abstract, divorced from the different communities they served, can reinforce a homogenized interpretation of mass consumer culture as a standardized experience. But the dramatic regional variation in self-service experimentation demonstrates that this was not the case for American shoppers before 1940. Given the significance of Piggly Wiggly in the history of self-service, there has been surprisingly little consideration of the extensive experimentation with self-service in the South.[40] Connecting the southern Jim Crow origins of self-service to the national history of this mass retailing method shows that promoters of self-service linked their stores to a rhetoric of American democracy but that they were also built to serve systems of inequality.

This book is organized into thematic chapters with a chronological framework that explains different stages in the process of invention—from initial invention in the early twentieth century, and entrepreneurial experimentation during a developmental phase in the 1920s, to a final stage of invention during the Great Depression when the success of supermarkets marked a turning point in the history of self-service stores. Analyzing the physical store arrangements that operationalized self-service shopping, mapping the national distribution patterns of self-service stores, and reconstructing particular social contexts of self-service experimentation documents the complexities of inventing self-service as a regional vernacular process in the development of a mass consumer society.

Chapter 1, "Machines for Automatic Selling," explains how the first generation of self-service stores proliferated in the economic dislocations of World War I and argues that self-service stores evolved as a specialized form of retailing in the 1920s, distinct from the open display principles used in most modernizing grocery stores at the time. In the initial invention stage, vending machines and cafeterias were the most important influences in self-service store design.

Chapters 2 and 3 focus on the history of Piggly Wiggly from its founding in 1916 through its expansion into a national self-service chain during the 1920s. The eventual success of Piggly Wiggly as a corporate chain has obscured the grassroots invention process Clarence Saunders used to create his version of a self-service store. Chapter 2, "Inventing Piggly Wiggly, 1915–1923," focuses on how Saunders took a full year of experimentation, tearing out and rebuilding store interiors in a trial-and-error process with his Memphis customers, before his self-service system worked well enough to franchise. His struggle to secure a patent documents how Piggly Wiggly was ultimately understood as a machine for automatic selling. Saunders was ousted from the company in a stock scandal in 1923. Chapter 3, "Selling the Store, 1918–1933," focuses on how franchisees built Piggly Wiggly into a national self-service chain and used newspaper and magazine advertising in innovative ways to sell the store during the 1920s. Most Piggly Wiggly stores were owned by independent franchisees with five or fewer stores, not the central Piggly Wiggly Stores, Inc. The Piggly Wiggly Operators Association launched an unusual national advertising campaign in consumer magazines from 1927 to 1933. Historians have misinterpreted company ads as representative of consumer experience. A comparison of the physical Piggly Wiggly terrain and the symbolic landscape constructed in the chain's advertising reveals the distinctiveness of the self-service chain in consumer history.

Chapter 4, "Navigating the Self-Service Landscape, 1920–1940," takes a deeper look at the entrepreneurial phase of self-service store development. During this phase self-service stores developed through a large-scale national process driven by independent store owners and local or regional chains. Self-service stores were not simply created by chain store organizations and imported into the countryside. Local store owners built their own self-service arrangements in trial-and-error processes of experimentation. The advantages of self-service stores as machines for automatic selling especially appealed to small-town inventors searching for predictable profits. I argue that, although the corporate supermarket eventually came to define the globalization of American mass retailing, the American self-service store originated in the highly competitive and unstable conditions of small-business capitalism on Main Street in the early twentieth century.

Shopping in a self-service store was a starkly different experience than shopping in a counter-service store. To understand how self-service stores operated as a specialized form of retailing, Chapter 5, "The Purchase-Inducing Force of the Store," goes inside the store to evaluate the physical features and operational logic of self-service store arrangement. Store patents document varied experiments with a diverse technologies and approaches to store arrangement, but they also demonstrate shared underlying principles as inventors worked to systematize the shopping pathway, mobilize merchandise, compartmentalize the self-service retail space as a specialized system, and automate salesmanship through sensory retailing.

Chapter 6, "Mechanizing Paternalism: The Southern Origins of Self-Service," examines the invention of the self-service store as a social process with meanings that were contingent on particular cultural contexts. The appeal of low prices is not sufficient to explain the popularity of self-service experimentation in the poorest region of the country. Chapter 6 analyzes the social experience of diverse southern customers to consider how the radically equalizing practice of self-service shopping was invented in a culture of segregation. Self-service stores automated the authority of the merchant and offered protections to African American customers and southern White women that traditional forms of retailing did not. I argue that self-service stores embodied stark dichotomies of democracy and White supremacy.

Chapter 7 examines the 1930s as a critical turning point in the history of self-service when the application of self-service retailing to huge "super market" store spaces generated a new round of experimentation during the economic crisis of the Great Depression. This chapter connects the origins of supermarkets to the long-term experimentation of independent store owners and small local or regional chains that continued to invent influential and enduring self-service methods throughout the 1930s that shaped the ways that supermarkets worked. Store operators reimagined the mechanisms for systematizing the shopping pathway, mobilizing merchandise, and silent salesmanship. Integrating service departments, especially the butcher counter, along the self-service pathway and connecting them to a centralized checkout process helped to ensure that large store spaces worked effectively as orderly machines for automatic selling. It is tempting to look for the origins of supermarkets in large stores. But when they built their self-service grocery departments, supermarket entrepreneurs followed the lead of small store owners who had been experimenting with self-service systems for decades.

The book's conclusion marks the end of the developmental stage of self-service store invention. Embraced as an industry standard by the new Super Market Institute at their fourth annual meeting in 1940, self-service achieved technological momentum. Self-service stores stopped being physically compartmentalized as specialized retail spaces, and the grocery industry began the widespread conversion to self-service retailing led by supermarket expansion after World War II. The store design process shifted from local vernacular experimentation to corporate financing and policy making.

Not until 1946 did Carl Dipman, editor of *Progressive Grocer*, declare, "self-service food store operation is no longer on trial."[41] The dominance of supermarkets built by large corporations in the second half of the twentieth century has obscured the role of small firms in the invention of the American self-service store. The broad conversion of consumer landscapes to self-service in the twentieth century was driven by multiple factors. We know more about the external factors that made it possible—the rise of prepackaged brand name products, the spread of the automobile and new technologies like the cash register and refrigeration, ideas of scientific management and business efficiency—than the social interactions that shaped how self-service worked inside stores. The chain store owners and independent grocers who invented the self-service store in the early twentieth century produced lasting cultural, technological, and business changes that transformed the practice and meaning of shopping. *Beyond Piggly Wiggly* documents the essential role that small-town American grocers and their customers played in that process before 1940, when self-service was still on trial.

# Machines for Automatic Selling

The foremost inventor of his time, Thomas Edison was among the earliest to take on the challenge of self-service store design. In 1910 the *New York Times* featured Edison's work on an "automatic clerkless shop."[1] "This is the machine age," Edison declared as he described the organized efficiency of a candy factory where one worker operated multiple machines to produce standardized chocolate drops "faster than he could count." That the most prominent American inventor at the turn of the century considered store design a test worthy of his attention demonstrates both the importance attached to improving how stores worked and a widely shared faith in technological solutions for problems of distribution. Small-town merchants incorporated new inventions into their strategies for selling. Telephones expanded the reach of the store. Cash registers and adding machines systematized bookkeeping in what one historian has described as "the first step toward automating retail and customer transactions."[2] But Edison and others bemoaned the fact that all of these new technologies had done little to change the ways that stores were physically designed to sell.[3] Clerk wages represented one of the biggest fixed costs for grocery stores. Workers who served crowds of demanding customers during early morning and evening rush hours often stood idle as customer traffic dwindled over the course of a workday. Could stores be designed to work without so many clerks? Edison claimed dramatically that "in an automatic store one man could do the work which is now done by fifty grocers."[4]

Stores were a focus of attention at the turn of the century because of the high cost of living. Despite dramatic changes in the industrialization of food production between 1880 and 1930, working-class people spent as much as half their income feeding their families.[5] Stores were an artifact of a distribution system that some observers believed had failed to keep up with the innovations of mass production. *The World's Work* echoed the general consensus: "The cost of producing what we eat, wear, and use is often not as great as the cost of selling these things to us."[6] "Are there too many retail stores?" economist Paul Nystrom asked in his study of retailing.[7] Nystrom complained, "Production has been the object of solicitous scientific study in laboratory and school, while distribution . . . has been left largely to itself."[8] Government researchers, business experts, and a variety of other industry stakeholders from advertisers to home economists promoted new strategies for improving the ways stores worked.[9]

The idea that retailing could be organized using scientific principles increasingly shaped store operation. Practices that became known as scientific retailing included setting fixed prices for products, organizing store spaces into departments to improve worker efficiency, and emphasizing volume sales and high turnover of merchandise as measures of business success beyond the gross profit margin.[10] New concerns about sanitation and germs created unprecedented demands for cleanliness inside stores. These features came to define what it meant to be a modernizing retailer. Scientific managers studied workers' movements to improve store arrangement for increased efficiency. But only a small, specialized segment of the grocery trade embraced self-service as a volume strategy during the 1920s. Self-service stores took scientific retailing to new extremes by creating store interiors that functioned as coordinated systems for automatic selling. Ironically the small store owners who were so often portrayed as the cause of inefficiency in the distribution system became the most important architects of the modern self-service store.

It is useful to apply the stages of invention defined by historians of technology to evaluate the phases of inventing the self-service store before 1940. During the phase of initial invention in the World War I era, self-service stores appeared as oddities, a temporary response to wartime economic hardships. In the 1920s, self-service stores entered an important experimental stage of development, described by historian of technology David Nye as "a social process through which inventions are adjusted to suit the needs of specific users and ensure affordable cost of production."[11] Although store designers made reducing overhead costs a high priority, the process of experimentation was capital-intensive and the result in profit uncertain. Industry leaders promoted open display principles as a method for improving clerk efficiency rather than fully systematized self-service store arrangements. Dozens of self-service store designs were patented, underscoring their reputation as a specialized form of retailing during this developmental stage.

At the turn of the twentieth century, numerous industrialized societies experimented with new forms of self-service retailing as a strategy for lowering the costs of distribution and speeding up the sales process inside the store. Food service retailers led the way, experimenting with automatic restaurants and cafeterias in the early 1900s in Germany, South Africa, the United States, and elsewhere.[12] As historian Angelika Epple has argued, self-service retailing "has a polycentric history involving many unknown tinkerers, and it is a history that can be told only as a transnational venture among various industrialized societies."[13] Grocers initially looked to vending machines and cafeteria precedents for design inspiration to rethink how to organize their store spaces as systems for automatic selling. Though important design influences came from international sources, the cafeteria-style self-service store would ultimately prevail in American store design. As self-service stores became linked to national narratives of modernity and democracy in a context of wartime patriotism, cafeteria-style self-service stores became popularly understood as uniquely American inventions of the machine age.

## Edison and the Automat

In 1910 there was no fixed idea about what a self-service store should look like. When Edison planned his clerk-less store, he did not include open shelving or market baskets as part of his store design. Instead, he filled the selling floor with dozens of vending machines. At the time, retailers included self-service display features in their stores. Marshall J. Bailey composed treatises on store fixtures for *System: The Magazine of Business* and wrote, "The ideal is a fixture from which the customer can select goods without assistance, pay the cashier and leave the store."[14] A few other early writers shared this goal. In recommending price marks in 1909, *American Grocer* maintained that customers "like to be at liberty to inspect the goods, find the price and make a decision as to purchase without being interfered with by a clerk."[15]

What distinguishes Edison's store from these examples is that he went beyond a focus on improving a single store fixture. He did not try to invent a better vending machine; he conceptualized store fixtures as one element of a larger coordinated retail system. Edison's invention extended the standardization, codification, and rationalization of production processes (in what historian Lindy Biggs calls the "rational factory—one that could run automatically as though it were a grand machine") to the organization of retail space.[16]

Edison organized his automatic store on two floors like a typical turn-of-the century factory. Products would be delivered to a second-floor storage space where a series of chutes connected the storage bins to the vending machines on the selling floor below. Electro-magnets, not people, drove the system. Edison organized the bins, chutes, and vending machines into a system for automatic selling. He ensured that the store could work without clerk assistance in urban neighborhoods with large immigrant populations by labeling each vending machine on the selling floor with signs that identified the products they contained in half a dozen different languages. Products could be organized into categories or departments to enable customers to locate the items they sought quickly. In stark contrast to ordinary grocery stores, there was no store counter and no price negotiation with a clerk. Products were available only in fixed, pre-measured quantities. "Suppose a patron wants beans," Edison explained. "He will go to the series of openings that represent the vegetable department. He will look for the sign bearing the legend 'Beans.' He drops a nickel in the slot and a neatly tied package containing 5 cents worth of beans will drop through the opening." To simplify things even more, everything in the store could be sold in pre-measured amounts of five cents. Edison had already assigned draftsmen to the project and the illustrations accompanying the reporter's interview featured Edison at work in his Menlo Park laboratory alongside a conceptual rendering of his automatic store full of customers. It offers a striking juxtaposition—the concept of a store as a machine that could be invented in a laboratory. "Selling and distribution," Edison argued, "are simply machines for getting products to consumers. And like all machines, they can be improved with great resulting economy."[17]

Edison's automatic store presents several important insights about the origins of the American self-service store. The idea that a store could be a mechanical invention worthy of attention at the Menlo Park laboratory helps to explain the context in which the Patent Office ultimately approved dozens of patents for self-service stores. Most people agreed with the USDA that "principles of self-service can not be patented, being nearly as old as distribution itself."[18] But there were different mechanisms for implementing self-service, and the idea that self-service store improvements could be patented proved persuasive. Between 1917 and 1940, more than seventy patents were issued to inventors from twenty-three states for self-service store designs, 73 percent of them in the 1920s. Although other inventors used different technologies and design ideas, Edison's emphasis on organizing store systems for automatic selling represents a distinguishing characteristic of self-service stores.

Edison's invention is also important because he understood that developing a successful self-service store would require both mechanical ingenuity and social persuasion. He thought the mechanical part of the process would be easier than the social part. In mechanical terms, Edison emphasized that the machines to make self-service work already existed. Many big grocery stores already used machines to automatically weigh and package bulk flour. The vending machines that distributed goods to customers in the retail space had already automated some aspects of food retailing. "As a mechanical proposition it's simple," Edison declared. But persuading customers to serve themselves was a different kind of challenge. To demonstrate the benefits of his store, he imagined building a prototype in a New York tenement district and calling it "The Samaritan Market" because it would dramatically reduce the cost of living for poor people. Although he believed that his invention could work in any grocery store, Edison anticipated resistance. "Pride would be altogether too powerful a factor. Even a mechanic who makes his $2.50 a day would be too proud to patronize one of these nickel-in-the-slot stores." In fact, the mechanical and social challenges of inventing self-service stores were not separate problems. They were closely interrelated. For that reason, the physical design of self-service stores turned out to be more challenging than Edison anticipated. Inventing self-service stores was risky because it not only meant physically coordinating store counters and shelves to automate salesmanship; it also required social engineering to produce new roles for clerks and consumers.

With its reliance on vending machine technology, Edison's automatic store links American experiments to a larger international context of self-service retail experimentation. The first automat opened in Berlin in 1896. Operated exclusively by vending machines, with the slogan "you absolutely help yourself," there were 125 successful automatic restaurants in Germany before World War I. But automats met with limited success in the United States. Horn & Hardart first opened in Philadelphia in 1902 using German vending machines but invested considerable resources in tinkering with the German prototype to find a version that would appeal to American consumers.[19] The company ultimately patented a drum mechanism consisting of a massive cylinder that took considerable effort for workers or customers to rotate in order to load or remove food from the chamber. The physical exertion required to use the machine worked against the goal of speed in making sales or maximizing worker efficiency and so suggests the importance of other priorities in self-service experimentation as well. According to historian Alec Shuldiner, the drum design Horn & Hardart developed for vending prepared food operated like a "giant cash register," ensuring that customers paid the precise amount for their food selection and that workers did not have access to the cash drawer.[20] The experimental focus on controlling the exchange of money reflects the larger history of self-service store experimentation with the checkout process. For more than a decade of sustained experimentation and considerable cost, Horn & Hardart worked to improve a vending machine that not only reduced wages but also controlled workers, concerns documented in other types of self-service store designs.

The expense of automat technology helps to explain why small-business owners in the United States did not adopt it as the basis for self-service store design. Setting up a single automat restaurant based on Horn & Hardart technology could cost upwards of $350,000—one hundred times more expensive than the cost of opening a typical grocery store.[21] During the 1920s the self-service restaurant chain created a unique hybrid format by combining their automat technology with the widely popular cafeteria, adding steam tables and bringing workers into the main dining room to serve customers on the line. Horn & Hardart was most successful in the end when it combined the self-service features of the fully automatic vending machine with cafeteria-style steam tables served by humans, not machines.[22]

## Groceterias, the New Help Yourself Stores

In contrast to the limited success of automats in the United States, cafeterias were widely adopted in a variety of contexts at the turn of the century to feed large numbers of people quickly and cheaply. Americans initially experienced cafeteria self-service at the World's Columbian Exposition in 1893, where John Kruger's buffet-style eatery (said to be inspired by the Swedish smorgasbord) served hungry crowds.[23] Kruger adopted the term "cafeteria," which a linguist studying American speech in the 1920s traced to a Cuban-Spanish word for coffee shop. The scholar associated the cafeteria with "a poor man's club" that had only recently achieved respectability. The specific origins of the term were murky, but "one should look for the extension into polite society," he wrote, "from water-front dives, the original home of the tango and the Charleston, both of the name cafeteria, and of the procedure of self-service."[24] If cafeterias had dodgy origins, they became the epitome of middle-class respectability in the United States.

The self-service cafeteria was an innovation particularly suited to the gender and class dynamics of the new urban white-collar office worker. Whereas earlier self-service restaurants had served working-class men in a disorganized scramble at an open lunch counter, the hallmark of the cafeteria was the self-service line of customers traveling in single file to select standardized portions of food. Cafeterias served masses of customers quickly and affordably. While cafeteria chains fed thousands of hungry urban store clerks and office workers, the format became ubiquitous in institutional contexts as well, from factories to schools and hospitals. The Bureau of Labor Statistics reported, "The cafeteria method of serving seems to be especially desirable where large numbers must be taken care of in a short space of time. . . . One company states that 1,500 people are served by this method in nine minutes and another that 1,300 are served in six minutes."[25] Feeding diverse crowds from utilitarian factory lunchrooms to more lavish department store dining rooms, cafeterias evoked democratic ideals, genteel respectability, and modern efficiency and connected self-service to a larger national narrative about democracy and modernity. As a *Washington Post* writer exclaimed, "The crowning glory of the quick lunch room as an American institution is its democracy. The Wall Street banker and the Wall Street newsboy regularly eat . . . at the same place. With all its faults, the quick lunch room is an American institution of which we ought not to be ashamed."[26]

The cafeteria design principles of orderliness, speed, visual display, and democratic access help to explain why self-service store designers looked to cafeterias for inspiration. They sought to devise more systematic methods for volume sales than the frenzied world of the bargain basement. For example, Filene's department store in Boston is recognized as a pioneer in reduced-cost retailing. In January 1909 Filene's debuted a bargain basement that displayed discounted merchandise on open tables and racks with minimal service compared to the department store upstairs. Shopping in the bargain basement was a chaotic experience. "On a typical busy Saturday, seventy-six thousand shoppers passed through its doors. Once inside, people grabbed, pushed, and shoved."[27] In his application for a patent, vending machine designer Judson B. Hurd explained that his self-service invention was designed to overcome the chaos of the bargain basement: "At bargain-counters and in the sale of hurry lunches, &c., the articles vary so much in size, form, and price that they cannot be handled with an ordinary vending-machine, yet here is where a machine is most needed, here we have the crowd, confusion, and consequent loss. It is impossible to provide a clerk for each customer, yet without it some must wait and the crowd becomes congested."[28] Self-service inventors worked to find an affordable solution to coordinate crowds of bargain-hunting shoppers. Designed with machine-like efficiency, using partitions to organize customers into an orderly line where the food sold itself lavishly displayed on steam tables, cafeterias offered new inspiration.

Lewis Mumford, American architectural critic and philosopher of technology, in his essay "Machinery and the Modern Style" went so far as to argue that the cafeteria best evoked American modernism. Mumford affectionately described the Childs cafeteria chain, where he was a regular customer, as "nearer to the source of a contemporary style than a building by Richardson, White, or Cram," the premiere architects of the day—designers of the modern skyscrapers, department stores, and public buildings that redefined the monumental cityscape of the early twentieth century. Childs had opened its first New York restaurant on Broadway in 1889, and by the mid-1920s the chain operated over one hundred restaurants in twenty-nine cities, in sharp contrast to the automat chain Horn & Hardart, confined to stores in only Philadelphia and New York.[29] For Mumford the cafeteria best represented American modernity because it worked like a well-oiled machine. Mumford enthused, "Its excellence is due to the fact that it has been made by a machine, and that it exhibits the accuracy, the fine finish, and the unerring fidelity to design which makes machine work delightful to everyone who knows how to take pleasure in geometrical perfection."[30] The machine-like efficiency of the cafeteria made it an attractive model for store designers who wanted to automate selling.[31]

In 1916 the Patent Office approved Bostonian Albert Weston's cafeteria design as a patentable "serving device for eating houses."[32] Figure 1.1 shows that Weston's systemized arrangement comprised a track designed to guide removable trays past food "depots arranged in sequence" according to "the ordinary order of service of food at a meal." The plan provided controls for entry and exit, and the track served the dual purpose of collecting food selected by customers and guiding them along a predetermined path. The design ensured that customers had to traverse the entire line, moving single file in one direction, before exiting with their trays into the dining room. Though the space was wide enough for "any individual to pass others ahead of him at will... no individual can pass from the entrance to the portion B [dining room] without going to the end of the passage." The payment process was organized at the end of the line where, an "inspector" (labeled 14 in the floor plan in figure 1.1) totaled the food items on each tray and issued a check for the amount due.

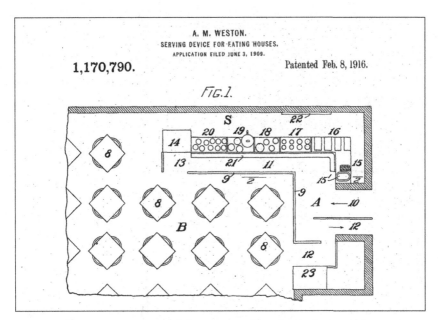

FIG. 1.1. Albert M. Weston succeeded in patenting his cafeteria design as a "serving device for eating houses" that enabled patrons to be "served in a semi-automatic manner." *Source:* Weston, Serving Device for Eating-Houses patent.

Diners paid the cashier (at station 23) upon exiting the dining room through a controlled passage (labeled 12 on the floor plan). The Weston patent created an important precedent for the patentability of self-service store arrangements as mechanical systems that enabled customers to serve themselves and documents the transferability of key elements of cafeteria design to self-service stores, including spatial strategies for organizing customers into a line and centralizing payment at the exit. Using cafeterias as their design inspiration, self-service store inventors created store spaces that organized the crowd into orderly, disciplined shoppers.

Though Americans were widely familiar with cafeterias, the first self-service stores were such a departure from the typical shopping experience that they were perceived as curiosities that required explanation. Self-service stores were so new and different from existing stores that the word "grocery" did not seem to adequately describe them. The *Classical Weekly*, observing the spread of the cafeteria across the United States and the new slang words it spawned wondered, "Lately a sister institution has sprung up in the *groceteria*, but would women ever frequent it were it called a *selfservegrocery*?"[33] The

FIG. 1.2. H. G. Hill Grocery Company ad. The H. G. Hill Grocery chain introduced Nashvillians to self-service in two downtown locations, on Broadway and on Church Street. H. G. Hill was the largest grocery chain in Nashville, and the majority of their stores elsewhere in town operated using traditional counter-service methods. Hill called his two self-service stores "Hill's Groceteria" to alert customers to their self-service format and distinguish them from other stores in the chain. *Source: Tennessean* (Nashville), 10 July 1918.

linguists who documented ways that the new stores were changing modern American speech explained, "Everyone knows by this time that a cafeteria is a 'help yourself' restaurant. Apparently in the popular mind the ending *teria* or *eteria* has come to indicate such a process."[34] Typically advertising their stores as "groceterias," "basketerias," or "marketerias," the first self-service inventors alerted shoppers before they entered the door that they should be prepared to serve themselves.

California soon became known as the place where self-service grocery stores were invented.[35] In 1915, for example, newspaper readers in Asheville, North Carolina, were reading about "Groceteria" stores operated by a single clerk as the "newest thing in the Santa Monica bay district." The article explained, "When you go into a 'groceteria,' you fill your basket with what you find you need, then go to the cashier's desk and have your purchases checked up."[36] But Californians were not the only first adopters. As Angelika Epple argued regarding the international context of self-service experimentation, the American self-service store "has a polycentric history involving many unknown tinkerers" who opened stores across the United States.[37]

Wherever they opened, self-service stores alerted customers that they were not typical grocery stores by including some reference to self-service in the store name or advertisements. In 1914 *Simmons' Spice Mill* covered the Lutey Brothers "marketeria" in Butte, Montana, for its readers in the grocery trade. "The marketeria was never intended to displace the ordinary grocery, where deliveries are made as a matter of course, but it seems to have met a demand where quality and quantity rather than service are desired. Grocers in other cities have adopted the idea," the magazine observed.[38] In Nashville an ad for Hill's Groceteria explicitly linked its inspiration to California, explaining that "as far back as 1914, one D. E. Stanton of California, started the Self-Serve Grocery under the copyrighted name of the 'Groceteria.'" Besides these examples there were numerous lesser-known local experiments in self-service store design in the World War I era, such as the Ohio grocer who advertised his self-service store several months before the first Piggly Wiggly opened.[39] But the most successful self-service store inventor of the era was Clarence Saunders, who opened the first Piggly Wiggly store in Memphis in 1916.

## Market Basket Patriotism

Saunders understood the importance of the social challenges for selling self-service as an unfamiliar technology. He began to sell Piggly Wiggly franchises nationally in 1918 as the United States was becoming increasingly involved in war in Europe. Saunders marketed his self-service store as a patriotic war measure that worked as an anti-hoarding device.

World War I created conditions that fueled the expansion of self-service stores. Experimentation in these stores had begun in a context of high inflation in food prices that increased political pressure to reduce the costs of distribution. Working-class people typically paid as much as half their weekly income for food.[40] Between 1910 and 1913 food prices surged dramatically, sparking consumer protests from urban immigrant housewives, middle-class women's clubs, and small-town shoppers.[41] High food prices were a major campaign issue in the presidential election of 1912 and contributed to the defeat of the incumbent William Howard Taft. The issue of the high cost of living engaged reformers, social scientists, and business researchers looking for

FIG. 1.3. Clarence Saunders used innovative methods to advertise his newly patented self-service store. In a story that circulated nationally, he promoted self-service shopping as "Market Basket Patriotism" linked to Food Administration rationing efforts during World War I. Saunders featured the newly patented Piggly Wiggly aisles, his patented hanging price tags, and curious crowds on opening day as the Memphis chain began to sell franchises nationally. *Source: Daily Capital Journal* (Salem, OR), 25 June 1918.

causes and solutions to the problem. The American Academy of Political and Social Science published studies focused on "reducing the cost of food distribution."[42] But it was not until the food and labor shortages of World War I that we see self-service stores become a recognizable trend. After war broke out in Europe in 1914, the cost of living more than doubled over the next five years. A poor grain crop in 1916 and wheat exports in support of European food needs contributed to food shortages in the United States. Food riots and boycotts in New York, Chicago, Philadelphia, Boston, St. Louis, and Baltimore in the spring of 1917 put pressure on the Woodrow Wilson administration to address the inflation.[43]

Congress declared war on April 6, 1917, and Wilson used the wartime emergency to launch the Food Administration with Herbert Hoover, who had made a name for himself combating starvation in war-torn Belgium as head of the Belgian Relief Organization. The Food Administration focused especially on food conservation through voluntarism. Promoting "Meatless Mondays" and "Wheatless Wednesdays," Hoover declared, "Food will win the war." He mobilized the support of grocers like H. G. Hill, who admonished Nashville shoppers at his Groceteria: "Food Will Win the War—Don't Waste It" (fig. 1.2).

Saunders capitalized on the Food Administration initiative to begin the process of selling Piggly Wiggly franchises nationally. He scored an interview with John Allen Murphy of the influential trade magazine *Printer's Ink* to discuss his plans for expansion. Murphy's article noted the success of California's groceterias and emphasized that Piggly Wiggly was worth watching because of Saunders's plans for franchising his patented self-service store system. Murphy provided an overview of the licensing policies for entrepreneurs interested in investing in the new store concept.[44]

In his innovative national newspaper campaign, Saunders linked "Market Basket Patriotism" to the Food Administration's efforts to curb hoarding and reduce food prices. Picturing himself as if in collaboration with Food Administrator Herbert Hoover, Saunders promoted the Piggly Wiggly system as a specialized type of cash and carry store. "A complete reversal of thrift methods of our grandmothers' time in matter of household buying, one designed to check food hoarding in family larders, will undergo public test in Washington soon," Saunders wrote, fostering anticipation. "Right under the observation of Food Administrator Hoover, who asserted that 'the food hoarder is working against the common good and even against the very safety of the country,' a number of public pantries on the 'piggly wiggly' plan will be opened to demonstrate that one of the wasteful ways of the housewife is the purchase of quantities of groceries." Without officially rationing food, the Food Administration promoted voluntary limits on food consumption. Saunders advertised Piggly Wiggly as an anti-hoarding device: "The public pantry plan, with piggly wiggly aisles is said to reduce the cost a fifth at least below the time honored 'general grocery,' reduce the time required in market basket buying according to the government's wishes, and particularly reduce the wasteful hoarding and accumulation of things and individual investment in groceries to an entirely new level."[45]

In promoting Piggly Wiggly as a mechanism for reducing hoarding, Saunders revealed the social engineering purposes of self-service store designers. The self-service store, and particularly the Piggly Wiggly version of self-service, was a powerful tool for changing the behavior of shoppers. Saunders distributed to the state offices of the Food Administration a list of "twelve patriotic reasons for Piggly Wiggly stores."[46] Top on the list was that the stores served "to check food hoarding in individual pantries." Additionally each store was said to offer important advantages for a wartime economy by saving fuel, rent, and lighting costs and helping "the labor situation" by "releasing the grocer's clerks for more essential work."[47]

Piggly Wiggly rode the war tide to dramatic expansion. By the end of 1918, the chain had opened dozens of stores beyond Memphis and used advertising in innovative ways to establish itself as the most recognizable self-service store nationwide. But Piggly Wiggly had plenty of competition, and it was not clear whether self-service stores would survive when the war ended. "When the Government and essential industries took thousands of clerks and delivery men away from the regular stores, the self-serve variety multiplied so rapidly that there are hundreds of them now scattered all over the country," observed Perry F. Nichols in *American Magazine*.[48] Nichols invited the consumers who read his article, "Tell us how the idea . . . strikes you[.] Will it make a 'go'? All sorts of new things are being hurried along as a result of the war. Is this one of them? Or will it die out? You will decide. Stores have got to be run to suit you." Similarly, John Allen Murphy had wondered in his *Printers Ink* coverage of Piggly Wiggly, "The extraordinary times through which we are passing have favored the development of stores of this type, but when conditions are restored to normal will it be possible for any system of retailing to keep its selling costs down to such a low figure as has been shown by this Memphis chain?"[49] Customers were willing to forego the services they had been accustomed to in the patriotic fervor of wartime, particularly the convenience of delivery, but would that behavior endure once the war ended?

Self-service stores were considered by many observers to be a temporary response to wartime shortages and inflationary conditions. The links between self-service and patriotism also created associations between self-service and wartime sacrifice and deprivation. In its first year of publication, *Progressive Grocer* magazine studied self-service stores and displayed a mix of curiosity and skepticism. "Was cash and carry only a war baby?" one article asked. "During the years of continually rising prices . . . the serviceless stores presented an ideal method for combating the high cost of living[,] and housewives throughout the country flocked to such markets. . . [But] the hardness of war days has passed and [the housewife] is ready, in many cases, to resume once more the conveniences of pre-war days."[50] Grocers particularly felt the pressure to return to the profitable trade of telephone orders, delivery, and credit services.[51]

On the other hand, some grocers who had switched to self-service during the war planned to continue the practice after the war. William Warfield, a Pensacola, Florida, grocer, saw his business grow from $70,000 in 1919 to $181,000 in 1920, after the conversion to self-service, and he had no plans to go back to service and delivery. *Progressive Grocer* reported, "He feels that the critical conditions under which most parts of the country lived have served as an economical awakening, and that . . . the consumer will continue to be a saver [even after prosperity returns]."[52] With seventeen years in the grocery business, Warfield declared that he had never seen so many well-to-do people willing to forgo services: "You can stand in the front of the Warfield store and you will see poor and rich alike line up and take their turn to make their selections from the neatly arranged shelves. All walks of life represented in Pensacola's population come in and wait at the cash register to be checked out with well filled baskets. Everyone is bent on one mission—to secure good, fresh food at a saving. And they do not hesitate to fall in line with the crowd in order to do it."[53] The future of self-service seemed promising, and many observers in government and business studied how it evolved during the 1920s. But the consensus throughout the interwar years was that self-service stores were a specialized form of retailing that could not be implemented everywhere. The mainstream grocery industry focused on open display principles, not self-service store operation. Close examination of an influential model store promoted by the Commerce Department in 1929 helps to explain the difference between the open display techniques that were widely embraced and the specialized retailing system embodied by self-service stores.

## Uncle Sam Builds a Model Store

When the Department of Commerce convened a conference of grocery industry executives in Louisville, Kentucky, in February 1929, they invited the recognized expert on store arrangement, Carl Dipman, to design a model store that would represent best practices in store operation. Dipman had been the editor of *Progressive Grocer* since it began publication in 1922, and that gave him a front row seat for studying innovations in grocery store design during a decade of tremendous change in the grocery business. After he died in 1954 the *New York Times* memorialized him as a food trade editor who "helped develop the self-service store"—he had written several books on the subject.[54] But the model store Dipman designed for the Commerce Department in 1929 was not a self-service store.

Dipman promoted the advantages of his store design in an article advocating the use of open displays that would encourage shoppers to circulate through the store and serve themselves. He emphasized that "90% of the package groceries sold in this store" were "are out where women [could] handle them."[55] Thousands of visitors toured the model store in Louisville, and Dipman declared that open display was no longer an experiment. "The principles are long tried. There have been thousands of such stores built the country over."[56] But the open display principles that became a hallmark of modern grocery arrangement in the 1920s were not the same thing as systematized self-service store operation. While open displays encouraged customers to handle merchandise, stores that incorporated them did not necessarily automate the retailing process from the assembly of merchandise to the checkout counter. Dipman's recommendations for store arrangement in 1929 reflected the broad agreement among business experts of the interwar years that self-service was a specialized retailing method, not a general standard for grocery design.

The same year that *Progressive Grocer* published its first issue, Walter S. Hayward and Percival White coauthored one of the earliest textbooks on chain store management, and the U.S. Department of Agriculture published a comprehensive study of self-service store operation.[57] Dipman elaborated on his ideas about modern store design in his first book on grocery store arrangement in 1931. Together these publications document the curious but wary approach experts took to self-service stores at that time.

Hayward and White were experts on the application of scientific management in retailing and "among the earliest to articulate a consumer orientation as the key to success in marketing," so they might have been expected to enthusiastically embrace self-service stores.[58] But they considered the self-service store to have an uncertain future. Though they admired the successes of Piggly Wiggly, Hayward and White concluded, "Long enough time has not yet elapsed to demonstrate the exact possibilities inherent in such a scheme." They presented self-service stores as a specialized type of chain store, giving weight to the idea that self-service was primarily a chain store innovation.[59]

The Department of Agriculture studied the impact of self-service stores on food distribution and offered advice for would-be self-service entrepreneurs in its report "Self-Service in the Retailing of Food Products."[60] The department's researchers saw self-service as an important strategy for lowering the costs of food distribution. But they emphasized, "The advantages and disadvantages of self-service are marked, so much so, in fact, that it seems apparent that the principle of self-service can not be applied in a haphazard way to any store at any location or under any management and be entirely successful."[61] Key advantages included low operating expense, higher volume sales compared to cash and carry or credit-and-delivery stores, and improved ability to handle customers during rush hour. But these advantages were not guaranteed. To achieve the advantages of self-service, the USDA writers warned, "A considerable amount of study previous to installation is necessary, and in order that the disadvantages do not offset the advantages an efficient management is essential."[62] Most of the report detailed this specialized knowledge for self-service success—including different considerations for buying merchandise, particulars of store arrangement, concerns about inconveniencing customers, and how to curtail thievery. Effective store arrangement was even more consequential for the self-service store than for the service store because there were no sales staff on the floor to push merchandise.

To understand why these business experts saw self-service store operation as risky business in the 1920s it is important to consider the fierce competition and volatility of the grocery business at the time. With their slim profit margins and high competition from stores around every corner, grocery stores faced a very thin line between success and failure. In Louisville, for example, one study discovered that "45% of all the groceries started between 1921 and 1928 failed in the first year of their life." The authors noted: "It is interesting that this was not due merely, if at all, to chain store competition for almost exactly the same proportion of new grocery stores failed during a comparable period back in the '90s, and this not only in Louisville but [also] in several other cities surveyed."[63] The reduced overhead costs of self-service were supposed to result in lower prices to the customer, thus giving self-service a competitive advantage over higher-priced service stores. But this meant that profit margins for self-service would be even smaller in a business where all retailers typically operated on margins of 3–5 percent There was not much room for error.

The USDA offered a hypothetical example to show that small fluctuations in business would have a greater impact on self-service stores than on to traditional store operation.[64] In the first scenario the self-service store and the service store both earned the same net profit of $1,400. The service store charged higher prices to cover the costs of service and achieved a 4 percent

**TABLE 1.1**

|  | % of net profit | Total Sales | Net Profit |
| --- | --- | --- | --- |
| Service Store | 4 | $35,000 | $1,400 |
| Self-Service Store | 2 | $70,000 | $1,400 |

SOURCE: F. E. Chaffee and Kerbey McFall, "Self-Service in the Retailing of Food Products," United States Department of Agriculture Bulletin 1044, Washington, D.C., April 19,1922, 40.

**TABLE 1.2**

|  | % of net profit | Total Sales | Net Profit | % Loss |
| --- | --- | --- | --- | --- |
| Service Store | 3 | $35,000 | $1,050 | 25 |
| Self-Service Store | 1 | $70,000 | $700 | 50 |

source: F. E. Chaffee and Kerbey McFall, "Self-Service in the Retailing of Food Products," United States Department of Agriculture Bulletin 1044, Washington, D.C., April 19, 1922, 40.

net profit on sales of $35,000 per year. Meanwhile, the self-service store lured more customers through low prices to double the total sales of the service store. Despite the difference in total sales, however, both stores netted the same profit. The self-service store's low 2 percent margin meant it had to do twice the business of the service store to achieve the same income.

Though the self-service store seemed to have a tremendous selling advantage, its lower margin on every sale made it especially vulnerable to small changes in business conditions.

To demonstrate this the researchers offered a second scenario illustrating what happened to the same investors if the net profit decreased by only 1 percent, starkly revealing the higher risk of the self-service merchant. If both these stores experienced a decrease of profits (because fewer customers came to shop or they left the most expensive merchandise on the shelves, for example) or an increase of expenses (because rent or wages went up or wholesale costs rose, for example), even small fluctuations in business had a much bigger impact on the net profit of the self-service store than on the service store. Although the total sales remained the same in the two stores, a 1 percent drop in the margin of profit resulted in a 50 percent loss in income for the self-service store investor compared to the 25 percent loss for the service store.

The higher profit margin of traditional counter-service stores offered more cushion to weather business losses. Thus, though self-service stores routinely outsold counter-service stores, converting a traditional counter-service store to cafeteria-style self-service could be very risky business indeed. It was not a failsafe strategy for volume sales for the typical neighborhood grocer.

The majority of modernizing grocers opted for more open displays, not self-service operation. In 1927 executives at the J. Walter Thompson advertising agency discussed the importance of counter selling as a marketing device and overall trends in retail merchandising:

> We know that for years the Woolworth stores have been very successful in what is called "counter selling." They place all the goods out on a counter and let the people come in, look at them and handle them. In recent years the grocery stores have become slightly conscious of that fact. There has been a trend, a movement toward so-called "counter merchandising,"—taking the goods off the shelves, removing the counters, putting in tables and aisles, etc., where people can serve themselves or at least handle and see the goods—that is a very definite trend.[65]

The counter and wall system of turn-of-the-century stores, mostly arranged with open space at the center of the store and long banks of counters in front of wall shelving, was giving way to table displays and open shelving. The advertising executives cited Carl Dipman as the recognized expert on grocery store design. "Mr. Dipman of *Progressive Grocer* said that in the last year and a half, ten thousand independent grocers had changed over their design from the old-fashioned grocery type to the counter type of retailing."[66] Though customers might be able to handle products displayed openly on the counter, there was a big difference between what retailers called "counter selling" and a fully operational self-service store.

Given the issues raised by the USDA study about the unique complexities of self-service store operation, it is significant that Carl Dipman's first book on modern store arrangement did not contain a single chapter focused on self-service store design. Moreover, Dipman offered only one example of a self-service store floor plan in his book about the modern grocery store, identifying the plan as an isolated example of a "type of store popular in the South."[67] Even this example included an order counter at the rear of the store "for economical operation of the service part of the business." A comparison with the model store Dipman promoted nationally can clarify the important difference between a store arranged to encourage self-service using "open display principles" and one designed as an automatic selling machine based on systematized self-service.

At first glance the plans of two stores shown in figures 1.4 and 1.5 look almost identical. Both are configured for narrow street frontage and deep interior spaces. The self-service store (fig. 1.4) is slightly larger (at almost 1,300 square feet) than the Louisville model store (at about 856 square feet) in figure 1.5. The two stores have similar product placement, with fresh produce to the right after entering the front door and meat departments at the rear of the store. Both arrangements show open shelving lining the walls for display of canned foods, biscuits, and bottled products. The key difference is at the center of the store. While customers who entered the Louisville store were welcome to turn either right or left, customers in the self-service store were compelled to move left at the entrance. An eight-foot rail blocked access to the passageway on the right, systematizing their route through the store. Customers picked up a basket from a bin at the entry to collect their purchases. The Louisville store offered no receptacles for customers to assemble their own orders.

Dipman's model store design demonstrated the principle of "island display" by grouping merchandise on tables around the center of the floor.[68] In the Louisville model store the island was formed by a group of low display tables and showcases arranged to form a narrow two-foot passageway. But island display was not intended as part of a self-service store system. Significantly, the aisle formed by the display tables was too narrow for the circulation of customers at rush hour and was intended as a workspace for clerks. A large coffee mill, operated by the clerk, anchored the display table configuration. "It is generally best," Dipman explained, "to arrange the island so there will be a working space for salespeople in the middle of it or at the rear of the equipment." The intention of the island display was to bring the store merchandise "into view and within reach of the customer." Dipman wrote, "Now the housewife can to some extent wait on herself."[69] But the focus of the design was on efficient clerk service. In contrast, instead of the island at the center of the retail space, the self-service store included three shelves arranged to form aisles in the middle of the store that were wide enough for customers to circulate, collecting their purchases.

Finally, one of the most important differences in store arrangement and operation in the two stores is the configuration of the checkout process. In the self-service arrangement, the cash register was located at the front of the store, configured so that customers were required to exit through a checkout line at the end of their shopping route. A scale on the checkout counter made it possible for a single clerk to weigh produce without having to staff the produce department. The basket bin was within reach of the checkout counter, making it possible for the cashier to toss empty baskets into the bin after each sale, ensuring that baskets would always be available for the next customer entering the store. Dipman made no mention of the scientific efficiencies of this configuration. Instead, his model store located the cash register on the counter at the rear of the store, where the most rapidly moving merchandise was shelved *behind the counter*, "so that orders can be put up quickly and with the least amount of footwork [by store clerks assembling customer orders]."[70] Dipman did not recognize these work efficiencies of the plan.

Recommended by the Commerce Department, *Progressive Grocer*, and their industry partners, Dipman's model store with its open display principles became the most influential industry standard of the interwar years. It influenced modernizing chain and independent store owners alike. For example, Albon Holsey, secretary of the National Negro Business League, toured the model store in Louisville and reported that it could handle "an annual gross business of from $75,000 to $100,000 with an average stock of $3,000."[71] Holsey promoted the model store arrangement as a competitive advantage for the newly formed Colored Merchants Association (C.M.A.) and enlisted C.M.A. member James A. Ellington to build a model store in Winston Salem, North Carolina, using plans and specifications Holsey had secured from Dipman. Ellington's store became a research hub for Black businessmen with a conference organized to coincide with the grand opening on May 4, 1929.[72] Students from Hampton Institute and Bluefield Institute traveled to Winston Salem to study it. Carl Dipman wired his "hearty congratulations" of the model store event.[73] The National Negro Business League promoted the model store arrangement in all C.M.A. stores as the ideal of modern grocery operation. Two years after he designed the Louisville model store, Dipman declared, "There are 35,000 grocery stores in America that have been completely modernized in the past three years—changed from old-fashioned stores with side counters and cases to modern island stores with open displays."[74] These modernizing stores using open display principles should not be confused with self-service stores.

Dipman's model store exemplified the conservative approach to self-service taken by most progressive grocers of the 1920s. It was designed to encourage customers to handle merchandise, read labels, and even serve themselves by taking products from the island displays or open shelves to the rear counter if they were inclined, but the primary purpose of the arrangement was to speed up a clerk's assembly of customer orders. The open display principles promoted in the model store increased sales and worker efficiency, but the store

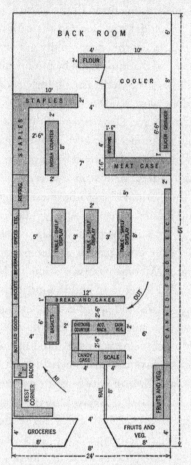

The Modern Grocery Store

A floor plan for a combined self-serve and service store. This type of store popular in the South. The order department at the rear makes for economical operation of the service part of business. The checking and wrapping counter in the front is for convenience of cash and carry customers.

56 ·

FIG. 1.4. This is the only self-service floor plan Carl Dipman included in his first book on modern store arrangement. Customers entering the store were physically routed past the basket bin. Customers exiting the store were required to traverse a narrow pathway past the checkout counter. None of the other floor plans in the book included arrows indicating a directional flow of customer traffic. *Source:* Dipman, *The Modern Grocery Store*, 56.

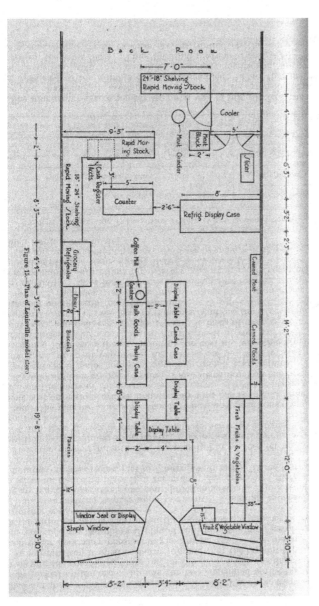

Back Room

7'-0"

24"-18" Shelving
Rapid Moving Stock

Cooler

Rapid Mov-
ing Stock

Meat
Block

Meat Grinder

Slicer

5'

2'

9'-3"

Cash Register
Racks

18"-24" Shelving
Rapid Moving Stock

Counter

5'

2'-6"

Refrig. Display Case

8'

Grocery
Refrigerator

Coffee Mill

Counter

Bulk Goods

Baking Case

Display Table

Candy Case

Display Table

Display Table

Display Table

Canned Meat

Canned Foods

Fresh Fruits & Vegetables

Flour

Biscuits

Fancies

12"

Window Seat or Display

Staple Window

Fruit & Vegetable Window

Figure 15—Plan of Louisville model store

8'-2"     3'-4"     8'-2"

FIG. 1.5. Carl Dipman's Model Store Plan. In the preface of his first book on modern grocery layouts, Carl Dipman emphasized that old-fashioned stores with side counters and cases ought to be modernized with open shelving and displays that improved service, arranged so that orders could be "assembled with greater rapidity." Dipman himself created this recommended model store arrangement that located the fastest-moving merchandise behind the counter at the back of the store for efficient clerk service. *Source:* U.S. Department of Commerce, *Louisville Grocery Survey*, 63.

design did not shift the work of assembling purchases from clerks to customers. According to Dipman, the greatest advantage of the plan was faster service. "Orders can be assembled with greater rapidity," he wrote, and "for the counter customers there is less waiting."[75] But a few entrepreneurs embraced the challenge of designing store interiors that could go beyond speeding up clerk service to sell products without relying on human salesmanship. Dozens of them succeeded in patenting their store designs.

## The Patented Self-Service Store

Few business records survive to document self-service store operations during the interwar years, but store patents represent an invaluable source of information about the intentions and design ideas of their inventors, though most self-service stores were never patented. Store patents of the time included many different fixtures and technologies—cash registers, turnstiles, vending devices—but they focused on coordinating all of the different parts of the store into a spatial system that automated selling. The mechanical parts of the self-service store included the turnstiles that regulated access to the selling space; the price-tagging systems that made prices clearly visible to customers for each individual item; adding machines and cash registers that made rapid and impersonal checkout possible; automatic scales for weighing fresh produce; display cases and racks of various kinds that made products both visible and accessible; and eventually conveyor belts and shopping carts that sped up the collection and movement of goods. But the subject of store patents is circulation—how to move people and products through the store as rapidly and efficiently as possible to the final point of sale. This is documented in floor plans that map the flow of goods and customers through the store space. Though many of the store patents assert that their self-service improvements might be applied to any type of retailing, they all explicitly reference grocery stores as the target of the invention.

Self-service store patents represent idealized spaces. As historian Geof Bowker asserts, it is important to keep in mind that all patents "give internalist and Whig accounts of the development of the process or apparatus that they describe, and as legal instruments they attempt to impose that interpretation on the material world."[76] Patents trace the internal processes of invention by ensuring individual inventors' claims to specific solutions to particular technical problems. Like Whig interpretations of history, patents present inventions as a march of technological progress. Store patents are always presented as improvements compared to existing store designs. They always work, at least on paper. Nevertheless, reading the patents between the lines, we can glimpse the practical and social challenges of operationalizing self-service. Patents address such problems as controlling entrance and egress of consumers; how to avoid product damage and pilferage; and how to minimize customer confusion or congestion at rush hour. They document the ways that store spaces served as laboratories for observing customer behaviors. For example, some inventors categorized shoppers as browsers whose openness to looking and willingness to spend time in the store were encouraged in the layout. Other designs took into account the shopper who came in to buy one or two specific items and created pathways that would not alienate shoppers in a hurry. Most importantly, store patents offer evidence of distinctive spatial challenges for making self-service work in a practical and social store context. Store patents can be read as evidence of this social process at work inside the store.

Thomas Edison never patented his self-service store, but an inventor who worked in his lab did. In 1923 Miller Reese Hutchison, a professional inventor best known for his dictograph, Klaxon horn, and Acousticon for the deaf, added his new and improved self-service store to his inventory of patented inventions.[77] Hutchison was hired by Edison in 1910 (the same year that Edison had been interviewed by the *New York Times* about his automatic store concept) to work on the storage battery and was promoted to chief engineer of the Edison Laboratory three years later. By 1917 Hutchison had formed his own company as sole distributor of Edison batteries. Several devices Hutchison successfully patented were intended for use in self-service stores, but he also succeeded in patenting a self-service store design in 1923.[78] Hutchison's store patent demonstrates basic characteristics of all of the patents included in this study.

Like Hutchison's patent, all store patents included floor plans showing how the various elements of the store were intended to be arranged. Like most self-service designers, Hutchinson used turnstiles to control the store entrance and exit. Typically store patents document different kinds of technologies for moving people or products—conveyor belts, wagons, turntables, and even automobiles! Customers in Hutchinson's store collected their selected products in wire baskets attached to a monorail system that established a predetermined pathway through the store. After circumnavigating the store, customers paid for their purchases at the checkout counter at the front of the store and exited through the turnstile. Though self-service store designers did not invent the idea of a checkout counter, they configured the checkout

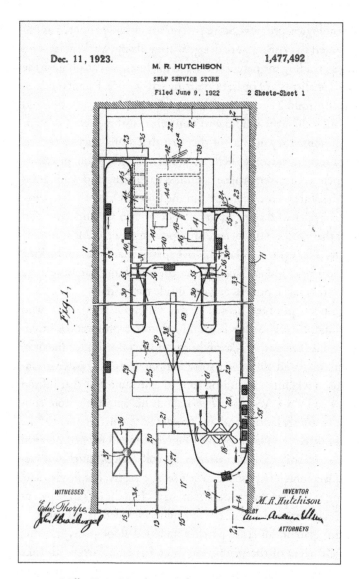

FIG. 1.6. Miller Reese Hutchison's floor plan showed a monorail system automating shopping in his self-service store. The monorail wound around the store and determined the path customers took through the store and ensured that customers saw everything on display. The one-way path started as customers entered the turnstile at the righthand side of the plan and linked a basket to the monorail, rolling it around all of the displays and ending at the checkout counter (labeled 25 on the plan). Clerks could automatically return baskets to the starting point on a monrail that linked the checkout counter to the entry. Customers exited the retail space through a second turnstile after paying for their purchases. *Source:* Hutchison, Self-Service Store patent.

process in new ways, and the final payment process generated considerable experimentation.

While Hutchison's patent demonstrates some of the common characteristics of store patents, his identity as a professional inventor is unusual compared to the other patentors. Before World War II, self-service store design was the purview of vernacular designers with diverse occupational experience.[79] They were not specialists in architecture or even in retailing. Occupational profiles of self-service patent holders for self-service stores show that at least half had direct experience in retail. In addition to grocers, there were retail store merchants in dry goods, shoes, or drugs. Others worked in a variety of occupations, including an automobile factory worker from Flint, Michigan, a real estate broker from San Diego, and an auto salesman from Nashville. At least one patentor was a woman, Annie Laurie Moseley of San Antonio, who patented a self-service automobile grocery store in 1922.[80] James Carroll, who held at least four patents for self-service stores, first became interested in self-service while working for the U.S. government during World War I, when he was responsible for "establishing the self-service methods employed in the commissaries at the various cantonments" in Europe.[81] He contracted with the Nifty Jiffy chain to build his self-service store in Atlanta. William McCarty put his self-service plan into practice in his own Jitney Jungle chain in Mississippi and was sued by Piggly Wiggly for patent infringement.[82] A. W. B. Johnson was a successful dry goods merchant best known as the founder of the first cafeteria chain in Birmingham, Alabama—Britling Cafeteria—in 1918.[83]

The Piggly Wiggly chain clearly used the patent as part of a corporate strategy for expanding and for protecting its distinctive self-service identity. Inventor James Carroll worked as a consultant to implement his version of self-service with the Nifty Jiffy corporation. A few self-service inventors assigned their patents to regional chains or contracted with them to implement their ideas. For example, Edwin Trapp assigned his patent to Jenny Wren Stores, Inc., of San Francisco, and Charles Rorrer and Albert Mitterer assigned their patent to Stadium Stores, Inc. of Denver. The majority of these self-service inventors also held other patents. Grocer Edward Stiles of Des Moines held ten patents related to improvements for a meat slicing machine. John Smiley of Dallas, who listed his occupation as advertising, also patented a baseball board game. Grocer Lorenzo Anderson of Hawkinsville, Georgia, patented an invention to slow drivers down at railroad crossings. Thus, the entrepreneurs who patented self-service store designs fit the larger history of patent innovation in the early twentieth century. Overall, "the number of U.S.

patents issued to individual inventors outnumbered those issued to corporations until 1933."[84]

The occupational diversity of the entrepreneurs who patented self-service innovations produced a variety of technical and technological sources for self-service design. Self-service grocery stores were a specialized form of retailing during the 1920s, but the technology used to create them was widely available. Though cafeterias were an important design inspiration, self-service stores could look dramatically different from each other. The developmental stage of invention was marked by great variety of approaches to store design.

Clarence Saunders was the first person to successfully persuade the Patent Office that a self-service store could be a patentable invention. When he secured the first patent for a "self-serving store" in 1917, many entrepreneurs who had already created self-service stores thought their inventions were not patentable. Saunders cultivated a public identity as an inventor, associating his Piggly Wiggly invention with steam engines and electricity and asserting its transformative impact as a revolutionary link in the chain between producer and consumer.[85] He described his store as "an apparatus for the vending of merchandise."[86] Saunders went on to secure more patents for self-service stores or related technologies than any other entrepreneur in the 1920s. Saunders's business success made him something of a celebrity, featured in news media that targeted a diverse audience, including businessmen who read *The Magazine of Wall Street*, *Forbes*, and *Financial World*; advertisers who read *Printer's Ink*; tinkerers who read *Popular Science*; young readers of YMCA's monthly magazine, *Association Men*; and home economists who read *The Mother's Magazine*.[87] "Most of our effort at economy has been expended on production. The bigger field for economy is in selling," *The World's Work* magazine declared. "In this field the Piggly Wiggly stores are an interesting and hopeful experiment."[88] Saunders's extensive use of advertising and penchant for publicity made Piggly Wiggly a household name and the best-documented self-service store of the 1920s. The notoriety of Piggly Wiggly as a self-service chain has contributed to an overemphasis on chain stores as the originators of self-service. Before Piggly Wiggly became the largest self-service chain of the 1920s, it started with a few stores in Memphis. To understand the local design process behind the first self-service store patent, we need to take a closer look at how the first Piggly Wiggly was invented in Memphis in 1916.

# Inventing Piggly Wiggly, 1916–1923

Patent reviewer T. A. Hostetler took one look and flatly denied Clarence Saunders's application for a self-service store patent as a duplication of the principles embodied in the cafeteria. "These claims all savor of a method of doing business . . . shown in Weston," Hostetler wrote.[1] Saunders did not take "no" for an answer and overcame Patent Office rejections to become the first inventor to patent a self-service store. He persisted because the patent was such an important element of his expansion plans. Saunders opened a factory in Jackson, Tennessee, that produced Piggly Wiggly store interiors and shipped his patented "apparatus for vending merchandise" to eager franchisees across the country. Max M. Zimmerman, founder of the Super Market Institute, would later declare, "No book on food distribution can be written without discussing Clarence Saunders, who made a definite contribution to the Super Market through Piggly Wiggly."[2]

Saunders was a successful inventor not only because he created a workable self-service store arrangement but also because he was such an effective salesman. He invented Piggly Wiggly as both a physical and a symbolic space. His "market basket patriotism" campaign was just the start. Under Saunders's leadership the chain pioneered new ways of using advertising and news media to sell the self-service store as a cutting-edge business model and a space that evoked American egalitarian ideals. In the process the public began to think of the chain, with its recognizable standardized interior and catchy name, as the way self-service stores worked. Though he never made the claim, it was as if Saunders had invented self-service retail itself and not just a particular kind of self-service store. In the origin story of the supermarket, Piggly Wiggly is still often erroneously described as the first self-service store.[3]

The corporate success of the Piggly Wiggly chain has obscured its grassroots origins. Saunders designed the first Piggly Wiggly interior in a local trial-and-error process in his downtown Memphis store. His experience in trying to create a self-service system that actually worked in practice shows that self-service store design was not obvious or intuitive. He experimented with different design elements based on direct observation of customers and workers. With an intention of franchising his patented store interior, he also carefully studied different store locations, using Memphis as a laboratory for testing the output of Piggly Wiggly stores in different types of neighborhoods to determine the right conditions for making self-service profitable. To understand the origins of the self-service store as a vernacular invention, we need to start with Saunders, the most successful inventor of the interwar years.

## A Man of Ambition

Clarence Saunders was a drummer. Not the kind who played blues on Beale Street, the kind who rode the rails drumming up business for wholesalers. At the turn of the century, traveling salesmen like Saunders visited small-town and urban stores to build distribution networks for the products managed by the wholesalers they worked for.[4] Saunders perfected his sales technique as a drummer for a series of wholesale companies in Memphis and Omaha between 1904 and 1913. Within two years of starting work in Memphis, Saunders boasted, it was written, that "he was known personally to almost every grocer in the territory" and that "every wholesaler had heard of him."[5] He reportedly developed a reputation as a pushy salesman among some of his clients, who complained to Memphis wholesaler Shanks, Phillips & Company about the pressure tactics he used to increase their orders.[6] So when he later promoted self-service by emphasizing that customers who waited on themselves didn't have to negotiate with a pushy clerk, he knew what he was talking about from personal sales experience.

Most importantly, Saunders's career as a drummer offered daily encounters with grocery stores all over his extensive territory. Shanks, Phillips was one of the largest wholesalers in the South, and Saunders must have witnessed a wide range of store conditions, from modernized interiors with new electrical lighting operated by teams of white-aproned clerks to neighborhood stores where grocers and their families lived above the shop and old-fashioned country stores with sawdust scattered on the floor to absorb the tobacco juice male customers spat as they gossiped around a pot-bellied stove. Drumming offered a self-taught course in grocery store practices at the turn of the century, and Saunders turned out to be an avid student.

He began his move to the other side of the counter in 1913, when he persuaded twenty-one grocers who were among his wholesale customers in Memphis to form a cooperative chain to negotiate better deals with wholesalers. Each grocer retained ownership of his store but relinquished buying and advertising control to Saunders who continued to work for Shanks, Phillips. They named the cooperative chain United Stores and implemented a uniform storefront and color scheme to visually coordinate their stores. United Stores implemented the best management strategies of the day to cut overhead expenses, including cash-only sales and chain store economies of scale in purchasing and advertising. Finally, in June 1914, Saunders became a grocer himself when the chain opened a new United Store in Memphis, jointly owned by all the grocers, and managed by Saunders.

Housed in a commercial block on a busy downtown street at the center of the wholesale cotton trade, the 79 Jefferson Street store became the flagship for the United Stores chain and a laboratory for Saunders's experiments in store design. For all their modernization, United Stores were still designed to work as traditional counter-service stores. In an August 1916 United Stores ad, Saunders seemed to describe himself as he mused in his grandiloquent advertising style, "He in whose bosom pulsates the thrilling throbs of ambition sets not in a place where the decaying timbers of yesterday supported a magnificent edifice—whether the edifice be a brick building or an antiquated business method. Looks this man of ambition to newer and more advanced ideas."[7] A few days later, Saunders closed his Jefferson Street United Store and hired a construction crew to gut the old-fashioned counters and reorganize the interior.

Saunders's keen salesmanship was on full display in newspaper ads that stirred up curiosity about what was going on inside the store and stoked public anticipation. "Piggly Wiggly will be born in a few days," he promised, "not with a 'silver spoon' in his mouth, but with a work shirt on his back."[8] It took longer to build the new store interior than Saunders had anticipated, as he worked with the carpenters to create the new self-service system. "The Piggly Wiggly will establish a new fashion," Saunders proclaimed as he began to formulate a personality to sell the store brand. "His costume has taken longer to be designed and finished than the dressmaker thought it would take. He did not care to make his debut unless in full dress, and as he is only partly dressed now he is ashamed to be seen yet awhile."[9] The construction crew worked for about two weeks before the store was ready to open its doors to paying customers on September 11, 1916. Saunders had reconfigured his traditional full-service store to compel his customers to serve themselves.

Saunders was always intentionally mysterious about the direct sources of inspiration for his self-serving system. His biographer, Mike Freeman, has identified at least three possible self-service stores outside the South that Saunders may have personally encountered, either by visiting the store or by studying trade literature.[10] First, the Lutey family of Butte, Montana, claimed that Saunders visited their self-service store sometime in 1914 or 1915 to learn about the operation they had started in 1912. Saunders would have had access to the wholesaler's trade magazine *Simmons' Spice Mill*, which wrote about the Lutey brothers self-service store in 1913.[11] The Luteys ran Montana's largest retail, wholesale, and mail-order grocery chain, and William Lutey served as the state's food administrator during World War I.[12] The Luteys reportedly had thought about patenting their store design but been discouraged by a lawyer who told them that a self-service store wasn't a patentable idea. Instead, they secured trademark status on May 27, 1913 for using the words "cafeteria," "marketeria," and "groceteria" as labels for Lutey's grocery products such as coffee, tea, and flavoring extracts.[13]

Second, Saunders launched Piggly Wiggly not long after he visited an innovative grocery in Terre Haute, Indiana, probably one of the stores in Hollie Oakley's Economy Store chain, which may have introduced self-service features as early as 1912.[14] Oakley launched his grocery business in 1909 and implemented innovative business practices, but it is unclear whether Oakley's shift to self-service predated the Piggly Wiggly design. Finally, Saunders probably studied examples of self-service described in trade magazines such as the story Lee McCrae wrote for *Illustrated World* in January 1916, about Albert Gerrard's grocerteria in Pomona, California. The article described features that were similar to Piggly Wiggly, including an entry turnstile, the arrangement of store fixtures into aisles that formed a pathway for customers to follow, and a centralized checkout station at the exit, where a checker itemized their purchases and a cashier handled their payment using a cash register.[15] In his patent application Saunders admitted that he was aware of self-service experiments in California.

But Sanders's inspiration may not have come exclusively from direct observation of specific store installations. He probably got some of his ideas on his lunch break in a cafeteria line. Thompson's cafeteria style restaurant, one of the largest self-service lunchroom chains of the early twentieth century, opened in Memphis in 1915 at 11 South Main Street, just a block away from the Jefferson Street United Store.[16] The patent reviewers cited Albert Weston's cafeteria patent as a precedent, and in his patent application Saunders acknowledged that he was familiar with "the well-known cafeteria dining room" and that "the underlying purpose in such a dining room" was the same as in his self-service design for Piggly Wiggly.[17]

Whatever his design sources might have been, it is clear that Saunders worked out his own original version of a self-service store on-site at his 79 Jefferson Street store. Saunders had to make his ideas work in practice inside his 1,125-square-foot store space. But he did not invent Piggly Wiggly in two weeks. Working out the kinks in his design went on for months after opening day, as customers tried to use his self-service system. Local experimentation in Memphis was essential not only for improving the configuration of the store interior but also for evaluating the unique challenges self-service presented for store location before the company began to market the patented interior to franchisees nationally. It took a full year before Saunders had a self-service store arrangement that worked well enough to begin expanding the company beyond Memphis. Because Saunders was the first to successfully patent a self-service store, it is important to take a closer look at how he was able to convince patent reviewers that his store design was a patentable invention. His success in patenting a self-service store design documents the ways that the concept was understood as a specialized retail system.

## The Store as Laboratory

Saunders hired one of the best patent lawyers in the country to shepherd his application through a rigorous review process. E. W. Bradford was senior member of the law firm Bradford & Doolittle, with offices in Washington and Indianapolis, specializing in patent and trademark law. He was joint author of a manual on the Federal Trade Commission published in 1916 and served as secretary of the patent and trademark section of the American Bar Association. Bradford also completed two terms as president of the American Patent Law Association.[18] He was instrumental not only in negotiating revisions in the first Piggly Wiggly application that secured Saunders's first store patent but even more importantly for winning approval for a highly disputed second patent for an improved store design that was crucial to Saunders's franchising efforts. The Saunders patent case files make Piggly Wiggly the best-documented example of a self-service store design process. Affidavits submitted in support of the patent document the social mechanics of inventing a self-service system in operation.

Saunders filed his first application for a store patent in October 1916 only a month after the King Piggly Wiggly opened.[19] By February 1917, patent examiner Theodore A. Hostetler's rejection of the application seemed decisive. Going beyond the grounds that it duplicated Albert Weston's cafeteria patent, Hostetler declared the store design to be inherently unpatentable, asserting that Saunders's claims were simply "a method of doing business and as such are not patentable."[20] Undaunted, Saunders and Bradford met personally with Hostetler, and Bradford followed up with a letter. "[We wish] to briefly recapitulate the grounds on which we base our contention that the application embodies not only invention but [also] invention of the best type, and of a type that is entitled to the protection of a patent."[21] Bradford explained that Saunders freely acknowledged that "the idea of making the customers wait on themselves [was] not in itself a new idea." He nevertheless asserted that Saunders's self-service design went far beyond the basic idea of open shelving or the operating mechanisms of the cafeteria.[22] Piggly Wiggly was "more than a means for requiring customers to wait on themselves."

Saunders claimed that what the Piggly Wiggly design achieved was a novel combination of store features that systematized selling in a way that substantially increased store profits and reduced store overhead. It worked as a retailing machine that actually induced sales. Saunders offered before-and-after sales data to support his claims about dramatic reduction in overhead and increase in volume sales. Using a traditional counter-service store arrangement in his United Store, customers had purchased an average of thirty-five cents worth of merchandise per visit, but in the same square footage the Piggly Wiggly system produced more than double the sales: "Each customer purchases eighty-five cents worth of goods at each visit." The Piggly Wiggly system not only persuaded customers to buy more, it was also capable of serving more customers at a dramatically lower cost than the United Store had in the same store location. Bradford emphasized the potential for Saunders's invention to dramatically lower the cost of distributing groceries. "As a matter of fact," he emphasized, "most accurate figures prove that the cost of distribution by the 'Piggly Wiggly' store service is approximately four percent as against fourteen to eighteen percent under the old methods." This line of reasoning was especially powerful in a wartime context of high inflation when food costs were a politically charged issue. Bradford never mentioned the food shortages and wartime context explicitly, but he presented Piggly Wiggly as an invention that served the public interest: "It is thought that if any class of inventors are justly entitled to the protection of a patent it is the class that create things which are of great public benefit, such as the invention forming the subject-matter of this application."

The lobbying effort succeeded, though patent examiner F. W. Holt grumbled, "At best applicant has only made a more extended application of the underlying principle of the cafeteria." He added, "The novel feature of applicant's construction as viewed by the Examiner resides in his arrangement of shelving."[23] The Patent Office approved an amended set of claims focused on the arrangement of fixtures that formed a continuous one-way path through the store. The approved patent described Piggly Wiggly as "an apparatus for the vending of merchandise" defined by a shelving arrangement "whereby a circuitous path is provided through which the customer must pass from the entrance to the exit."

The patented mechanical store consisted of a variety of parts linked together—a gate to control entry and exit, customized shelving for displaying different kinds of products, a one-way path that ensured all customers were "required to review the entire assortment of goods carried in stock," and a centralized checkout station at the end of the circuitous path (see fig. 2.1).[24] In explaining how his system worked, Saunders emphasized the automatic features of the design. The entrance and exit gates were weighted to close and lock automatically behind the customer. Refrigerators were fitted with automatically closing hinges to ensure that the careless customer could not inadvertently leave the cooler open.

While the one-way path controlled the movement of customers through the space, the design also reorganized the work patterns of store clerks. Saunders highlighted a gallery feature atop the shelves that served as an elevated passageway for clerks, to be "used by a 'floor-walker,' or other employee of the establishment, for the purpose of directing or instructing those . . . not acquainted with the method to be followed while actually in the aisles." The floor-walker could provide surveillance of customers and keep track of shelves that needed restocking "without interfering with those . . . in the aisle-ways making purchases (see fig. 2.2)."[25]

Work that was typically performed to order in front of the customer in the traditional grocery store was rendered invisible in the Piggly Wiggly self-service system. For example, the stockroom was not only intended as a

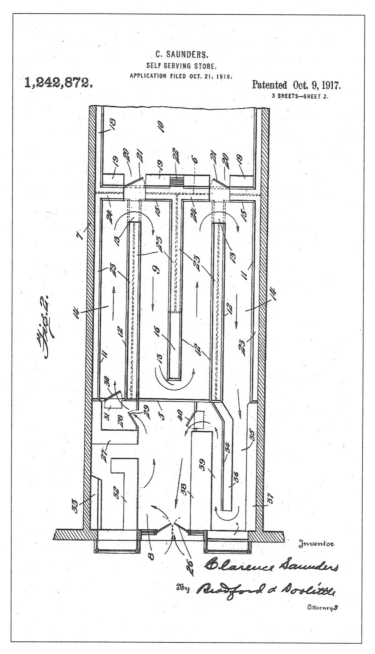

C. SAUNDERS.
SELF SERVING STORE.
APPLICATION FILED OCT. 21, 1916.

1,242,872.

Patented Oct. 9, 1917.
3 SHEETS—SHEET 2.

Inventor
Clarence Saunders
By Bradford & Doolittle
Attorneys

FIG. 2.1. The first Piggly Wiggly patent. Arrows indicate the direction of the one-way path from the entrance at the left to the exit on the right. Once customers entered the gated pathway the only way out was to fully traverse the store and exit past the checkout counter. Saunders, Self Serving Store patent 1,242,872.

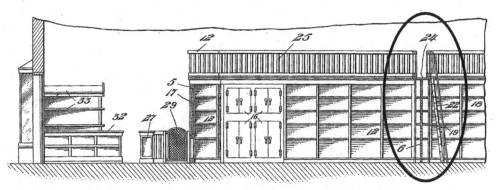

FIG. 2.2. Clerks reached the galleries on top of the store shelves by climbing an integrated ladder (labeled 24). *Source:* Saunders, Self Serving Store patent 1,242,872.

place to store products on their way to the retail shelves, it also housed an important counter system for weighing and packaging bulk products into standard-sized packages. Advertisements assured customers that they no longer had to question whether a clerk had accurately weighed their purchases: "Packages in all Piggly Wiggly stores are weighed by an automatic weighing machine without a human hand touching the contents and with absolute accuracy in weight as to pounds and ounces."[26] It was a store that seemingly operated itself. Saunders called it "The Piggly Wiggly Self-Serving System" and promoted it as a new kind of machine for automatic selling. The problem was that the system didn't work.

Patents represent an ideal. They describe innovations and improvements. They present inventions that always work on paper. But the first Piggly Wiggly store arrangement broke down on opening day, when 968 people made purchases, and "hundreds of sightseers" who didn't make purchases crowded into the one-way path.[27] Perhaps more of the sightseers would have bought something if they had been able to get through the checkout line. On October 1, 1916, a newspaper ad informed Memphis readers, "A change in the checking system will be in effect Monday morning which will relieve the congestion that has sometimes resulted in the last aisle." Saunders assured them, "Naturally some changes were expected to be made from the first start."[28] Irl C. Rainwater, manager of the King Piggly Wiggly, reported that the self-serving system worked fine "when the crowds were small but during busy periods as on Saturdays and busy hours during other days, it was impossible to keep the crowd moving by the checking desk with sufficient rapidity

FIG. 2.3. The perspective drawing in Clarence Saunders's first patent centers on the lobby space. Customers entered the controlled retail space through a gate at the left. At the right, a two-stage checkout counter with adding machine and cash register was stationed at the end of the circuitous path. In the first checkout step a clerk totaled and wrapped the purchases, and in the second stage a cashier accepted payment and made change. The system ensured that only one clerk had access to the money. Only after settling with the cashier could customers pass through the exit gate into the lobby of the store. The location of the checkout counter created traffic flow problems between shoppers trying to exit the store against the flow of incoming traffic. *Source:* Saunders, Self Serving Store patent 1,242,872.

to avoid congestion in the aisles." It was a fatal flaw if customers couldn't complete their purchases and decided to take their business elsewhere. The stalled checkout line "resulted in many complaints by customers and was a trouble that was recognized by all of those connected with the store," Rainwater said. By the time Saunders won his first store patent in August 1917, he had already begun the process of revising the store design significantly in an effort to improve the way the store handled rush-hour business. Inventing Piggly Wiggly was an ongoing, trial-and-error process based on the practical experience of operating a crowded store full of curious, confused, and demanding shoppers.

John A. Covington, the contractor Saunders hired to build the first Piggly Wiggly interior, testified in the patent review that Saunders worked closely with him to fix the checkout clog: "These experiments covered a period of nearly a year and consisted in building, tearing out, and rebuilding checking counte[r]s of various plans and arrangements time after time" until they achieved a workable solution. Covington emphasized "that this experimental work was expensive in character and according to his judgment several thousand dollars were expended in the development of this single feature of the store fixtures by Mr. Saunders before the invention . . . was finally perfected and approved by him."[29] Hubert T. McGee, an architect who had worked with Saunders since August 1916, drawing plans and specifications for his store interiors, emphasized that he had played a limited role in the design process, making "drawings for Mr. Saunders for a number of different schemes" to find a fix for the checkout problem. Much of the work took place at night, when Saunders's "different schemes were installed, tried out, discarded and other[s] substituted from . . . time to time during a period covering nearly a year."[30] All of the affidavits supported the fact that it was Saunders himself who finally invented the workable solution. Mr. Rainwater explained that "many experiments were tried out from time to time but no satisfactory solution was found" until Saunders hit upon a configuration "making it possible to divide the line of customers and use two or more checking crews." Then "the trouble was overcome[,] and it was possible to keep the crowd moving through the single exit with sufficient rapidity to avoid any objectionable congestion."[31] Just as Thomas Edison famously assembled teams of chemists, mathematicians, and engineers to work in his Menlo Park laboratory, Saunders coordinated his team made up of an architect, a draftsman, carpenters, and a store manager in an experimental problem-solving process that used the store space as laboratory.

In the process of experimentation, Saunders created a competition to elicit customer participation for store improvement ideas. All three winners suggested changes that would make it easier to find what they were looking for. First-place winner Mrs. G. Greif recommended that "at the beginning of every aisle place a list of every item on same in alphabetical order. I know from my own experience that it is hard to find every item one wants in such a large stock as you handle." Second-place winner Jeanette Kemp agreed: "It is a little inconvenient to find the articles which I want. Would it be possible to arrange goods alphabetically?" Thinking about potential problems of alphabetical arrangement, she admitted, "Of course I understand that goods which need to be kept cold would have to be out of line, but the majority of things would

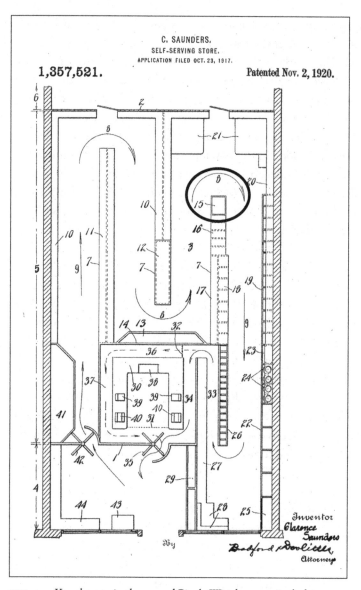

FIG. 2.4. Key changes in the second Piggly Wiggly patent include the use of turnstiles in place of the original gated entry and exit, and a reconfigured U-shaped checkout station that made it possible to divide customers into two checkout lines to accommodate high traffic. A double-sided cabinet (labeled 15) ensured repeated views of the merchandise from the third and fourth aisles. *Source:* Saunders, Self-Serving Store patent 1,357,521.

be easy to find." Alternatively, she suggested that a store directory might help. "I am sure that it would not take long for me to learn where articles are if only I had something to go by."[32] In his updated patent, Saunders seemed to acknowledge the role his customers played in refining the self-service design when he asserted that the revised design was intended "to meet the demands of an intelligent and critical public."[33]

The revised design retained the continuous one-way pathway but made several key changes in the layout to make it work more efficiently. The updated patent documents a variety of improvements in addition to the reconfigured checkout system. The unwieldy entry and exit gates have been replaced with a more mechanically inspired turnstile that would become the corporate symbol for Piggly Wiggly in the 1920s. The revised store design maximized display space with specialized shelving to increase the variety of stock the store could make visible. For example, the cabinet numbered 15 in figure 2.4 was designed to hold bacon and other cured meats. It opened on either side of the case so that customers could select meat from either the third or the fourth aisle. The patent emphasized that this configuration was a product of experience based on observation of how customers interacted with store fixtures. Saunders explained, "This manner of displaying meat . . . facilitates its sale since the customer is obliged to view [the meat twice] when passing through the third and fourth aisles[,] and thereby repeated display of these goods is had. The arrangement also makes it possible for double the number of customers to view the articles and select therefrom at the same time."[34] The rationale for invention highlighted the role the display cabinet played in relationship to the continuous pathway. The claim for invention was not an improved double-sided display case, which would not have been a novel idea. It was the dynamism between cabinet and pathway that created repeated display of the meat.

The most important difference in the two store designs was the reorganization of the checkout process. The initial plan had built the checkout counter into the lobby space where customers exiting the store flowed against the traffic entering the store (see fig. 2.5). This configuration had allowed for only a single checkout line and described an exit lane formed by a low "basket-resting shelf" where customers could rest their full baskets while standing in the checkout line. The revised design integrated the checkout counter into the retail space, creating clear pathways for customers entering and exiting the store (see fig. 2.6). Most importantly a new U-shaped checkout counter made it possible

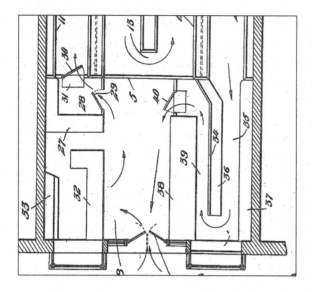

FIG. 2.5. Closeup of checkout counter (labeled 39 on the plan) from the first Clarence Saunders store patent. The arrows show how the flawed design directed customers into one narrow exit route that backed up traffic inside the store and created congestion in the lobby space as people exited the store against the flow of incoming traffic. *Source:* Saunders, Self Serving Store patent 1,242,872.

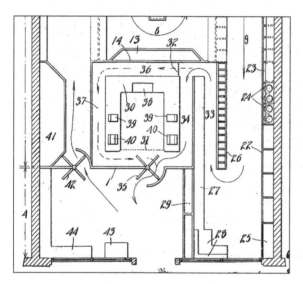

FIG. 2.6. Close-up of the new U-shaped checkout counter that routed customers into two checkout lines exiting through a single turnstile in Clarence Saunders's second store patent. *Source:* Saunders, Self Serving Store patent 1,357,521.

to multiply checkout lines during peak hours of operation. Saunders did not claim to have invented the concept of a checkout line. His emphasis was on the way that the checkout counter worked "to increase the sales capacity of the store, utilizing the labor of the employees to the best possible advantage and thus still further cut down the overhead expense of running the store and enable goods to be sold at prices commensurate with such saving."[35]

The first patent had set the precedent that a self-service store could be a patentable invention. But it was the second patent that was crucial for Saunders's ongoing efforts to franchise his system, and it took twice as long to win approval from the Patent Office. Saunders filed the initial application on October 23, 1917, almost exactly a year after he had submitted his first patent application, and he pursued his case aggressively for the next two years. Unconvinced by detailed rationales provided by Saunders's patent lawyers, affidavits from key employees, and direct observations of a Piggly Wiggly store in operation, the patent reviewer F. W. Holt repeatedly denied his appeals and revised claims on the grounds that the changes represented commonsense application of existing ideas rather than a new mechanical invention.

Holt visited Piggly Wiggly to observe the store in operation but was unconvinced that it met the criteria of invention, arguing, "It is perfectly obvious that a plurality of passage ways will accommodate a greater number of people than a single one. . . . It is the fixed opinion of the Examiner that the device presents a clear case of duplication of parts."[36] Saunders's lawyer E. W. Bradford contested Holt's decision, explaining that the checkout lines were not simply duplicated, they were configured to be served by a single cash register and a single exit. The innovation did not simply speed up the checkout line, the counter was configured to ensure that workers could always be efficiently deployed as business ebbed and flowed throughout a workday. A single clerk could operate the checkout counter when traffic was low, while the other clerks could keep busy weighing and marking packages in the stockroom or restocking the sales room. "These clerks are called one by one from the stock room, as they are needed to keep the line moving and the store from becoming congested."[37] The final design improved the efficiency of the whole store. Saunders submitted photographs documenting the operation of the improved Piggly Wiggly checkout counter with multiple lines of customers served by a single cashier.

Saunders argued that his revised checkout counter design did not merely create duplicate lines with duplicate exits. It systemized the work of store clerks and monitored the flow of cash in new ways. He stationed adding

FIG. 2.7. Photograph submitted by Saunders to document the operation of the improved Piggly Wiggly checkout counter, with multiple lines of customers served by a single cashier. Customers entering the store were steered through the left turnstile past the basket bin. Library of Congress

machines on two sides of the U-shaped counter. At rush hour, customer traffic could be routed around the counter to create two checkout lines. Saunders patented a perforated tape for adding machines as part of the new checkout system. Clerks totaled each sale and placed one side of the tape on the customer's package, filing the other side of the tape to create an account record for tracking inventory. Customers in both lines were then routed past a single cashier, centralizing the exchange of money at one cash register that served both checkout lines. "By this system, there is no way for 'leaks' to develop in the store without collusion between the checking clerk in control of the adding machine, the customer himself and the cashier," Saunders explained. Coordinating the work of recording the sale and collecting the payment also sped up the checkout process. Saunders pointed out that "in a busy place, where there are a number of customers standing in line to be waited upon, the time required to punch the keys of the cash register and wait for the cash drawer to open is saved, which . . . enables the store to wait upon a proportionately larger number of customers."[38] Creating this coordinated checkout system was the result of extensive experimentation.

To counter Holt's assertion that simply multiplying checkout lines was an obvious solution for speeding up the checkout process, Elmo Pullin, superintendent of Piggly Wiggly stores in Memphis, testified that many experiments had been made with different types of checking counter before the U-shaped counter solved the problem "and that the experiments leading to this invention covered a period of a number of months and were carried on at considerable expense, probably several thousands of dollars." Pullin reported that the improved counter had increased the productivity of the store, enabling it to handle more customers and double daily profits.[39]

Holt was unmoved: "In various places of amusements and etc., it is common to have a plurality of entrances and exits to accommodate the crowds. It is perfectly obvious if one passage will not accommodate a crowd a plurality will."[40] He categorically denied the patent application. Bradford and Saunders appealed the decision all the way to the Board of Examiners-in-Chief and made their case in an oral hearing. By the time they submitted their brief to the board in April 1919, Piggly Wiggly was operating in about one hundred cities and towns in the United States. They argued that some Piggly Wiggly stores served twenty-five hundred customers a day "with a force of only five persons in the store." While the average cost of running a typical cash and carry grocery store was around 15 percent of cash receipts, "Piggly Wiggly stores are being operated on approximately 3 per cent of the receipts and few if any exceed the 5 per cent limit."[41] To counter Holt's logic about duplication of checkout lines, Bradford described an Indianapolis department store, L. S. Ayers and Company, that had opened a grocery department in the basement that, "among many others throughout the country," had been "fashioned somewhat after the Piggly Wiggly type of store." When the department store experienced the same problem with congestion at the checkout line, it had the space to simply open up a second checkout counter with a separate exit. Bradford carefully pointed out, "Such a scheme, however, requires a complete duplication of crews to operate, as well as a complete duplication of parts." Each new checkout line required a separate crew to function.

By comparison, Piggly Wiggly's solution was far from an obvious duplication. The U-shaped checkout counter handled multiple lines of customer traffic with one crew, one exit, and one cash register. It was the result of repeated design experimentation and failure. Observing the store in action was central to the design process. "If it only required the making of two passage-ways to be used in lieu of the one passage-way," Bradford reasoned, "it seems strange that Mr. Saunders should have spent all of this time and all of this money, with the assistance of a competent architect and a competent builder, as well as the assistance of others, who were daily using the system, before he succeeded in evolving and perfecting an apparatus that would overcome the difficulty and solve the problem."[42]

The examiners-in-chief found Bradford's argument persuasive, overruled reviewer Holt's objections, and approved the second store patent application in May 1919. They agreed that it took so much effort and expense to devise the new checkout system that the improvement met the threshold for invention. "Experiments were conducted extending over a period of nearly a year and at an expense of several thousand dollars before the construction disclosed in this application was reached." The examiners-in-chief concurred with Saunders that the changes "involved more than an obvious expedient."[43] It was the second time Saunders had successfully convinced the Patent Office that his self-service store was a specialized machine for automatic selling.

In addition to the fixture arrangement, Saunders individually patented several key elements of his system. His hanging price tags made it possible for customers to see the price of each item without picking up the packages to find a price mark—cutting down on the wear and tear on the merchandise. The diamond-shaped numbers were designed to hang from the shelves by hooks and keep traffic moving smoothly along the self-service pathway. "Customers

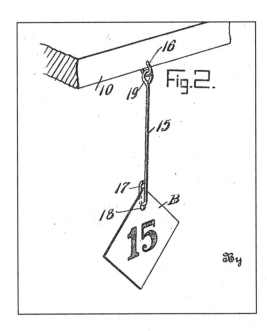

FIG. 2.8. Saunder's patented price tag hanging system was designed so that the preprinted diamond-shaped tags hung from hooks that could not be easily dislodged by customers retrieving items from shelves. *Source:* Saunders, Price-Tagging Means patent.

may readily see in making their selections and with the same glance by which they locate and observe the goods, what prices they are expected to pay for different articles."[44] A perforated tape for adding machines made it possible to speed up the checkout process and produce duplicate sales records to ensure accurate record-keeping for the store and keep cashiers honest.[45] The floor-walker gallery was replaced by a patented lighting system consisting of an electrical conduit mounted above the cabinets with transverse arms to illuminate multiple aisles, "bringing the lights to the points where most needed." This made it easier and cheaper to install lighting when the Piggly Wiggly interior was installed "in buildings not provided with modern electrical equipment."[46] The only thing Saunders doesn't seem to have thought much about improving was the common market basket. His shelving design integrated resting shelves periodically along the pathway for customers to occasionally relieve the weight of a full basket, but even the original list of required store equipment franchisees were required to purchase did not include a set of market baskets. Subsequent self-service inventors would spend considerable time and effort working out how to make it easier for shoppers to collect as much as possible as they worked their way through self-service pathways.

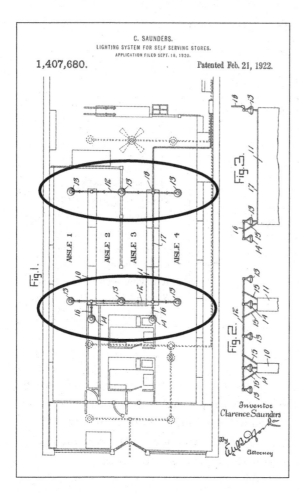

FIG. 2.9. Saunder's patented lighting system shows how a lighting conduit above the shelves lit the full store pathway and made it cheaper to install electricity in existing store spaces and effectively illuminate the factory-built interior. *Source:* Saunders, Lighting System for Self-Serving Stores patent.

Saunders did not just focus on how the store interior worked. As he built his Piggly Wiggly chain in Memphis, Saunders selected different locations and types of buildings, keeping careful records of store productivity to study the urban contexts that might make self-service stores profitable. King Piggly Wiggly was in a commercial block building in the heart of downtown Memphis. His second store, Prince Piggly Wiggly, opened in a well-established grocery store that served a prosperous residential neighborhood of Victorian-era mansions. [47] "Piggly Wiggly the Third" opened in the warehouse district, near a hotel and train station. Saunders had built the first Piggly Wiggly interiors in a trial-and-error process inside the store. By

December 1917, after opening the first three stores, he had begun building store interiors at a Memphis warehouse on Front Street.

One of the most important store location experiments in the first year of operation was on the outskirts of Memphis. Saunders was particularly interested to see how well a self-service store might work in an area with lower population density. He opened a Piggly Wiggly in the new Memphis suburb of Binghamton, "a sparcely [sic] settled town of only about twelve hundred people." Saunders explained, "The Binghamton store was established more for the illustration it would give of what could be expected of a poorly settled and small populated area comprising a village, without much bankable worth in its citizenship."[48] It was a daring move given the stiff competition in the neighborhood from the Bowers chain and several other stores. Duke Bowers had built a successful cash and carry chain of more than forty stores in Memphis—the biggest chain in Memphis at the time.[49] The suburban Piggly Wiggly store ultimately offered convincing evidence of store sales for recruiting small-town franchisees. But by the first anniversary of the King Piggly Wiggly, the self-service company was still a small local chain.[50]

On the first anniversary of the opening of King Piggly Wiggly, Saunders published sales figures for his nine Piggly Wiggly stores, showing that the average Piggly Wiggly customer spent 75 cents for a typical store visit and that stores had averaged sales of $510.45 per day.[51] Even the suburban Binghamton store, though less profitable than the downtown locations, had sold an average of $200 of groceries per day, at a time when "according to the most authentic information obtainable," Saunders claimed, "the ordinary chain cash grocery store" had "average sales of between $400.00 and $500.00 per week."[52] Saunders estimated that, taken together, his nine stores brought in over $4,000 every day. At that rate he projected annual sales of $1,339,252.72. Such sales figures help to account for investor interest in the company and the growth of the chain beyond Memphis. The patent lent an important aura of reliability that mitigated the risks of implementing self-service. The sales data provided powerful evidence that Piggly Wiggly was a reliable machine for automatic selling.

Between October 1916 and October 1917 Saunders had mostly worked out the kinks in his self-serving system. He had nine successful stores in operation in Memphis, and he was ready to start selling Piggly Wiggly stores to as many buyers as he could attract.[53] Saunders's work had caught the attention of observers beyond Memphis, and the first article about Piggly Wiggly

Fig.2.10. Clarence Saunders copyrighted the first national advertisement for Piggly Wiggly as he began selling store franchises nationally. *Source: Collier's,* 18 May 1918, 22–23.

appeared in *Printer's Ink*, the premiere trade magazine for advertisers, in December 1917. "Perhaps no chain of stores that has been organized in recent years has been the object of so much curiosity and speculation as the Piggly Wiggly stores, which were started in Memphis, Tenn., in 1916," John Allen Murphy declared.[54] Murphy acknowledged other precedents in self-service. "The 'groceterias,' of California, have been very successful in using this plan," he suggested. "Clarence Saunders, however, has introduced so many oddities into this method of selling groceries that his system is attracting national attention." The patent transformed the store from a space of consumption to an object of consumption.[55] Saunders turned his attention from store design to launching a new approach to chain store operation by franchising his patented store interior.

## Piggly Wiggly All Over the World

Inventing Piggly Wiggly was a capital-intensive process, and Saunders recruited investors to expand the chain. In June 1918 he formed a partnership with Memphis wholesaler Leslie Martin Stratton. Stratton's managers took over the daily operation of the Memphis stores, freeing Saunders to build the franchising operation. The two men founded the Piggly Wiggly Corporation in August 1918, and the board appointed Saunders to serve as president.[56] Saunders sold the corporation the rights to his patents and trademarks for $550,000 and fifteen thousand shares of Piggly Wiggly common stock. The new company slogan declared Saunders's goal: "Piggly Wiggly All Over the World."

In May 1918 Piggly Wiggly took the unusual step of launching its national franchising campaign with an advertisement in *Collier's*, the national weekly magazine. It wasn't just a small notice in the corner of a page. It was a lavish two-page panoramic view inside the store. And it didn't look like a grocery ad. There were no weekly deals, no seasonal specials. With prices, tastes, and supply chains that varied from place to place, that would have been meaningless on a national stage. Furthermore, *Collier's* was an unlikely place for a grocery store ad. With an impressive slate of journalists and writers from Jack London and Ernest Hemmingway to Upton Sinclair and Ida Tarbell, *Collier's* had an established reputation for news reporting and promoting progressive reform. It was serious journalism for a weekly readership of over a million men and women. But the ad wasn't designed to sell food; it was selling the store.

A new process of invention had begun for Piggly Wiggly—the social process of persuading customers, potential franchisees, and grocery shoppers alike to adopt the new retailing method. With its origins in Memphis and its namesake connections to the hog, a mainstay of the southern diet, Piggly Wiggly has been interpreted as an emblem of southern culture.[57] However, that was not how the company marketed the store during the interwar years. The smiling pig wearing a butcher's white hat did not appear as a symbol for the brand until the 1930s, when Piggly Wiggly worked to establish a reputation for selling high-quality fresh meat. The self-service chain initially cultivated a brand identity that emphasized its national (and even international) ambitions rather than its regional origins. "Piggly Wiggly All Over the World" the *Collier's* ad declared. *Printer's Ink* called it an "odd slogan."[58] It was also a bold proclamation for a little Memphis chain with only a few dozen stores at the time.

Saunders named the corporate newsletter after the turnstile, the gear that made the patented circuitous pathway work. It symbolized the experience of movement and the high-speed efficiency of the self-service machine. The emphasis was on the mechanical elements of the patented design, and the store was promoted as a new kind of merchandizing apparatus for the machine age, not as a regional icon of southern culture. The cost for buying a franchise included a licensing fee, calculated on a sliding scale based on a town's population and monthly royalties.[59] Startup costs also included the expense of all store fittings ($3,500–$4,000 for a store), plus the merchandise needed to stock the shelves for opening day ($4,000–$5,000). Store rental, advertising, and installation fees including the services of an official home office representative to ensure the proper installation of store fixtures added to the bottom line. Altogether the company estimated, "The total investment, therefore, for the opening of the first store in a town will approximate Ten Thousand ($10,000.00) Dollars."[60] That was a steep capital investment in an era when neighborhood grocery stores offered the most affordable opportunity for owning an independent business. In stark contrast to the standardized oak fixtures that composed the Piggly Wiggly interior, many grocers at the time created their own store fixtures out of various materials. Such economies were considered good business practice for cost-effective grocery interiors. *Progressive Grocer* often provided their audience of modernizing businessmen instructions for building their own display stands, such as a "fixture for fruits and vegetables" made out of old cracker boxes.[61]

The success of Piggly Wiggly does not easily fit the idea of self-service as primarily a cost-cutting strategy. It may have lowered operating costs, but a Piggly Wiggly store interior cost more than double the expense of installing the Louisville model store sponsored by the Commerce Department. Carl Dipman estimated that the average cost for one of his model stores, including all fixtures and equipment (such as scales and cash register) was $3,686. The grand total could be as low as $2,755. If you included refrigerated cases for a meat department, Dipman estimated that at the highest end the cost of installing a model store interior totaled $5,520.[62] By contrast, the *minimum* cost of opening a Piggly Wiggly store was $10,000 in 1918, and it did not include a meat department. The Piggly Wiggly interior was also expensive compared to other chain store interiors. In 1912 A&P launched a dramatic expansion of the chain based on a standardized cash and carry store concept they called "the Economy Store." Though it was a traditional counter-service store, the

A&P Economy Store shared the goals that drove self-service experimentation—streamlining store operations, eliminating the cost of delivery service, and reducing the number of clerks needed to operate a busy store. At $2,500 for store fittings and inventory, the A&P Economy store cost a fraction of the cost of a Piggly Wiggly franchise, which required the purchase of a factory-built interior, approved inventory, and franchising fees.[63] Given the considerable capital investment for a small business, the rapid growth of the self-service chain in a war economy is dramatic testament to Saunders's salesmanship.

Despite its high price tag, demand for store interiors soon outpaced the capacity of the Front Street warehouse, and Saunders bought a furniture factory in Jackson, Tennessee, located on a railroad line about ninety miles from the Memphis headquarters. "This factory makes the fixtures for every Piggly Wiggly store that is established whether it be in Bath, Me., or Butte, Mont., or Tuscon [sic], Ariz.," the new Piggly Wiggly corporate newsletter reported.[64] By the end of 1919 the Piggly Wiggly Corporation had sold hundreds of store franchises across the country. Saunders formed Piggly Wiggly Stores, Inc., with additional investors, with an objective of consolidating management of Piggly Wiggly franchises. The corporation issued 150,000 shares of common stock, raising nearly $6 million to buy up privately owned Piggly Wiggly franchise stores, but privately owned Piggly Wiggly franchise stores would always outnumber stores owned by Piggly Wiggly Stores, Inc.

Company literature emphasized that Piggly Wiggly stores were standardized: "There must be exact reproduction in style and arrangement of each individual store unit so that the general appearance of every Piggly Wiggly store shall be to the average eye exactly the same."[65] Standardization extended from the approved list of name-brand products to their location on the shelves. The product placement policy that "coffee in each Piggly Wiggly store must be in the same place" was intended to make it easier for customers to find the products they were looking for.[66] However, the claim of standardization presented enormous practical challenges in implementation. Complete standardization of the store interior was more ideal than reality. Piggly Wiggly franchises opened in diverse regional markets, and company literature suggests that stores carried at least some different merchandise based on local taste preferences and the fact that not all branded products were available everywhere.[67] Piggly Wiggly interiors had to be adjusted to fit store spaces that came in a variety of shapes and sizes.

The Piggly Wiggly Home Office did work with architects to build new stores in Tennessee, and sometimes investors built new buildings when they bought a franchise, but the prevailing expectation was that franchisees would lease existing commercial spaces. The Jackson factory customized store interiors to fit specifications submitted by franchisees.[68] Exact measurements were crucial, so the corporation published a twenty-three-page booklet titled *Store Buildings and Equipment Instructions*, to establish guidelines for franchisees that ensured the factory had the right kind of information to build an interior that would fit.[69] The pamphlet explained how to prepare an existing space for the installation of the factory-built self-service interior.

Saunders's patent indicated that the floor plan could be scaled up or down, and the Piggly Wiggly factory produced store interiors of different sizes. An article in *Woodworker* reported, "Piggly Wiggly stores are planned to conform to either one or the other of two standard layouts. These are called the three-line and four-line stores, meaning stores with three lines or four lines of shelves. Fixtures for these stores are standardized and interchangeable. Variations in the size of store rooms are taken care of by varying the number of standard-size display cabinets and the length of panel railings."[70] The factory ultimately produced stores with as few as one line of shelves. For the first generation of Piggly Wiggly stores, it was said, "A store that has a width of less than 18 feet, a depth of less than 60 feet and a height of ceiling less than 12 feet can under no circumstances be used as a Piggly Wiggly Store."[71] Even this apparently ironclad rule had exceptions: "In case, however, it is not possible to have the proper depth, if the building is sufficiently wide, say 35 feet, so that 15 feet can be partitioned off on the side for the stock room, that kind of a building can also be utilized."

Retrofitting existing stores spaces also meant that franchisees would likely incur additional costs for labor and materials beyond the investment in the factory-built interior. Building instructions emphasized the importance of accuracy in measuring the existing store space to ensure proper fit of the customized fixtures and required that drawings be submitted by a qualified draftsman. Potential franchisees had to submit a variety of documentation for their rented spaces in the early days. Saunders emphasized, "Don't send a pencil sketch of any building drawn by any one not an expert and don't send information with regard to any building merely stating that the building has straight walls inside, but in every case send in exact measurements made by an experienced draughtsman."[72] It was crucial to have exact measurements.

The factory had to take into account "positions and dimensions of all openings, projections, offsets, columns, posts, stairways, trap doors, elevators, partitions, heighth [sic] of ceiling and its condition, condition of floor and walls, location of lavatory, sink and toilet."[73]

The company suggested that franchisees try to get the building landlord to cover remodeling costs such as rewiring, but remodeling was not optional and had to be completed to Piggly Wiggly specifications even if the landlord refused to cover the costs. The home office required that all electrical work be performed by union labor and discouraged do-it-yourselfers. "It must be understood by every Operator that he must not under any condition in order to save a nickel or save a dollar or several dollars, undertake to do work about a building himself that an experienced mechanic should do."[74] All of these remodeling costs could add significantly to the initial $10,000 price tag.

The store interior arrived like a kit and was assembled like a jigsaw puzzle, with parts labeled to correspond with a customized floor plan furnished by the home office. The home office also sent a representative from the Jackson factory to oversee every store installation. "Work absolutely by the floor plan furnished by the Home Office," the instructions emphasized. "There is a reason, and a good one in every case, as to why certain equipment shall be placed in a certain position. All of this has been learned by practical experience, and if instructions are followed to the letter, the result of the work done in installation of the complete equipment will be in accordance with what you will like best after it is done."[75] The arrangement of store fixtures in every customized location was carefully planned by the factory to ensure that every Piggly Wiggly store worked effectively as a machine for automatic selling.

In the early years of expansion, the factory produced about one and a half stores a day, so it must have worked overtime to complete the interiors for the twenty-six stores that opened in Washington, D.C., all on the same day in May 1920.[76] In 1922 the factory was enlarged. "Now it can turn out fixtures for three stores in an eight-hour day," W. H. Rohr explained when he covered the factory operation for *Woodworker*.[77] After the factory expansion, *The Turnstile* proudly declared, "Four cars of fixtures are shipped daily from Jackson. Each car contains a complete set of fixtures for a Piggly Wiggly store."[78] Experimentation with self-service design continued long after the franchising process started. The expanded factory became a laboratory for testing self-service design ideas. Workers built a model store inside the factory that helped to sell franchises by showing potential operators how the self-service system worked and by ensuring that any new equipment would work with the overall self-service system.[79]

Selling Piggly Wiggly stores made Saunders a rich man. By April 1922, Piggly Wiggly Stores, Inc., had sold fifty thousand new shares of common stock at $43 a share, earning over $2 million. The chain achieved its international ambitions when it crossed the border and opened a store in Montreal.[80] But the young company soon faced a critical turning point. A highly publicized failure of franchisees in New York had major repercussions for the chain, still in its early expansion efforts. Manhattan franchisees optimistically declared, "Piggly Wiggly is probably better suited to metropolitan habits than any other section of the country. New York people are interested not only in saving money but also time and annoyance."[81] The Manhattan Piggly Wiggly Corporation opened four stores in New York City in April 1922, with ambitious plans for opening at least three hundred stores in Manhattan and surrounding boroughs.[82] Claiming they could check out three customers per minute, Manhattan Piggly Wiggly assured busy urbanites, "You save TIME through self-service."[83] But New Yorkers turned out to be a hard sell. Before the year was out, the corporation had filed for bankruptcy, sending shock waves south to the home office in Memphis. The failure of such a prominent franchisee created public confusion about the structure of the chain. "This is distinctly the Manhattan branch of Piggly-Wiggly," the home office wrote, trying desperately to distance itself from the failed venture in New York. "Piggly-Wiggly stores are all over the country, and are operated under separate franchises in group arrangements." From the perspective of the home office, "The financial difficulties of the [Manhattan] company are due to having over-extended itself. It set up too many stores in too short a time."[84]

The trade press wondered, though, whether the Manhattan failure signaled more intrinsic limitations of self-service retailing. *American Food Journal* acknowledged, "Various Piggly Wiggly companies which operate in different parts of the country are all separate organizations," but it nevertheless attributed the Manhattan failure to larger systemic and cultural weaknesses in the self-service plan rather than to local Manhattan mismanagement. "Failure of the Manhattan chain of Piggly Wiggly self-service stores, followed by the $1,000,000 failure of the Piggly-Wiggly Eastern Corporation, which operated stores in Newark, N.J., and suburbs, does not seem to be regarded with much surprise in the food trade." The trade magazine reported, "[The industry] regards the venture more as a stock-selling development than a legitimate grocery chain." Acknowledging that Piggly Wiggly stores had been successful in the South and West, the magazine observed, "Conditions are not the same in the East."[85] In particular, the high rent for large store spaces required to install the patented floor plan and the facts that shoppers could not buy bulk goods and that store owners could not customize product offerings in variable neighborhood settings were factors that limited the success of the chain in the urban Northeast. The polyglot neighborhoods of the city were not hospitable environments for self-service stores where shoppers were required to navigate signs and labels in English and choose from a limited selection of standardized products for homogenized tastes.

Saunders felt that stock traders took advantage of the publicity from the New York failure to unfairly lower the price of Piggly Wiggly stock on the New York Stock Exchange. In an ill-advised attempt to raise the price, he began buying up shares. When he was unable to meet the stock exchange margin call, his effort to corner the market brought the corporation to the brink of bankruptcy and set off a legal battle between Saunders and his board of directors. The inventor who had become the public face of company resigned in August 1923 and was banned forever from using the Piggly Wiggly name.[86] But by then the name of the store had taken on a life of its own.

## A Name Plucked from Originality

Saunders's inventive name for his self-service chain demonstrates his flair for selling. Most grocery stores were known only by their street addresses or the names of their proprietors, so Piggly Wiggly stood out from the crowd—and that was the point. The name alone captured the curiosity of the public before they ever entered a store to experience the one-way path.[87] Just as he never fully explained where he got his ideas about self-service, Saunders never explained the origins of the store name, even though he was asked repeatedly asked about it. "To the query from whence came the name the answer is 'From out of chaos and in direct contact with a single individual's mind,'" the Piggly Wiggly Home Office playfully declared.[88] Saunders, ever the consummate salesman, deliberately cultivated an aura of mystery about the origins of the name, even after he was ousted from the company. "Piggly Wiggly is a name plucked from originality. It has no kinship with any other name under the sun. Solitary and alone it stands out immeasurably different and unique in euphony." Corporate documents simply stated, "It was necessary to have a name that was original and that would mean only one thing everywhere.

Hence—PIGGLY WIGGLY. Sounds easy—spells easy—is easy."[89] Saunders trademarked the name and pursued violators relentlessly. In 1920, the company sued Hoggly-Woggly Company in St. Louis for trademark infringement and issued public statements emphasizing the centrality of the chain's name to its store brand. *Simmons' Spice Mill* reported, "The Piggly-Wiggly Co. declare its name to be 'fanciful, arbitrary and distinctive,' and the invention of Charles [*sic*] Saunders of Memphis, its president. Piggly-Wiggly says Hoggly-Woggly is impairing its business and that housewives are buying from Hoggly-Woggly, attracted by the ads of Piggly-Wiggly."[90]

The silliness and mystery of the name did the trick. It generated word of mouth. The absence of an origin story left people free to make up their own meanings, and the name seemed to demand some kind of explanation from the start. "The queer name, 'Piggly Wiggly' was selected because of its attention-getting value and because it is difficult to imitate," *Printer's Ink* declared. As the chain spread beyond Memphis, new stories emerged. *Chain Store Age* speculated that the store name was based on an old English idiom: "Everything about Piggly Wiggly is original. The name is probably a corruption of an old English idiom higgledy-piggledy or at sixes and sevens. The name is more than a name. It is now a word in the English language, copyrighted, and its use limited to those authorized, but to the public it means only one thing—a Piggly Wiggly store. The display, shelving, the price tickets are all original."[91] *Judicious Advertising* said the name had a "Mother Goosey sound" and suggested that "the wiggly course of [Saunders's] store aisle probably helped suggest the name, which has a certain appropriateness on account of this feature."[92] It communicated that serving yourself was fun, not work.

As customers reported on the new experience of self-service shopping, popular interpretations of the chain name circulated in local newspapers and revealed new vernacular processes of invention. Such grassroots processes of interpretation combined with company advertising to make the Piggly Wiggly brand synonymous with self-service during the interwar years. Newspapers began to use the chain name in lower case letters, rather than capitalized as a proper name, especially as an adjective to describe the aisles. "The name describing the system, 'piggly wiggly,' may be said to have originated from the circuitous or 'piggly wiggly' aisles through which customers pass in direct contact with shelves filled with grocery items with plain price tags hanging in front of each item," explained Oklahoma's *Daily Ardmoreite*.[93] Similar references to "piggly wiggly aisles" appeared in newspapers from Ogden City, Utah, to St. Joseph, Missouri.[94] J. R. Falconer, for example, reported to readers of the *Ward County (ND) Independent* in Minot about his recent trip to Sidney, Montana, a growing county seat. "[Sidney has] what we consider the most complete and up to date department store we have yet seen in the west. In the basement of this store there is maintained a grocerataria [*sic*], or what is termed in the South a piggly wiggly store," Falconer explained. Five years after the first Piggly Wiggly store opened, it had become the generic equivalent of the self-service groceteria. The novelty of the self-service store made it a tourist attraction worthy of reporting back home. Falconer explained to his Minot neighbors, "['Piggly wiggly store'] means] a store or department where the customer enters a swinging gate, secures a basket, and helps himself, the goods being arranged conveniently and marked in plain figures. We were informed by the manager of the grocery department on the first floor that anyone desiring to make their purchases in the basement could effect a saving of from 10 to 12%."[95] Though Falconer admired Sidney's "many handsome business structures," it was the experience with self-service that made it a "model city" for Falconer. Navigating the "piggly wiggly" aisles may not have gotten the heart racing like a thrill ride at the amusement park, but the novelty of the Piggly Wiggly system had a recreational appeal.

The concept of "piggly wiggly aisles" as a generic representation of self-service cash and carry helped make the chain a household name. "As a result of the government's advertising of 'fair food prices' the 'Cash and Carry' idea has been developed into a type of standardized self-serve grocery stores with 'piggly wiggly aisles,'" the *Daily Ardmorite* explained. "Data furnished the state food administration of Oklahoma, concerning this revolutionary type of retail grocery stores, indicates that the distribution of food at retail under the pressure of war necessities, has turned in a sweeping way to the self-serve type as hundreds, even thousands of 'piggly wiggly' stores are being established in the United States."[96] Not all of those stores were actually Piggly Wiggly franchises. Thousands of self-service stores did indeed make their appearance after America's entrance into World War I, but Piggly Wiggly was well on its way to becoming the recognized standard for self-service in both the popular imagination and the trade literature.

The well-publicized failure in New York and Saunders's ouster came at a particularly vulnerable moment for the fledgling company. The wartime economy that had provided the initial boost for self-service innovation was giving way to a "return to normalcy," increasing pressure for expanding retail services. Given the expense of opening a Piggly Wiggly store, how would the corporation attract buyers after the novelty of self-service wore off? Would the impressive sales figures continue after the war ended and shoppers demanded a return to the conveniences of full-service stores? Ultimately the company weathered the financial fallout of Saunders's stock manipulations and thrived despite the exit of its famous inventor. Piggly Wiggly may have failed in New York City, but small-town shoppers and franchisees would make it a Main Street icon of modern consumption during the 1920s. The success of the company during the 1920s would be based on the work of local franchisees and innovative use of advertising to sell the store brand.

# Selling the Store, 1918–1933

Store franchisees built Piggly Wiggly into an iconic national brand during the 1920s by installing Piggly Wiggly interiors on Main Streets from coast to coast and by constructing symbolic advertising narratives to sell self-service as a new shopping practice. More than any other firm, Piggly Wiggly shaped the way Americans thought about self-service shopping in the interwar years. Franchisees made an extraordinary commitment to advertising in both local newspapers and national consumer magazines. It can be easy to mistake Piggly Wiggly as a typical grocery chain of the era, but the entrepreneurs who bought Piggly Wiggly franchises remained committed to the advantages of the factory-produced store format as a specialized machine for automatic selling. They did so even as they faced significant changes in grocery retailing that were not easily incorporated into the original patented store design. A photograph of a Piggly Wiggly store in Sacramento in 1923 and an advertisement representing a Piggly Wiggly store in Chicago in 1929 offer important insights about the contradictions between the physical store as a specialized retailing system and franchisees' symbolic representations of it as a nationwide consumer experience. These two stores also document how franchisees adjusted the patented Piggly Wiggly self-service system to compete in a changing food retailing landscape during the 1920s. Connecting the physical and symbolic Piggly Wiggly terrain reveals the distinctiveness of the self-service chain in American consumer history. Throughout the spring and summer of 1923, the *Sacramento Bee* ran stories about Clarence Saunders's stock manipulations and his chaotic downfall. By August Saunders had resigned from the company, leaving its future in doubt. Despite the turmoil in Memphis, business continued as usual for Piggly Wiggly franchisees around the country. In November the *Bee* announced the grand opening of the second Piggly Wiggly in the city. Andrew Williams, who worked for the Pacific

Coast franchise, had scouted the location in the new Public Market, a stylish building designed by architect Julia Morgan near the state capitol. "On his first visit to the Sacramento Public Market," the *Bee* reported, "Mr. Williams was instantly impressed with its great possibilities and decided at once to install a Piggly Wiggly grocery store in a prominent location on the main floor."[1] Williams set up a three-line store inside the market where shoppers entered through the turnstile and traversed the self-service pathway, gathering prepackaged products and exiting through the checkout line like they did in any Piggly Wiggly store.

In figure 3.1, the photographer peered into the store from above, making it possible to see how this Piggly Wiggly store worked as a compartmentalized machine for automatic selling in the larger space of the Public Market. Its specialized self-service retailing system could not easily accommodate many kinds of fresh foods offered by other vendors in the market. Bakeries, delicatessens, and greengrocers sold products that required clerk service, slicing,

FIG. 3.1. Piggly Wiggly three-line store inside the Sacramento Public Market. The patented lighting system was installed atop the shelving to light the circuitous pathway around the compartmentalized self-service space. The photograph is attributed to Bjarne Dahl, an architect on Julia Morgan's staff. *Source:* Julia Morgan–Sara Holmes Boutelle Collection, MS0027, Special Collections and Archives, Kennedy Library, California Polytechnic State University, San Luis Obispo.

weighing, and wrapping items to order. Also housed in the market, the strategically named Market Service Grocery offered convenient delivery, telephone orders, and mail-order services for customers who did not have time to come to the store.[2] The only way to buy groceries from Piggly Wiggly was to come to the market and traverse the patented pathway in person. During the 1920s, larger "combination" grocery stores integrated these products and services more readily into larger store spaces arranged around counters operated by clerks, and Piggly Wiggly franchisees were challenged to adapt the original patented Piggly Wiggly pathway.

The Sacramento Piggly Wiggly served customers in the heart of the city. At the end of the decade a *Ladies' Home Journal* ad documented the successful transition Piggly Wiggly franchisees made to the suburbs, selling the store as part of an elite leisured landscape north of Chicago bordering Lake Michigan. The ad presented self-service shopping as the vogue of modern independent women "who enjoy[ed] the freedom of choosing for themselves." Featuring the kind of new commercial development that attracted investors, the fine print invited "men who control sufficient capital to finance a number of stores" to inquire about the "unusual opportunity to own and operate a profitable local business with the merchandising co-operation of a national organization."[3] Thus the ad sold the store to a national audience of consumers and potential franchisees.

At first glance, the Chicago Piggly Wiggly in figure 3.2 appears to be a typical chain store. The ad draws a familiar picture of White middle-class suburbanization, the expansion of chain stores, and the development of mass consumer society in an urbanized United States during the 1920s. The ad promotes self-service as a popular shopping method promoted by millions of women. But this picture is incomplete and misleading. The suburban store featured in the 1929 magazine ad was still the specialized machine for automatic selling pictured in the Sacramento Public Market. Piggly Wiggly continued to play a specialized role in the history of self-service retailing throughout the 1920s. Landscape historians and cultural geographers have studied the ways that the built environment is not only physically constructed but also how it functions socially and ideologically. The physical, social, and ideological constructs of cultural landscape can interact in ways that reinforce or contradict each other.[4] A clearer understanding of the intersection between the physical and symbolic Piggly Wiggly terrain shows that self-service shopping was not the widespread consumer experience that consumer magazine ads claimed or that historians have assumed.

FIG. 3.2. The J. Walter Thompson advertising firm designed a series of full-page ads featuring Piggly Wiggly stores in different locations around the United States. The Chicago ad associated a North Shore suburban Piggly Wiggly with tony social gathering spots in the neighborhood, including Sky Harbor, "unique airport and night club combined," a summer season Thoroughbred horse show, and opera in the park. *Source: Ladies' Home Journal*, September 1930, 184.

Because self-service was so unfamiliar to most shoppers, Piggly Wiggly ads articulated ideas about shopping more explicitly and extensively than any other ads of the era. As a result, they have also powerfully shaped the ways historians have understood consumer culture in the early twentieth century. Piggly Wiggly ads have been variously interpreted by historians of advertising, consumer history, and gender as broadly representative of national patterns of mass consumption in the interwar years.[5] Historian Eric Foner highlights a Piggly Wiggly ad, with its emphasis on the freedom to choose, as emblematic of the ways that consumption in the Progressive Era came to symbolize freedom and citizenship.[6] It is ironic that a store so carefully designed to control the movements of shoppers and workers has come to symbolize the freedom of the American marketplace.

The Chicago Piggly Wiggly ad was professionally designed by the influential J. Walter Thompson advertising firm, and so it is not surprising that it echoes familiar themes in other ads of the period.[7] Configuring the consumer as the affluent White woman that represented advertisers' idealized target market, the ad evokes familiar advertising narratives of the 1920s about the democracy of goods that enabled American consumers to enjoy the pleasures of modern convenience.[8] Historians have interpreted Piggly Wiggly ads as broadly representative of consumer experience because they featured women as independent household managers who embraced self-service shopping.[9] Overlooked in this emphasis on representativeness, however, is the fact that the ads document an important turning point in modern retail history. Self-service shopping was still new and unfamiliar to the majority of consumers during the 1920s. It is highly misleading to interpret Piggly Wiggly ads as representing national consumption practices during the interwar years. Instead, the store space and the company advertising worked together to differentiate Piggly Wiggly as a new kind of shopping experience.

The Chicago Piggly Wiggly ad was part of a national campaign sponsored by the Piggly Wiggly Operators Association that brought the self-service chain into direct competition with A&P, the largest food chain in the nation at the time. It was a unique advertising competition, designed to sell the store brand at a time when ads typically sold brand name products, not the chain stores that sold them. A&P and Piggly Wiggly both faced significant challenges in rethinking store design as the profitability of small stores during the wartime economy faltered in the 1920s. In competing sales pitches, A&P and Piggly Wiggly ads document the ways both chains adjusted their store designs during the decade. The different routes they took demonstrate the social difficulties of selling the self-service store in the interwar years.

When Piggly Wiggly opened in the Sacramento Public Market, there were over twelve hundred stores in the chain operating in forty-one states and in Canada.[10] Franchising got off to a fast start, but growth of the chain was modest during the decade. By the end of the 1920s the *Ladies' Home Journal* ad for the suburban Chicago store revealed that there were 3,200 Piggly Wiggly stores in more than a thousand towns and cities. In comparison, A&P had a national distribution of 16,000 stores and by 1929 had become the first retailer ever to sell $1 billion of merchandise in a single year.[11] These were two very different kinds of chain organizations. In contrast to the highly centralized A&P organization, the Piggly Wiggly terrain was ultimately created in a grassroots process by the cumulative choices of local franchisees rather than a centralized planning process in the Memphis Home Office. Small-town franchisees each crafted a landscape that demonstrated the specialization of self-service retailing during the 1920s and recruited a diverse clientele that reflected the popularity of self-service for modernizing small-town consumers. While the patented interior looked the same no matter where it was located and the Piggly Wiggly chain had a national reach, franchisees' reliance on self-service retailing methods shaped the Piggly Wiggly terrain in distinctive ways.

## Mapping the Piggly Wiggly Terrain

Because the home office relied on the initiative of local entrepreneurs to buy the store interior, the chain developed a varied profile of small and large independent owners who built Piggly Wiggly into the only national self-service chain during the 1920s. They established the versatility of self-service retailing in different geographic and commercial contexts during the 1920s. While the largest franchises were in Chicago and Los Angeles, the typical Piggly Wiggly store was owned by a small-town franchisee with fewer than five stores. Studying the franchising history of Piggly Wiggly is complicated by the fact that many franchisees formed their own independent companies. The home office in Memphis ultimately owned only a fraction of Piggly Wiggly stores. The Piggly Wiggly chain also included the New Mexico Piggly Wiggly Company, the Piggly Wiggly Valley Company of Louisville, and the Piggly Wiggly California Company, to name a few.

Initially only towns with a minimum of five thousand residents were eligible for Piggly Wiggly franchises, but Saunders speculated that the self-service store would eventually work even in towns as small as one thousand people once the public became more familiar with the advantages of the system.[12] Because self-service required lots of foot traffic to ensure profitability, the franchising contract specified that the highest priority was "to obtain central locations in the downtown districts and in the suburban districts as will make possible a large volume of trade per store."[13] The capital-intensive store location strategy added to the price tag for the expensive patented interior, but it also created high visibility for the growing chain.

Piggly Wiggly opened in downtown Raleigh, North Carolina, within view of the state capitol, attracting hundreds of visitors on opening day in the spring of 1921 (see fig. 3.3).[14] It was the only grocery store in the 100 block of Fayetteville Street, the central commercial artery of the capitol city, drawing a busy trade daily and pulling in customers from the countryside on Saturdays. The downtown location served diverse customers doing business at the courthouse or shopping at other stores in the central business district for decades. The Piggly Wiggly focus on high-rent locations in the heart of the central business district stands out from the crowd. Significantly, other grocery chains in downtown Raleigh at the time chose cheaper locations and did not stay long at the same address. Flexibility in moving stores was a strategy for maximizing store profitability as business districts and neighborhoods evolved. For example, A&P had a strict policy to only take short-term leases, and that could limit a choice of prime locations. As late as 1933, 94 percent of all A&P store leases ran for only one year.[15] In Raleigh, A&P operated in more affordable territory than Piggly Wiggly, several blocks farther out on Hillsborough Street and Person Street, closer to an affluent residential neighborhood. The Person Street A&P moved once between 1924 and 1930. The Hillsborough Street store moved three times between 1924 and 1947. With its reliance on standardized interiors custom fitted to specific store dimensions, Piggly Wiggly was less mobile than A&P. But the downtown location worked. City directories show that Piggly Wiggly operated continuously at the Fayetteville Street location until at least 1950.

Given the stringent aims of self-service retailing methods to lower overhead costs as much as possible, the Piggly Wiggly emphasis on high-rent locations is notable. The self-service chain reasoned that the high rent could be offset by volume sales at a given store. As John Burch, the nationwide Piggly Wiggly advertising manager explained, the store itself was the most

FIG. 3.3. "Fayetteville, Street, Raleigh, NC, looking north toward the State Capitol, ca. 1923." Piggly Wiggly occupied a prominent location in downtown Raleigh, North Carolina. Opened in 1921, it was the only grocery store in the 100 block of Fayetteville Street, the central commercial artery of the city. *Source:* Carolina Power and Light Photograph Collection, PhC.68, State Archives of North Carolina. Courtesy of the State Archives of North Carolina.

convincing advertisement of all: "Once [a customer] enters a Piggly Wiggly store, she will continue to return, as the privilege of selecting goods without interruption or persuasion from any one, appeals to most housekeepers, and the cleanliness and orderly arrangement of the goods unconsciously has its effect on the customer."[16] The high visibility of stores in prominent locations was worth the cost to give the maximum number of people an opportunity to try out the system.

With its highly publicized track record of store sales that promised predictable profit, Piggly Wiggly was surprisingly appealing to small-town entrepreneurs, despite the considerable franchising and location costs. By 1923 Piggly Wiggly had established a foothold in at least forty-one towns with under five thousand residents, including a few towns with fewer than one thousand people, such as Hugo, Colorado; Taylorsville, Kentucky; and Plainview, Texas. Fully a third of Piggly Wiggly stores were located in towns with less than ten thousand residents. The patented interior took the guess work out of store arrangement, and the home office sent support personnel to get the store up and running when working with new franchisees. Just as in larger cities, small-town franchisees located their stores at the heart of the business district. In a postcard of Hickory, North Carolina, Piggly Wiggly serves as a visual front door to downtown, with the only legible store sign on Union Square (fig. 3.4). Local town boosters worked with postcard companies to highlight particular features of downtown scenes or erase elements like crowded sidewalks to present an orderly business district, so it is noteworthy that the only store identified by name in the Hickory postcard was Piggly Wiggly.[17] Of course, small-town main streets were full of chain stores. J. C. Penney, for example, built more than half of its stores in towns with less than five thousand residents.[18] But the decentralized ownership of Piggly Wiggly stores made it a different kind of national chain. It would be harder to claim Woolworth, headquartered in New York City, as a local institution. A franchising process that supported independent ownership of store units was appealing for small-town entrepreneurs. Featuring Piggly Wiggly as the only legible chain on Main Street offered Hickory town boosters an opportunity to link their modernity with their localism.

Long before an anti-chain movement would generate chain store taxes in twenty-eight states, Piggly Wiggly franchisees emphasized their local ownership of the stores, especially in parts of the country where the anti-chain movement would be the strongest.[19] The role of independent store owners in the chain became a central part of the narrative Piggly Wiggly told in local

FIG. 3.4. This postcard of downtown Hickory, North Carolina, with Piggly Wiggly in the foreground, was postmarked 18 August 1939. The chain was first listed in *Miller's Hickory City Directory* in 1925. *Source:* Durwood Barbour Collection of North Carolina Postcards (PO77), North Carolina Collection Photographic Archives, Special Collections, Wilson Library, University of North Carolina, Chapel Hill.

small-town newspapers. As they opened their second Piggly Wiggly store in El Paso, Texas, the local franchisee touted advantages of a company with national scope. The El Paso Piggly Wiggly joined stores in sixty-three cities enjoying the advantages of shared operating expenses that meant lower prices for El Paso shoppers. Nevertheless, they assured their small-town readers, "While Piggly Wiggly is a National institution, the El Paso stores are owned and operated under license by El Paso men whose homes are here and by El Paso money."[20] Local control meant that stores could cater to the regional tastes of their customers and to the republican rhetoric of small town, antimonopoly opinion. The home office developed a list of approved, standard, brand name products, but independent units purchased from wholesalers in the regions where their stores were located, so the products offered on Piggly Wiggly shelves reflected the tastes of local communities. In Raton, New Mexico, the local franchisee emphasized, "The New Mexico Piggly Wiggly Company believes in New Mexico, and, with equality in quality and prices, purchases the products of the state, and buys from those wholesalers who maintain offices and warehouses in the state."[21] Such rhetoric reflected the unique business model of the Piggly Wiggly chain. The Piggly Wiggly Home Office actually reduced the number of stores it owned, even as the chain expanded among independent franchisees. In 1923 Piggly Wiggly, Inc., owned 659 stores.[22] By 1926, after weathering the financial fallout from Saunders's stock debacle, Piggly Wiggly, Inc., owned 490 stores.[23]

In the fall of 1925, independent operators and representatives of Piggly Wiggly Stores, Inc., met in Chicago, not Memphis, signaling the influence of the largest national franchisee. The convention brought together independent operators from all over the country to form the Piggly Wiggly Operators Association. A. C. Jones, owner of Piggly Wiggly California Company, one of the largest independent owners in the association, became its secretary. Jones reported his analysis of the self-service chain's steady progress for readers of *Chain Store Age* following the Chicago conference. In less than a decade the chain had grown from a few units in Memphis to 1,850 Piggly Wiggly stores in operation across the country. Jones's report revealed a varied profile of store owners, "whose only bond of union is their contractual obligations with the parent company and their membership in the Piggly Wiggly Operators Association."[24] The chain consisted of 266 independent owners who operated 1,360 stores. Some independent owners established multi-state holdings. For example, the Grimes Company owned 64 stores in Colorado and a unit of 19 stores in San Francisco.[25] Most Piggly Wigglies, however, were operated by small independent owners with five or fewer stores. "There are 52 independent operators who have 6 stores or more, and 214 who have 5 stores or less," Jones reported. Jones himself owned 59 stores, and he touted their consistent performance as an example of the attractions of becoming a Piggly Wiggly franchisee: "Speaking generally, I think I am safe in saying that the sales per store throughout the entire Piggly Wiggly chain are uniformly higher than those enjoyed by any other type of chain grocery store. In my own chain, we average per store per week about $2,200 in groceries and green goods the year around, and from figures I have received from other Piggly Wiggly operators, I know that most of them make about the same showing."[26] Jones echoed the rationale Clarence Saunders had used successfully with the Patent Office. The Piggly Wiggly store design was a reliable machine that produced volume sales.

To attract the customers that drove those sales figures, the Piggly Wiggly franchising contract specified that franchisees buy "at least a half page advertisement" in the local newspaper announcing a new store opening.[27] Store openings took on a carnival atmosphere, with some standard rituals. Handing

FIG. 3.5. "Opening Day, Sat. Nov. 7, 1925. Piggly Wiggly Store No. 2. Yakima [Washington]." It is easy to see why traffic congestion was such a concern for self-service store inventors when stores were filled with customers. On opening day, not everyone came to shop. Sometimes curious sightseers came to see how the store worked. They filled the aisles and left without spending a dime. *Source:* Piggly Wiggly Grocery Store Collection, Memphis and Shelby County Room, Benjamin Hooks Central Library, Memphis Public Libraries.

out roses or carnations to shoppers, for example, became a strategy for feminizing grocery shopping and recruiting affluent local customers. The home office routinely reported store operators' opening day statistics in the company newsletter, often distinguishing the numbers of actual shoppers from the numbers of merely curious. More than half the population of Carlsbad, New Mexico, turned out to experience the small town's first self-service store.[28] In Meridian, Mississippi, rain couldn't dampen the turnout for the Piggly Wiggly opening where J. A. Ross reported, "Opening sales $325.05, customers seven hundred four." Besides paying customers, the opening attracted sightseers. "Somewhere in the neighborhood of three thousand visitors passed through store and seemed overjoyed to see such an up-to-date store with cheap prices. Number of customers said other stores are holding them up," Ross wrote. D. D. Williams reckoned that his store opening in Miami in May 1919 attracted about thirteen hundred paying customers and another six thousand curious visitors.[29] The company encouraged store managers to open the store to sightseers because they were so confident that once people experienced self-service they would come back to shop regularly. Photographs of store openings corroborate the claims of large turnouts, with customers standing shoulder-to-shoulder bringing the circuitous path to a crawl. With their attention-grabbing name, prominent store locations, and publicity, Piggly Wiggly stores were designed to be a tourist attraction.

Piggly Wiggly interiors were installed coast to coast, but there were definite regional patterns of adoption. Customers could shop at the Piggly Wiggly in Bridgeport, Connecticut, and Atlantic City, New Jersey, and even East Greenwich, Rhode Island (with 3,290 residents), but the chain was least successful in New England and the Mid-Atlantic. Though the chain downplayed its southern origins in its marketing strategy, Piggly Wiggly was located on twice as many southern Main Streets than in any other region. Texans were the most enthusiastic Piggly Wiggly adopters outside Tennessee, with stores in forty-four towns (twice as many locations as any other state), from Abilene to Yoakum. Independent owners with fewer than five stores made the self-service chain a Main Street icon during the 1920s. But regional patterns of Piggly Wiggly store distribution highlight the fact that shopping at Piggly Wiggly was not a representative shopping experience for most Americans.

Even so, Piggly Wiggly became a popular culture symbol of modern American consumption in the 1920s. Sinclair Lewis's best-selling novels *Main Street* (1920) and *Babbitt* (1922) evoked a widely recognized stereotype of downtown America, whether it was celebrated by real estate developers and urban boosters or vilified by what *Harper's* editor Frederick Lewis Allen called "the revolt of the highbrows." Allen observed in his informal history of the decade, "The intellectuals had only to read Lewis's books to realize that the qualities in American life which they most despised and feared were precisely the ones which he put under the microscope for cold-blooded examination. It was George F. Babbitt who was the arch enemy of the enlightened, and it was the Main Street state of mind which stood in the way of American civilization."[30] Babbitt's wife shopped at the Piggly Wiggly, symbol of the economizing strategies and new domestic labor of the respectable middle-class woman. She complained to her husband, "I get so bored with ordering three meals a day, three hundred and sixty-five days a year, and ruining my eyes over that horrid sewing-machine, and looking after your clothes

**TABLE 3.1**   Piggly Wiggly Store Locations by Region

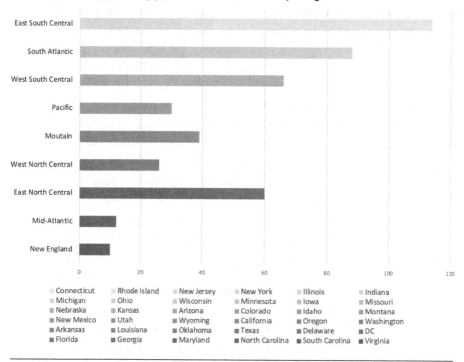

| | | | | | |
|---|---|---|---|---|---|
| Connecticut | Rhode Island | New Jersey | New York | Illinois | Indiana |
| Michigan | Ohio | Wisconsin | Minnesota | Iowa | Missouri |
| Nebraska | Kansas | Arizona | Colorado | Idaho | Montana |
| New Mexico | Utah | Wyoming | California | Oregon | Washington |
| Arkansas | Louisiana | Oklahoma | Texas | Delaware | DC |
| Florida | Georgia | Maryland | North Carolina | South Carolina | Virginia |

SOURCE: Compiled from store opening announcements in *Turnstile* newsletters, 1922–1923.

and Rone's and Ted's and Tinka's and everybody's, and the laundry, and darn-ing socks, and going down to the Piggly Wiggly to market, and bringing my basket home to save money on the cash-and-carry and—*everything*!"[31] The Memphis Home Office may not have appreciated Lewis's use of the brand as a symbol of the drudgery of modern domestic labor, but they would have cel-ebrated his choice of the chain as a symbol of middle-class respectability. By 1922 Piggly Wiggly was a household name at home in the fictional midwest-ern city of Zenith and on the Main Streets of readers who shopped in towns across America. The company's extensive use of advertising built a symbolic landscape that extended the cultural reach of Piggly Wiggly beyond its phys-ical store locations. One community newspaper at a time, local franchisees built a national brand identity and shaped how Americans thought about self-service shopping in general.

Piggly Wiggly ads did not simply report the weekly sales items like most grocery store ads. The unfamiliarity of self-service shopping methods spurred the company's creative uses of advertising to explain how the stores worked and to create a persuasive narrative about the advantages of self-service. One Piggly Wiggly promoter called it "building the story of Piggly Wiggly."[32] Piggly Wiggly ads are important because they went far beyond price appeal to attract customers. They offer the best evidence of the symbolic story-telling small-town franchisees used to attract customers to self-service shopping.

Piggly Wiggly became a darling of advertising trade magazines *Printer's Ink* and *Judicious Advertising* when it launched its national franchising campaign with an ad in *Collier's*. They celebrated the chain's use of advertising as something new because existing chains had not taken advantage of the power of advertising to sell the store brand. Chains did not buy much advertising, and when they did, "it was advertising of products rather than of the institution," *Printer's Ink* complained. In contrast, Piggly Wiggly ads sold the store. *Printer's Ink* admired the way Piggly Wiggly ads were designed to "to familiarize the public with the name, the character and the appearance of the stores and thus to pave the way for the more rapid expansion of the system." It made sense to advertise nationally: "The idea here is to tie all the local Piggly Wigglies together and to let the public know that the store they are patronizing is part of a big national organization.[33] But national magazines like *Collier's* were expensive, and Piggly Wiggly focused its advertising resources on local newspapers where franchisees could directly recruit customers to the new stores they were opening. *Judicious Advertising* noted admiringly, "Newspaper advertising has been really the backbone of the [Piggly Wiggly] system's success."[34]

Piggly Wiggly advertising was unprecedented compared to the limited advertising investment of most grocery stores at the time. John Burch, the advertising manager for the Piggly Wiggly Home Office, offered an astonishing inventory of the company's sustained investment. "Piggly Wiggly uses each week an average of 10,000 inches or 140,000 lines in the daily papers in the 150 cities in which we operate stores," Burch reported in 1920, after only two years of franchising. Burch explained that daily newspapers offered the best results because they reached so many readers in local communities and could reflect price fluctuations in local markets. He added, "We also know that this form of advertising constantly brings new customers."[35] Regular advertising was especially important for self-service, not only to recruit new customers to an unfamiliar shopping method but also to keep them coming back to the store again and again. While the home office developed a variety of advertisement designs, local franchisees had choices about which designs to use, and they added information about store location, prices, and products that were relevant to local markets. Piggly Wiggly standardized slogans and trademarked headlines to construct a national identity, but the company adjusted its local newspaper narratives to appeal to the variety of community contexts where stores were located.

In California, franchisees commissioned their own advertising booklet to coordinate advertising on the West Coast.[36] A. C. Jones, president of his independent Western States Piggly Wiggly Company, began a long-term collaboration with advertising consultant H. H. Lestico in 1922 to create professional ads for his stores in the Los Angeles area. Lestico devoted his career to chain store grocery advertising, and he considered that Piggly Wiggly's self-service store format created a special need for advertising—not simply because customers were unfamiliar with self-service but also because clerks did not perform the traditional sales role in a self-service store. "Piggly Wiggly is almost entirely dependent upon advertising," Lestico explained, "for the reason that employees have little opportunity to sell. The consumer must be interested through what she sees and reads. Therefore it is quite important that what she reads be effective."[37] But simply relying on the manufacturers to advertise the products on Piggly Wiggly shelves would not distinguish Piggly Wiggly from other stores offering the same products. Readers needed a reason to choose Piggly Wiggly over any other chain. Lestico stressed the importance of persistence and consistency. "It takes months of constant telling, interestingly and truthfully, to influence a sufficient number of minds to gather together enough momentum to realize definite results," he emphasized.

In 1926 Lestico built on his collaboration with the Los Angeles–based Piggly Wiggly California Company to publish a set of ads for Piggly Wiggly franchisees. *Building the Story of Piggly Wiggly* was intended as "a practical system of Piggly Wiggly advertising used by prominent operators throughout the United States in selling the Piggly Wiggly story to the consuming public." The book included testimonials from Piggly Wiggly operators who had used his services beyond Los Angeles, such as the Piggly Wiggly Puget Sound Company in Seattle; Piggly Wiggly of San Francisco; the Home Piggly Wiggly Company of Arkansas City, Kansas; and Piggly Wiggly Pacific

Company in Oakland.[38] Local franchisees' commitment to advertising was instrumental in creating narratives that forged the chain's national identity.

A core advertising message centered on the democracy of self-service. On one spectacular opening day in Washington, D.C. where twenty-six new Piggly Wiggly stores opened their doors at the same time, the chain proclaimed, "Thus comes Piggly Wiggly . . . into the midst of Washington's workers, into the midst of its society, into the midst of its Governmental activities." Appealing to workers and socialites alike, the message evoked the socially equalizing effect of the self-service store: "Everyone is received alike, everyone is able to buy alike and at the same price, everyone is to be allowed that same freedom of choice and of movement throughout the store and in all of these things not one time on any day will there be one solicitation that any person make a purchase."[39] It was not just a strategy for the seat of national government. The El Paso Piggly Wiggly emphasized that the store "has been visited by the society class, the banker class, the wage-earner class, and the PLAIN American class—all of whom have said that they liked the Piggly Wiggly way."[40] In the Piggly Wiggly store, self-service was both democratic and aspirational. It elevated all shoppers to the same fashionable affluence of the Washington socialite or the banker class.

Piggly Wiggly ads explicitly engaged small-town caste systems, weaving together themes of egalitarianism, frugality, pride, and quality with the reassurance that all customers would be treated with equal respect and have access to the same quality of merchandise as the well-born. It was an especially appealing narrative for small-town customers where the privileges of rank could influence the speed and quality of store service. An Oklahoma City ad emphasized that all classes of people served themselves at Piggly Wiggly: "It was made for her who is just a plain woman. It was made for her who goes about in silks. It was made for her who rides on street cars. It was made for her who rides in automobiles. It was made for her who does her own washing. It was made for her who has her washing done. It was made for her who uses a gingham apron while she gets ready for the homecoming of her man. It was made for her who lets the cook prepare the meal for the man of the house. A Piggly Wiggly was made for everybody."[41]

The Oklahoma City ad assumed a female customer, but store location strategies in central business districts and photographs of store interiors document a more diverse clientele. Self-service attracted plenty of businessmen to the store, and Piggly Wiggly franchisees appealed directly to Black customers in towns and cities of the Great Migration. In Columbia, Missouri, Piggly Wiggly was the only chain store to advertise in *The Colored Directory*, assuring Black housewives, "Think of Piggly Wiggly as the last word in modern food distribution—Quality, Cleanliness, and Self-Serve are the real features."[42] Hollie T. Sims, editor of the *Negro Star* in Wichita, promoted Piggly Wiggly when local manager G. W. Holden hired porter Charley Ivy. "This young man comes to the city from Shelby, Miss., from a splendid family. He is the first Negro employee of the Piggly Wiggly Stores here. Mr. Holden promises many good things if we will but patronize his stores." Holden placed an ad in the *Negro Star* in the summer of 1922, offering several reasons why African American customers should do their shopping at the new downtown Piggly Wiggly store. "FIRST, when you go in most any Grocery in the country YOU generally are not seen until you are disgusted or every one else is waited upon. SECOND, When you ask for this or that you are shown something that is not moving well, and the clerk supposes It's good enough for you."[43] Though the new store was the eighth Piggly Wiggly in Wichita, the ad specified that *Negro Star* readers should make note of the new location. It did not include the addresses of the other seven Piggly Wiggly stores around town. While they promoted the equality of self-service shopping, Piggly Wiggly franchisees built and promoted their stores with the local knowledge of a racially segregated landscape.

The symbolic egalitarian narrative fit the new spatial experience of self-service shopping. For decades department stores had fostered a connection between democracy and consumption through open access to the store and the right to browse whether or not you actually bought anything. Open access to store displays cut across race and class lines. Workers and bourgeoisie mingled shoulder to shoulder in palatial store spaces. In effect, department stores democratized desire as working-class, immigrant, Black, and White shoppers browsed the merchandise. But historian Traci Parker has shown how the racialized democracy of the department store service differentiated customer experience and "shaped the ways that race and class were imagined and employed to create both worker and consumer identities."[44] Department stores upheld the class and racial order by ignoring or underserving Black customers and relegating the working class to bargain basements. Self-service redefined the relationship between democracy and consumption by equalizing not only the access to store space but also the shopping experience itself. An Ogden, Utah, Piggly Wiggly franchisee declared, "At Piggly Wiggly there is no 'class,' there is no difference." The first-come, first-served operation of the self-service checkout line stood in stark contrast to counter-service stores where clerks offered preferential treatment.[45]

Piggly Wiggly constructed a self-service narrative to attract the masses. But the company was especially careful to avoid being typecast as a cheap, working-class store. "The richest people are generally the most frugal," one ad moralized. "They acquired their money by hard work and don't throw it away." Advertising narratives sometimes described "sightings" of wealthy local customers:

In a Piggly Wiggly store a few days ago were seen the wife of a man owning several millions of city property, the daughter of a banker, the president of a big down-town department store, and others of wealth and position. They were getting the best food products, but they were paying for FOOD, not for SERVICE and DELIVERY. They weren't ashamed to do their grocery buying themselves. People like this don't have to be ashamed—they are a law unto themselves—they now have money and position because they did not spend all their days "aping" after some so-called society leader.[46]

These narratives played on small-town social networks and hierarchies, simultaneously applauding the common sense and thrift of affluent shoppers who embraced self-service and shaming those who were too "uppity" to carry their own grocery basket. Piggly Wiggly locations on prominent Main Streets and central business districts reinforced mass access while safeguarding the status of affluent customers.

Above all, Piggly Wiggly ads repeated a narrative of freedom in the self-service aisles that emphasized the social rather than practical advantages of self-service. "One of the reasons for Piggly Wiggly's popularity is its democracy and freedom from clerk domination, each customer is his or her own boss," the Ogden, Utah, franchisee emphasized.[47] With seemingly unfettered access to store merchandise, with no pushy clerk to talk them into buying something you didn't need, with the freedom to move at their own pace along the circuitous path, customers now had all of the privileges of access once reserved exclusively for the merchant himself.

As franchisees built a persuasive narrative of equality and freedom in their advertising, they faced new challenges in maintaining the original patented store interior as a machine for automatic selling. If stores had only increased in size, the Piggly Wiggly factory might simply have built additional shelving to expand display space. But grocery stores not only got larger, they also began to offer products that had not traditionally been sold in grocery stores. New "combination stores" promoted their advantages for modern women by focusing on the convenient one-stop shopping they offered. It was an approach to food retailing that both chain and independent grocers increasingly embraced in the 1920s. Instead of multiple trips to butcher shop, bakery, and greengrocer or public market, shoppers could make one trip to a combination stores that offered them fresh meat, produce, and baked goods under one roof, sometimes conveniently located in the suburbs so one didn't have to make a trip downtown. The problem for Piggly Wiggly franchisees was that all of these products were considered at the time to be impossible to sell through self-service methods. Franchisees had bought a machine for automatic selling when they purchased a Piggly Wiggly interior, and any physical changes to the store design had to be carefully integrated to maintain the advantages of the specialized self-service system.

## Adapting Piggly Wiggly for a New Food Retailing Landscape in the 1920s

A&P and Piggly Wiggly both launched their explosive chain expansion with small cash-and-carry store concepts created in a wartime inflationary economy, but the grocery business changed dramatically during the 1920s. Both companies had to make significant changes to store operations to keep up with the competition. They chose different strategies in store design that illustrate the unique challenges of self-service retailing. From the street, Piggly Wiggly looked like any other chain, and it was often included with other chains in business literature of the day. Standardized company colors—for Piggly Wiggly it was blue and yellow, for A&P it was red and white—made it easier to distinguish otherwise interchangeable store fronts. But once inside the door, the shopping experience was fundamentally different. Although the average Piggly Wiggly store sold twice what the average A&P store sold, A&P focused its volume strategy on economies of scale, with large numbers of stores, volume discounts from food producers, and vertical integration of supply chains. Piggly Wiggly franchisees remained committed to self-service store design and faced distinctive challenges in adjusting the one-way path to incorporate products that were difficult to sell through self-service methods.

The mid-1920s have been described as a time of crisis for A&P. Although overall profits rose, sales volume per store did not.[48] A&P found it increasingly difficult to increase sales by lowering prices, and far-flung stores created new management challenges. In the late 1920s, A&P reorganized the company and began to build larger stores with modern equipment for butchering and storing fresh meats. Between 1922 and 1926 A&P added nearly nine thousand

FIG. 3.6. Interior view of an A&P combination store with a meat counter. Note the hams hanging on the wall to the left. A side of meat hangs on the back door waiting to be cut to order. The entire store is arranged for counter service. *Source:* Caufield and Shook Collection, CS 091203, 1928, Archives & Special Collections, University of Louisville Libraries.

stores, becoming the nation's largest chain.[49] A store in suburban Louisville offers an example of the new combination store format. In the photo in figure 3.6, canned goods line the shelves behind wooden counters to the right of the center aisle for easy retrieval by clerks. To the left, refrigerator cases offer fresh meats, while hams hang on the wall. At the rear of the store a large side of meat hangs in front of the freezer door. The Louisville store shows how even relatively small store spaces could be organized as combination stores. In larger stores, multiple counters arranged around the floor space departmentalized the store products and offered a wider selection. While the small World War I–era "economy store" was operated by one or two clerks, combination stores required more staff and the expertise of a butcher. The A&P combination store in Winchendon, Massachusetts, for example, had at least six employees: a store manager, three clerks, a meat manager, and a meat cutter.[50]

Store design oversight for A&P was assigned to the division managers, and at an A&P divisional president's meeting in 1927 the chairman of the Southern Division reported that "they had adopted the Self-Service Method in some stores in Texas and [that it had] proved very successful."[51] A few months later, in January 1928, several other division sales directors reported some success with self-service in carefully selected locations, including the Chicago area, and recommended that more divisions experiment with self-service store formats. But these experiments have not been well documented, and economist M. A. Adelman reported that "nothing more was heard of these early trials" beyond the brief discussions at the divisional meetings.[52] A&P would not begin conversion to self-service until 1936, under pressure from new large-format self-service supermarkets. Writing in 1959 at a time when supermarkets symbolized the innovation and global dominance of American capitalism, Adelman criticized A&P's reluctance to embrace self-service in 1927 as the result of a backward-looking defensive reflex, even as the company was at the height of its success. "How else can we explain the failure to try any more such experiments at a time when everyone in the company professed to be worried about falling sales . . . and when liquid funds were so ample and profits so large as to be embarrassing?"[53] A&P may not have been on the cutting edge of store design innovation in the 1920s, but the chain was following the best practices in grocery design of the day, emphasizing a store arrangement that fostered efficient clerk service. A&P represented the mainstream approach to combination store design in the 1920s.

For Piggly Wiggly franchisees, adding fresh meat and produce presented special challenges because incorporating counters for clerk service created

FIG. 3.7. During the 1920s and 1930s, Piggly Wiggly adjusted the original patented store design to incorporate a fresh produce department, typically located at the front of the retail space where window displays pulled customers into the store. Fresh produce was difficult to sell using self-service methods. A clerk probably helped customers use the large white scale stationed in the produce department to weigh and mark produce purchases. *Source:* Piggly Wiggly Grocery Store Collection, Memphis and Shelby County Room, Benjamin Hooks Central Library, Memphis Public Libraries.

points of congestion for the self-service pathway. Although the chain experimented with a few Piggly Wiggly Meat Markets during the late 1920s, those stores remained separate operations from the standard Piggly Wiggly store. The main change franchisees made to the patented interior during the 1920s was an expansion of fresh produce departments. The factory-built interiors that defined the brand increasingly made space at the front of the store for fresh produce and promoted the store with seasonal produce displays. For example, a Piggly Wiggly in Tacoma, Washington, had what was described as "a typical Piggly Wiggly fruit department arrangement, according to standardized layout," with a compact footprint for seasonal fruit display that could efficiently serve as a front window display.[54] "Why shop around?" a Piggly Wiggly ad asked customers in Oakland. "Piggly Wiggly has over 1500 articles of Nationally known merchandise. (The ordinary grocery store carries about 400 items.) A complete line of Quality Groceries, Fresh Fruits and Vegetables, Produce, Milk and Cream, etc., will be found on all Piggly Wiggly shelves." The California franchise added that some stores even had bakeries and meat markets.[55] Piggly Wiggly franchisees appear to have been more open to self-service methods for selling produce than most other grocers. As late as 1937, Myrtle Lohner studied grocery store practices in Chicago and found that "many stores, because of the large amount of spoilage of produce by customer handling, would definitely prefer to operate this department entirely on a service basis if they could at the same time keep customer good-will."[56] Meanwhile, the customer response to self-service produce was mixed. Lohner found that the majority of the women she interviewed preferred a combination of service and self-service in the produce department. Piggly Wiggly franchisees had to relax the stringent self-service rules that had defined the chain in its earliest days to offer customer assistance in the produce department.

The 1920s also witnessed significant changes in the retail landscape outside the store. Speculative real estate developers who were experimenting with shopping centers to serve as suburban destinations found Piggly Wiggly stores a useful addition to include in the mix of stores they recruited to lure customers away from downtown business districts.[57] The fact that Piggly Wiggly advertised regularly helped to entice shoppers to new suburban shopping centers. With its success in making self-service appealing as a middle-class activity, developers featured Piggly Wiggly stores in some of the most prominent suburban shopping centers of the interwar years. The Kansas City real estate developer J. C. Nichols included Piggly Wiggly in his new Country Club Plaza shopping center, one of the first, most influential shopping centers in the United States. Nichols carefully chose tenants he considered to be best suited to the affluent residents of his Country Club district and with the name recognition to attract customers.[58] By 1924 Piggly Wiggly was a leading tenant with three different store locations in the Country Club Plaza. But Piggly Wiggly was not the only grocery store in the shopping center. Nichols also included a full-service grocery option to cater to his affluent suburban market. While the Piggly Wiggly interior was a standardized model produced in the Jackson, Tennessee, factory, local grocer Fred Wolferman hired his own architects to design the building that housed his Country Club Plaza store and included a full-service bakery and meat counter in addition to the grocery department, which was served by clerks who assembled customer orders in the store. In contrast to the self-service Piggly Wiggly, Wolferman's grocery offered home delivery and promised customers that the suburban store would "carry just as complete a line of merchandise as is carried in their downtown store."[59]

Piggly Wiggly was also a prominent tenant in the influential Washington, D.C., Park and Shop neighborhood shopping center. Located next door to an A&P store, customers at the shopping center could choose whether they wanted counter service at A&P or self-service at Piggly Wiggly as their method for grocery shopping.[60] The competition between Piggly Wiggly and A&P shopping experiences played out not only on the ground in new neighborhood shopping centers but also in a national advertising campaign during the late 1920s that featured the new retail suburban landscape. Read in juxtaposition to each other, the A&P and Piggly Wiggly ads offer important insights into the cultural construction of food shopping at a time when self-service was still a specialized form of retailing and an unfamiliar social practice to many readers of national consumer magazines. Their ads drew stark differences between shopping experiences in the two chains that help to explain why they were not interchangeable chain stores in the suburban shopping center.

## A New Nationwide Movement?

At their Chicago convention in 1926, Piggly Wiggly independent operators agreed to contribute five dollars per month per store to create a fund dedicated to a new national advertising campaign.[61] It took several years to raise enough money to launch the campaign. H. H. Lestico observed in his multivolume *School of the Chain Store* that "space in the Saturday Evening Post, in color, runs around $12,000 a page for the one issue, and pages in similar magazines are almost as expensive."[62] Piggly Wiggly ran full-page ads monthly in the *Post*, *Ladies' Home Journal*, and *Good Housekeeping*. A. C. Jones reported, "The average Piggly Wiggly operator, I am told, and I agree from my own experience with them, is more willing to spend money for advanced ideas in merchandising and operation than the average chain store grocer."[63] That enthusiasm for advertising stemmed directly from the need to educate consumers about self-service methods and the imperative for attracting a steady stream of repeat customers inside the store to ensure the profitability of the system. A&P had been running full-page ads in national consumer magazines regularly since the beginning of the decade, portraying the store as "the little red school house of American retailing."[64] Between 1927 and 1933 Piggly Wiggly franchisees took on the world's largest chain store with monthly ads promoting the advantages of self-service shopping. The campaign was designed by the Chicago office of the J. Walter Thompson Company, who described it as "a striking new method of presentation for a campaign." The agency promoted self-service shopping as "a very definite trend in the buying of foods," and they featured particular Piggly Wiggly stores representing "areas and customers in typical cities" as the nucleus of the new campaign.[65]

Piggly Wiggly Stores, Inc., magazine ads created a new narrative about self-service for a national audience, one that simplified and gentrified the varied newspaper narratives that Piggly Wiggly franchisees had been promoting for the past decade. Consumer experts of the day centered their attention on middle-class White women as the primary household consumers. The J. Walter Thompson agency estimated in 1918 that women constituted 89.1 percent of grocery store sales.[66] And home economist Christine Frederick estimated similarly that women were responsible for 87 percent of food purchases.[67] "Women have sponsored a nationwide movement—a wholly new type of store," the first ad declared to readers of *Saturday Evening Post* in October 1927. It would be the recurring campaign theme. The ads attributed the growth of the company to "the amazing record of how American women have adopted and supported this new method of household buying."[68]

Each month Piggly Wiggly ads showcased store locations in some of the most glamorous neighborhoods of the United States, illustrating the national reach of the self-service chain. In addition to the Chicago North Shore ad (fig. 3.2), the series featured stores in San Diego's Mission Hills and Milwaukee's Whitefish Bay.[69] "Snobbish cars with custom bodies draw up at Miami's Piggly Wigglys," one ad said.[70] In Washington D.C., Piggly Wiggly stores served Massachusetts Avenue downtown and "aristocratic suburbs" like Chevy Chase where "famous hostesses" followed the "marketing vogue."[71] Likewise in Denver: "Piggly Wiggly finds such favor with the young hostesses of Park Lane and the Country Club district."[72] The national ad campaign declared, "Each smart center the country over has its Piggly Wiggly stores, where the wealthy (and thrifty) women of that community shop daily."[73] The national campaign constructed a selective landscape—emphasizing new suburban shopping centers and tony urban neighborhoods, not small-town Main Streets where most Piggly Wiggly stores were located or the diverse customers who shopped in them. However, if numbers of stores were the measure of popularity, A&P, not Piggly Wiggly, was the overwhelming choice of American shoppers.

Comparing the ways that the magazine ads featured the two different store interiors brings these consumer choices into sharp focus. An A&P ad from

FIG. 3.8. This store interior view depicting friendly counter service was prominently featured in an A&P ad (detail). *Source: Ladies' Home Journal*, February 1927, 69.

February 1927 features the store counter as symbolic of the food shopping experience in its stores. The visual message emphasizes the orderly arrangement of brand name products on shelves arranged around the perimeter of an impeccably clean store. Although fresh fruits and vegetables are displayed within reach of the customers, no baskets were provided to encourage the customer to collect more than she could hold by the handful. Behind the counter, a white-coated clerk serves a well-dressed mother accompanied by a child. The carefully arranged brand name products are visible but not accessible to the customer. One A&P ad from 1928 suggests that in the combination store the customer could either serve herself or ask a clerk for service. "She is privileged to personally select her order from A&P's wide variety of fine foods," the ad explained, "or she can have the manager make her selections."[74] Self-service was optional, not mandatory. On a practical level it was not possible for customers to help themselves to more than a few items at a time, carried to the counter to be packaged by the clerk, while a customer moved back and forth around the store. No receptacles were provided in the store for the collection of groceries by customers.

In contrast, no clerk and no counter appear in the Piggly Wiggly ad from June 1929 in figure 3.9. Instead, two fashionably dressed White women are

FIG. 3.9. The J. Walter Thompson agency depicted self-service shoppers absorbed in the silent reverie of self-service shopping, their seemingly weightless market baskets brimming with groceries. The hanging price tags signal distinctive Piggly Wiggly store methods, while fresh produce spilling into the aisle in the shopper's path evokes changes in the original patented system. *Source:* Piggly Wiggly ad (detail), *Ladies' Home Journal*, June 1929, 114.

enthralled by the self-absorbing experience of self-service. Brand name products are signaled by uniform packaging arranged on orderly shelves. Diamond-shaped paper tags hanging in front of items on the shelves demonstrate the patented Piggly Wiggly price-tagging system. Fresh produce virtually leaps off the page in the foreground, suggesting the updated convenience of one-stop combination store shopping. Theatrical lighting dramatizes the freedom and independence of serving yourself at a leisurely pace. If these women are mothers, they left their children at home. In the bourgeois fantasy constructed by Piggly Wiggly ads, self-service shopping was an independent (even isolating), depersonalized (even antisocial) experience. The ad presented self-service as an internal, imaginative experience and emphasized the autonomy of women as self-service shoppers. The shoppers interact only with the products on the shelves, not with clerks and not with other customers. They are not mothers accompanied by children.

It is no coincidence that A&P, the chain store behemoth whose price-cutting competition threatened the survival of local stores, constructed an image of a friendly neighborhood store with polite clerks, while the self-service Piggly Wiggly, icon of modernization on small-town Main Streets, exploited the daily frustrations of the neighborhood store, where interaction between clerk and customer could be stressful. Customers often experienced conflict over prices, short weights, and the quality of goods, or difficulties over credit. Piggly Wiggly ads highlighted the advantages of the absence of clerks: "Here, with no clerks to persuade them, women make their own decisions as they shop. There are no salesmen in the Piggly Wiggly Store." While A&P presented the clerk as the friendly expert offering helpful information about new products or assisting errand-running children, Piggly Wiggly emphasized the clerk as pushy salesman talking customers into buying things they didn't really want. Moreover, in a service store you had to wait for the clerk to fill orders ahead of you during rush hour. At Piggly Wiggly in contrast there were "no clerks to wait for—no hurry—no delays."[75] One Piggly Wiggly ad appeared to voice direct customer experience, "'I like to browse around, without a clerk at my elbow—and pick things out for myself.' So one woman summed it up recently."[76]

The different ways that A&P and Piggly Wiggly ads dealt with motherhood demonstrate some of the cultural challenges of selling the self-service store to American women. One of the key services offered by many grocers was telephone orders and delivery. A home economist from the University of Chicago advised, "If her time is mortgaged by small children or an outside job, or if the cash-and-carry store is not conveniently located, its disadvantages may outweigh its possible economies. The homemaker may then be far wiser to patronize a dependable dealer who will deliver and from whom she can order by telephone."[77] Even if a store did not accept telephone orders for home delivery, a key advantage of clerk service was the ability to send your child to the neighborhood store to pick up a few items. This was such a standard practice that ads of many product manufacturers featured children running errands at the grocery. "A Child Can Carry a Year's Supply" claimed A.P.W. Paper Company, promoting the company's toilet paper that was "packed in a carton so compact that even a small child could carry it."[78] In an APW ad, a grocer hands the carton of toilet paper to a child barely tall enough to see over the counter, no mother in sight. A&P, which resisted telephone orders in many of its stores, cultivated the convenience of errand-running children as an advantage of clerk service. "Priceless . . . This Confidence of American Mothers. . . . Daily to A&P they send their little ones, supremely confident that the genial manager of the store will treat them as he would his own—wait upon them promptly—give the 'little shoppers' that which they ask for—and then securely wrap their packages and send them homeward with foods of established goodness."[79] Given the widespread and convenient habit of sending children to the neighborhood store for a box of soap or baking soda as needed, it is telling that no children are pictured in Piggly Wiggly magazine ads, not even accompanied by shopping mothers. Self-service was a shopping method for adults only.[80]

Local franchisees sometimes sought to explicitly reassure their customers that children were welcome at Piggly Wiggly. The *Santa Ana Register* ran a Piggly Wiggly ad encouraging mothers to send their errand- running children to Piggly Wiggly, where friendly clerks would "show them how to find what they are looking for and . . . make shopping an interesting game." In the ad, a clerk fills a market basket for the children, reaching for products on the tallest shelf before they wheel the groceries home in a toy wagon and deliver correct change to their mother.[81] Self-service methods required that such messages be explicit for a practice that was understood as routine at counter-service stores.

According to historian Katherine Parkin, food advertisers emphasized the theme of "food is love" and the selflessness of family provisioning and traditional nurturing role of women in the home.[82] Anthropologist Daniel Miller has studied the meanings modern supermarket shoppers attach to their work and argues that routine provisioning "can be understood as a devotional rite."[83] His theory of shopping "suggests that there is an important component of gender that is foundational to this ritual practice, and that most female shoppers become identified with this sense of gender when they carry out mundane shopping." But Piggly Wiggly ads sold self-service by recasting the message of women's responsibility for homemaking with an emphasis on women's independence, describing self-service as a "fascinating way to shop," emphasizing the internal and imaginative aspects of self-service.[84] The ads fantasized about having the liberty to take your time: "You come and go as you please—dash in, with the motor still running—or linger for a real shopping tour."[85] The experience of self-service was presented as a special stimulus to good home management and creativity. "What useful ideas for your menus come to you while you look over the richly laden shelves!"[86]

The self-service shopping experience at Piggly Wiggly did capture customers' imaginations in new ways. Blurring the distinction between physical and

FIG. 3.10. In this ad for the A.P.W. Paper Company, a friendly-looking grocer hands a box to an errand-running child. The add asserts that a year's supply of the company's Satin Tissue toilet paper was packed "in a carton so compact that even a small child could carry it." *Source:* A. P. W. Paper ad (detail), *Ladies' Home Journal,* January 1924.

FIG. 3.11. The Piggly Wiggly franchise in Santa Ana, California, trained its clerks to help unaccompanied, errand-running children find what they were looking for and "make shopping an interesting game." The store assured mothers that their children would return home with correct change for their purchases by providing small sealable envelopes especially for that purpose. *Source: Santa Ana Register,* 18 January 1929.

symbolic space, nurses at Saint Thomas Hospital in Nashville transformed their workstation into a Piggly Wiggly store in a process of gift-giving ritual and play. In a story titled "A Matrimonial Piggly Wiggly," the Piggly Wiggly corporate newsletter reported the impending marriage of the local manager of Piggly Wiggly Store No. 12 in Nashville to one of the Saint Thomas nurses. Her coworkers surprised her with a themed bridal shower. She arrived at work to find "that a complete Piggly Wiggly store had been arranged with a turnstile, counters, etc. She was presented with a basket upon entering the turnstile and was told to help herself to the beautiful gifts placed on the counters by her workers and friends. Just over the door a sign which read: "The Road to Happiness Through Piggly Wiggly."[87] In a reference to her fiancé, the whole display was capped by a large sign: "Piggly Wiggly All Over the World. Store No. 12."

The nurses employed the chain's key slogans and defining material features of the self-service store—the turnstile and the market basket—to transform the counters of the nurses' station into a self-service fantasy that blurred distinctions between shopping for everyday necessities and the more personalized process of gift giving. Scholar James Carrier points out that mass-produced commodities sold in self-service stores "are almost aggressively anonymous." Indeed, the Piggly Wiggly ads pictured packaged products without identifying any particular brands. "There is, then," Carrier asserts, "a conflict between the anonymous commodities that people confront when they go out and buy things, and their need to have personal possessions to transact in the gift relations in which they are involved. To deal with this conflict, people have to convert the former into the latter. Doing so is the work of appropriation, the work of making a personal possession of the anonymous commodity."[88] The nurses at Saint Thomas Hospital, represent a historical moment when self-service was changing the meaning of shopping. Re-creating the self-service store interior was central to this imaginative work of appropriation. Their bridal shower suggests that women did indeed fantasize about self-service shopping, though less as a devotional rite of family provisioning than as a therapeutic personal fantasy. The competing messages in Piggly Wiggly and A&P ads document a historical process of selling different shopping methods. How and where people shop was becoming as central to the construction of identity in a consumer society as what they bought.

National advertising promoted an affluent, feminized ideal for the brand. But through small-town newspapers and store location strategies based on the local knowledge of franchisees, the chain built a diverse clientele. Piggly

Wiggly became a popular culture icon. Its complicated social reception is suggested by stark contrasts. On the one hand, Piggly Wiggly established a reputation of middle-class respectability. George Babbitt's wife shopped there in Sinclair Lewis's fictional midwestern town of Zenith. On the other hand, it served as the licentious backdrop for Charlie McFadden's blues song "Groceries on the Shelf." "My name is Piggly Wiggly, I got groceries on my shelf . . . Don't let these Cadillac women make no flat tire out of you," McFadden intoned. Even as Piggly Wiggly ads sought to cast self-service shopping as the modern choice of fashionable White women, its local advertising took on small-town caste systems and appealed to consumers across the color line. The symbolic Piggly Wiggly space promoted personal freedom and fulfillment. The physical machine for automatic selling promised small-town franchisees a predictable profit.

The Piggly Wiggly model of self-service was the most famous and iconic of its day. National ads and the broad geographic reach of the chain made Piggly Wiggly recognizable even in towns and cities without a local store. By the end of the 1920s, Piggly Wiggly was synonymous with self-service. By extension, self-service appeared to be a chain store innovation. When the U.S. Department of Agriculture studied self-service, authors of the subsequent report remarked that Piggly Wiggly dominated the public imagination at the mention of self-service. "There is a common belief among the retail grocers of the country and the general public, especially in the East, that the term self-service is used only in connection with a certain corporation operating a number of self-service stores," they wrote. Piggly Wiggly need not be mentioned by name for readers to understand the reference. "The corporation referred to does hold certain patents covering floor plans and certain interior arrangement of their stores, but principles of self-service can not be patented, being nearly as old as distribution itself."[89] Besides Piggly Wiggly, the report identified other cooperating self-service stores that provided data for the study of self-service distribution, with less-familiar names such as Hillman's (Chicago), Liberty Market and L. S. Ayres & Co. (Indianapolis), Groceteria (St. Paul), Acme Stores (Los Angeles), the Emporium, (San Francisco), Groceteria Stores Company (Seattle), Gerard Grocery (Pomona, California), and U-Save Stores (Cambridge, Massachusetts). To understand the complex origins of self-service store design, we need to go beyond the history of the iconic chain most closely associated with self-service. Clarence Saunders was the first entrepreneur to successfully patent a self-service store, but he would not be the last.

# Navigating the Self-Service Landscape, 1920–1940

It turns out that the Piggly Wiggly terrain reflected broader geographic patterns of self-service experimentation. When self-service stores first appeared during World War I, observers expected that they would only be viable in cities because their low profit margin and lack of delivery services required considerable population density to sustain a business. Clarence Saunders had begun his expansion strategy in 1918 by limiting franchises to towns with at least five thousand residents. Piggly Wiggly franchisees who located stores in high-traffic business districts demonstrated a broad consensus that self-service was a specialized form of retailing that required distinctive store location strategies. But local franchisees also made Piggly Wiggly a small-town icon in the 1920s. Their success reflects the larger significance of small-town entrepreneurs experimenting with self-service.

The 1920s and 1930s represent an entrepreneurial phase in the development of self-service stores. Census records, store patents, photographs, newspapers, and other sources document the diverse origins of self-service stores and the important role small-town businesses played in the invention process during this developmental phase of self-service retailing. Store inventors came from Los Angeles but also from Hazel, Kentucky, and Rolling Fork, Mississippi. Successful stores opened in downtown central business districts, small-town main streets, suburban neighborhoods, and even rolling stores that served a country trade. The invention of the self-service store was a large-scale national process, but self-service stores were not evenly distributed across the United States. During the interwar years, self-service evolved as a distinctively regional practice with multiple clusters of experimentation. Chain and independent grocers played different roles in experimentation depending on where their stores were located.

An innovative minority of small-town grocers who had the financial resources to invest in reconceptualizing their store arrangements overcame the mainstream resistance to self-service as a high-risk retail strategy because they embraced the unique management and selling potential of self-service stores in their local contexts. They increasingly faced intense competition not only from the expansion of national chains on Main Street but also from the metropolitan commerce generated by suburban development. As machines for automatic selling, self-service stores represented a promise of predictability in a volatile market. Store patents document the ways these inventors created store designs that served small-town business needs.

The historical process of creating mass retailing changes when we consider the dynamic of small-town and urban inventors as co-creators of self-service retailing. Self-service stores seem incongruous in a rural landscape where the mail-order catalog and the general store have been the most widely recognized agents of mass retailing for consumers at the crossroads or the county seat, the mailbox or the company store.[1] Widespread Model T ownership and improved roads helped to extend the reach of self-service as a mass retailing strategy into the countryside. Historians of technology and consumer history emphasize the agency of small-town and rural Americans in resisting or reshaping urbanizing technologies as they adapted the automobile and the telephone to country life.[2] But the American self-service store was not simply an urban invention of chain stores exported to the countryside and adjusted to small-town contexts. Self-service stores were created in a process of invention that often *originated* on small-town Main Streets where local stores served as laboratories for social, technological, and economic experimentation. Dramatic regional patterns of experimentation demonstrate the grassroots origins of self-service as a new social practice.

When he launched his discount variety chain in 1962, Sam Walton expanded his business by targeting small towns in Arkansas, Louisiana, Missouri, and Oklahoma. Focusing on the rural beginnings of the global superstore, historian Bethany Moreton confronts what she calls the "Wal-Mart paradox": "How did the world's largest corporation grow from the most violently anti-monopoly section of America?" Moreton argues that Wal-Mart succeeded in rural America by cultivating a rhetoric of independent republican manhood and home-based management: "In order to make its home in the old Populist countryside, Wal-Mart had to overcome the twin objections to chain distribution: its remote, faceless ownership and its threat to white rural manhood."[3]

But the rural origins of Wal-Mart seem less paradoxical when viewed as part of the longer history of self-service innovation.

To fully understand the rural origins of Wal-Mart, we need to reach further back in the twentieth century to consider the relationship between rural and small-town Americans and the self-service roots of mass retailing. By the time the first Wal-Mart opened, rural shoppers in the Ozarks had been serving themselves for decades. Enterprising entrepreneurs in Poplar Bluff, Missouri, and Fort Smith and Hot Springs, Arkansas, had all opened Piggly Wiggly franchises by 1923. In its early years, Wal-Mart built a corporate identity that emphasized its regional, hillbilly origins as a strategy for overcoming the anti-monopolism of small-town consumers. By contrast, the Piggly Wiggly chain de-emphasized its regional beginnings in the 1920s, centered its rhetoric on American democracy, and proclaimed its global ambitions in a corporate slogan that declared "Piggly Wiggly All Over the World." But its franchising strategy allowed small-town store owners to assert their identity as local businesses.

Piggly Wiggly was not the only self-service store in the Ozarks during the interwar years, nor were the self-service stores of the Ozarks imported by distant faceless chain organizations. Self-service grocers went beyond low-price appeals to craft advertising narratives that sold self-service based on small-town values of democracy, frugality, and self-reliance. The success of self-service store entrepreneurs in the small-town South and West during the interwar years shows that Wal-Mart's rural origins in Populist country were built on the foundation of a deeper history of self-service innovation in the countryside. Though it eventually came to define the globalization of large-scale American mass retailing, the American self-service store got its start in the precarious conditions of small-business capitalism on Main Street in the early twentieth century.

## Not a Neighborhood Proposition

Experts agreed in the 1920s that self-service stores could not work everywhere. "The principle of self-service can not be applied in a haphazard way to any store at any location or under any management and be entirely successful," declared a USDA study of self-service retailing in 1922.[4] Because self-service stores competed by offering low prices to make up for the lack of services, volume sales were essential for profitability. Business management textbooks agreed that the self-service store was "more adapted for downtown sites than for suburban."[5] And government researchers asserted that the self-service store was not "a neighborhood proposition."[6] Self-service also had limited appeal for middle-class shoppers who craved the customer services that reinforced social respectability. It comes as a surprise that self-service stores actually turned out to be more successful in the countryside and less successful in urban working-class neighborhoods than experts had originally anticipated.

In the low-margin business of food retailing, the longer products sat on store shelves, the higher the cost of doing business. Thus, the number of "store turns" as it was known in the trade, was an important measure of efficiency, productivity, and profitability for any store regardless of operating method. Department of Commerce researchers intensively studied twenty-six stores in Louisville between 1928 and 1929, finding that the number of times per year that stores turned over their stock ranged between 10 and 34 in the study sample. Researchers determined that "the location of the store is the most important in its effect upon turnover."[7] Larger stores in affluent neighborhoods had more store turns than smaller stores in working-class neighborhoods. For the purposes of comparison, a 1929 Federal Trade Commission investigation found that the average A&P store turned over its stock twenty-five times in a year.[8] Piggly Wiggly stores reportedly averaged thirty-nine turns yearly.[9] Though self-service was widely recognized as a retailing method with a potential to produce high stock turnover, none of the stores studied in the Louisville sample operated through self-service methods.

A key reason for the limited use of self-service store arrangement was that most groceries were neighborhood operations serving a clientele that lived within a few blocks. In their extensive study of retail grocery stores from 1914 to 1918, Harvard's Bureau of Business Research reported that neighborhood stores depended as much on phone sales as they did on walk-in counter sales.[10] A decade later the Louisville study also found that phone sales remained an important strategy for increasing store turns, making it possible for a store to operate with a limited inventory. Most of this sales work was initiated by store workers whose routines included calling customers for daily orders as early as 5:00 a.m. in working-class neighborhoods. According to the study, "The suggestion of the order taker is frequently accepted by the customer on the other end of the wire. Her failure to specify brand, a frequent occurrence, permits the manager to concentrate inventory among the products of fewer manufacturers, especially those whose goods move rapidly."[11] Since phone solicitation was often the job of the grocer's wife, researchers noted, it contributed significantly to store turnover without adding overhead costs.

In contrast to the importance of phone solicitation for neighborhood stores, self-service grocers depended on a steady, daily stream of customer foot traffic in the store. The Department of Agriculture advised, "In order that full advantage may be taken of all of the possibilities of self-service, a maximum volume of trade must be obtained. In order to obtain such a volume, the location of the store should be such that its patrons will be drawn from a considerable territory rather than from a radius of a block or two, as is often the case with the smaller grocery stores of the 'corner' type."[12] The ubiquitous neighborhood corner store was widely perceived to be a poor candidate for conversion to self-service.

Chain stores too were wary about self-service, using it strategically in targeted locations rather than as an overall operational principle for every location. Grocery chains increased stock turnover through a variety of management strategies, including careful consideration of store location, inventory control that emphasized a limited selection of fast-moving products, centralized discount purchasing, and reduced overhead through improving store efficiencies. Leading market researchers Walter Hayward and Percival White described one chain store operator who experimented with self-service in an unidentified city. Though he managed multiple outlets in different neighborhoods, he chose only his downtown location to convert to self-service in an experimental trial. He reported that it worked better for rapidly handling the afternoon rush than his other stores. Despite the success of the downtown store, however, he had no plans to convert the entire chain to self-service. "For a residence neighborhood," he explained, "we feel the self-service store would never work."[13] With self-service stores' low margin and streamlined operation, business experts agreed that they worked best in downtown locations.

This expectation was so strong that it led the Department of Commerce to question the results of its business census of self-service food stores. Interested in understanding the nationwide scale of self-service stores operations, the Commerce Department led "a complete field canvass of retail stores throughout the United States" collecting data for the calendar year 1939.[14] The standard questionnaire canvassers used to collect data asked store owners to reply yes or no to the question "Is the grocery department SELF-SERVICE?"[15] Researchers couldn't believe how many small independent stores answered yes. They wondered whether the store owners who completed the survey had misunderstood the directions. Researchers reasoned, "The schedules of some of the smaller independents . . . suggest the possibility that in small stores the term self-service may have been confused with the fact that the store is operated by the proprietor himself, without paid salespeople."[16]

While there was as yet no standardized version of a self-service store, the field canvass had established a basic definition of a self-service store, in the hope that it might ensure some consistency for interpreting the data. Focusing on store arrangement and methods of operation, the Commerce Department definition of self-service specified: "The grocery department is self-service if (1) it is physically arranged to lead customers along rows of open shelving and displays, where they are free to select and assemble their purchases; and (2) there is a minimum of personal attention of salespeople. Usually the customer carries the selected merchandise to a cashier's desk where it is wrapped and the sale completed."[17] This definition certainly left a lot of room for interpretation. It went beyond the idea of open display to indicate a store arrangement that was systematized to "lead customers" through the store. But it left open the question of how much clerk service might be provided in a self-service operation and how the process of customer checkout might be organized. One might have expected many grocers with open shelving to reply yes to the question as to whether their store was self-service. Instead, fewer than 10 percent of grocers answered yes. Of the 387,337 grocery stores in the United States at the time, only 31,183 store owners identified their businesses as self-service operations. If there was confusion among some grocers about what self-service meant, it does not seem to have been particularly widespread. Given that chain stores have been widely considered pioneers in promoting self-service store methods, it is astonishing to note how few of them reported that their grocery departments were organized for self-service in 1939. The final tally documented a retailing landscape in which self-service stores remained rare. Large or small, independent or chain, self-service stores were still the exception rather than the rule in the food retailing landscape in 1939.

Store patents, business photographs, and local newspapers document the significance of small-town self-service operations and suggest that Commerce Department researchers should have been able to place more confidence in the census schedules completed by those smaller independent store owners. An itinerant photographer traveling through South Texas in 1934 captured numerous examples of small independent and chain store self-service operations like that of A. L. McWhorter and his son Jack.[18] Their store offers important corroboration of the role of small-town independent store owners in self-service experimentation.

FIG. 4.1. Model Grocery and IGA Store, Sinton, Texas, 1934. A. L. McWhorter, owner, in white striped shirt and suspenders, stands at the checkout counter. His son, Jack McWhorter, is in the white IGA apron at his shoulder. Sinton, Texas (about thirty miles north of Corpus Christi) had fewer than two thousand residents in 1930. *Source:* Itinerant Photographer Collection, Harry Ransom Center, University of Texas at Austin.

The photographer who took the picture in figure 4.1 did not have his own studio. He worked the streets to make a living and probably walked in the door like any customer and asked if McWhorter would like a picture of his store. The photograph he took spontaneously captured an ordinary business day. The grocer and his son posed at the cashier's desk with almost as many aproned workers as small-town customers. But this was not a mom-and-pop counter-service store operation. McWhorter physically organized the floor space with rows of open shelving that formed aisles where customers circulated to assemble their own purchases. The basket bin ensured that customers had the right equipment to serve themselves and carry their assembled merchandise to the cashier's counter at the front of the store. The name of his business proudly proclaimed McWhorter's identity as an independent business owner and his store as a model of modern business methods. His store arrangement certainly fit the Commerce Department definition of a self-service store.

The story that has dominated the history of self-service is the rise of new supermarkets in the 1930s. Indeed, business census data showed that about two-thirds of the largest grocery stores operated using self-service methods, and these represented an increasing share of food sales.[19] Chains operated 79 percent of the most profitable self-service stores, with sales of more than $100,000.[20] If we stop here, with the aggregate numbers in 1939, then the history of self-service appears to be a chain store phenomenon closely associated with the rise of the supermarket. Though the main purpose of the Commerce Department study was to take stock of the new large "super markets" that were changing the food distribution landscape, the resulting store census actually revealed a complicated picture of the variety and geographic distribution of self-service stores three decades after they had first appeared. Most importantly, regional differences in store size and the role of independent store owners show how most customers of the 1920s and 1930s experienced self-service shopping in small stores whose interiors were built on-site. McWhorter's IGA Store was in the heart of self-service country.

## Self-Service as a Regional Practice

Observing the strong regional patterns that emerged from the data, census researchers concluded, "Self-service itself, regardless of size of stores, proves to be less acceptable to the public or slower of development in some sections than in others." The region with the greatest resistance to self-service overall was New England, where the census reported: "Only 16 percent of the grocery and combination store business is done in self-service stores, compared with a ratio of 29 percent for the country as a whole." Self-service was most popular in the South, Southwest, and Pacific West, where 50–62 percent of food retailing business was in self-service stores. The census reported, "In California alone the ratio exceeds 69 percent."[21] The report simply documents the diffusion of self-service in different regions without posing any explanations for why the retailing method might have succeeded in some parts of the country and failed in others. The question, however, is not as simple as why did self-service succeed in California and fail in Connecticut?

In 1922 the *American Food Journal* explained the failure of Piggly Wiggly in New York and New Jersey as evidence of regional differences in the economic viability of self-service retailing: "While the theory of self-service may appeal to Southern and Western consumers, . . . conditions are not the same in the East."[22] The trade journal emphasized the high rents necessary to lay out the self-service interior, the lack of bulk goods that were important to working-class customers, and limited stock of packaged goods as disadvantages of self-service for the eastern marketplace. Yet, despite the high cost of installing self-service fixtures, Piggly Wiggly succeeded in high-rent downtown locations throughout the poorest region of the country. Economic explanations alone are insufficient to explain the regionalism of self-service retailing in the early twentieth century. Because self-service was a new social practice, variable social factors in different local and regional contexts determined its success or failure. The reasons why self-service was popular in Texas do not necessarily explain the most important factors for its success in California.

The new retail history focuses on the importance of local contexts of stores and the social processes and power relationships that shaped them as scholars have begun to build a picture of the importance of local and regional variations in the creation of a mass consumer society. As historian Tracey Deutsch argues, "In important ways seeing the localness of stores enlarges our vision of the systems that intersect in retail firms and that shape their success."[23] For example, in her study of department stores in upstate New York, historian Sarah Elvins found that merchants constructed company identities, operating methods, and advertising appeals to customers based on the community context of western New York State. Elvins argues that "locality remained fundamental to the way in which American consumers negotiated the mass market well into the 1920s and 1930s."[24] No retailers were more important in that process than grocery stores, where American customers negotiated the mass market daily. This emphasis on localness and the particularities of the communities in which stores operated is essential for making sense of the regionalism of self-service. Small-town retailers' focus on building a local market was a decisive factor in the decision to adopt self-service methods. While local contexts determined the different rates of diffusion of self-service stores, the Commerce Department's canvass reveals the complexity of self-service store experimentation as a large-scale national process.

The business census presents only a snapshot of a single year. Nevertheless, in 1939 it recorded a strategic turning point in the history of self-service store innovation. Applying self-service store arrangement to large stores was a recent development, but grocers had been experimenting with small self-service store designs for at least thirty years. The geographic dynamic of newer, larger self-service stores the Commerce Department hoped to understand was dramatically different from the older regional patterns of experimentation in smaller stores. The largest self-service stores with the highest annual sales volume ($300,000 and over) were in the Mid-Atlantic (where Michael Cullen had opened one of the first supermarkets in the United States in 1930) and in the East North Central states.[25] The Mid-Atlantic had more than three times as many of the largest self-service stores as the Pacific, where self-service stores were more numerous and had a longer history of success. This geographic pattern is reversed when we focus on the smallest self-service stores. While small self-service stores were rare in the Mid-Atlantic, they were common in western and southern states. Almost 60 percent of self-service stores (18,374) were small stores selling less than $50,000 annually, and they represent longer-term patterns of self-service store experimentation in regions that had adopted self-service during World War I.

The census snapshot also documents significant regional variations between the role of independent store owners and the role of chains in self-service experimentation. The census showed that nationally most self-service stores were operated by independents, not by chains. Of the 31,183 self-service stores across the United States, 19,642 (63%) were independents. Ninety-three percent of self-service stores selling less than $20,000 annually were independently owned. Historian Susan Spellman has shown that independent grocers had long been important innovators in store technology and modernizing business practices. For example, they were among the first to adopt cash registers in the 1880s, and they played a vital role in technological changes that made cash registers more responsive to the practical needs of daily store

**TABLE 4.1**  Largest Self-Service Stores by Region
Total Stores = 6,221

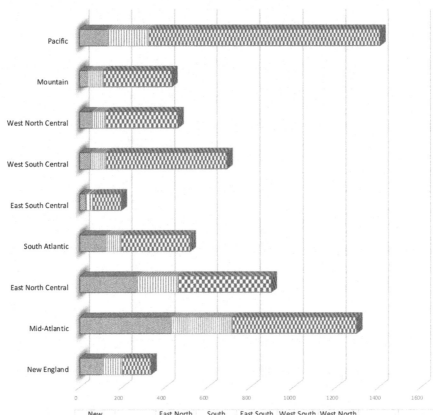

|  | New England | Mid-Atlantic | East North Central | South Atlantic | East South Central | West South Central | West North Central | Mountain | Pacific |
|---|---|---|---|---|---|---|---|---|---|
| ▦ $300,000 and over | 105 | 426 | 265 | 124 | 26 | 50 | 59 | 36 | 133 |
| ▯ $200,000 to $299,999 | 93 | 288 | 194 | 69 | 34 | 74 | 63 | 76 | 192 |
| ▨ $100,000 to $199,999 | 135 | 579 | 437 | 323 | 135 | 566 | 338 | 320 | 1,081 |

SOURCE: "Census of Business, 1939, Retail Trade: Supermarkets and Self-Service Food Stores." In U.S. Department of Commerce, Bureau of the Census, *Sixteenth Census of the United States: 1940* (Washington, D.C.: 1941). *Table:* Self-Service Grocery and Combination Stores, by Size of Store by Geographic Division.

**TABLE 4.2**   Smallest Self-Service Stores by Region
Total Stores = 24,962

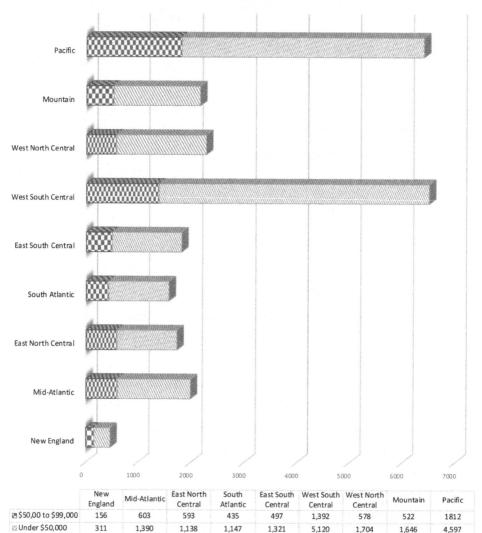

| | New England | Mid-Atlantic | East North Central | South Atlantic | East South Central | West South Central | West North Central | Mountain | Pacific |
|---|---|---|---|---|---|---|---|---|---|
| ▨ $50,00 to $99,000 | 156 | 603 | 593 | 435 | 497 | 1,392 | 578 | 522 | 1812 |
| ▨ Under $50,000 | 311 | 1,390 | 1,138 | 1,147 | 1,321 | 5,120 | 1,704 | 1,646 | 4,597 |

SOURCE: "Census of Business, 1939, Retail Trade: Supermarkets and Self-Service Food Stores." In U.S. Department of Commerce, Bureau of the Census, *Sixteenth Census of the United States: 1940* (Washington, D.C.: 1941). *Table:* Self-Service Grocery and Combination Stores, by Size of Store by Geographic Division.

operation.[26] Thus experimentation with self-service was part of an established history of technological experimentation for local grocers. While chain store owners built regional supply chain networks and economies of scale, small independent grocers experimented with the self-service interiors that automated mass retailing inside local stores.

The choices of independent store owners depended on where they lived. Self-service stores in the Northeast were more likely to be owned by chains, while those in the South or West were far more likely to be owned by independent store owners. Since the census classified stores with more than three outlets in the chain category, many stores listed in the chain category represented local, vernacular contexts rather than large regional or national organizations. Even a firm as small as Robertson's Self-Serving Grocery and Market, with six stores in Dallas, have been counted as a chain.[27] Overall, most self-service stores were in states where the anti-chain movement was strongest. Twenty-eight states passed chain store taxes during the 1930s, the vast majority of them in the South and West.[28] Focusing on store size and the role of independents compared to the role of chains, we can begin to understand why self-service was most popular in the regions where the anti-chain movement was strongest. Self-service stores in anti-chain territory tended to be small, independently owned, or operated by small local chains. Only in the Mid-Atlantic, New England, and East North Central regions were self-service stores more likely to be operated by chains than by independent owners. Thus, local case studies of stores in these regions would exaggerate the role of chains in the invention of self-service retailing. The pronounced regional differences in self-service experimentation offer a more nuanced picture of self-service innovation that highlights how independents and small regional chain owners engaged in the process of renegotiating, as historian Sarah Elvins notes, "the very definition of what was 'local' and what was "national."[29]

By 1939 the typical self-service store was not in an urban working-class neighborhood surrounded by tenements, it was on Main Street in a small town in the South or on a new West Coast highway. The consumer economy and increasing automobile ownership in the countryside reorganized rural space in the 1920s and 1930s.[30] Farm families came to town more often to do their shopping, and small-town merchants had new opportunities to expand their clientele, but they also faced increasing competition as customers traveled greater distances to find the best deals. American economist and sociologist Thorstein Veblen observed in a 1923 essay about small-town capitalism that rural towns were sites of fierce retail competition. It was possible

**TABLE 4.3**     Self-Service Chain and Independent
Stores by Region

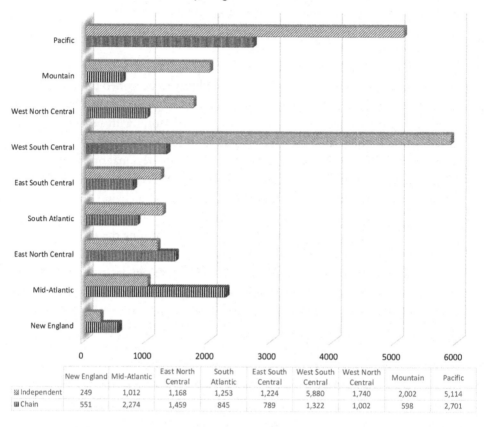

| | New England | Mid-Atlantic | East North Central | South Atlantic | East South Central | West South Central | West North Central | Mountain | Pacific |
|---|---|---|---|---|---|---|---|---|---|
| ⬚ Independent | 249 | 1,012 | 1,168 | 1,253 | 1,224 | 5,880 | 1,740 | 2,002 | 5,114 |
| ⬚ Chain | 551 | 2,274 | 1,459 | 845 | 789 | 1,322 | 1,002 | 598 | 2,701 |

SOURCE: "Census of Business, 1939, Retail Trade: Supermarkets and Self-Service Food Stores." In U.S.
Department of Commerce, *Bureau of the Census, Sixteenth Census of the United States: 1940* (Washington,
D.C.: 1941). *Table:* Self-Service Grocery and Combination Stores, by Types of Operation by Geographic Division.

to make a comfortable living in small-town retailing. "[But] the average returns per concern or per man are quite modest," Veblen explained, "and the less successful ones are habitually doing business within speaking distance of bankruptcy."[31] Chain stores infiltrated small-town main streets, while newly organizing real estate developers redefined suburban development and created shopping centers that competed with commercial business districts. Sociologist Roderick McKenzie, who studied urban trends in the 1920s and 1930s, described a new type of metropolitan community. "Formerly independent towns and villages and also rural territory have become part of the enlarged city complex," he wrote. Rural space represented a new type of "metropolitan community" shaped by the reach of automobiles, offering more flexible transportation options than a countryside previously organized around railroad lines. McKenzie asserted that metropolitanism was the new "communal unit of local relations throughout the entire nation."[32] The process of metropolitanism made the volume strategy of self-service retailing a viable option on Main Street. The farmers who came to town on Saturday shopped in the central business district, not the neighborhood store. Self-service offered both opportunity and risk to merchants accustomed to doing business "within speaking distance of bankruptcy."

## The Fluidity of Self-Service as a Business Practice

To humanize the census data, Sylvan Goldman's boom-and-bust experience in the grocery business offers a useful example for understanding some of the challenges and attractions of self-service for small-town entrepreneurs during the 1920s. Goldman is best known for patenting a shopping cart design that became one of the most influential supermarket technologies of the 1940s. But long before supermarkets, Goldman was among the first generation of small entrepreneurs to introduce rural customers to self-service in the Southwest. His career illustrates the circulation of information about self-service methods across regions and shows the fluidity of the self-service landscape in the 1920s and 1930s, as he alternated between traditional counter-service methods and self-service methods in the local chain stores he created in Oklahoma. Goldman competed with a host of other lesser-known self-service store innovators around Tulsa and Oklahoma City in the interwar years. He made and lost more than one fortune in the process.

Goldman returned from his army service in Europe during World War I to launch a wholesale grocery business with his brother Alfred in Breckenridge, Texas, in 1919. Bad roads made it difficult to reach rural stores, and an economic downturn in the local oil industry put them out of business. With family support the brothers moved to Los Angeles, a recognized center of food retailing innovation at the time, to study chain store retailing methods, with the ultimate goal of opening a grocery business in Oklahoma. The Goldman brothers spent a year learning the complexities of chain store management. They studied the administrative side of the business by meeting with supervisors, meat managers, produce operators, and chain executives. But most importantly they experienced the business on the job by working in combination stores where produce, fresh meat, and grocery departments were often owned and operated by different business concessions that leased space in the store. There was no centralized checkout line in these combination stores, and the Goldmans worked the counters filling customers' orders and collecting payments at the separate departments. It is unclear how much the Goldmans knew about self-service before they went to California, but in Los Angeles they also studied the different management challenges of self-service store operations compared to those of the counter-service stores where they worked.[33]

In 1926 the Goldman brothers moved to Tulsa to open their first grocery store, but they did not simply introduce Los Angeles self-service to Oklahoma. By then, self-service stores were already a familiar experience in town. Franchisee Julius Cytron had opened Tulsa's first Piggly Wiggly in 1919, and by 1923 he was operating four Piggly Wiggly stores around town.[34] Besides Piggly Wiggly, there were Liberty stores created by R. E. Streeter in 1923 and promoted as a self-service "chain of grocery stores established by Tulsans."[35] In fact, the Goldmans did not even start their business as self-service. Their first four Sun Stores operated by traditional counter-service methods.[36] Not until the fifth Sun Store did the Goldmans implement self-service operation. It worked so well that they rebranded Sun Stores as a self-service chain. By their first anniversary, business was good for the Sun chain, which had expanded to twenty-one stores. The Goldmans kept it simple compared to the big combination stores they had studied in Los Angeles. As self-service operations, Sun Stores were initially small and focused on groceries excluding fresh meat and produce. They emphasized economy in their advertising and store promotion efforts to convince customers that self-service was a fair trade for giving up delivery and credit services. The Goldmans adapted their self-service stores during the 1920s to compete in the combination store trend. By 1925, Sun

Stores averaged a generous five thousand square feet of selling space and combined fresh meat and produce concessions with self-service groceries.[37]

Tulsa was a booming oil town during the 1920s. The population had exploded from 18,182 residents in 1910 to 72,075 in 1920, and it doubled in size again by the 1930s. Significantly, the Goldmans did not confine themselves to the city limits. They created a metropolitan chain by successfully expanding the self-service Sun chain to small towns within a few miles of Tulsa. "By the spring of 1928, Sun stores had opened in towns extending southward from Tulsa to Henryetta, fifty-five miles away, and including Kiefer, Mounds, and Beggs. A second line reached as far southwest as Chandler and featured stores in Sapulpa, Bristow, Stroud, and other towns."[38] It was a rapid expansion. Within two years there were fifty stores in the Sun chain in and around Tulsa. In contrast to booming Tulsa, the countryside was experiencing the agricultural depression of the 1920s, with rising rates of tenant farming.[39] The Sun chain's economizing message appealed to debt-strapped farmers. "Protect your future," a Sun Grocery Company ad declared to Okmulgee shoppers, who could choose to shop at two Sun stores, one on West Main and another on East Main. "The Sun Stores System of no Delivery—Buying Direct from Producer to Consumer is a Profit Sharing Plan. Visit your SUN Store daily and receive your dividend."[40]

The Goldmans were important rural pioneers in self-service innovation, but they were not the first to introduce rural Oklahoma customers to self-service. Self-service was not simply an urban import from Tulsa to the countryside. A. V. Ellis opened his first Help Yourself Grocery in Henryetta, Oklahoma, in 1920. By 1922 he had rebranded his growing chain as the A and E Grocery and expanded to Okmulgee. Ellis reported, "We have people who come to us to do their trading from Nuyaka, Beggs, Mounds, and half way to Muskogee on the east. . . . We cover a radius of about thirty miles." A and E offered delivery service, fresh produce, and a meat counter along with their self-service grocery department, but plenty of people came directly to serve themselves. "Nearly forty-five hundred persons made purchases at the store" during a single week in February 1923, and Ellis estimated that "at least twelve thousand five hundred persons were fed out of his store" in Okmulgee (with a population of 17,430 in 1920).[41] In addition to A and E, the Korn Krib Self-Service Stores urged customers in Shawnee, Oklahoma, to "buy just what you want and leave what you don't want" in 1922.[42] Watts Cash and Carry Grocery announced its conversion to self-service in Blackwell, Oklahoma, in 1924. Anticipating resistance to the change, Watts promised lower prices, saying, "In changing over to the self-service system we are enabled to sell at even a much lower price [than] we have been accustomed to making—and that seems like doing the impossible—but all we ask is a trial and we will convince you."[43] Rural Oklahomans were accustomed to self-service long before supermarkets entered the picture.

The Goldmans sold their profitable Sun Stores chain to Skaggs-Safeway in 1929, giving the growing regional Safeway chain its first foothold in Oklahoma. But the Goldmans did not have long to enjoy their newfound leisure as monied stockholders. When the 1929 stock market crash wiped out their Sun sale fortune, they once again faced the prospect of starting over. The brothers moved to Oklahoma City and bought a small bankrupt chain of five stores at one downtown location and four suburban locations. But the Goldmans did not immediately try to repeat the success they had had with self-service in Tulsa. They returned to counter-service store operation, considering store locations without parking access and a customer base that was accustomed to clerk service.[44] They took a methodical approach to store conversion as leases expired and new stores opened. The small downtown store, with a twenty-five-foot by fifty-foot salesroom, had a separate identity as the Standard Food Store, while the suburban stores were named the Sunshine stores.

After the downtown store was destroyed by a food riot, the brothers rebranded the stores as the Standard chain and converted them all to self-service. Three hundred unemployed hungry men stormed the Reno Avenue store in January 1931 while seven hundred more protesters filled the street. Their relief petition had been denied by city hall just down the street from the store. The store manager, H. A. Shaw, with his five clerks lined up behind him, reasoned with the crowd leader. "If you'll have all your men go out but about six, I'll pass out food to them, but I want to keep a check on what's going out," Shaw reportedly said.[45] Instead of the orderly line Shaw hoped to create, "the clerks and Shaw were rushed against a counter and held" as the store was looted. The newspaper reported, "The mob began tearing food from the shelves. The store was strewn with broken packages and piles of cans. The plate glass display window was broken." It is unclear what role, if any, the riot played in accelerating the Goldmans' return to the kind of social controls provided by self-service store arrangement. Standard did not build its first supermarket until 1934.

The Goldmans embraced self-service store operation as a modern retailing method, but as practical businessmen they applied it situationally and strategically. They understood experimentation as a business advantage for a small company. Sylvan Goldman reportedly said, "It isn't the size of a company that counts, but the advantages of being flexible, using good judgment and being able to grab opportunities while larger operations must debate or wait on company routine and red tape for decisions."[46] Switching back and forth from counter service to self-service operation was more challenging than it might at first seem. As a specialized form of retailing, self-service store arrangement was not interchangeable with counter-service store operation. Sylvan Goldman did not simply reproduce what he had learned about how self-service worked in Los Angeles. He developed new self-service methods in his local context. For example, Goldman's Standard stores were among the earliest to introduce self-service produce departments, as distinct from counter-service produce concessions. Goldman's explanation of his management strategies made it clear that self-service produce required display, pricing, and labor management strategies different from those of traditional produce counters.[47] He advocated for self-service produce departments because of their labor-saving advantages. One produce manager could effectively coordinate trimming produce and replenishing displays in his largest produce departments. By comparison, in a counter-service store, Goldman explained, "you not only need this same amount of help we use to prepare this merchandise for sale but also many additional clerks for selling, plus the extra selling help for weekends."[48] Self-service offered the potential for reduced labor costs, but you had to know how to use the workers you hired effectively to ensure a profit.

The popularity of self-service for rural independent store owners might be chalked up to their desire for cost-cutting simplicity. The USDA observed, "The fixtures used in the average self-serve store are simple and inexpensive." This was because store owners usually substituted simple tables and shelves for elaborate display cases.[49] At first glance, store interiors like that of A. L. McWhorter's Sinton, Texas, store (fig. 4.1) demonstrate the thrift of self-service interiors: simple wooden shelving, handmade lattice bins, and chamfered railing that might have looked familiar bracing local porches. But the affordability of store fixtures belies the sophisticated retailing knowledge required to make self-service profitable. Furthermore, the technologies for moving people and goods through the store could add substantially to the costs, and self-service store patents often proposed expensive solutions.

The specialized knowledge for operating self-service stores did not come from business schools. There were no published textbooks that detailed the ins and outs of successful self-service store arrangement. It was a knowledge developed in the daily practice of running a store. None of the self-service store innovators in Oklahoma patented their store designs, but they certainly experimented with the details of self-service store operation. Sylvan Goldman adjusted what he learned about self-service in large California stores to suit the small-town context of rural Oklahoma. He experimented with new practices in self-service retailing of fresh produce and used self-service strategically in his chain of stores. Though he did not patent a full self-service store design, Tulsa entrepreneur Julius Cytron patented an improved gate design for self-service stores, which suggests the variety of local experimentation. His gate worked automatically by a foot tread and included a mechanism for raising a sign panel that could be used to direct customers, "such as directions for the patron to take one of the baskets supplied by the store for use in carrying his merchandise to the checking counter." Cytron's experimentation was the result of careful observation of his patrons. The moving panel was more powerful than a sign attached to the wall because it caught the attention of customers when it rose automatically in front of them as they entered the store.[50] The local experimentation of store owners around the United States is documented in their patented store designs. Store patents corroborate the regional patterns of self-service and offer important evidence of the attractions and challenges of self-service retailing for small-town inventors.

## Efficient and Practical in Use

From 1917 through 1929, the Patent Office approved seventy-five patents for self-service grocery stores. Though store patents were filed by inventors from every region, the vast majority came from the Pacific and southern regions where self-service stores were most numerous. Given the purposes of self-service as a mass retailing strategy, it is unsurprising that the inventors came from large cities such as Los Angeles and San Francisco and growing New South cities like Birmingham, Alabama, and Atlanta. But many of the inventors also came from smaller cities, like Hammond, Indiana, and Wichita Falls, Texas, and a significant proportion lived in towns of less than five thousand people, like Hawkinsville, Georgia; Hazel, Kentucky; and Rolling Fork, Mississippi. The smallest place a patent holder called home was Cedar Bluff, Mississippi, with 228 residents in 1920. Overall, during the 1920s more than half of patent filers came from cities with populations less than fifty thousand, and a sizeable minority (22 percent) came from towns of fewer than five thousand people.

**TABLE 4.4**     Self-Service Store Patents by Region, 1917–1937

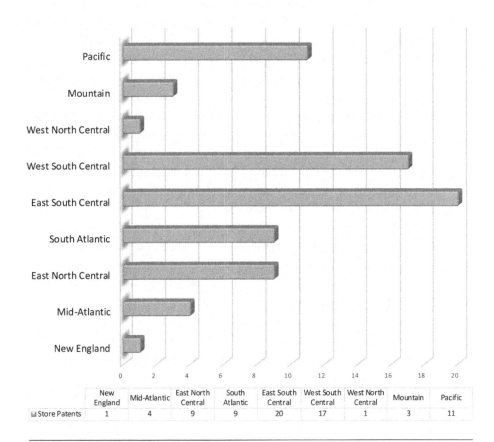

| | New England | Mid-Atlantic | East North Central | South Atlantic | East South Central | West South Central | West North Central | Mountain | Pacific |
|---|---|---|---|---|---|---|---|---|---|
| Store Patents | 1 | 4 | 9 | 9 | 20 | 17 | 1 | 3 | 11 |

SOURCE: Compiled from store patents, 1917–1937.

Patents document the role of small-town businessmen as self-service inventors and deepen our understanding of self-service stores as tools of modern merchandising. Nelson T. Sharp summed up inventors' basic goals: "My invention provides a store arrangement. . . which may be installed economically, and one which will be efficient and practical in use."[51] Though he also described his invention as simple, it took three diagrams with seventy-five labeled features to explain how his self-service store worked. The systematized design of self-service interiors, with their careful consideration of customer flow and product layout, created special challenges for fitting stores into the changing commercial landscapes of the 1920s. Patents document distinct concerns of small-town businessmen that reflect the challenges of doing business on Main Street, especially maximizing the use of small store spaces and ensuring the portability of store fixtures.

One of the advantages of self-service design was the ability to maximize display space without changing the square footage of a store. Patented stores were designed to fit small spaces, but that created challenges for coordinating display space and customer pathways through the store. Alexander C. Robert of Desdemona, Texas, explained that "the primary object" of his invention was to design a self-service store "in which the shelving and other equipment [would] occupy as small an area as possible and thus conserve the floor space and yet provide ample means of access to the goods."[52] Similarly, Lorenzo Norwood Anderson of Hawkinsville, Georgia, said his invention was designed "to economize space without limiting the display of goods or the paths traversed by the customers from one part of the store to the other." He claimed that his shelving system that ringed the perimeter of the store in a zigzag pattern actually "materially increased" the store space.[53] His claim echoed the USDA assertion that many of the reduced expenses generated by self-service were largely attributable to the "greater volume [of trade] evidently possible under self-service than under the cash-and-carry plan, even though both utilize[d] the same floor space."[54] Patents often stated that floor plans could be adjusted or expanded for different spaces. Indeed, flexibility of design was essential to account for the variety of spaces that might be refitted for self-service. Nevertheless, over and over, self-service store patents reveal a veritable obsession with maximizing or economizing floor space—a problem that comes into clearer focus when considering the typical small-town commercial spaces.

Whether chain store or independent, urban groceries were typically designed to fit existing deep, narrow, commercial block store spaces that could

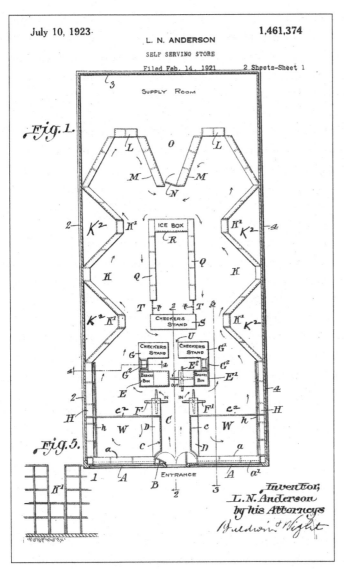

July 10, 1923.

L. N. ANDERSON

SELF SERVING STORE

1,461,374

Filed Feb. 14, 1921          2 Sheets-Sheet 1

Fig. 1.

SUPPLY ROOM

Fig. 5.

FIG. 4.2. Lorenzo Norwood Anderson's zig-zag shelving arrangement accomplished multiple goals: maximizing display space, store surveillance, and economizing space. "The checkers or attendants of the store may at all times have the shelves and bins in view and may keep watch of the customers as they pass through the store," Anderson explained. Customers could enter through left or right turnstiles with pathways following the wall shelving toward the back of the store and then circulating back toward the front around central displays leading to the checkout counter. The exit was controlled by a third turnstile connecting two u-shaped checkout counters at the front of the store. *Source:* Anderson, Self-Serving Store patent.

be found on any small-town Main Street or urban shopping district in the 1920s. Store owners rented commercial space and set up store interiors to display their products to best advantage. Self-service store patents document designers' efforts to make store interiors adaptable to variable store envelopes. Interiors were designed to be portable because the turnover rate in commercial property was high. Not all of that turnover was a result of business failures. In a study of tenant turnover in Bridgeport, Connecticut, during the 1920s and 1930s, the authors declared that moving was "a Main Street norm."[55] Lease terms varied greatly from street to street, and relocating stores was a common practice for ensuring profitability. The Bridgeport study found that turnover had averaged more than seventeen Main Street stores per year in the 1920s. The ability to move your store was critical to business success.[56]

Such frequent location changes were especially common for chain stores. A&P cut costs by adhering to a strict policy of signing only short-term leases. As late as 1933, 94 percent of all A&P store leases ran for only one year.[57] To secure the most advantageous rents, A&P moved stores frequently as leases expired. In Winston-Salem, North Carolina, for example, the chain had eight locations in 1925, half of which would move to new locations by 1930.[58] In 1925, Lynchburg, Virginia, had seven A&P stores, only three of which were in the same location by 1930. A&P centralized decision-making control for locating stores, using detailed statistical information from real estate experts and store sales to evaluate the profitability of locations based on pedestrian traffic and neighborhood income. As leases expired, the company reevaluated the profitability of each location and moved stores to secure more favorable lease terms, larger spaces, or better visibility. Even a move of a few doors down was considered to be worth the effort. Construction teams could build store interiors within days.[59] In Grangeville, Idaho, a Safeway store manager moved the store to a new location "which was only sixty feet from the old location," one weekend in June 1929.[60] "In order to keep up the Safeway spirit and have 100 per cent attendance in moving the store, Mrs. Vittetoe, wife of the manager, served a chicken dinner to all who participated. The only thing to mar the day's pleasure was that things tasted so good it took the boys an hour and a half to pick the bones instead of the usual 45 minutes for noon lunch—and then it rained all day." Even though the lunch break went long, the new store was open for the next workweek.

Because self-service stores were designed as systems for automatic selling, portability presented significant challenges. Self-service store inventors designed for portability of store interiors in a variety of ways to ensure that standardized systems could travel in search of prime retailing locations. For example, Herman A. Weiman of Dallas, Texas, designed a store interior that could be "disassembled if desired when moving."[61] In Hammond, Indiana, Thomas Crawford designed store fixtures that could be installed "without their being nailed to the walls or floor of the building so that they [could] remain the personal property of the occupant of the store and not become a part of the realty which would transfer their ownership to the landlord of the building." Crawford's store was also designed to be adapted "to any store building regardless of its shape."[62]

Patents articulated modular design components to ensure that if store interiors had to be relocated, the systematic features of the machine for automatic selling would not be lost in transition. John Briggs of Wichita Falls, Texas, emphasized that his patented self-service store consisted of "units or sections" that permitted "rapid and convenient installation." The store fixtures were constructed to interlock and form continuous rows of shelving with special locking devices. "They cannot only be quickly erected and assembled, but also very easily detached and removed from the store without drawing a nail or taking out a screw, or splitting a board."[63] Hastings P. Howard of Memphis designed shelves that were all mounted on rollers. "The portability of my cabinets or display units . . . permits the cabinets to be arranged within the salesroom as the shape or size of the room or the circumstances may suggest or require."[64]

A special subset of self-service store patents took mobility to its logical extreme by mounting the whole store on wheels. Rolling stores served a rural and suburban trade, but most were not designed for self-service operation. Large firms served extensive regional markets. W. T. Rawleigh Company, headquartered in Freeport, Illinois, sent out traveling "Rawleigh men" to distribute to rural customers the medicinal products they manufactured. Similarly, J. R. Watkins Medical Company distributed the medicinal products and flavoring extracts they manufactured in Winona, Minnesota, through direct sales using vehicles that served as portable stores.[65] Town merchants also sometimes used rolling stores to drum up rural business or deliver to suburban customers. The Louisville Grocery Survey documented the rising importance of such suburban delivery routes to small-town and mid-sized city grocers and reported that city deliveries within two miles of a store routinely made a daily profit of fifty dollars, while deliveries that ranged beyond town to expand the store customer base to outlying suburban districts had the potential to bring in much more. "[But] there is a social element which can not be divorced from the delivery job," the report on the survey said. Delivery staff socializing with customers ate into potential profits. Stopwatch tests of several delivery routes showed that stops ranged from thirty seconds to nearly ten minutes. One delivery man spent fifteen minutes at a stop delivering a special type of Canadian potato seed for a farmer on his route who asked him for advice about how to plant the unfamiliar seed. Even with the lost time discussing farming, the suburban route brought in about $57 daily. The delivery man cultivated customer loyalty in a variety of ways, the report said. "He mails their letters, cashes their checks, and does other little favors quite foreign to his position as grocery clerk. This is expensive in time but it is doubtful if he could keep all his customers unless he were gracious in these particulars."[66] The habits of delivery men, who worked in relative autonomy to control the route and pace of delivery, determined whether stores actually made money on their routes.

Self-service rolling stores offered special advantages for extending the authority of the town merchant to regulate the pace of suburban trade routes and promised the independent itinerant merchant higher sales.[67] In January 1921 Clyde Martin of Little Rock, Arkansas, and Leonard Hoffman of St. Louis, filed for a patent on their "itinerant vending and sales vehicle."[68] They took the risk of alienating some rural customers by reducing the social element of shopping and designed a self-service rolling store in which the driver did not even have to leave his seat to collect payments. The interior was essentially arranged as a two-aisle store. Customers entered the vehicle through a turnstile. Because the same opening served as both entrance and exit, the turnstile was designed to "revolve in one direction only," so that the driver could "keep count of the number of patrons in the store and . . . be assured of any one leaving the car without paying for collected goods." A handrail that ran the length of the interior organized customers into a single line and directed their path, preventing them from moving back and forth inside the vehicle. Customers completed their circuit at a checkout counter where they paid the driver clerk for their purchase. The patent explained that their vehicle embodied "a complete salesroom" with all of the important features of self-service stores and that it was intended to enable small-town and rural shoppers "the same privileges in the making of their purchases as is now enjoyed only by the people of more thickly settled portions of the country."[69] Martin and Hoffman also claimed that their mobile self-service store was cheaper to operate than typical versions in town. If self-service rolling stores worked like their counterparts on Main Street, rural customers bought more when they had the chance to walk through the salesroom loaded onto the truck bed and choose for themselves.

Store patents document the distinctive concerns and challenges of small-town inventors who modernized Main Street stores and introduced rural

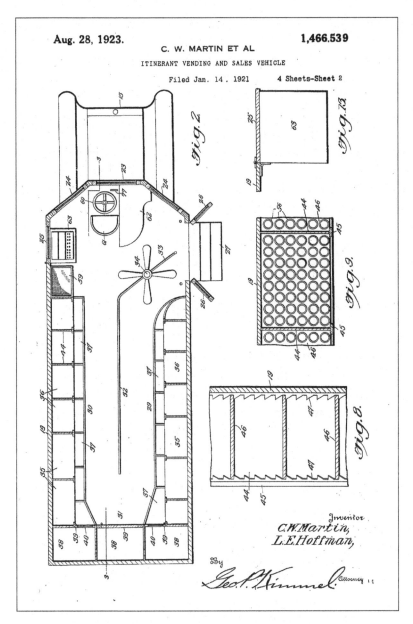

Aug. 28, 1923.

1,466,539

C. W. MARTIN ET AL

ITINERANT VENDING AND SALES VEHICLE

Filed Jan. 14, 1921

4 Sheets-Sheet 2

FIG. 4.3. Clyde W. Martin and Leonard Hoffman's Itinerant Vending and Sales Vehicle patent. Customers entered the rolling store through the turnstile and served themselves from open shelving. A railing created two aisles in the center of the truck that established a one-way traffic pattern and ensured that customers would see all of the products on offer as they passed through the store. *Source:* Martin and Hoffman, Itinerant Vending and Sales Vehicle patent.

customers to self-service shopping. For the entrepreneurs who took the risk, self-service stores offered an edge in the competition. They especially offered a reassuring sense of control in a context of commercial unpredictability, with the promise to deliver reduced wages, special controls for workers, and more sales within the same square footage than traditional or cash and carry stores. With the imprimatur of the Patent Office, patented systems asserted that they "worked" and offered store arrangements that had been tested. Most self-service store owners did not patent their store designs, and the 19,642 independent store owners who reported that they used self-service methods in 1939 left few records to document the reasons why they experimented with self-service. The history of "M" System stores, a successful self-service chain marketed to individual store owners in the South and Southwest, suggests why self-service stores were so appealing to independent entrepreneurs in a region where self-service experimentation was popular.

## "M" System and the Small Business Appeal of Self-Service

Elgan H. Carlton created the first "M" System store in 1922 in Clovis, New Mexico, a town of less than five thousand residents. Later accounts emphasized the hands-on local origins of the store "invented by a practical grocery merchant" who spent a year experimenting with the design in Clovis before expanding his business.[70] Company representatives explained that the store name came "from the shape of the fixtures which are laid out to form a perfect letter 'M' and [also] from our system of Modern Merchandising Methods."[71] Carlton trademarked the fixtures and store brand name and, after success with twelve stores in New Mexico, moved the company headquarters by 1924 to Fort Worth, Texas, where he opened a factory to build "M" System fixtures and began selling franchises.[72] In contrast to the national and international ambitions of Piggly Wiggly, the "M" System franchising effort focused squarely on a regional market. The company rapidly expanded in Texas and by 1925 established a second headquarters in Atlanta, where they opened another factory to build store interiors for the southeastern market.[73] By 1928 the firm had added a third branch office and factory in Kansas City, Missouri.[74] By 1929, "M" System stores operated in fourteen states.[75]

The self-service chain succeeded by marketing its store interiors as scientifically designed to address the practical concerns of small business owners.[76]

FIG. 4.4. "M" System Store No. 842 in Refugio, Texas, in 1934. Refugio had a population of just over two thousand people in 1930. The "M" System was named for the M-shaped shelving arrangement pictured in this photograph. The zigzag shelving arrangement made it possible for the clerk at the front checkout counter to have a clear view of customers in the store. *Source:* Itinerant Photographer Collection, Harry Ransom Center, University of Texas at Austin.

When they began selling stores in North Carolina, marketers emphasized the competition small-town grocers were facing from chain stores. In one North Carolina town, they claimed, residents made half their food purchases from chain stores in larger towns nearby. Company policies restricted licenses to one owner per town, ensuring that "M" System stores would not undercut each other. The company reassured franchisees unfamiliar with self-service retailing methods of ongoing support after they had purchased the fixtures: "The company gives continuous co-operation in buying, advertising, etc., and stands ever ready to give quick attention to any problem that may arise with the operators."[77] The "M" System fixtures took the guesswork out of self-service store design, and the centralized service department ensured that stores would be stocked with the most affordable merchandise. Marketers explained that the "M" System "originated with the idea of enabling the individual grocery merchant to own and operate his own business, and yet at the same time compete with the largest chain stores in the country."[78] The "M" System offered the competitive advantages of a chain organization and the autonomy of independent ownership.

The "M" System interior did not come cheap. Installing a full set of "M" System fixtures and equipment could be as high as $4,500 for one store. Company salesmen nevertheless declared, "The 'M' System is the only Grocery System that will allow the man with a small capital to enter the field on the same basis as the larger operator."[79] To make the franchise more affordable, the company allowed grocers to reuse some of their existing store merchandise and equipment. Store promoters wrote, "While considerable capital is required to enter the 'M' System on a cash basis, where a merchant is already in business and has a stock of merchandise with suitable items of equipment, such as cash registers, scales, refrigerators, etc., the investment is greatly reduced."[80] They estimated that, when grocers reused equipment, a store conversion might cost less than $2,000. "M" System marketers in North Carolina asserted that the store's strong record of profitability made it easier for small-business owners to find financing. "Carolina Bankers . . . are financing men for the 'M' stores that they would not for a moment consider financing for an old line credit business."[81]

It seemed like a low-risk investment. If a grocer could find the financing to buy into the system, the M System was a well-designed machine for automatic selling that offered predictable profits. The zigzag "M" shape of the store arrangement was scientifically designed to maximize display and "make stealing unknown" because "from the checking stand the operator [could] see at a glance every inch of shelving and floor space." The efficient store design processed customers and sales more rapidly than traditional store arrangements. "With fifty people in an M System store trading[,] a customer can go in, make a purchase and get out in seven minutes. Thirty minutes or more are required in the old style service stores."[82] Compared to a typical grocery operation earning $1,500 per week, offering credit and delivery to customers, operated by three clerks, a bookkeeper, a cashier, and two delivery wagons, the "M" System promised to halve overhead expenses.[83] Promoters assured potential buyers that two people could successfully handle an "M" System store doing a healthy business of $8,000 per month.[84] An *Atlanta Constitution* ad addressed to "every Grocery Merchant—or expecting to be soon—Anywhere in the South or Southeastern States" declared, "The fixtures are not only self-serving and *self-selling*, but also are a vital item in slashing overhead expenses of all kinds."[85] The main reason to buy an "M" System interior was its reliability as a machine for automatic selling.

The flexibility and affordability of store conversion was attractive to small-business owners. Thurston Cole, in Bryan, Texas, converted his traditional service store to the "M" System self-service in 1929. He was an experienced grocer who had worked in the grocery business for two decades.[86] Mrs. A. E. Nelson installed the "M" System in her Blackstone, Virginia, grocery store, joining "several women operators, who for years, have been making wonderful earnings [using the "M" System] in face of keen chain-store competition."[87] In North Carolina thirty-four stores had converted to the "M" System by 1928. "Generally speaking," it was reported, these were "old line merchants who . . . changed to the 'M' System, although a number [were] operated by men who were formerly employed by large chain organizations."[88] The former chain employees were presented as men who bought "M" System stores to become independent owners. "M" System stores were also reportedly bought by people who had never operated a grocery store.[89] Some franchisees bought multiple "M" System stores, creating their own local chain networks. In Amarillo, Texas, for example, banker C. W. Furr, opened the first "M" System store in town in 1924, and by 1931 he owned thirty-seven "M" System stores throughout the Panhandle. In 1927 Furr bought the Amarillo Piggly Wiggly Company, which operated in fifteen Panhandle-Plains cities, merging the two self-service systems into a single local company, "M" System–Piggly Wiggly Corporation, with himself as president.

The *Amarillo-Globe* described it as a "100 per cent Panhandle-Plains company, every officer and stockholder being an actual, bona fide resident and believer in this country."[90] The marriage of "M" Systems and Piggly Wiggly in the Texas panhandle was a fitting union of localism and self-service with the power of chain store management.

Systematized sales brought an aura of predictability in an unpredictable and highly competitive marketplace. Patented self-service designs offered the further reassurance of systems that were tested and could be counted on to work without specialized knowledge or training. If they were capital-intensive in the upfront costs of interior fixtures, site design, and inventory, self-service stores promised higher sales per square footage and cost savings over the long term. Self-service features routinized and simplified business procedures such as taking inventory, cleaning the store, and stocking shelves. The autonomy of operating a store with minimal staff and the advantage of a store design that facilitated the management of workers and customers held strong appeal to small-business owners.

With its emphasis on modern systems, efficiency, and scientific merchandising, and its popular identification with a single national chain, self-service might have become a symbol of chain store competition for the anti-chain movement. Instead, the success of self-service store experimentation in Populist country like Texas requires a rethinking of the modernizing role of small-town grocers. Anti-chain sentiment gained steam during the 1930s when anti-chain taxes were enacted in twenty-eight states, the vast majority of them in the South and West, the same states where self-service stores were most successful. Most anti-chain protesters were merchants, many of them independent grocery store owners, who argued against what they saw as unfair trading practice of chain stores with distant urban headquarters. "Keep Ozark Dollars in the Ozarks," declared the Springfield, Missouri, chamber of commerce. Historian Daniel Scroop argues, "The anti-chain store movement was the most important outbreak of popular resistance to the rise of modern retailing in the history of the United States."[91] But it is a mistake to think of the anti-chain movement as anticapitalist or antimodern. As Scroop emphasizes, small-town merchants who opposed chain stores embraced a sophisticated ideology of localism that linked national identity and progress with self-government.[92]

With the decline of independent farming by the 1920s, the symbolic power of yeoman independence was threatened by the spread of chain stores that condemned their employees to the lifelong status of clerks. "The

FIG. 4.5. "He that is self-served is well served" declares the sign on the counter as an independent proprietor sits behind his respectable white picket fence. Hanging price tags on the shelves suggest the influence of Piggly Wiggly. The store location is unknown. Photo courtesy of Susan V. Spellman, private collection.

independence could adhere in other forms of proprietorship, provided the illusion of self-command remained," historian Bethany Moreton asserts. Anti-chain rhetoric invoked a critique of the machine. "[Chains] stifle opportunity for local boys. Their clerks stay clerks . . . [A chain] doesn't want bright boys—it wants plodders, dutiful machines," opined the *Reader's Digest* in 1938. Klansmen warned that chains threatened small-business ownership and turned young men into "automatons."[93] But self-service stores largely escaped the anti-chain, anti-machine rhetoric. In his sermon on human nature, Pentecostal preacher George Swann invoked Piggly Wiggly: "They have been eminently successful because they struck two chords in human nature that responded. One is PRICE and the other is FREEDOM in the store. They sell cheaper because they have no clerks, and each customer has freedom because he takes his basket, selects what he wants from things that are all priced, then comes by the cashier and pays."[94] Swann envisioned an autonomous male consumer taking up a market basket, making his own choices from store shelves with clear access the price he would pay of his own free will at the checkout counter—the same price other men would pay on an equal playing field. There was no love lost for the small-town grocery clerk in many communities—the over-bearing salesmanship, conflict over bill collection, distrust about the quality and freshness of products, and class tensions were part of daily business in the grocery store. On the other hand, from the small entrepreneur's perspective, the self-service store, with its scientific and mechanical precision, offered a powerful tool in support of the storekeeper's autonomy. Extending the rhetoric of self-sufficiency to his customers, the self-service grocer promised them that they would be the beneficiaries of self-service through lower prices and liberation from overbearing salesclerks, as the turnstile or gate locked behind them and they entered the self-service machine.

In 1930, still operating in the small town where it started, the "M" System promoted a republican rhetoric of independence and self-help to the residents of Clovis, New Mexico: "'M' System fosters the spirit of independence," an ad for the store declared. The "M" System had the power to inculcate core American values of democracy and efficiency. It embodied "the Soul of Democratic Institutions," teaching all to do for themselves. "Have you ever figured the time wasted while waiting to be waited on? At 'M' System you do not have to spend ten minutes listening to Mrs. Brown and a too talkative clerk arguing whether a private brand is just as good as an old established nationally advertised brand. Trade at 'M' System—Where you receive full values on every transaction."[95] The self-service store struck at the heart of small-town class and gender systems and reordered social relations inside the store. Pronounced regional variations in the popularity of the self-service store demonstrate that self-service was never only about improving business efficiencies. It was a social experiment as well.

# The Purchase-Inducing Force of the Store

The advertising rhetoric of self-service sold the new retailing method as a liberating and democratizing shopping experience. Those narratives were partly true. Compared to traditional counter-service stores, where the perceived social status of customers routinely affected the kind of service they received, self-service stores radically equalized the shopping process. But designing store spaces as systems for automatic selling required building in features to promote the volume sales that inspired self-service experimentation in the first place. Maximizing sales was not simply a result of improving business efficiencies in the self-service system. Store patents document the varied strategies self-service store inventors employed to socially engineer store interiors. Inventors explain how their designs automated salesmanship. through dramatically different sensory retailing methods. Replacing the social interaction of the counter-service store with the compartmentalized silence of self-service was an intentional design strategy for creating what Clarence Saunders called "the purchase-inducing force" of the mechanical store.[1]

The Piggly Wiggly store arrangement is the most familiar example of self-service store design before the supermarket, but it does not represent a standard self-service store layout. The arrangement of fixtures and mechanisms for operationalizing self-service varied so dramatically from place to place that a U.S. Department of Agriculture study of self-service groceries noted in 1928 that there were "nearly as many plans for the arrangement of fixtures and the display of stock as there [were] stores."[2] The great variety of designs reflected the experimentation of store operators during the developmental stages of self-service invention. Besides open shelving that defined aisles for shoppers to traverse through the store, there were zigzag shelving arrangements, baskets attached to monorails, and turntables that kept the store in motion. Not all stores were organized into aisles formed by open shelving. In the "Shopineze," customers came in and sat down in comfortable lounge chairs while the store rotated in front of them on a conveyor belt. In a Kentucky Automarket shoppers could drive their cars right through the store while customers on foot served themselves amid the exhaust fumes. Some store arrangements prescribed a specific path through the store, others left customers free to make their own routes in search of the product they were looking for. With few precedents and no fixed ideas about how self-service should work, the entrepreneurial phase of self-service experimentation was marked by incredibly imaginative strategies for creating stores that worked as machines for automatic selling. These stores are mostly invisible in the landscape of retail history.

When it comes to the small-business commercial architecture of Main Street, vernacular architecture historians tend to analyze stores based primarily on their appearance from the street. In his guide to American commercial architecture, Richard Longstreth classifies Main Street buildings based on the formal configuration of storefronts because they were designed to be seen from the front.[3] While storefronts are relatively stable fixtures of commercial streetscapes, store interiors are ephemeral by design. Commercial buildings were constructed as versatile envelopes for diverse tenants with different kinds of businesses. Storekeepers were the architects of store interiors, and they did not usually document their decision-making process. In her study of small-town commercial architecture during the 1930s, Gabrielle Esperdy focuses on the modernized storefronts funded especially through the Federal Housing Administration Modernization Credit Plan, offering a compelling argument that "they constitute a materially significant and highly symbolic portion of all New Deal building activity."[4] But a focus on the storefront obscures the important differences in operating methods inside stores. Esperdy emphasizes the role of chains in shaping American commercial landscapes of the early twentieth century, writing that A&P and the chains Kroger, American Store, and Piggly Wiggly were "self-service combination food stores selling produce, meats, breads and cakes, and canned and packaged goods under one roof" and generalizing that "these were *super*markets."[5] The emphasis on storefronts as the key symbolic feature of small-business architecture underestimates the centrality of store arrangement as a defining element of store function, symbolism, and shopping as a social practice. Longstreth points out, "Interiors may indeed be the most significant aspect in studying how specific kinds of commercial buildings developed and changed over time."[6] But analysis of small-business interiors lags behind the extensive scholarly analysis of large commercial spaces like department stores and supermarkets.[7]

FIG. 5.1. Automarket, Louisville, 1928. The checkout counter served both customers in cars and on foot. An automobile customer pays at the checkout counter, where bakery items on display could be weighed and wrapped at the end of the shopping pathway. A second cashier serves pedestrian customers exiting on the other side of the counter. *Source:* Caufield and Shook Collection, ULPA CS 090756, Archives & Special Collections, University of Louisville Libraries.

Store interiors are difficult to study. Most self-service stores were built on site by work crews that custom-fit shelving and other fixtures to rented store spaces. Small business owners did not leave detailed records about their store arrangements. While photographs of store interiors of the early twentieth century are myriad, they offer fragmented and decontextualized views of store operation. For example, it is not possible to see the systemized store arrangement of the Louisville Automarket from the isolated perspective presented in the photograph of the car at the checkout counter (fig. 5.1). Chester Liebs included it in his study of American roadside architecture. Liebs features the Automarket along with Piggly Wiggly as examples of "the self-service combination store." He presents Piggly Wiggly as the standard self-service interior and declares that the advantages of self-service were so self-evident that "the industry as a whole began a gradual changeover to self-service by the early 1920s."[8] But his brief description of the Automarket offers conflicting information about what made it a self-service store. Liebs explains that "customers threaded their automobiles along a narrow track," through the store and shopped "without ever having to leave their cars," but he also says "they were handed merchandise by a series of curbside salesclerks."[9] In fact, the checkout counter featured in the photograph is the only place in the store where auto customers interacted with a clerk. The store design automated self-service in the rest of the space with a coordinated system of turntables and market baskets on pulleys (see figs. 5.15–17). Classifying Piggly Wiggly and the Automarket as examples of combination stores erases the enormous challenges self-service store inventors faced in integrating products that were difficult to sell with self-service methods. The bakery counter pictured alongside the checkout counter in the Automarket is one example of how store owners experimented with strategies for spatially integrating products resistant to self-service retailing methods. Piggly Wiggly was not a combination store when it was first invented, and the original patented design had to be adjusted for selling fresh produce and meat in the 1920s and 1930s.

Self-service store interiors are not interchangeable with those of mainstream combination stores. They should be understood as a distinctive historical store type. They stand out in city directories of the early twentieth century because store owners typically signaled their specialized format in store naming practices—calling them groceterias (or grocerterias), basketerias, or self-service stores to distinguish them from regular grocery stores. They belong in the typologies of consumer spaces alongside shopping malls, arcades, corner grocery stores, farmers' markets, and variety chains like Woolworth.[10]

But to make self-service stores visible we need a better understanding of how store arrangements worked. Their variety and novelty during the experimental phase of invention has made it hard to see them as a related type of shopping space. Store patents offer vital evidence for understanding self-service stores as a specialized store type.

Historians of technology evaluate invention as a sociological process shaped by both inventors and consumers. Historian Ruth Schwartz Cowan defines the "consumption junction" as "the place and the time at which the consumer makes choices between competing technologies." She emphasizes the importance of evaluating the process of invention "from the inside out," to consider "which elements stood out as being more important, more determinative of choices, than the others, and which paths seemed wise to pursue and which too dangerous to contemplate." Consumers play an integral role in determining which new inventions ultimately succeed or fail. Cowan argues that it is important to consider the diversity of consumers as an essential "complicating factor" for evaluating the consumption junction and emphasizes that "we must define consumers in terms of the artifact about which they are making choices (as, for example, 'a prospective purchaser of a washing machine') as well as by other appropriate socioeconomic variables (for example, 'middle class,' or 'rural')."[11]

We are not used to thinking of stores as technologies in the same sense as a washing machine, but that is exactly how their inventors described them. Store patents often identify self-service stores as vending machines, apparatuses, or mechanical stores. The prospective customers of store patents were the entrepreneurs who might buy or invest in the invention. In contrast to newspaper and magazine advertisements that promised store shoppers the freedom to choose, store patents promised store operators control features that guaranteed maximum sales. The grocers who were early adopters of self-service store operation designed store systems that reshaped the work routines of clerks and the ways that shoppers interacted with products in the store. The patent process itself promoted variability since only innovations could succeed in being patented.

Patents offer the opportunity to study the invention of self-service stores "from the inside out," as Cowan urges. Inventors from across the United States included floor plans showing design details and explanations of how the arrangement was intended to work and what problems it was designed to address. At first glance their tremendous variability can obscure their shared operational logic. Store designs may have incorporated different mechanisms for automating selling, but they were not haphazard. Representing a time when self-service store arrangement was not well-documented in business texts, patents offer vital evidence of the rationale for store design. Despite their great variety, self-service stores were not simply random oddities. Their variability represents a coherent phase in the entrepreneurial development of self-service stores as a new technological and social practice.

Self-service interiors were shaped by four key principles. First, as specialized machines for automatic selling, store spaces were physically enclosed or compartmentalized to separate their carefully crafted systems and route customers to enter and exit the space at the right point. Second, whatever mechanisms inventors employed to automate selling, their floor plans always included directional arrows documenting intended store pathways that organized retail space into a coordinated selling system. Third, long before the rolling shopping cart became a standard feature of supermarket operation, self-service store inventors experimented with a wide variety of strategies for mobilizing merchandise to promote volume sales. Finally, inventors experimented with strategies for automating salesmanship that engineered new sensory environments designed to generate consumer desire. These shared principles shaped self-service stores whether their designs were patented or not.

Serving ourselves has become such a standardized experience that we do it today without a second thought, so it can be hard to imagine how stores worked before the late-twentieth-century retail conversion to self-service. For customers long accustomed to having clerks do the heavy lifting of order assembly, self-service was a disorienting and unfamiliar experience. If some customers found it liberating, others found it degrading to do the work of hired clerks. The memoir of a grocery clerk who worked at a large grocery store in Massachusetts offers a vivid record of how the compartmentalized self-service space operated as a specialized retail system in the store. His description of how shopping worked very differently in the counter-service and self-service parts of the store brings into vivid relief how self-service shopping was intentionally designed to be a fundamentally new kind of shopping experience.

## Compartmentalized Retailing: The Store within a Store

Upham's Corner Market in Dorchester, Massachusetts, founded by John and Paul Cifrino in 1915, served a diverse Polish, Lithuanian, German, Italian, and Irish clientele at the nexus of six different streetcar lines in South Boston.

The store reflected the 1920s trend toward larger spaces that combined meat, fruits and vegetables, and packaged groceries for one-stop shopping as the brothers expanded the store several times during the decade. By 1927 Upham's encompassed over fifty thousand square feet of retail space—a size that dwarfed the largest Piggly Wiggly store.[12] The large store was arranged in departments, each organized around separate counters—bakery items and vegetables and fruits, with glass shields to protect the produce. There was not simply one meat counter; the store was large enough to house different counters for lamb, poultry, pork, beef, and fish. William Marnell, who started out in the store as a bundle boy, remembered with admiration the skilled and knowledgeable staff who blended custom tea mixes, consulted on the right cut of meat for a roast, or advised cooks about the best bean variety to use for baked beans. "One must picture each counter adequately manned at all times, with clerks massed in phalanx formation at the great rush hours," Marnell recalled. Despite its grand size and departmentalized arrangement, Marnell emphasized nostalgically and somewhat disdainfully in his memoir *Once upon a Store*, "There was nothing faintly suggestive of the self-service concept that underlies the modern supermarket." He was there when the Cifrino brothers converted the grocery counter to self-service. According to Marnell, the Cifrino brothers studied the methods of an unnamed self-service chain.[13] Piggly Wiggly had three stores in Boston by 1922 and was a likely source of inspiration.[14]

Marnell had worked at Upham's through multiple expansions and considered that the self-service grocery department conversion was more complicated than any of the previous remodels. The grocery department was based at a long L-shaped Victorian counter, with glass display cases and shelves lining the walls behind the counter, with "only the width the clerks needed to move around." The Cifrinos closed off a substantial section of the store, and construction crews worked mysteriously behind a plywood wall to reconstruct the space. When the renovation was completed, the new grocery department was, in Marnell's word, "a miniature store within The Store."[15] The new self-service compartment had a pile of baskets by the separate entrance for customers to collect their groceries. In place of the bulk items that had been weighed and measured by clerks at the Victorian counter, canned and packaged products lined open shelves that formed three aisles. Customers completed their transactions with the cashier at the exit of the partitioned space. Shopping in the new grocery department was dramatically different than in the rest of the store.

In the open counter-service area of the store it was a chaotic and noisy scene at rush hour, as crowds of customers pressed toward the various counters, jockeying for the attention of the clerks. The store was a cacophony of voices, neighbors chatting in their native Polish, others speaking in heavily accented English, still others struggling to negotiate with "the most meager fragments of broken English." Clerks shouted instructions to each other so that they could be heard over the noise of the crowd. Customers haggled over the quality of meat cuts and sought advice about cooking techniques from knowledgeable staff. Once the deal was struck at one counter the customer moved on to the next counter and began the shopping process all over again. Some stores handled payment at each counter, but Upham's organized the payment process so that customers did not have to carry packages from one counter to another. It was a technology-assisted process. As she moved from counter to counter, the shopper collected sales slips. Clerk did not have to take the time to wrap the merchandise at every counter. They marked the sales slip with a colored pen and loaded it into a metal basin along with the customer's purchase. As the basins circulated the store, "an overhead conveyor belt kept moving by electrically operated rollers beneath it. The basin nodded and bobbled and lurched along until it reached its destination, sliding usually with one ultimate whirl down a shute to a shelf from which a bundle boy lifted it, wrapped it, affixed the sales slip with a bit of brown sticking paper, and left it on a shelf to be delivered to the lady when she presented the original sales slip."[16]

Since the basins were in the habit of tipping over as they circulated the store, the butter and egg counter was the only one with its own bundle station. Once she had finished shopping, the customer took her collection of sales slips to the cashier, who stamped them as paid. There were three color-coded bundle counters, and the customer had to locate her purchases according to the streak of color each clerk had put on her sales slip. This too was a noisy transaction. Marnell recalled that bundle boys were required to double-check the accuracy of cashier's addition and said that their vocal complaints about clerks' indecipherable sales slips "could be shrill and even piercing." A single customer might be served by half a dozen clerks before exiting the store.

Given the number of clerks it took to handle the transaction of a single customer, one might imagine that cutting labor costs was a primary goal of the Cifrino brothers self-service renovation. In the new self-contained grocery department there was no need for color-coded sales slips or multiple bundle stations. There were no overhead conveyor belts with unpredictable bobbing basins. A single clerk and cashier operated the whole system. However, though staff for the grocery department was reduced, the clerks who had worked the grocery counter were moved to other jobs in the store.[17] The chief attraction of the renovation for the owners was that the self-service space sold more groceries than the clerks had. Free access to the products and silent concentration on the task of shopping intertwined to increase sales in the new self-service grocery department even though no salesclerk was handy to push a new product. But the Cifrinos did not consider self-service generally applicable for the whole store. Marnell observed that, with a clerk and cashier running the self-service section, "price could move down a bit and profit still go up. . . . [but] the partners never considered extending the self-service concept to other counters, and never did so as long as The Store was theirs."[18] They understood self-service as a specialized form of retailing for prepackaged grocery products.

Transforming the grocery department into a machine for automatic selling produced a shopping experience completely different from the din and tumult on the other side of the store. In contrast to the rush of crowds vying for position at the various clerk-service counters, customers picked up a market basket from the bin and entered the compartmentalized self-service pathway one at a time. A turnstile set a controlled pace by admitting customers in turn and launching them in the right direction onto the self-service pathway. It was a silent journey through the aisles, focused on looking at the products on the open display. Marnell observed that self-service customers initially felt fearful about taking products off the shelves and putting them in their baskets: "There was a general agreement among the nicer customers that at first it seemed like stealing, putting things in your basket yourself." Their unease suggests a sense of exposure, their inexperience on display to be observed by others. But the open access to the products and the silent engagement with the visual display soon had its intended effect. "She would spot a package of rice and remember that she was out of rice," adding it to her basket. Without distractions the shopper noticed things she hadn't seen before behind the glass counters and made unplanned purchases.

Marnell believed that self-service appealed to the shoppers because the mental absorption with shopping tasks made the time go faster. "She had kept moving all the time, she wasn't bored waiting for her turn to be served as she had to at the old grocery counter," he reasoned. Some customers liked direct access to the products because they could "size up things more carefully, read what the labels said before they made their selections, . . . compare prices more easily, and most important of all, see things they needed but had not thought of, and so make their shopping more efficient." He did not explain how shoppers who couldn't read English navigated the self-service system. Perhaps they avoided it altogether and submitted their grocery orders to clerks staffing the Order Department counter on the other side of the store.

Converting the grocery department to self-service reconfigured the social relationship between clerks and customers at Upham's. Rather than standing at counters, customers moved along a pathway defined by the placement of store fixtures, collecting products as they circulated the store, finally arriving at a centralized checkout counter where they paid and exited the space with their purchases. It standardized customer experience. In contrast to the individual negotiations across the counter, every customer in the self-service compartment walked the aisle with basket in hand and stood in line on a first-come, first-served basis to check out. Self-service levelled the playing field—and that felt empowering to some shoppers and degrading to others. Marnell described the reactions of customers encountering self-service for the first time: "Imagine having to go around a labyrinth of aisles . . . hauling with you a heavy basket, stopping to get cans off shelves, having to look for everything you want to buy, having to do all your own work as if you were a clerk and not a customer, and then paying just as much for it as you ever did." Evoking the charged class dynamic between clerks and the elite women they served, Marnell wrote, "It made you, the lady from the very best part of The Town who had wads of middle-aged money and a seven passenger Packard touring car in the carriage house, one of the help."[19]

Upham's was an unusually large grocery store for the 1920s. Most grocery stores were only large enough for a few counters, and they didn't need the basins circulating around the store on conveyor belts or the color-coordinated bundle stations to keep up with customer purchases. But the cacophony of rush hour would have been familiar to their clerks and customers. In Louisville, one tiny neighborhood store routinely served seventy-six customers between 8:00 and 8:30 a.m., mostly public-school children from across the street buying refreshments or school supplies. In working-class neighborhoods, stores opened as early as 5:00 a.m., and the first customers "most frequently bought products directly related to the usual breakfast requirements, such as bacon, eggs, milk, etc."[20] Across the city, groceries experienced a "three-peak day," with the highest customer traffic corresponding to mealtimes. Customers shopped according to the rhythms of their appetites. Rush hours were more pronounced in working-class neighborhoods than in wealthier suburbs where customers could afford the cost of delivery and thus did not have to physically go to the store to do their shopping. With one grocery counter to serve all of the customers at peak shopping times, the hubbub of socializing and bargaining would no doubt have been considerable, even in these smaller neighborhood stores. Yet the system that customers of the 1920s found the most confusing to navigate was not the cacophonous counter-service store at rush hour but the silent order of the self-service store. Social interaction and sensory engagement in the "store-within-a store" offered stark contrasts to the counter-service norm.

The Upham's "store within a store" demonstrates how compartmentalization ensured that self-service stores could work as enclosed systems for automatic selling. Compartmentalization was a defining characteristic of self-service stores throughout the 1920s and 1930s, even in small stores, where the selling space was routinely fenced off from the lobby (see, for example, figs. 4.1 and 4.5). Store owners worried about theft in self-service stores, but that is not the main reason their inventors designed them as separate spaces. Self-service stores were built as contained, compartmentalized spaces so that they worked effectively as specialized systems for automatic selling. Controlling the entry and exit ensured that customers started out on a path that would focus their attention on the products for sale and end their shopping trip at the cashier's counter to pay before exiting the store.

There were several different spatial strategies for compartmentalizing self-service installations during the interwar years. In Butte, Montana, the Lutey brothers created "duplex" stores, opening counter-service and self-service stores in contiguous downtown storefronts.[21] Some chains opened self-service and counter-service stores in separate locations. For example, H. G. Hills positioned self-service stores downtown and counter-service stores in residential neighborhoods in his Nashville chain.[22] Using different brand identities as a compartmentalizing strategy, the Rogers chain in Atlanta bought the self-service Nifty Jiffy stores while maintaining counter service at Rogers stores. A Rogers ad (fig 5.2) explained to Atlanta shoppers that the two stores were part of the same chain: "If you like to be served by courteous, efficient sales clerks, of course you will visit a Rogers Store. If you like to step into a roomy, attractive store and walk around and wait upon yourself—then, Nifty Jiffy will appeal to you."[23] Larger regional chains used this compartmentalizing strategy on a bigger scale. For example, when Kroger and Safeway bought Piggly Wiggly franchises they did not convert all of their stores to self-service. Their newly acquired Piggly Wiggly stores offered a self-service option,

FIG. 5.2 Rogers chain ad, Atlanta, 1928. Nifty Jiffy, based on the patents of James H. Carroll, claimed to be the first self-service store system ever organized in Atlanta. The first store opened in 1924 with plans to expand the chain nationally. President and general manager E. F. Newell had experience as a district manager of Piggly-Wiggly Stores, Inc., in Dayton, Ohio, and Atlanta. By 1928 Nifty Jiffy had been absorbed into the local Rogers chain. There were 150 traditional counter-service Rogers stores in the city and twelve Nifty Jiffy stores maintained as specialized self-service stores in the chain. *Source: Atlanta Constitution*, 30 June 1928.

while Kroger and Safeway stores retained counter service. Whether they isolated self-service store locations as distinctive outlets in a larger chain system, physically separated a self-service grocery department from the counter-service parts of a larger store, or simply fenced off the retail space from the lobby, store designers compartmentalized all self-service grocery spaces as enclosed, specialized retailing systems.

Upham's organized the self-service grocery department into aisles of open shelving and provided market baskets for customers to do the work of shopping. But designing a fully operational self-service store turned out to be more complicated than simply arranging shelving into aisles and turning customers loose in the store. Store inventors across the United States tried out different technologies and methods to reconfigure store spaces into systemized customer pathways that coordinated multiple store functions. Though shoppers seemingly had unfettered access to product displays, once they came through the turnstile and entered the self-service machine, their routes were carefully engineered to generate desire.

## Patenting Pathways

Self-service inventors designed interconnected spatial systems that sorted consumer labor, store management, and the work of store clerks to overcome significant challenges in small store spaces. Store designers did not invent the machinery they used to build their automated selling systems. Turnstiles, conveyor belts, monorails, cash registers, adding machines, and refrigerators were already used in various retail settings and industries. When he patented an improvement in the self-serving store that he described as an apparatus, inventor John Smiley acknowledged, "I am aware that association of a roller conveyor with shelving is not broadly new."[24] Self-service store systems organized these existing technologies in new ways, and store patents document a variety of goals—maximizing sales, effective inventory control, and monitoring workers and shoppers. Whether or not a store design offered customers options in making their own pathways through a store, all created an interconnected set of elements from entry to exit intended to direct customers to see, select and transport products, and take part in a centralized payment process before leaving the store.

The floor plans that mapped patented self-service systems envisioned store space in entirely new ways that differed from traditional counter-service stores and modern stores that combined open display with counter service. To understand what was so new and different about how self-service store systems worked, it is helpful to compare the working pathways of a typical clerk-service store to a self-service pathway. Using a common method for evaluating business efficiency at the time, government researchers in Louisville timed workers completing specific tasks in their 1928 study. In several Louisville grocery stores, researchers used stopwatches to time how long it took clerks to complete a specific order. The final report included maps of their work process. Figure 5.3 shows the process a clerk used in assembling an order with nine items. The researcher mapped the progress of order assembly as the clerk moved repeatedly back and forth across the space, using the main counter to collect the items on the list. The order assembly map shows three counters or shelves lining the walls of a small store, with open space in the center of the

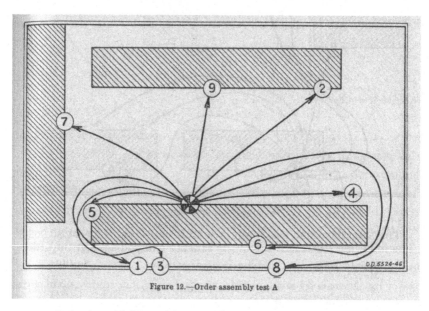

Figure 12.—Order assembly test A

FIG. 5.3. Order Assembly Test A. This map of store counters and shelving shows the multiple paths a store clerk took to collect a customer order with nine items. It took him twelve minutes and forty-two seconds to complete the order. *Source:* U.S. Department of Commerce, *Louisville Grocery Survey*, 65.

store. The nine products on the order list were located all over the store, and some of them may have been staples that required weighing and measuring, which added to the time it took for the clerk to complete the order. It took the clerk twelve minutes and forty-two seconds to assemble the nine items in the order from the moment he picked up the list to the completion of the packaged order ready for delivery. Notice that the clerk repeatedly covered the same ground as he worked his way down the list. He might have picked up item 3 while he was in the same location for item 1. Instead, he crossed to the opposite end of the store to collect item 2 and then returned to the location of item 1 to collect item 3. The researcher determined that the cost of assembling the order was higher than the total purchase amount of the order, leaving the store with a net loss of 7.25 percent.[25] The timed test took place in an empty store under ideal conditions. Imagine the clerk attempting to fill this order under normal conditions at rush hour with the store full of customers. Weaving through the crowd and interacting with customers would certainly have increased the cost of order assembly.

In addition to this clerk, researchers timed and mapped the order assembly process of several other Louisville grocery clerks in different stores with a similar haphazard collection process, suggesting that this order assembly map in figure 5.3 represented the typical pattern of operation in counter-service stores. All of the clerks used the store spaces in the same way, moving back and forth from shelves to counter, collecting one item at a time. To improve worker efficiency and store profits, the researchers urged a new understanding of the connection between store space, work routines, and profit margins. "The most striking possibility for cost reduction does not seem to have yet occurred to the retail grocer," they concluded. "This possibility involves the present administrative misconception of the function of the retail selling space."[26] The report stopped short of recommending that grocers convert their stores fully to self-service, however. "Service to customers is a function with which the manager will be wise to do little experimentation. He may school his clerks in politeness and in the art of persuasion, but he will not wisely attempt to control the time, and consequently the cost, of the service. This lies within the province of the customer only, and she may resent any evident effort to hurry her."[27] Carl Dipman's model store, with its open display principles and improved arrangement for worker efficiency, was the result of the Louisville grocery study.

But self-service store inventors took to heart the idea that efficient store layout was the key to generating improved profit margins. Their store arrangements document the radical rethinking of store space required to operationalize self-service store systems. If we consider the order assembly map in a traditional counter-service store as the typical method of operation for a traditional counter-service store, the self-service store presented a very different concept map for store arrangement and operation in the same basic building envelope (figs. 5.4 and 5.5). Traditional stores were designed for gathering customers at the counter, not spreading them out or moving them through the store. If the store had open displays, a customer might assist the clerk in assembling the order by carrying an item or two to the counter. But the act of shopping in such a store primarily involved the social and financial transaction at the counter. Direct interaction between customer and product was minimal. In stark contrast, the back-and-forth movement of clerks in the counter-service store was replaced by the organized forward movement of customers searching for products on their own in the self-service store. The act of shopping became a process of perusal and personal selection.

One way of understanding the self-service pathway, as business historian

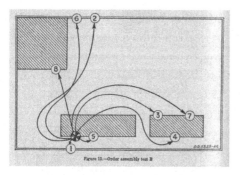

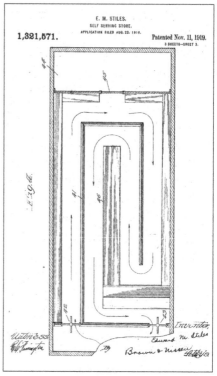

Figure 13.—Order assembly test B

FIGS. 5.4 and 5.5. Comparison of traditional counter service floor plan with a typical self-service floor plan. Both plans map different arrangement of store fixtures and fundamentally different concepts of movement through store space. FIG. 5.4: Order Assembly Test B. [*Source*: U.S. Department of Commerce, *Louisville Grocery Survey*, p. 66.] FIG. 5.5: Self Serving Store, Patent No. 1,321,571, Edward M. Stiles, November 11, 1919.

Richard Tedlow asserts, was the organization of business efficiencies: "Traffic flow through the store now became a key to productivity."[28] But the variety of designs demonstrates that traffic flow was more than a logistical problem or an issue of business efficiencies; it was a problem of social engineering as well. Store designs go beyond concerns about reducing the expense of wages to document an array of practical problems in converting small, narrow store spaces to maximize display space, increase the number of customers the space could contain, ensure accessibility of the merchandise, and facilitate traffic flow during peak hours of operation.

Inventors experimented with how much choice to give customers in their design of self-service pathways. When Robert Tribble submitted his application for a self-service patent in March 1919, he provided four different floor plans to show variations for installing his "vending apparatus" composed of a store arrangement that formed an "arcuate passageway" (fig. 5.6). Tribble's design was intended to overcome flaws in Clarence Saunders's one-way path.

"In the Saunders structure," Tribble explained, "customers are required to pass along a predetermined and definite path and substantially in single file past all of the shelves." The problem with this system was that it treated all customers exactly the same way. It didn't offer customers any choice of direction in the store. "It is frequently the case that a customer, upon reaching, we will say, salad dressing," wrote Tribble, as if he had tried out the Piggly Wiggly system himself, "sees a certain brand of salad dressing but has in mind some other brand that he or she prefers and, in looking to see if this other brand is in stock, they pass beyond the salad dressings and if they do not find the brand desired they attempt to return to the brand first seen." Customers trying to back track clogged the system in narrow aisles. "Since other persons are constantly seeking to pass through the aisles, this causes confusion and congestion. Furthermore, it is frequently the case that one customer is selecting goods to fill a large order while other customers may desire only a few articles and desire to pass through the aisles more rapidly. Here again interference is caused." Tribble's "arcuate passageways" offered wide paths on either side of a central partition to "enable customers to move about freely in selecting their goods without interfering with or obstructing each other" and to "change the direction of travel of this large body of persons from rear to front without confusion or congestion."[29] All four floor plan variations offered customers more flexibility of movement than the Piggly Wiggly one-way path while still defining a customer path through the store, from the turnstile at the entrance to the turnstile at the exit.

Tribble's store arrangement was patented as a "vending apparatus" because fixtures were systematically coordinated to automate the sales floor—"to display to each and every customer substantially the entire stock of goods; to keep the body of purchasers moving substantially continuously in the same direction in order to avoid confusion and congestion; to utilize all available space to the best advantage . . . and finally to cause each purchaser to pass a common point at which the goods selected may be checked up and collected for."[30] Patented pathways linked elements of the selling system into an interconnected network designed to promote continuous forward motion of shoppers (and merchandise) from the entrance to the exit.

Turnstiles became the control mechanism of choice for launching customers in the right direction onto the self-service pathway and preventing them from exiting before paying. As Robert Tribble explained, the entrance was "controlled by a turnstile or storm door of such construction as to permit the passage of customers in one direction only into the interior of the store."

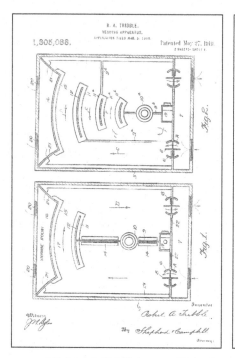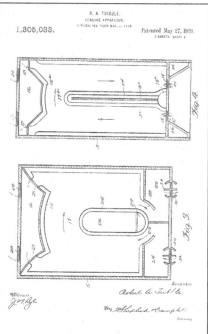

FIG. 5.6. Robert A. Tribble's 1919 self-service system avoided the Piggly Wiggly circuitous pathway by using curved shelving to create an arched path rather than forming multiple aisles. His patent included four variations on the "arcuate passageway." In each case clerks were stationed at the central counter to check out customers.

Though Tribble emphasized that customers might move more than one direction in the store, the arrows indicate the ideal direction of traffic in the store. *Source:* Tribble, *Vending Apparatus* patent 1,305,033.

Turnstiles were widely used in other urban settings—theaters, ballparks, streetcars, and anywhere crowd control and collecting tickets from paying customers was desirable. They steered customers, organized them into single file, deterred theft, and prevented clogs in the forward-moving pathway to maximize sales.

Self-service store pathways always terminated at the checkout counter. Small grocers had adopted cash registers by the thousands at the beginning of the twentieth century to "stop leaks" and institute new accounting controls. As one social scientist put it, "Petty thieving and carelessness among employees are hard to detect and very difficult of correction."[31] Self-service store inventors created a centralized location for payment as an important strategy for keeping both customers and workers honest. Robert Tribble claimed that using his arcuate passageway prevented mistakes and asserted, "The many losses incident to the conduct of business wherein a large number of clerks are required to add up amounts due from customers, often in great haste, will be avoided."[32] Although the widespread adoption of cash registers was a precondition for the creation of checkout lines, the invention of a centralized checkout process was the result of considerable independent experimentation.

Inventors conceived self-service pathways as multilayered to coordinate the movements of customers and the work processes of clerks. The work of restocking shelves was particularly problematic. To achieve volume sales, shelf stocks had to be replenished as shoppers depleted them, and this was mostly likely to happen at rush hour when the stores were full of customers. But the work of restocking shelves interfered with the movement of consumers through the carefully configured store pathways. Nelson Sharp designed a store with hidden pathways behind the shelves so that clerks could restock them "without being observed by purchasers in the shopping area of the store." Strategies for separating work from shopping were based on the need to keep shoppers moving forward toward the checkout station as efficiently as possible. "It is an outstanding feature" of the store arrangement, one patent claimed, "that the customers and the attendants never interfere with each other and that the attendants are in a position to assist the customers at any point of the stand or counter."[33] Another inventor claimed that his revolving shelf system made it possible for clerks to take an inventory of stock "during working hours in the day time without interrupting service to customers and without requiring overtime work."[34] The most technologically ambitious designs used turntables and conveyor belts to layer different pathways for customers and clerks.

Albert Fritsche of Los Angeles, California, established a prescribed pathway through the store using the mechanism of the one-way conveyor rather than aisles defined by shelving configurations that determined a customer's route through the store. The conveyor in Fritsche's design extended from the back of the store to a circular sorting counter at the front of the store. In Fritsche's conveyor belt store, customers carried coupon books rather than market baskets. Customers selected items from shelves, tagged them with the adhesive coupons, and placed them on the conveyor belt, which deposited the marked items on a turntable at the center of the checkout system. Each coupon book contained coupons labeled "last." The customer attached that label to the last item they selected, then placed it on the conveyor. Theoretically, the clerk,

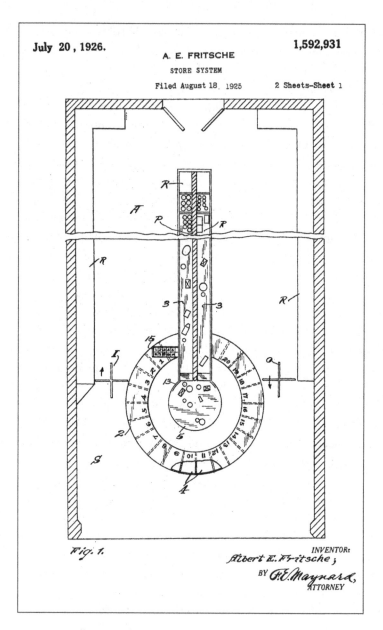

July 20, 1926.                                          1,592,931

A. E. FRITSCHE

STORE SYSTEM

Filed August 18, 1925          2 Sheets-Sheet 1

*Fig. 1.*

INVENTOR:
Albert E. Fritsche;
BY G.E. Maynard,
ATTORNEY

FIG. 5.7. In Albert Fritsche's 1926 Store System patent, clerks worked inside the center counter space sorting customers' selections into numbered bins. Customers entered the store through the "ingress turnstile" labeled I and selected items from store shelves labeled R that lined the walls. Shelving units were also built over the central conveyor belt to maximize display space. Customers retrieved their purchase order and paid at a cashier's stand beside the "exit turnstile" labeled O. *Source:* Fritsche, Store System patent.

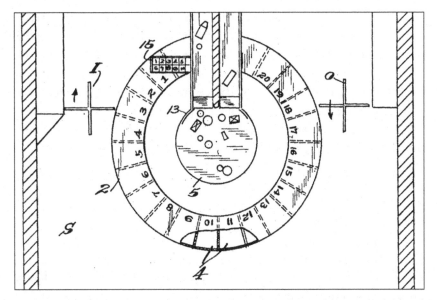

FIG. 5.8. Closeup of the central turntable and numbered counter bins in Fritsche's self-service system (fig. 5.7). Items placed on the conveyor belt (labeled 3) by customers were delivered by the conveyor belt to a turntable at the center of the counter space (labeled 5). Clerks staffing the central circular service aisle retrieved the selected items and sorted them into twenty numbered bins around the outer circular counter based on adhesive coupons attached by the customers to each item they selected.

alerted by the item with the "last" sticker, tabulated the finished order before the customer arrived at the cashier's stand. Clerks sorted customer selections from the turntable and organized them into the separate "counter box" corresponding to the customer's coupon number. The customer retrieved items in their bin using the remaining coupons as identification for the purchase order. Clerks kept a running tabulation of items as they retrieved them from the turntable and moved them to the tagged bin. Thus, Fritsche emphasized, "The time of the customer is conserved and waiting and crowding at the cashier's desk is eliminated."[35]

At first glance, the customers in Fritsche's store would appear to be replicating the same haphazard pathways that the clerks had demonstrated in the Louisville study, retrieving one item at a time and placing it on a counter, traveling repeatedly back and forth across the shop floor. But the different parts of Fritsche's store configuration worked as a system to keep merchandise moving along the pathway from the time the customer entered the "ingress turnstile" to the final purchase at the exit turnstile. Furthermore, whereas the inefficiency of store clerks reduced the profit margin, the inefficiency of the customer's route could be a useful strategy for increasing sales. Relieved of the weight of a heavy market basket, "A customer will thus tend to go in a leisurely manner around the store and select more and heavier goods than will be the case if she has to carry the loaded market basket from shelf to shelf."[36] Self-service inventors went far beyond the mainstream methods of basic cash and carry stores. They spent a lot of time working on strategies for mobilizing merchandise in the effort to maximize sales.


## Mobilizing Merchandise

The market basket was the carrier of choice for most self-service stores through-out the 1920s. Most urban customers shopped every day and purchased only a few items at a time. Wicker baskets were relatively lightweight and sturdy, not easily damaged by the rough handling of customers and clerks. Though they did not add significantly to store overhead costs, the size and weight of the market basket hindered volume sales because it limited the amount of goods a customer could carry. Not everyone was physically able to carry their own basket. Fritsche, who combined a series of rotating shelves and conveyor belts in his self-service store, explained, "In such a class of stores [self-service] the customer carries a basket or receptacle and as this is filled with chosen goods it soon becomes objectionably heavy to carry, particularly by children and old folks, and frail females, and all crippled and weak customers. When a customer finds that a load is too heavy he or she may tire before completing purchasing and thus the store loses the business."[37] Inventors experimented with a variety of approaches for lightening the customer's load.

The freewheeling shopping cart first appeared in the mid-1930s and was only possible in the largest self-service stores. Throughout the 1920s, the small size of most grocery stores did not leave much room for easy circulation of shoppers, clerks, and carts in cramped quarters. Customers also needed to quickly understand how to work the new and unfamiliar shopping system or else merchants could lose their business. Thus, shopping receptacles tended to be small and physically integrated into the overall store plan. They were considered part of the overall self-service store apparatus, and they were often physically attached to it. In 1920 Shiker DeBakey installed wagons on tracks that ran around the perimeter of the store, "30 inches above the floor," for convenient access of

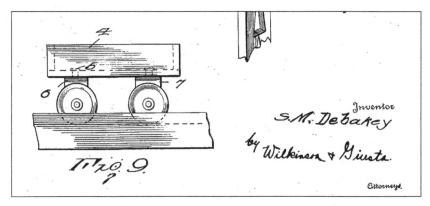

FIG. 5.9. Shiker DeBakey said his 1920 store design could be operated by two employees, a cashier and a clerk. His "light wagons or buggies" were "particularly designed to promote the convenience of children and ladies in shopping." The buggies were loaded onto an inclined track held in place by a loop of wire. A customer could release the first wagon in the line by removing the looped wire and dropping it in front of the next wagon in the stack. *Source:* DeBakey, Home Store patent.

customers.[38] DeBakey explained, "The wagons or cars are of suitable size to hold the various commodities purchased by any one customer." He added: "The customers are compelled to follow a course through the store following the track . . . and drawing the buggy or wagon . . . after them."

Such vehicles served a variety of purposes, all in an effort to maximize sales by relieving the weight of the shopper's load, directing the customer on a prescribed path through the store, and modulating the shopper's pace. The simplest mechanisms involved a shelf system that closely mimicked the idea of the cafeteria. With its cafeteria-based plan, Piggly Wiggly had offered shelf resting stations periodically through the circuitous path, especially as the customer neared the end of the path and had to wait in a checkout line, when the basket was heaviest. Robert Tribble built a shelf along the entire path of his store. "Upon this," he said, "customers may place their baskets and move them along as they travel down the one side of the store and up the other."[39] An added value of the shelf was that it kept traffic moving in one direction. In a more technologically complicated solution, John Smiley added a "roller carrier" above a continuous track in front of the grocery shelves.

Customers connected their market basket to lift it from the track and relieve the weight of the load. When a customer encountered a shopper along

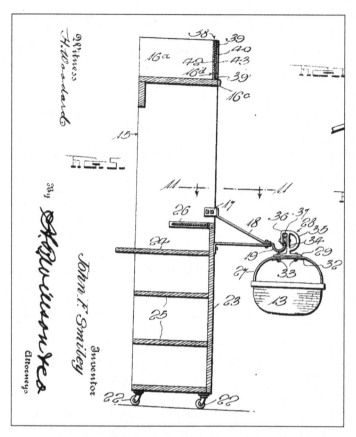

FIG. 5.10. Detail view of John Smiley's 1925 design for attaching baskets to a roller carrier that traveled at about waist height around the store cabinetry and could be lowered to the checkout counter at the end of the pathway. *Source:* Smiley Self Serving Store patent.

the path who was in the way, the basket could be unhooked so the faster customer could pass the slower customer. Again, the mechanism for lightening the load also helped to direct the movement and focus of the customer. "Since the purchaser in moving the basket along the basket track will pass all of the shelving, the attention of the customer will be attracted to all of the goods on sale and many articles which might otherwise have been overlooked will be placed in the basket."[40]

James Carroll's endless conveyor solution (fig. 5.11) dramatically illustrates the sort of technology-enhanced strategies self-service inventors used to facilitate the movement of products from grocery shelves to final purchase. Carroll's strategy encompassed both the movement of people (the shoppers who used market baskets to assemble their purchases) and the endless movement of products along a conveyor belt. Customers who entered Carroll's store in 1919 came through a turnstile and picked up a market basket just as they might do in any self-service store, but then they faced a choice. They could walk around the perimeter of the store collecting groceries in their basket, or they could move to the center and sit down to watch the products rotate past them on a conveyor system that filled the center of the store, selecting items to place in their basket as they moved along the conveyor.[41]

Conveyor systems in particular went beyond creating a predetermined path through the store to influence the speed of the shopper. Store patents explored the relative advantages of either speeding up shoppers or encouraging them to slow down and spend more time in the store. If inventors could do both in the same design then they could attract shoppers with different purposes—browsers with time to linger or target shoppers who needed to pick up a few specific items. Leonard Clerc was a factory foreman in Detroit, home of the original assembly line, when he applied his mechanical skills to self-service stores. His design brought new meaning to the idea of a mechanical store (fig. 5.12). Unlike factory workers who stood at their stations on an assembly line, customers at his "Shopineze" literally shopped from the comfort of armchairs. They selected merchandise to place in shopping baskets at their feet while a conveyor belt circulated the store space and "the entire selection of merchandise in the store" moved past them.[42] Customers could fill as many baskets as they liked while seated, and clerks carried the full baskets to a ramp that led to a booth where a cashier bagged the items and tallied the sale. The system had the advantage of being a moving advertisement. The store's front window offered constantly changing displays. If you stood on the sidewalk long enough in front of the store you could watch the whole store roll by

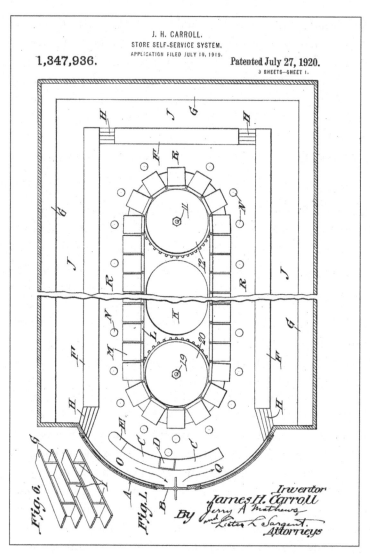

FIG. 5.11. In James Carroll's 1920 self-service system, the cashier was stationed right in front of the entrance at the desk labeled D. After entering through the turnstile, a customer could choose to "wander around through the aisles R and J at will selecting whatever goods [might] appeal to her." Or she could "take a seat on one of the stools N and select goods from the display racks M as they [were] successively moved along in front of her in their endless course." The front desk, C, contains stations for the bundle wrapper, E, and the cashier D, and was "positioned so as to provide a narrow passage along which the customers [had to] pass in single file." This ensured proper crowd control at peak times. No one escaped the notice of the cashier on her way out the store. *Source:* Carroll, Store Self-Service System patent.

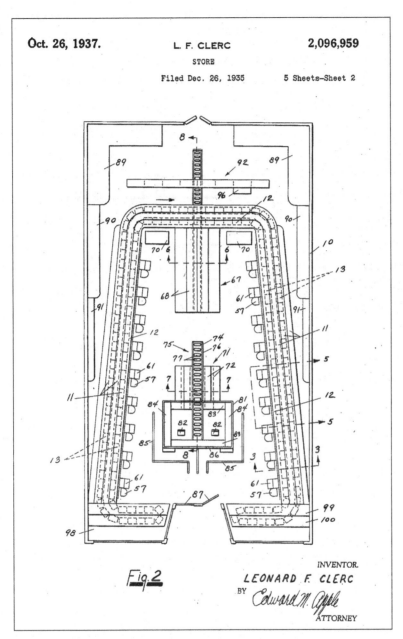

Oct. 26, 1937.          L. F. CLERC                    2,096,959

STORE

Filed Dec. 26, 1935          5 Sheets—Sheet 2

Fig. 2

INVENTOR.

LEONARD F. CLERC

BY Edward M. Apple

ATTORNEY

FIG. 5.12. In Leonard Clerc's 1937 patent, notice that the conveyor belt system was connected to window displays labeled 99 and 100 in this floor plan. Clerc explained, "This feature forms an attractive window display since it is constantly changing and since it enables outsiders to see the entire stock move through the window space." *Source:* Clerc Store patent.

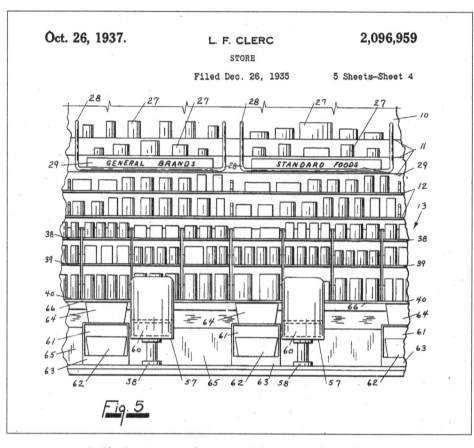

Oct. 26, 1937.               L. F. CLERC              2,096,959

STORE

Filed Dec. 26, 1935       5 Sheets—Sheet 4

FIG. 5.13. In Clerc's 1937 patent, the moving shelves were within reach of seated customers. Those who couldn't find a seat could walk the store shopping from stationary shelves (labeled 12) out of reach of the seats. The highest shelves (labeled 11) were for empty boxes that served to advertise the store's product classification system, to make it easier for customers to find what they were looking for. The difficulty of distinguishing between "General Brands" and "Standard Foods" speaks to the challenges of creating classification systems that enabled shoppers to locate specific products without clerk assistance. *Source:* Clerc Store patent.

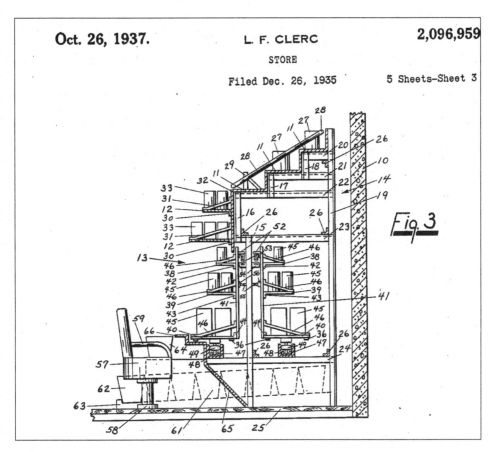

Fig. 3

FIG. 5.14. Also in Clerc's 1937 patent, notice the baskets outlined by dotted lines in a basket rack (labeled 62). "The rack is inclined . . . so that a plurality of empty baskets placed therein will automatically slide by gravity into a position where they can be readily reached from the customer's chair." Customers could fill as many baskets as they liked without lifting a loaded basket. *Source:* Clerc Store patent.

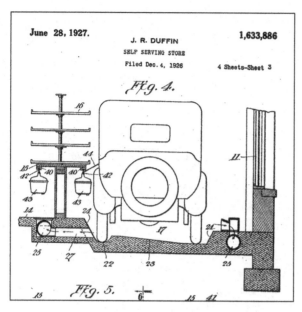

June 28, 1927.

J. R. DUFFIN

1,633,886

SELF SERVING STORE

Filed Dec. 4, 1926

4 Sheets—Sheet 3

*Fig. 4.*

*Fig. 5.*

FIG. 5.15. In James Duffin's 1927 patent, notice that the car is "locked" into a predetermined path by the trough that guides the inner wheel through the store. This diagram shows the conduits for ventilating exhaust fumes (labeled 25), the trough that determined the path of the vehicle (labeled 22), and the baskets hanging from a carrier system attached to the vehicle with a cable (40, 42, 43, and 44). The baskets attached to the interior carriage system defined the pathway for pedestrians on the other side of the turntables. *Source:* Duffin Self-Serving Store patent.

because the conveyor system extended from the retail space to the front window. At the Shopineze, the main attraction was "the ease, comfort, and speed with which the customers may shop."

In James Duffin's self-service store in Louisville (fig. 5.15), shoppers never had to leave their cars to serve themseves. His Automarket offered customers the opportunity to drive their car through the store and serve themselves from rotating shelves affixed to a semicircular counter. Products were arranged on a series of turntables (fig. 5.16) mounted on a U-shaped counter that defined the perimeter of the store. The store was designed to serve "two classes of customers," pedestrians and drivers: "[Both] have free access to all the goods, and neither interferes with the other." Pedestrians entered the store through a turnstile and secured a basket to a carriageway that circled the inner side of

FIG. 5.16. Automarket, Louisville, 1928. The turntable displays served automobile customers driving around the perimeter of the store and pedestrians shopping in the middle of the store space. *Source:* Caufield and Shook Collection, Archives & Special Collections, University of Louisville Libraries.

FIG. 5.17. A drawing of Duffin's Automarket in operation, 1928. Duffin's patented floor plan showed an empty central space, but the drawing appears to show the center used as storage space. Customers on foot entered a lobby space with seating and a narrow entry to the retail space on the right. Turntables displaying products were accessible by customers on foot or in their cars. A fence blocked pedestrian customers from accessing the central storage or display area. *Source:* Caufield and Shook Collection, Archives & Special Collections, University of Louisville Libraries.

the turntable shelves. Shoppers in vehicles followed a route defined by a driveway that ringed the perimeter of the store. The driver entered the store and attached a basket suspended from a carriage with a cable to the car. The patent explained, "[The driver] then traverses the driveway and secures from the different rotatable shelves the articles desired, the basket being pulled along by the automobile until the cashier's and wrapping table are reached."[43] A news article about the store said that the display racks were motorized rather than entirely hand-operated. "The idea is to parade the merchandise before the eyes of the public, as it helps to sell it, and people buy a lot of stuff they see which they would not buy otherwise."[44] According to the patent, "Towards the exit of the driveway the rotatable shelves may be dispensed with, and the counter suitably arranged for vegetables, dairy produce and refrigerated materials."[45] Thus, Duffin integrated products like bread and meat that had to be

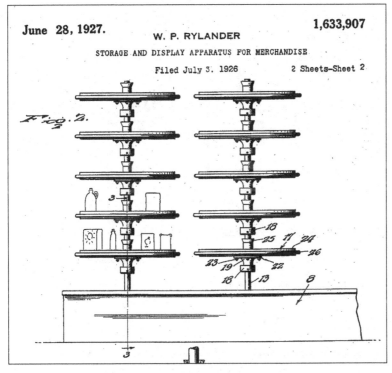

FIG. 5.18 William Rylander's turntables. A customer could interrupt the motion of one of the turntable shelves to inspect or retrieve the merchandise.
*Source:* Rylander, Storage and Display Apparatus for Merchandise patent.

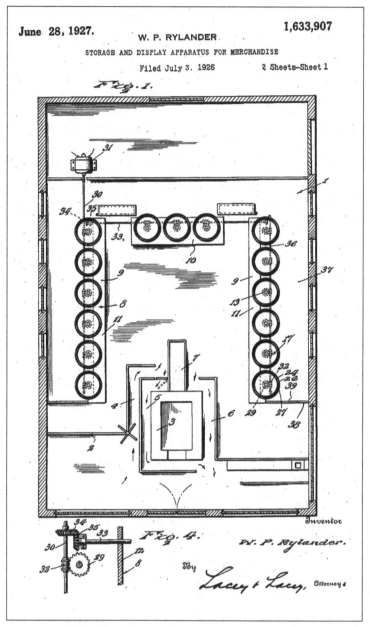

June 28, 1927.

W. P. RYLANDER

1,633,907

STORAGE AND DISPLAY APPARATUS FOR MERCHANDISE

Filed July 3, 1926

2 Sheets—Sheet 1

*Fig. 1.*

*Fig. 4.*

*Inventor*

*W. P. Rylander.*

*By*

*Lacey & Lacey,* *Attorneys*

FIG. 5.19. Rylander's 1927 floor plan. An electric motor out of sight to customers (labeled 31) kept the rotating shelves moving continuously, seemingly magically. *Source:* Rylander, Storage and Display Apparatus for Merchandise patent.

sliced, weighed, and wrapped by clerks at the end of his self-service pathway with the checkout counter.

William Rylander's store full of turntables kept the displays in continuous motion but allowed for selective interruption of the shelf motion by the customer to inspect the goods. "It is a well-known fact," Rylander explained, "that a moving display attracts more attention of the observer."[46] Rylander's entire store was in motion with a coordinated system of revolving turntables. A customer might interrupt the spinning of an individual turntable without stopping the motion of the other displays. Customers could circulate freely through the center of the store, targeting turntables that displayed the merchandise that interested them most. Clerks at the passageway at the perimeter and rear replenished the rotating shelves. The system physically separated the space the clerks used for work and the space customers used for shopping. Rylander's efforts to design a selling system that activated the visual attention of customers suggests some of the ways that self-service systems automated salesmanship.

A California Piggly Wiggly ad concept of the 1920s played with the theme of efficiency and flow of customers through the turnstile.[47] It was a machine age fantasy of the standardized consumer—an army of well-dressed White women with cash to spend and a family to feed (see fig. 5.20). Certainly a million customers would not fit into Piggly Wiggly or any other small self-service store all at the same time. But, coordinated in single file, hundreds could shop on the same day because the self-service systems were designed so efficiently to move customers through the store. . The click, click, click of the turnstile, was the sound of the self-service machine at work. Such representations of self-service evoke the turntables and conveyors Florenze Ziegfeld Jr. used to move the interchangeable performers in his synchronized song-and-dance productions of the 1920s. Historian Joel Dinerstein has described Ziegfeld as the inventor of "mechanized choreography": "In the Ziegfeld Follies, and later in Busby Berkeley musicals, women functioned as cogs and punch cards in immense, mechanically-rotated tableaux of lavish fantasy."[48] The chorus line routines emphasized the standardized interchangeability of performers. The emphasis was on orderly synchronized movement. Like so many interchangeable performers on a Ziegfeld chorus line (or turntable), fashionable women in the Piggly Wiggly ad performed their carefully choreographed march along the predetermined path of the self-service machine.

Though ads often emphasized shoppers' freedom to move through the store and their unfettered access to store shelves, patented designs for self-service

FIG. 5.20. Concept for a Piggly Wiggly advertisement. *Source:* Lestico, *Building the Story of Piggly Wiggly*.

stores document merchants' strategies of persuasion and outright coercion. They hoped to influence not just the direction customers took through the store but also their desires. Sales volume increased not only because customers moved faster or took their time along the patented pathways but also because the self-service machine worked, seemingly magically, to motivate customers to buy more. Though its architects promoted the self-service store as a modern machine made for mass distribution, it was above all a new kind of spatial experience. "No description that can possibly be made; no drawings or photographs could with full measure tell all there is to know about a Piggly Wiggly store," Clarence Saunders declared. "It is only in the atmosphere of the store itself in actual physical contact with its many parts, that there can be a true mental grasp of the fundamental soundness of the elements working toward a certain definite result."[49] Self-service pathways mobilized merchandise and improved worker efficiencies, but, as machines for automatic selling, compartmentalized self-service retail spaces created environments that automated salesmanship by activating (or deactivating) customer senses.

## Automating Salesmanship through Sensory Retailing

A Piggly Wiggly ad from 1928 (fig. 5.21) theatrically suggests the new sensory experience of self-service shopping .[50] The prominently featured picture of a disembodied hand holds a gleaming can. Is it peas or peaches? No matter, the actual product is immaterial. The self-service experience is what is being advertised. The picture is instructive. It features the chain's patented hanging price tag in clear focus against the blurred background of a display cabinet. The ad text explains, "Everywhere the big square tags to tell you each price at a glance." The play with different levels of focus in the picture evokes the different ways of seeing in a self-service store—sometimes shifting from a close-up focus needed to read labels or locate items on a shelf to recalibrate for a sweeping view of the store to assess the arrangement of the space. The hand was obviously meant to communicate freedom to touch the goods, but touch was problematic in food shopping. It might require handling dusty cans or dirty produce. The gloved hand also operated symbolically, connoting class. In the early twentieth century, clean white hands "affirmed the woman's status as part of the 'leisured' middle class." Such women did not have to do hard manual labor. Gloves offered a practical way to "hide one's labor" and a symbolic way to "prevent class slippage."[51] The cultural work of the glove transformed food shopping and self-service into the fashionable work of middle-class women. What is absent in the ad is as important as what is in sight. "There are no clerks at Piggly Wiggly." This was meant to reassure. "Just help yourself. Pick up what you like, look it over, arrive at your own decision *purely on merit.*" In the bottom left corner of the ad a woman inspects the shelves alone in silent contemplation. Self-service shopping was intended to be a solitary business, an act of mental calculation. Perusing the shelves in uninterrupted thought sparked imagination, and imagination produced sales. "See what fine ideas come to you for your menus!" None of this was accidental. Self-service store designers spatially engineered the sensory experience of shopping to enhance the selling power of the store. Self-service systems were especially designed to eliminate sound, manage touch, and coordinate sight.

FIG. 5.21. Ad designed by J. Walter Thompson Company for Piggly Wiggly Stores, Inc. The disembodied gloved hand and the hanging price tag symbolized the vogue, economy, and modern efficiency of self-service. The ad is designed to sell the self-service shopping experience rather than the anonymous product. *Source: Ladies' Home Journal*, December 1928, 111.

*Silence: The Soundscape of Self-Service*

The silent salesmanship of a self-service store presented a profound contrast to the raucous environment of the counter-service store. Socializing with other customers slowed down the one-way path through the store and thus the pace of sales. Conversation was discouraged by design in self-service stores. Clarence R. Ball explained that his self-service store arrangement made it "wholly unnecessary for a customer to have any oral dealings with a clerk or attendant."[52] Silent salesmanship was an increasingly popular idea in the 1920s, broadly applied to product packaging and store display techniques, whether or not the store was arranged to be self-service. Promoted by advertisers and manufacturers who desired control over the messages customers heard about brand name products, silent salesmanship implied a critique of hired clerks whose skills and enthusiasm for selling were in doubt. As one display case manufacturer asserted, "Any clerk can sell the customer the goods she came in and asks for, but it takes a 'Silent Salesman' All-Glass Show-Case to sell goods that the customer never knew she wanted until she saw them displayed."[53] Packages that were effectively designed for selling had the added advantage of portability, extending the sales message to the world beyond the confines of a store display. "Packages act as silent salesmen on the dealer's shelf and in the home," declared Richard Franken and Carroll Larrabee in their popular book, *Packages That Sell*.[54] Effectively designed packages could perform their seemingly effortless sales magic in any store where they were displayed. The silent salesmanship of the self-service store, however, extended well beyond the colorful packaging on store shelves.

The self-service store increased the scale of silent selling techniques from individual displays to encompass the entire space of the store. Advertiser Emerson P. Harris described the self-service store as "a silent vending machine in that it has no audible voice." But he added: "It is an instrument which may have a potent influence with consumers."[55] Store designers promoted a soundscape of silence that enveloped the store as a whole and required significant behavior modification of workers and customers. In her study of modern architectural acoustics, historian Emily Thompson explains that soundscapes are spatially and culturally constructed: "Like a landscape, a soundscape is simultaneously a physical environment and a way of perceiving that environment; it is both a world and a culture constructed to make sense of that world."[56] Silence was considered a key ingredient for spatially automating salesmanship. Intended to promote control and efficiency, it was also one of the features that characterized the modernity of the self-service store. In the early twentieth century, new technologies generated both new kinds of sounds and different ways of listening. While one might think first of new inventions that produced sounds—the telephone, the phonograph, the radio, or the microphone, technologies that changed the perception of sound in the Machine Age—the self-service store produced a new soundscape of consumption. Thompson convincingly demonstrates the importance of efficiency and control as defining elements of the modern soundscape in the early twentieth century.[57]

Researchers used scientific instruments to measure impact of noise on worker productivity. In 1927, for example, an industrial psychologist at Colgate University chemically analyzed the exhalations of clerical workers to determine how noise affected the efficiency of typists and published his findings in the paper, "Noise *Does* Impair Production."[58] He compared the productivity of typists working under both quiet and noisy conditions and determined that "the best typists worked about 7 percent faster in a quieter environment."[59] Engineers and architects used new noise abatement technologies and materials to control sound in the built environment. Self-service grocers who rented spaces did not always have the kind of control necessary for installing sound buffering insulation, but they arranged stores to eliminate the need for conversation.

The appeal of silence for the shopper, as Piggly Wiggly ads repeatedly emphasized (see fig. 3.9) was the advantage of shopping in freedom from the hard-sell techniques of pushy sales clerks who tried to talk you into buying things you didn't want. But silence had important practical purposes for the grocer. From the perspective of the grocer, the fixed price and silent selling meant that the grocer didn't have to haggle with assertive female shoppers who complained about prices or quality of merchandise. Chain grocers sought to standardize store policies and emphasize low fixed prices to attract middle-class women and reduce their demands.[60] Grocery stores increasingly instituted cash and carry policies and price-marked packages and displays. World War I inflation had accelerated the change: "A new inflationary economic culture encouraged the spread of a bargain-hunting ethos as shoppers searched for good deals. Whereas bargaining had previously revolved around 'clever talking,' bargain hunting now was based on shrewd comparison shopping and close scrutiny of prices."[61] These trends were not limited to self-service stores but creating silent salesmanship was especially important for the goals of self-service store designers.

Silence focused the attention of shoppers on the products that lined their route through the store. It transformed shopping from a social exchange with clerks or other customers to an internal, psychological experience of the individual shopper. The "extra time involved in ascertaining the location of certain articles" in the self-service store was "usually offset by the time consumed in conversation" in the counter-service store, according to the USDA study of self-service.[62] With an uninterrupted focus on the displays, shoppers were more likely to see products they wanted without assistance. Above all, silence facilitated movement through store aisles. Customers who stopped to talk with neighbors or ask a clerk about a product impeded the flow of traffic through the store, slowing down sales. Edward da Roza emphasized that his design minimized "the congestion which might result from the loitering or visiting of customers while they are within the paths, and yet gives the greatest possible privilege to neighbors and friends who may speak or chat with each other without necessarily retarding the progress of others who may wish to continue hurriedly from entrance to exit."[63] The soundscape of silence was an ideal that was difficult to achieve in practice.

The turnstile served as the voice of the self-service machine. Like the ring of a cash register, "Every time the turnstile CLICKS, we know we've made a new friend or sent a regular customer on her way, more than ever, satisfied with the goods she bought and the price she paid," a California Piggly Wiggly advertiser enthused.[64] Even at the end of the self-service line, where shoppers encountered the human worker at the cash register, the click of the machine symbolically substituted for conversation between cashier and customer.

*Within Easy Reach: Managing Touch*

In its study of self-service practices, the USDA promoted buyers' physical access to the merchandise as one of the most popular features of self-service. "Another psychological appeal in self-service which can not be overlooked," researchers wrote, "is the natural satisfaction which most people derive from getting behind the counter. The average person generally wishes to handle the goods on a grocer's shelves and enjoys the opportunity to do so."[65] On one hand, being able to touch the merchandise increased the incentive to buy, but letting customers handle merchandise they hadn't bought yet also created perils for the grocer's bottom line. Customers sometimes damaged merchandise, and they contributed to the confusion of other shoppers when they misplaced items in a carefully organized store display system. Self-service designers thought carefully about how to manage customers' open access to store products while protecting their investment in the merchandise.

Clarence Ball's self-service store is a case in point. Ball's patent said, "[It is designed] to provide an arrangement whereby customers may select their purchases without actually handling the goods or articles comprising the stock on hand so that the goods will not become shop worn or damaged through handling, and articles of food or toilet articles will not be liable to contamination." He achieved this by displaying samples "entirely separate from the actual stock of goods." The displayed products were numbered. Prices were clearly marked and descriptive information was displayed. "[This is] so that all necessary information is afforded the prospective purchaser to the same extent as though he was brough" into actual contact with the stock of goods or articles and had their merits explained by a salesman."[66] Customers used order blanks to identify the product numbers they had chosen and submitted payment with their order. Clerks assembled the order in the stock room and delivered the wrapped order, with change, by conveyor belt to complete the transaction. It was "self-service" because, even though the customer never handled any merchandise until the sale was completed, there were no salesmen to interact with customers in the display room. Ball's store was a silent vending machine in action.

Selecting sturdy canned goods from an open shelf was one thing, but fresh produce presented tremendous challenges for self-service. Grocers of all kinds routinely experienced losses due to clerks who inaccurately weighed bulk products or charged the wrong prices or made errors in calculating the customer's bill. Natural processes of evaporation, deterioration, and spoilage eroded profits. And customers who handled the products damaged packages and bruised produce. The advantages of self-service in producing volume sales might be outstripped by the losses incurred when customers had open access to the shelves. *Progressive Grocer* recommended the strategy of one frustrated grocer who complained about the damage customers caused. "[He] gathered a basketful of fruit and vegetables that were about to be thrown out. He placed these in the center of his stand and put this large card over them: FOR SALE CHEAP. Spoiled by being fingered by shoppers. Please do not handle our Fruits and Vegetables."[67] Fresh produce was such a challenge to manage that even self-service stores created separate clerk-service departments to prevent customers from damaging too much produce sifting through bins to make their choices.[68]

FIG. 5.22. Biel Self-Service Store, Corpus Christi, Texas, 1934, and its large produce department stationed at the front window. Imagine the pungent odor of bananas and tomatoes ripening in the sunny window, while tender green produce is arranged on the unrefrigerated table farther from the window. Celery stalks are propped on a metal misting device fed by water tanks inside the cabinet. The photographer posed the store's meatcutter, J. W. Buster, in the space, but one can imagine any of the store's available clerks assisting customers in weighing and price marking their produce selections. *Source:* Itinerant Photographer Collection, Harry Ransom Center, University of Texas at Austin.

In their role as an agency that supported farmers, the USDA promoted self-service as a strategy for reducing the cost of fresh produce. The USDA researchers took issue with overly fastidious customers who did not like "self-serve stores because they sometimes make it necessary for the purchasers themselves to handle vegetables to which earth adheres or articles that may be dusty."[69] The researchers considered such customer attitudes to be frivolous. "Such customers obviously should go to the stores that are better fitted to give them the kind of service they require and they should be willing to pay the higher prices for the goods so received," their report moralized. A majority of the grocery shoppers the social scientist Myrtle Lohner interviewed in Chicago preferred a combination of service and self-service in the produce department. "Difficulty in handling was the most important reason why women found service more convenient for some produce even though they considered self-service more satisfactory on the whole," Lohner reported. They mentioned problems with weighing produce, soiled items, and bulky items that were "generally hard to handle." Nevertheless, the ability to pick out their own fresh produce was an important attraction for self-service customers she interviewed. Lohner reported that "the major reason given by those more satisfied with self-service was lack of trust in the clerk."[70] While some self-service customers found intrinsic satisfaction in serving themselves, the majority of customers in the Chicago study would have preferred service if they had enough confidence in the clerk to pick the highest-quality produce.

The biggest concern among grocers by far about giving customers free access to the merchandise was fear of shoplifting. At the turn of the century, shoplifting was a critical problem for all stores, and department stores were retreating from open display.[71] According to historian Elaine Abelson, shoplifting had become such a widespread problem that most displays "were fully under or behind glass" by 1910. The largest stores created new departments of detectives who kept an eye on customers and investigated thefts. The 1922 USDA report noted, "The question of thievery in connection with self-service has probably had more widespread publicity than any other feature." While all stores contended with shoplifting to some extent, self-service stores were considered to face an increased risk for theft "owing to the psychological effect of the store arrangement and the method of selling."[72] The appeal of the open shelves was irresistible, one observer claimed, and stimulated "unconquerable kleptomaniac instincts."[73]

Self-service store designers had unique challenges when it came to simultaneously stimulating customer desire and automating theft prevention

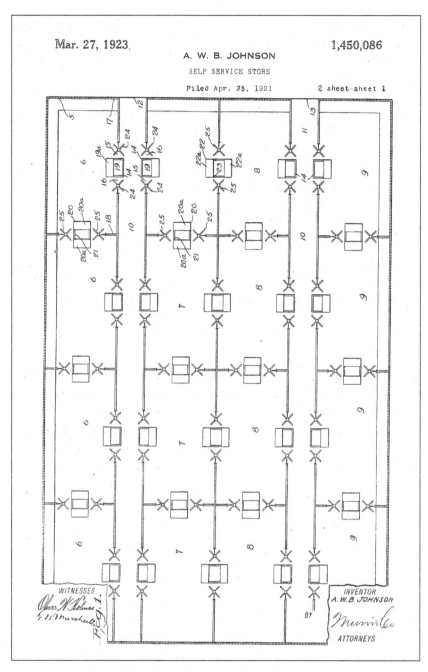

FIG. 5.23. The x's on Alva W. B. Johnson's floor plan represent turnstiles that controlled access to the astonishingly compartmentalized space. *Source:* Johnson, Self Service Store (1923).

strategies. In one of the most extreme designs for deterring theft, Alva Wright Boswell Johnson of Birmingham, Alabama, patented a store with sixteen compartments regulated by sixty-four turnstiles (see fig. 5.23).[74] While the customers could move from one compartment to another, Johnson sacrificed the speed of the shoppers' pathway in favor of customer surveillance. The primary purpose of the invention was to divide customers into small groups so that they could be watched more closely while serving themselves. Each compartment had a "service station" staffed by a clerk (indicated by the box between the turnstiles). Clerks at the service stations "face the interior of the compartment and watch the customers who are walking about in the compartment." The turnstiles could be configured to ensure that customers moved in a prescribed direction. The chief advantage of the system: "The customers may be watched in relatively small groups and from several sides by the clerks who receive money in payment of the sales of merchandise and who wrap the purchased goods." It would have required a minimum of thirty-two clerks to fully staff all of the "service stations" mapped in the patented floor plan!

## The "Clear Vision Store": Coordinating Sight

The compartmentalization of self-service spaces behind a turnstile-controlled exit was a key method for ensuring that customers did not walk out of the store without paying. But customers who were intent on stealing might defeat the turnstile without close scrutiny. Store patents show how engineering sight lines became an important strategy for protecting profits while encouraging free access to open shelves on the self-service pathway. The "clear vision store" was intended to make workers invisible to customers and, at the same time, to make customers highly visible to workers. Coordinating sight was important for both controlling inventory and enhancing silent salesmanship. Just as inventors had layered the pathways for workers and customers, they also layered store designs in an effort to coordinate different purposes and types of vision. Their systems sought to activate and deactivate sight for different purposes, including close reading of product labels, perspective-taking and comprehension of the whole store, and invisibility of work processes like customer surveillance or restocking shelves.

Self-service grocers especially turned to built-in strategies for enhancing store surveillance. The USDA recommended, "The store should be so arranged that an entire view of it may be had from either the cashier's desk or the stock room, or better, from both. The cashier should watch the customers during the hours of slow trade, and some one in the stock room during those hours in which the cashier is especially busy."[75] Inventors offered different mechanical strategies for achieving surveillance–zigzag shelf configuration that eliminated dark corners, placement of checkout stands to achieve a view of the entire store or watch the exit, adjustment of shelf height, and location of screens and partitions to direct traffic in predictable ways and make customers more visible. They debated the advantages and disadvantages of making customers aware that they were under surveillance. Would it alienate customers or keep them honest?

William McCarty, founder of Jitney Jungle in Jackson, Mississippi, explained the particular importance of increasing customer visibility and eliminating hiding places where shoplifters might have an advantage: "While a large number of customers are selecting merchandise from different parts of a store, a number of such customers are almost inevitably hidden from view of the comparatively few clerks or attendants, and this fact being realized by some of the weaker customers acts as a temptation for them to conceal some of the smaller (though perhaps expensive) articles in their pockets or clothing. Moreover, such a store is a standing invitation for the operations of professional shoplifters. Therefore, the consequent losses are sufficient to curtail the profits to a very considerable extent."[76]

McCarty made the case for discreet surveillance, reasoning that "the [visible] presence of such detectives or watchmen is repulsive to the majority of customers of integrity and tend[s] to exclude this more desirable class of customers from the store."[77] His design (fig. 5.24) integrated the surveillance function into the checkout counter and ensured open sight lines in the store by specifying a medium height for shelves in the center of the store. "The use of such fixtures affords a better view of the entire stock, is not so tiresome to the eye, and gives a much more pleasing appearance. Also, it allows less chance for thievery, as all customers are more easily seen by store employees and by each other."[78] An advantage of the design was that "the attendant at the desk serves also as a watchman or detective "without being considered as such by the customers."[79] The watchman was hiding in plain sight. H. H. Lestico reasoned, on the other hand, that customer awareness was an effective deterrent to theft. In making the case that stores should have peepholes in the storeroom for watching customers, he emphasized the advantages of making them prominent enough for customers to know they were being watched. "If the peephole is large enough for the people to see, it will be a sort of insurance. The idea of the peephole is not so much to catch people stealing as to keep

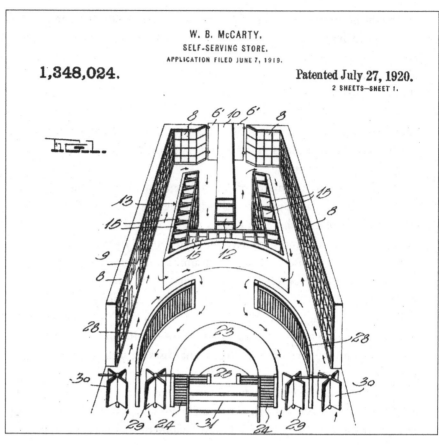

FIG. 5.24. William McCarty's plan for his Jitney Jungle patent application differed from Piggly Wiggly because it mapped two routes through the store. Customers who had time could take a long route through the whole store, and those who wanted a quicker route could cut across a shorter semi-circular route through the front third of the retail space. The floor plan featured a U-shaped "wrapping counter" at the front of the store where the cash register was positioned so that the clerk faced the store interior rather than the front door to facilitate surveillance of customers. *Source:* McCarty, Self-Serving Store patent.

those who want to from trying it."[80] Such deterrence was automatic whether or not a clerk was actually watching from the storeroom.

Above all, vision was considered the most important sense for automation of selling, and patents document a keen interest in enhancing and focusing the customer's visual work. At the most fundamental level, customers needed to be able to see the products on the shelves to serve themselves effectively. Saunders explained that a key purpose of self-service design was to create "a clear vision store whereby the purchase inducing force of the store due to the sight of the goods by the customer is greatly increased."[81] The mere sight of a product could prompt an unplanned purchase. The "clear vision store" encouraged both inspection and introspection. Creating visually open store spaces helped customers to decipher the arrangement of the store at a glance when they walked in the front door and understand what direction to take. Nifty Jiffy inventor James H. Carroll explained that his patented design was compact: "[This] brings every article easily within the range of vision of the customer, instantly upon their entrance, which means much time and trouble saved for the housewives in making their selections."[82] Beyond the basic purpose of making things visible on the shelves, inventors experimented with strategies for enhancing different aspects of seeing the store contents, including rapid comprehension of the store space and close study of product labels.

Henry C. Harvey of Huntington, West Virginia, created a store arrangement that facilitated three different kinds of vision. First "[The arrangement] permits the location of the different general classes of merchandise by the prospective customer at a distant point." His arrangement also promoted "the spontaneous notice of the customer," emphasizing the importance of speed and efficiency in shopping. And finally he wanted to promote a more leisurely type of visual browsing: "It will of course be understood that the customer may enter without having first located from the lobby the article or articles desired and may pass from one part of the sales room to another in search of such articles as may strike the fancy."[83]

Reading facilitated movement through the store. In lieu of asking a clerk for directions or information, customers were expected to find their own answers by reading the store layout or directional signs. Effective self-direction also entailed reading labels, and inventors worked to ensure that their lighting and store arrangement eliminated dark corners to enable customers to view products close-up, in detail. Reading labels was important for learning about products and making price comparisons. "Dozens of ideas for dishes and menus fairly jump at you from the shelves," declared a Piggly Wiggly ad.[84] The sensory engineering of self-service stores was carefully coordinated to spark imagination and desire.

Before 1940 self-service stores were designed as specialized, compartmentalized spaces for automatic selling. During this entrepreneurial phase of invention there was no standard format, and inventors' creative experiments with different technologies generated spectacularly diverse approaches to store design. Despite their variety, self-service stores demonstrated that inventors shared operational principles. They organized store spaces into coordinated pathways that separated the work of clerks and customers and ensured that customers had a chance to view everything in the store. They experimented with different technologies for mobilizing merchandise. And they engineered new sensory environments designed to heighten the psychological selling mechanisms of self-service spaces. The compartmentalized, self-contained, self-service retailing machine produced more sales than the traditional grocery counter by keeping people and merchandise moving along the systematized pathway and focusing shoppers' attention through strategies of sensory control. Patents document the internal design logic of store spaces, but they cannot explain why shoppers embraced or rejected self-service stores. To understand the invention of self-service stores as a social process we need to connect the store interior to particular social and community contexts. Grocery shoppers' responses to self-service varied tremendously by region. We turn next to evaluate the race and gender dynamics of the New South, where self-service stores were highly successful, to understand the attractions of the "purchase-inducing force" of the store in a culture of segregation.

# Mechanizing Paternalism

The Southern Origins of Self-Service

Albon Holsey, secretary of the National Negro Business League, spun a provocative story of self-service shopping in his article "White Folks First, Please."[1] "It happened on the opening Saturday night of a Piggly Wiggly store in a far Southern city," he wrote. The scene and its risks would have been deeply familiar to many of the African American readers of *The Messenger* magazine, themselves fresh migrants from southern cities in 1928. Saturday was the major shopping day of the week for Black and White customers alike, with pockets full from a week's wages. There was a crowd in the store. The physical layout of the space was central to Holsey's account. The customers were lost in thought and focused on the shelves, disregarding each other's presence in the racially integrated space, "each one—white and black alike— intent upon his or her purchases." The display spontaneously helped them remember what they needed. "At precisely the same moment two customers thought of onions and without a glance or thought of the other both bent over the onion box at the same time." Holsey inadvertently described the purchase-inducing force of the automatic selling machine.

Holsey's story brings new meaning to the reckless danger of touch when the two customers simultaneously reach into the bin "at exactly the same moment." He did not specify whether the hands physically connected; the mere sight of the White and Black hands in such close proximity was enough to provoke panic when the two customers realized that "the white arm was that of a woman and the black one that of a man." This was a perilous moment for both customers. The White woman feared for her reputation, the Black man for his life—"A panicky moment followed and then both stood erect and for the first time looked at one another." They realized they knew each other. The Black man worked as a handyman for the White woman.

She addressed him as "Uncle John"; he called her "Miss Simpson." Holsey built the tension and then diffused it. The two customers turned and walked away from each other. Holsey's main point was that Piggly Wiggly was a dramatically new shopping experience that leveled the playing field for Black customers. He emphasized that "ten years earlier 'Uncle John' would have waited until 'Miss Simpson' had been served before he even approached the clerk." Holsey made the moral of his story the positive impact of chain stores on Southern customs.

Holsey drew a landscape in which the chain stores had been imported from outside the South. "Piggly Wiggly, Penny, and other chain systems are now invading smaller Southern cities," he wrote. He emphasized that chain store practices created outside the region were transforming local customs and attitudes. Holsey enthused that their "lower prices, standardized service, and uniform courtesy to all customers" were "revolutionizing trade attitudes and changing Southern traditions."[2] This remains a familiar framework in southern consumer histories that present chain stores as national forms of modern consumption with standardized policies and products that undermined racial difference and local custom in the segregated South. Historian Grace Hale explains the problem southern store owners faced as consumer culture dislocated traditional paternalistic social relations: how to construct "a powerful and collective definition of whiteness within this new semi-public commercial sphere, which depended for its products upon northern manufacturers and for its profitability on both white and black buyers."[3] But Holsey's focus on Piggly Wiggly changes the frame. A decade earlier Piggly Wiggly had only recently begun to sell its patented store interior outside of Memphis. Throughout the 1920s and 1930s the chain that originated in a segregated New South city was the most influential and successful self-service store nationwide. Though nationally marketed brand name canned goods lined the Piggly Wiggly shelves, its self-service retailing system was homegrown in a culture of segregation. While the chain's advertising claimed its brand of self-service as a nationwide movement, the majority of Piggly Wiggly stores were installed on southern main streets. The invisibility of self-service stores as a specialized type of store has helped to obscure the southern origins of self-service retailing methods. It is important to finally connect the southern experiments in self-service store design to the larger national history of the modern retailing method.

It is hard to understand how the radically equalizing experience of self-service retailing could have been invented in the Jim Crow South. Piggly Wiggly was not a fluke. Southern entrepreneurs made the South one of the most active centers of self-service experimentation during the interwar years. Self-service inventors experimented at a time of historic shifts in the role of African Americans and White women as consumers in southern towns and cities. Holsey's story ultimately reveals that the affluent White women pictured in Piggly Wiggly ads shopped in crowded stores alongside African American customers. Inventors considered these new consumers especially susceptible to the purchase-inducing force of the self-service store. Although self-service was a profoundly equalizing experience for diverse shoppers, self-service stores were also built to uphold White supremacy and a patriarchal society. The physical store arrangement offers incomplete evidence for understanding how self-service store space was racialized. Only by evaluating the dynamic interplay of physical and experiential store spaces can we begin to understand how self-service shopping was not a standardized experience for every customer.

Invented at the same time that the assembly line evolved as a managerial tool for eliminating workers' control over production, self-service systems extended the "coercive architecture of production" into the realm of consumption.[4] As an intrinsically coercive architecture of control, self-service retailing sought to regulate the speed and movement of shoppers and monitor the work of store clerks through spatial systems of control. Self-service store inventors also included design features that could be used to differentiate customers. With its spatial strategies for the surveillance of customers, the major effect of the self-service store was to ensure what Michel Foucault calls "the automatic functioning of power."[5] Guaranteeing that shoppers were treated equally was not the purpose of self-service experimentation.

Engineered as machines for automatic selling, self-service stores automated the authority of the merchant and worked as a new spatial practice that reshaped social relations inside the store. For southern White women and African American customers, self-service stores created environments that offered personal protections that traditional forms of food retailing did not. While mechanized paternalism democratized and equalized the shopping experience, it also offered merchants new tools for social control and discrimination. Self-service stores did not disrupt traditional paternalistic social relations. They were intentionally designed to reinforce them—to make them automatic. Evaluating physical store arrangement, customer experiences, and symbolic representations of the store reveals the ways that self-service stores embodied stark dichotomies of democracy and White supremacy.

## "We Want the Business of the Colored Man"

Historians have documented the mass migration of rural African Americans and the impact they made on New South cities.[6] Urban wages generated purchasing power, and self-service grocers appealed directly for the business of African American consumers. As Albon Holsey's story "White Folks First" revealed, self-service stores offered special attractions for African American consumers. The depersonalization of the shopping experience in self-service stores automatically discouraged race-based incivility, and the checkout line systematized equality. The ability to select affordable, standardized brand name products offered added protections against inferior products substituted by clerks who filled grocery orders. But self-service stores were designed by White inventors, and they were not built to ensure racial equality.

From the initial stages of invention, self-service store owners directly recruited African American customers. When Blumenthal's department store in Savannah, Georgia, created a self-service grocery department in 1919, it reached out to the editor of the African American newspaper *Savannah Tribune* to attract customers. "We want you to learn that Blumenthal's is a store of true economy," the editor wrote on behalf of the store owners. "[Their] new self-service Grocery Department . . . will enable them to offer you all your groceries at exceptionally cut prices."[7] Low wages made African American consumers "persistent shoppers or bargain hunters" in the words of Fisk economics professor Paul K. Edwards. In *Southern Urban Negro as a Consumer*, Edwards reported, "55.4% of the housewives and family heads interviewed in Birmingham, 72% of those interviewed in Atlanta, and 75% in Richmond have mentioned price as the most important determinant of the direction of their trade." But Edwards emphasized that price was not the only factor Black consumers considered in deciding where to spend their hard-earned money. "Courteous treatment is a much more important factor than the merchant sometimes realizes," he wrote.[8] As chain stores expanded during the 1920s, they offered clean spaces and greater variety, and self-service stores offered systematized equality and depersonalization of the shopping experience that freed African American shoppers even further from the unpredictable treatment of store clerks.

Studies of Black consumers identified the distinctive appeal of self-service shopping. In his study of segregation patterns of the 1920s, African American sociologist Charles S. Johnson found that grocery stores depended "as much on the Negro buying public as on the white." "[Yet] the policies of stores vary widely, as do the relations between clerks and Negro patrons." Despite de jure segregation, which purported to clearly demarcate public spaces according to a strict biracial separation, day-to-day interracial customer experiences were defined by "constant uncertainty," and the treatment African Americans received varied greatly from store to store.[9] Johnson documented the instability of race by organizing his study of Black consumer experience in the segregated South into different types of commercial spaces—banks, department stores, grocery stores, and five-and-ten-cent stores—because African American consumers experienced different kinds of treatment in different kinds of commercial spaces. Beyond the incivility and disrespect that African American customers experienced daily from White customers and clerks alike, shopping posed the risk of outright physical harm for Black consumers. Edwards reported that one White store manager declared, "I'd rather have Negro than white customers, they are so much easier satisfied. But if one of them ever gets fresh with me, I'll crack him over the head with a chair."[10] Self-service store design offered African American customers a predictable social neutrality enforced by the systematized store arrangement. According to Johnson, "Negroes report that stores in which customers serve themselves offer fewer discriminatory practices than those in which customers must await the personal attention of a white clerk. The question of precedence of whites over Negroes does not intrude in self-service." Along with the advantages of equal treatment, Johnson added that self-service offered escape from "another practice which Negroes find obnoxious—that of being offered inferior goods laid aside especially for the purpose."[11]

Though it was published in 1943, *Patterns of Negro Segregation* was based on field research the African American sociologist Charles S. Johnson conducted in the 1930s while he led the Department of Sociology at Fisk University. His data for the urban South was collected in Nashville, Richmond, Birmingham, Atlanta, and Houston—all cities where Piggly Wiggly operated as one of the most familiar chain stores across the region during the 1920s. Johnson's methods included direct observation of "both normal and crisis situations" and "intensive interviewing" of both African American and White residents, with an effort to identify a diverse sample that included "Negroes of recognizably different social and economic classes."[12]

Johnson observed, "The most common type of response [among African Americans] to the personal implications of the race system is that of *avoidance*. Although this is most conspicuous in the efforts of upper-class groups to preserve self-esteem, it is a fairly common phenomenon among all classes and varies in degree with the situation and with the motivations involved." Avoiding the store was possible for African American women who had access to telephones to place their orders. In one interview, Johnson wrote, "An upper-class Negro woman said that she did much of her routine shopping by telephone since her voice and diction could get more consideration than her face in the store." Johnson emphasized that the strategy of avoidance was "not only a precautionary effort to avoid certain types of racial contact, but [also] an attempt to avoid conforming to the patterns of expected behavior."[13] The silent soundscape of self-service and the systemization of equality in a public space offered an incentive to come inside the store. The depersonalization of the shopping experience created space to avoid uncivil treatment.

The self-service store may have been attractive to many African American consumers not because they felt particularly liberated by serving themselves but because equal access to store products and equality in the checkout line were public demonstrations of equality. A photograph (fig. 6.1) of a busy Piggly Wiggly checkout line in Lexington suggests the tense experience of performative equality. A Black woman waits her turn in the checkout line as the White women in line with her throw hostile looks in her direction.

The fact that customers could select their own brand name products directly from the shelves without interacting with a clerk also meant that Black customers could inspect the quality of the merchandise before they bought it. Edwards offered evidence of consumer choices based on a series of careful surveys of African American consumers in Nashville and Richmond during the 1920s. Focusing on the response to brands nationally advertised with racist stereotypes, such as Aunt Jemima pancake mix and Rinso Soap Powder, Edwards concluded that the representation of race in advertising "can serve, on the one hand, to build up the Negro's good will toward, and interest in, a particular brand of merchandise, or, on the other hand, to build up his ill will and resistance to it."[14] When they served themselves, African Americans could choose not to buy racist brand name products. According to Edwards's interviews with hundreds of Black women shoppers, the majority of them, across all occupational classes, bought higher-priced brands: Maxwell House coffee, Calumet and Rumford baking powder, and Martha White, Pillsbury's Best, and Gold Medal flour.[15]

Piggly Wiggly franchisees bought advertising space in African American newspapers, directories, and other publications, directly recruiting African American customers at a time when other advertisers ignored Black consumers. According to historian Robert Weems, Kellogg's was one of the first major food companies to market directly to African American consumers in a

FIG. 6.1. Close-up of the racially integrated Piggly Wiggly checkout line in Lexington, June 20, 1931. *Source:* Lafayette Studios Photographs, Audio-Visual Archives, University of Kentucky Libraries, Lexington.

nonderogatory campaign in advertising Kellogg's Corn Flakes widely in the Black press during the mid-1930s.[16] Piggly Wiggly's direct advertising in the Black press preceded the Kellogg's campaign by more than a decade. Clarence Saunders opened a Piggly Wiggly store in the heart of the busy African American commercial district on Beale Street in the early years of operation in Memphis. On opening day in June 1919, Saunders assured Beale Street customers, "At Piggly Wiggly, white and black, rich and poor, young and old, receive the same goods, the same prices and same weights, and are accorded the same treatment as they pass in and out of this most democratic of all market places." Emphasizing that African American customers would enjoy the same treatment as White customers, a Beale Street store ad proclaimed, "Piggly Wiggly is just one kind of a store for every kind of people."[17] Store franchisees' slogans capitalize on the second-class treatment Black consumers faced and went beyond price appeal to emphasize the equality of self-service. "We Want the Business of the Colored Man," a Piggly Wiggly ad declared to readers of the *Negro Star* in Wichita in 1922.[18] Piggly Wiggly was the only chain that bought advertising in the *Negro Star*, and the same appears to hold true for advertising in other African American newspapers as well.[19] In Birmingham, Piggly Wiggly recruited African American customers with an explicit motto: "The One Price Store on Every Article to Every Race and Color and Kind."[20] It was the only grocery chain to advertise in the African American newspaper *Voice of the People*, where its ads declared Piggly Wiggly "the stores where all the people are treated alike."[21] An ad indicated that there were thirteen Piggly Wiggly stores in Birmingham, suggesting that African American customers could expect equal treatment in all of them, not just in the ones located in Black neighborhoods. In Montgomery, Alabama, Piggly Wiggly recruited African American readers of the *Emancipator* with the slogan "One Price to Everybody" and an emphasis on high-quality products: "More for Your Money and Better Groceries."[22]

Black customers used their importance as consumers to push for racial equality beyond the store space. After he left Piggly Wiggly, Saunders started another self-service chain he called "Clarence Saunders, Sole Owner of My Name Stores," relying on his name recognition as the inventor of Piggly Wiggly. He was legally prohibited from using the name of the company he had started. Even as he continued to court African American customers at his grocery stores, Saunders publicly campaigned against Black voters in the Tennessee governor's race of 1928. Operating as the Shelby County manager of the Henry Horton campaign, Saunders provoked a boycott from the African American community. On election day, Saunders escalated the conflict with a two-page campaign advertisement in Memphis's *Commercial Appeal*. Saunders urged White voters to go to the polls. "Show to the world that the white men and white women of Shelby County will not stand for Negroes to be called to the polls in a Democratic primary—show your white blood of resentment at the insult to your race." .[23] The *New York Age* described Saunders's diatribe as dangerous in a city with a history of racial violence: "He sought to incite the spirit of the whites . . . even at the risk of promoting mob violence and rioting."[24]

The response from the Black leaders in Memphis courageously demonstrated the ways that the power of the purse fused economic and political justice in the Black community. The *Commercial Appeal* reported that "almost the entire front page of an 'Election Edition' of *The Memphis Triangle*, leading negro paper," was an "inspired editorial attack" on Clarence Saunders's business. "We Know You, Mr. Saunders," declared the *Triangle* editorial title. "Mr. Saunders is a groceryman who has stepped outside of the realm of his business into a field where he is at a loss. He insults us in the public press." The *Triangle* editorial emphasized that Black customers had helped Saunders build Piggly Wiggly, "stuck to him when wrecked," and helped him rise again "to what is said to be the heights of a millionaire" by supporting his Sole Owner stores.[25] "We merely wish to remind you, Mr. Saunders, that hams and turnip greens can be purchased some other place than just your Clarence Saunders stores," the editorial said in a call for a boycott of Saunders's stores.[26] "Adieu Mr. Saunders! If you sell a ham for a nickel we don't want it."[27]

Black customers were well aware that fierce competition and low profit margins in the grocery trade meant that every customer mattered. Long before the first "Don't buy where you can't work" campaigns of the 1930s, Black Memphians connected their role as consumers to their political activism.[28] The fact that all customers regardless of race entered the store through the same turnstile made it a powerful equalizing symbol. "When the colored housewives of this community find it necessary to make the turnstiles click," the *Triangle* editorial declared, "they will remember that 'We Know You.'"[29] Black women assigned a distinctly political purpose to their use of the turnstile.

Grocery stores were among the most affordable small businesses for African American entrepreneurs. Edwards wrote, "More Negroes are engaged in the retailing of groceries in the urban South than in the retailing of any other type of consumer merchandise."[30] But before 1940, self-service stores were White-owned businesses. The risks and expense of self-service experimentation were prohibitive for most Black grocers. Besides the capital-intensive costs of franchising or store experimentation, discrimination in hiring meant that few African Americans had the opportunity to learn the grocery business on the job, much less the specialized retailing principles of self-service store management. Very few of the Black grocers Edwards studied in Nashville had any retailing experience before they opened their stores. Half of them "reported stock on hand valued at less than $800, which in some cases amounted to less than $100." The stores were in poor condition—"some dark and gloomy, others actually dirty."[31] The National Negro Business League promoted Carl Dipman's more-affordable model store as the best practice in store arrangement for African American grocers.[32] Though Piggly Wiggly advertised directly to African American customers, store franchise owners were White entrepreneurs. Holsey reported an important exception: "A Piggly Wiggly store in Tuskegee Institute, Alabama, is operated by a Negro manager and clerks." Perhaps this was a strategy for educating students at the college on self-service store methods.[33]

Given Saunders's very public White supremacist ideology, it is important to reconsider how physical self-service store spaces he designed relate to the symbolic equality he promoted in representations of self-service space. Historian Carolyn de la Peña argues, "We should think of race as an epistemology at play in all technological production and consumption." It is not simply that racist symbolism is applied to existing technologies. "Racial difference and whiteness are constructed through technology," Peña emphasizes.[34] White self-service store inventors designed retail environments that exerted control over the minds and bodies of their customers. H. A. Haring was one of the first White advertising executives to write about the buying habits of African American consumers in two 1930 articles for *Advertising and Selling* magazine in 1930.[35] Haring asserted that store owners with Black customers learned that "display is king." He asserted, "[The Black shopper] is short on abstract thinking, so that a mere description falls flat. He can visualize only what he sees with the eye. Better yet, what he touches with the hand."[36] Such attitudes about the powerlessness of African American shoppers in the face of open store displays suggests that White store owners considered their Black customers to be especially susceptible to the "purchase-inducing force" of the self-service store. The technical incompetence of people of color was a deeply ingrained idea for White Americans with roots in the history of slavery. "Rather than simply the shell or emblem of racist thinking," historian Bruce Sinclair writes, "defining African Americans as technically incompetent and then—in a kind of double curse—denying them access to education, control over complex machinery, or the power of patent rights lay at the heart of the distinctions drawn between black and white people in this country."[37] Considering the origins of self-service in the Jim Crow South offers an important opportunity to understand how the self-service store was designed and used as a tool of White supremacy.

## Inventing Self-Service in a Culture of Segregation

The machine age self-service store, dependent on the steady traffic of cash-paying customers, seems incongruous in a region that remained poorer and more rural than the rest of the country. Southern historians have emphasized the importance of the general store as the central economic institution in the cash-strapped region well into the twentieth century. General stores introduced rural southerners to brand name products and created systems of debt peonage that invented "a way for people to shop locally without money."[38] By contrast, Piggly Wiggly was one of the most expensive store interiors to install during the 1920s, yet southern franchisees embraced the brand. Although the costs of experimenting with self-service installations raised the economic risks for southern store inventors, White southerners were among the most enthusiastic inventors and promoters of self-service before 1940.

Self-service store patent applicants between 1917 and 1932 included merchants from fifteen states, but over 70 percent were issued to inventors living in the South.[39] Inventors came from cities like Birmingham, Atlanta, and Nashville but also from hamlets like Rolling Fork, Mississippi and Hazel, Kentucky. The majority of southern self-service entrepreneurs were independent store owners, but the region also produced some of the most successful self-service chains before 1940. Shoppers in Jackson, Mississippi, served themselves at the Jitney Jungle. In Atlanta, the self-service Nifty Jiffy store competed with Piggly Wiggly for consumer dollars. In Dallas there were nearly fifty Piggly Wiggly outlets around town competing with independent stores such as Long's Helpy Selfy, Robertson's Self-Serving Grocery and Market, and Killingsworth Self-Serving Store.[40] The only self-service store Carl Dipman included in his first book on modern store arrangement was an example from the South (see fig. 1.4). What accounts for the popularity of self-service among White southern grocers and their customers?

At first glance, a focus on economics might offer one answer—price appeal. Tenant farmers and sharecroppers sought the lowest prices in their trips to small-town stores, and factory and office workers earning cash wages in New South cities looked for stores that offered the best bargains, fueling the popularity of self-service. The low profit margin of self-service stores made self-service store owners more dependent on Black customers than other types of stores were. Put simply, every dollar counted. Historian Grace Hale argues, "The collective white need for superiority clashed headlong with white individuals' desire for greater income, and money often won."[41] As machines for automatic selling, self-service stores were the ultimate capitalist fantasy. With their focus on the efficient movement of customers through small store spaces, physically partitioning customers by race was not an option for self-service store designers. The inventors' goal of eliminating congestion and speeding up sales seemingly outweighed the social etiquette of segregation.

Most grocery stores were simply too small for the architectural strategies of exclusion that created fixed or fluctuating physical boundaries to separate "White" and "Colored" space in train station waiting rooms or the separate theater entrances for White and Black moviegoers. Architectural historian Robert Weyeneth explains that in physically integrated commercial spaces White supremacy was enforced through "behavioral separation," in which Whites enjoyed full access to store privileges while Black customers were restricted.[42] In traditional stores, White customers and clerks retained the ability to enforce White supremacy in the shuffle for service at the counter. As historian Stephen A. Berrey argues, "The practice of white people cutting in line not only racialized time and space; it was also a performative reinforcement of the social hierarchy."[43] But the amorphous and fluid customer lines that formed around a clerk counter in traditional service stores did not work the same way as the systematized checkout lines in cafeteria-style self-service stores.

During the 1920s and 1930s, self-service grocery stores were the only retail spaces designed to methodically organize customers into checkout lines. Cedarbluff, Mississippi, inventor Robert A. Tribble summarized the system in explaining the purposes of his store: "The self-service store aims to display the entire stock of goods to each and every customer, to keep the crowd moving always in one direction to avoid confusion and congestion, to direct all customers to a common exit and past a cashier's desk and to prevent the passage of customers from the store through any other than the last named exit."[44] Keeping the crowd moving, keeping them focused on the store displays and directing them toward the cashier's desk as a final shopping destination were features that characterized self-service stores as a specialized form of retailing. It was Clarence Saunders's year-long experimentation with the configuration of the checkout counter that convinced the patent examiners to approve his second store arrangement as a patentable invention. Customers in the Piggly Wiggly checkout line, especially when the store was full at rush hour, could not easily reorder the line (fig. 6.2). Insisting that Black customers always go to the back of the line would have wreaked havoc on the speed of the checkout process.

Store designers used different strategies to configure pathways, but, whether they followed a one-way path or chose different routes through the store, customers were organized into a checkout line that did not allow for social or racial hierarchies. Every customer checked out on a first-come, first-served basis. The self-service store was a relentlessly equalizing machine, and the rhetoric of entrepreneurs often emphasized that theme. Such a system seems antithetical to the goals of White supremacy. One can readily see why Black customers might be attracted to self-service stores that offered low prices and also publicly affirmed social equality. But affluent White women could afford to pay higher prices to avoid the racial equality of the checkout line. Why did they embrace a method of shopping that treated them as socially equal to African Americans? Moreover, the physical intimacy of racially integrated store spaces was potentially dangerous. The mutual panic of "Miss Simpson" and "Uncle John" in Holsey's story evokes the fear of social retribution (or worse) for customers who broke the rules of racial etiquette in the integrated space. In her study of the visual politics of spatial segregation, Elizabeth Abel downplays the homogenizing effect of capitalist space shaped primarily for the purpose of making money to emphasize the "diversifying effects of a built environment designed to accommodate a range of social needs."[45] Pocketbook issues were certainly a significant factor in consumer

FIG. 6.2. Faces in the Piggly Wiggly crowd. African American shoppers mingled with White men and women standing in line on a first-come, first-served basis. Close-up of Piggly Wiggly exhibit E photograph. Photograph by Clifford H. Poland; copyright by Clarence Saunders, 1918. *Source:* Library of Congress Prints and Photographs Division, Washington, D.C.

choice, but they cannot explain why different kinds of customers might choose self-service over counter-service chain stores. While low prices certainly attracted diverse customers, chain stores that did not operate using self-service methods also proliferated in the region and offered competitively low prices.

To understand why self-service stores were popular in the South among diverse shoppers, it is essential to consider how self-service stores offered different kinds of advantages to different social groups. French scholar Henri Lefebvre argues that spaces are not static backdrops for human activity, they are socially produced through the dynamic intersection of physical space, social experience, and conceptual representation. The material forms and functions of a space reveal *spatial practices*; *representations of space* are the conceptualized space of designers; and *representational spaces* are "space as directly lived" by inhabitants and users. To understand the history of space as a social experience it is essential to consider these three types of spaces in a dialectical relationship. LeFebvre emphasizes that the history of space "must account for both representational spaces and representations of space, but above all for their interrelationships and their links with social practice."[46]

Evaluating self-service stores as socially produced spaces requires interweaving different kinds of sources to reconstruct the intersectional dynamic of physical, symbolic, and experiential store spaces in historical context. The spatial practices that defined self-service stores included entry and exit turnstiles, technologies of mobility such as market baskets or conveyor belts, and configuration of fixtures for customer access to store products. Representations of space are documented in store patents and advertisements that explained designers' intentions and created symbolic meanings for store spaces. Holsey's story offers a glimpse of the lived experiences of different kinds of customers who used the space—the self-satisfaction of making personal choices from the open shelves and bins and the fear of breaking social taboos in the unfamiliar commercial space. Each of these types of space is incomplete considered in isolation and often contradictory considered in relation to the others. Store patents document the design intentions of the merchant but construct a generic customer and make no mention of race or gender. Consumer magazine ads construct a one-dimensional affluent White female customer and spatially decontextualize elements of the store design—featuring the hanging price tags, for example, without showing how they relate to the automatic selling system of the self-service pathway. Customer experiences are documented in a wide variety of sources, from personal memoirs to sociological studies of southern consumers that do not necessarily describe store spaces in detail. Interpreting these sources in relation to each other helps to reconstruct the dynamic interaction of the physical store arrangement, the cultural frameworks that conceptualized the spatial experience of self-service, and the customer experience in navigating social encounters along self-service pathways that produced the space of the store.

Reconstructing the ways that self-service was socially produced brings into sharper view the significance of regional difference in the invention and experience of self-service. In her essay on "spatializing culture," anthropologist Setha Low develops the concept of "embodied space" to understand how individuals produce meaningful space "through the patterning of everyday movements." Her ethnographic study of the Moore Street Market in Brooklyn, New York, showed how "it is the movement of . . . vendors, shoppers, pensioners, and visitors—differentiated by gender, age, class, ethnicity, and national identity—and their everyday activities: conversations, purchases, listening to music, eating homemade food, that makes the market space what it is. And it is through the embodied spaces of their social relationships that the market is simultaneously a local and translocal place."[47] Piggly Wiggly franchising contracts and advertisements emphasized that its standardized interior looked and worked the same everywhere. But evaluating self-service stores as spaces that were socially produced shows that shopping in Piggly Wiggly was not the same experience everywhere—and not simply because a two-line store was smaller than a four-line store. Self-service shopping in a racially and economically homogenous suburban Chicago Piggly Wiggly was not the same spatial experience as shopping in the racially integrated Piggly Wiggly in downtown Memphis. The factory-built store interior was standardized, but the representational space created by customers was different depending on community contexts. The meanings of shopping are unstable and contingent on personalized shopping geographies in particular locations and types of spaces.[48]

Self-service inventors situated their stores on Main Street to attract crowds—the tenant farmer in town on Saturday, the mill worker with pocket change, the housekeeper, even the downtown businessman on his way home from work. And especially they wanted to attract the "Miss Simpsons" to the store—not just because affluent White women made provisioning decisions for their families and had plenty of cash to spend. The presence of White women customers legitimized self-service as a respectable new social practice. Store owners used specific strategies to feminize their stores and recruit White women as customers, and these strategies involved both the physical store space and the cultural representations of self-service shopping. To be successful, self-service store owners had to do more than physically arrange their stores into systems for automatic selling. They had to reconstruct the gender, race, and class systems associated with food shopping and grocery spaces. They had to feminize the self-service store and racialize it as White space. Despite the equalizing experience of the systemized checkout line, the self-service store can still be understood as part of what architectural historian Robert Weyeneth calls "the spatial strategies of white supremacy."[49]

## The Aristocracy of the Market Basket

Clarence Saunders explicitly connected gender and class, berating women who refused self-service as comprising an uppity "High Heel Society" of Memphis, shaming them for being too proud to carry their own market basket.[50] But he also promoted self-service as something to do for fun, not work. During the opening week of the Jefferson Street Piggly Wiggly store in September 1916, Saunders recruited "the most beautiful of Memphis' Womanhood" to shop at Piggly Wiggly by staging the Piggly Wiggly Beauty Contest. He bought a full-page ad in the Memphis *Commercial Appeal* to publish the photographs of the nine winners. In addition to the five women who won "for the prettiest red hair," there were winners for the "noblest face expression," "prettiest eyes," and "prettiest hands" and for the "most stylish looking."[51] The portraits of each individual White woman were prominently featured, along with their names and addresses, conveying to newspaper readers that White women from fashionable and respectable neighborhoods all over town shopped at Piggly Wiggly. Only two of the winners were identified as "Mrs." The other seven were "Miss," suggesting that self-service shopping was an enjoyable activity and not simply an essential job of family provisioning. The beauty contest publicly launched Piggly Wiggly with symbolic associations with White womanhood.

At the same time that Saunders cast Piggly Wiggly as a populist space, not an elitist one. In traditional stores in the South, both White and Black customers experienced practices of social ranking, as store clerks made decisions about whom to serve first and required others to wait. Saunders exploited the social tensions of clerk service to explain the advantages of self-service in his first advertisements for Piggly Wiggly—"To have no store clerks to gab and smirk while folks are standing around ten deep to get waited on."[52] He emphasized that Piggly Wiggly was born with "a work shirt on his back," not with "a 'silver spoon' in his mouth."[53] Self-service stores promoted a herrenvolk democracy that elevated working-class White customers who experienced service equal to that given well-heeled society. Self-service was not simply a cheap alternative for poor people. An ad for Piggly Wiggly stores in Atlanta in 1920 redefined the cultural work of food shopping by invoking a new "aristocracy of the market basket." The ad offered a familiar list of reasons why "hundreds of thousands" of homemakers in Atlanta preferred to buy their groceries at Piggly Wiggly every day:

> They know they get full value in quality and quantity.
> They know they can select exactly what they want, not what somebody wants to hand them. No one to persuade, no one to suggest, no one to recommend what they shall or shall not buy.
> They know that at Piggly Wiggly they will not have to wait until Mrs. Extra Fussy, or Mrs. Can't Quit Talking, or Mrs. Perpetual Grouch have been waited on.
> They know that they save money. They know that they save time.
> They know that they get clean goods from a clean store.[54]

Getting quality merchandise at a good value, saving time and money, shopping in a clean store—these were typical expectations of grocery customers by the 1920s. But what makes this ad particularly distinctive in a southern context is the idea proclaimed in its title: "The Aristocracy of the Piggly Wiggly Basket." A nicely dressed though rather old-fashioned-looking White woman carries a market basket brimming with her purchases. The concept of aristocracy echoed an antebellum past, associating new forms of middle-class consumption with the affluence of a romanticized planter elite. The new urban middle class built its cultural authority on a fiction of continuity between the antebellum plantation household and the new consumer-oriented domesticity.[55] In the culture of segregation, the aristocracy of the market basket construed self-service as at once modern and traditional, democratic and paternalistic. One did not actually have to be a wealthy person to be a member of the market basket aristocracy. Self-service could elevate as well as equalize.

About a year after the Piggly Wiggly opened, Saunders explicitly requested the assistance of his customers in perfecting the way the store worked, offering cash prizes for the winning ideas in two categories—best suggestion for store improvement and best responses to the theme "Why the Piggly Wiggly Is All Right."[56] Frederick May was the first-prize winner in the second category for his explanation of the impact of the self-service experience. His essay offers insights from the perspective of a male head of household about why men supported self-service grocers' efforts to feminize grocery spaces. May particularly liked the fact that self-service had shifted the food shopping responsibility from domestic servant to homemaker, believing that the latter had greater incentive to pay attention to the family budget. "The prime advantage of PIGGLY-WIGGLY is that it makes the women market for themselves," he wrote. "Before the PIGGLY-WIGGLY the servant did the buying and the knocking down, without regard to price or quality she bought in jumbo quantities and 'toated' [sic] in proportion. It is no wonder banks prohibited overdrafts. Friend Husband could'nt [sic] stand the pressure." In addition to considering shopping as economic work, May's essay also signaled his attitudes about shopping as cultural work. Self-service was preferable to full service because his wife would not have to wait her turn: "She can reflect and select without interruption or embarrassment or waste or time. No first come first served here. It is the only place in the world where everybody is waited on at once."[57] Regardless of her economic class, every shopper could envision herself a member of the aristocracy of the market basket when she wasn't compelled by the social calculus of a clerk to wait for service at the counter. When she finished her shopping, she had her husband's equality publicly affirmed by the class neutrality she experienced in the checkout line.

When he opened the first Piggly Wiggly store in downtown Memphis, Saunders voiced his concerns about whether southern shoppers would be willing to serve themselves. "The North and the South—Is There a Difference?" he asked Memphis readers in the headline of one of his first Piggly Wiggly ads. He worried that the South was an unlikely place for self-service success. "Up North they said maybe a woman or a man would not be ashamed to go into the Piggly Wiggly and wait on themselves and then carry their purchases home with them, but not here in the South. Too much false pride, they said; too many folks who like to look and act like they imagine a millionaire ought to act. . . . They shook their heads and said it wouldn't work."[58] To recruit White women to self-service, southern inventors had to reconstruct the social role of the grocery store and the cultural work of food shopping in the region.

In practical terms, food shopping was time-consuming work at the turn of the century—a chore often performed by Black domestic workers. Elizabeth Howse, daughter of a Murfreesboro, Tennessee, grocer, remembered that Kank, the family's African American cook, performed the marketing early every morning: "In the spring, before she came to work; she had been all over town to see where the best greens were to be found, or, if the berries were ripe enough for a pie, or if anyone had a fat rabbit or chicken for sale."[59] Although southern White women of all classes continued to benefit from the underpaid domestic labor of African American women, historian Tera Hunter estimates that "between 1910 and 1920, the proportion of wage-earning black women in household work dropped from 84 to 75 percent."[60]

Writing during the scarcity of a wartime economy in 1919, Georgia suffragist Rebecca Latimer Felton romanticized her grandmother's self-sufficiency. She made her own starch and laundry soap and preserved the peaches from the orchards she cultivated in her own garden. But gardening and home production played an increasingly smaller role in putting food on southern tables. "The present generation lives in paper sack supplies," Felton complained. "They buy everything in paper sacks from a goober-pea to a small sack of meal." Though she expressed guilt about it, Felton admitted, "I am now buying peaches at thirty cents a dozen."[61] Modernizing grocers gradually reconstituted the gendered social role of grocery spaces in the region as food retailers focused especially on women as the provisioners of consumer households.

## The New Hangout of the (White) Women

Commercial business districts in the early-twentieth-century South were being redesigned to accommodate the new public roles White women were playing as consumers. Nineteenth-century entrepreneurs had transformed U.S. cities by creating new downtown spaces of public consumption for women in commercial business districts.[62] They relied on women as their major customers and intentionally designed department stores as female spaces from the beginning. Even on small-town public squares, department stores were the largest consumer spaces, built to cater to the social activities of women by including lunchrooms or cafeterias along with a wide variety of products for the home, family, and personal needs. Historian Ted Ownby explores the carnivalesque seasonal sales promoted by variety and department stores as a new kind of leisure that drew more women to stores in Mississippi than ever before. Ownby observes that the departmentalized organization and large store size was an essential element in encouraging southern women to become department store shoppers. "Having stores large enough to walk from department to department to shop gave women a freedom they had not enjoyed when they had to brave the overwhelming male presence to enter the old general store."[63] Department stores helped to feminize small-town business districts. Women in town might enjoy exploring a local department store, but grocery stores had a long, well-established role as male gathering spaces, and shopping for groceries was a daily necessity, not an occasional leisure outing or seasonal ritual.

As late as 1940, Jack Delano captured the traditional role of the grocery store as a male social space in Stem, North Carolina. In figure 6.3, young men dressed up for election day are seen smoking in leisurely conversation around a pot-bellied stove. They might have served themselves from the orderly open shelves lined with canned goods, but the space is the anthesis of a self-service system designed for the movement of customers silently intent on the work of shopping. In their access to the voting booth and their appropriation of the shop floor as an extension of the public square, the young White men claimed grocery stores as spaces of male privilege.

In the 1940s, O. S. Edmunds ran grocery stores in the Madison County towns of Mars Hill and Marshall, North Carolina. He also circulated a rolling store weekly to capture rural trade of customers who rarely came to town. Hal Edmunds, who worked as a clerk for his grandfather, later remembered a distinctly gendered divide in his town and rural customers: "Most all that traded in the regular store, they was mostly men. Men would come to the store and stay about all day[,] and their wives, whatever they wanted, they would write it down or tell the men. Women very seldom ever come to the store. Like in the rolling [store] business, it was all different. It was all women."[64] Rural southern women felt comfortable shopping from the privacy of their backyards or front porches as they made consumer choices from rolling stores. Though rural southern women were active consumers, their access to consumer spaces in town remained limited well into the twentieth century.

Eva Coffer's encounter with a drunken grocer in the spring of 1929 in Georgetown, Tennessee, offers a vivid example of the ways that traditional grocery stores threatened female respectability. Grocer Lee Atchley had been drinking all day when Eva Coffer came to shop. As Coffer struggled to break free of the grocer's drunken advances, Atchley's wife, at work in the store, suggested that she "take a wagon spoke to him." Coffer followed through on the advice by returning to the store a half-hour later with the heavy spoke of a wagon wheel and then, according to witnesses in the store, "beat the grocer to the ground as his child stood nearby, crying."[65] Atchley was treated by a physician but died several hours after the attack. "Clubbed to Death by Furious Woman," proclaimed one headline.[66] Coffer's trial was a news sensation across the Southeast. At the inquest Coffer relied on generations of tradition regarding White Southern womanhood. Testifying between "hysterical sobs," Coffer declared, "I was just trying to protect myself. I'd just as soon be dead as to lose my character." It turned out to be a convincing argument. When she was acquitted by the jury, "scores of the 700 spectators in circuit court rushed

FIG. 6.3. Grocery store in Stem, Granville County, North Carolina, "with high school boys dressed up because it's Election Day." Jack Delano photographer, May 1940.
*Source:* FSA/OWI Collection, Prints and Photographs Division, Library of Congress Washington, D.C.

forward to congratulate the 21-year-old slayer."[67] The fact that men drank and socialized in grocery stores made women reluctant to come to the store.

Perceptions that the grocery store was an inappropriate space for White women were widespread across the region in the early twentieth century. John Cutchins, who grew up in turn-of-the-century Richmond, Virginia, remembered that it was customary "in those days" that "the man—the head of the family—did the marketing."[68] Elizabeth Howse recalled, "All ladies called over the phone each morning for their order. It wouldn't have been considered 'nice' to get the groceries themselves."[69] Howse thought of her father's grocery store as a male space: "Many of [D]addy's cronies spent a good deal of time in the store. This being before any local clubs were organized, the store proved an enjoyable place to spend a pleasant hour or two."[70] Writer Eudora Welty remembered that her mother Chestina "never set foot inside a grocery store."[71] Chestina did her regular grocery shopping by phone rather than in person.

It was a very bold move when Clarence Saunders banned telephones from Piggly Wiggly stores and eliminated all delivery service. "The Piggly Wiggly does not advocate telephoning, and neither does it allow telephoning. Look in any telephone directory and you will fail to find a single Piggly Wiggly store listed therein," an ad warned Memphis women.[72] Piggly Wiggly customers would have to come inside the store and do their own shopping.

Chain store interiors appealed to the urban bourgeoisie because they were purposely designed for the efficient work of the modern housewife. They stressed themes of sanitation, order, and product quality, echoing the advice of popular magazines and domestic scientists that promoted new standards of cleanliness and sanitation in the Progressive Era. Memphis grocer Duke Bowers built his successful chain of cash and carry grocery stores in Memphis by physically and symbolically re-gendering the store. According to the local *Commercial Appeal*, when Bowers started in the grocery business "almost every grocery store had a bar in the rear, but Mr. Bowers would not allow a bar, nor would he allow his clerks to drink." This went against standard practice. "It was considered a slap at the good old constitution in those days to deny any man the right to drink as much and as often as he pleased. Mr. Bowers also would not allow tobacco to be sold in his stores."[73] Bowers opened his first grocery store in Memphis with three hundred dollars' worth of stock. By 1916 he operated forty-three cash and carry stores in and around Memphis. His ads capitalized on the domesticated store space and addressed homemakers as his target market, but he did not insist that they come to the store to do their own shopping. Bowers combined cash and carry with delivery, and prohibiting drinking was an effort to reassure mothers that it was safe for their children to run errands to his stores.[74] "We are favored with the largest number of 'children customers' of any commercial institution in the city," claimed one Bowers ad.[75] "Isn't it a most comforting thought, Madam, to know there is a grocery store in your neighborhood where you can safely entrust the family buying to your children? Where no loafing is allowed, no smoking, no tobacco of any sort is sold; where the influence is clean and wholesome?"[76]

Re-gendering the grocery store was a long-term process, and self-service inventors faced distinctive challenges. Even when grocery stores were considered safe and respectable for errand-running children, their mothers scrupulously avoided the store themselves. But the profitability of self-service depended on getting women inside the store. William Holman Jr. remembered that his family's early grocery store in Jackson, Mississippi, before it was converted to self-service, was the hangout for males in the neighborhood. "Women rarely visited the store. They shopped by telephone, and groceries

**Madam: Think This Over!**

Isn't it a most comforting thought, Madam, to know there is a grocery store in your neighborhood where you can safely entrust the family buying to your children? Where no loafing is allowed, no smoking, no tobacco of any sort is sold; where the influence is clean and wholesome? Isn't it worth a lot to have that kind of a store nearby? Even the candies, cakes, etc., are bought by us with the welfare of children in mind—to handle nothing but the purest and best.

FIG. 6.4. This detail from an ad for Mr. Bowers' Stores Incorporated assured Memphis mothers that they could "safely entrust the family buying" when they sent their children to Mr. Bowers' Stores in their neighborhood. *Source: Commercial Appeal* (Memphis), 29 August 1916.

were delivered by wagon to their homes. At the end of the month, the husbands came to the store and paid, or were supposed to!" The Holman and McCarty cousins opened their first self-service Jitney Jungle store in April 1919, on East Capitol Street near a Piggly Wiggly store.[77] Piggly Wiggly ultimately lost a patent infringement suit against the chain, and Jitney Jungle expanded as a competing self-service brand. William B. McCarty patented the store design in 1920.[78] In a striking transformation of the once male-dominated grocery space, where male college students pitched coins at a crack in the wooden floor, "Clerks were dressed down for failing to dress up. Ties were compulsory." McCarty and Holman domesticated the grocery business. The goal was to make the store "a super social institution, where ladies made appointments with each other to visit, drink a 'Coke,' and buy their bags of groceries," William Holman Jr. remembered. It took at least a decade.[79]

Their fourteenth store in Jackson opened a new chapter in feminizing the grocery store. The Jitney Jungle 14 was designed in the Tudor Revival style by a local architect in 1929 for the growing suburb of Belhaven, home to the families of local professionals, government officials, and businessmen.[80] Paying particular attention to attracting women to their new store, the Jitney Jungle 14 included a women's restroom. William McCarty's daughter later remembered, "When you entered the store there was a platform area to the left for the ladies to sit and visit before they shopped. There was a woman who taught knitting and the ladies would knit or read as they visited." There were also "chairs for children to sit in" while their mothers shopped. Besides groceries, the store sold house dresses, which came to be called "Jitney dresses."[81]

The store provided a measure of how successful self-service grocers had been in reconfiguring not only their grocery interiors but also the cultural role of food shopping. "No longer was the grocery store the haven of the idle male. It had become the hangout of the women!" William Holman Jr. declared.[82] Eudora Welty learned how to shop in the traditional neighborhood corner store, running errands so her mother could avoid going inside the store, but she became an avid self-service shopper and celebrated customer of the Jitney 14.[83] She especially remembered being attracted by the novelty of self-service: "This was the first store where you could actually go behind the counter to get what you needed. . . . I always felt it was named Jitney Jungle because it was like exploring to go into the aisles."[84]

The idea that women were especially susceptible to the influence of self-service was widespread in the grocery trade. Carl Dipman explained that the open displays in his Louisville model store were designed "to take advantage of the shopping instinct in women in such a manner as to increase sales." Just as White inventors considered visual display to have an irresistible effect on African American customers, Dipman emphasized the susceptibility of women shoppers. "Open shelving gives touch and sight a chance to work,—and as women see and handle so they buy."[85] Southern store inventors like Clarence Saunders and William McCarty designed automated selling environments as an intentional strategy for re-gendering the southern grocery store.

Defining the self-service grocery as a space purely designed for White middle-class female consumption, however, oversimplifies the social dynamic on the racially integrated selling floor. While self-service store inventors were ultimately successful in attracting more White middle-class women into their stores, plenty of men continued to shop in self-service stores. A photograph of a Lexington Piggly Wiggly store (fig. 6.5) documents the diversity of self-service shoppers. Self-service stores made stores physically safer for women by spatially controlling male clerks. Quoted in a national trade magazine, one Piggly Wiggly manager explained that self-service appealed to middle-class White women because it reduced their interaction with male clerks. "A woman does not like to run a gauntlet of clerks looking her over when she enters a store. This is sometimes the case in stores where the clerks are not busy and loll over the counter sizing up the ladies." Emphasizing the particular advantages of his chain's store design, he explained, "In Piggly Wiggly stores, this cannot happen for no one but the checker is in front and his back is usually to the door."[86] Self-service did not eliminate men from the store, but it disciplined their behavior. With men distributed in the aisles rather than collected

FIG. 6.5. Piggly Wiggly, 133 North Broadway and Short Street, Lexington, Kentucky, June 20, 1931. Source: Lafayette Studios Photographs, Audio-Visual Archives, University of Kentucky Libraries, Lexington.

in intimidating social circles, with their attention focused on shopping in sobriety, self-service stores were no longer spaces of unbridled male privilege, even when they did not actually become hangouts for women.

## A Well-Laid Trap

Albon Holsey's initial enthusiasm for self-service as liberating gave way to Black customers' increasing charges of unequal treatment as self-service store spaces evolved. Historian Bruce Sinclair emphasizes, "African-Americans have always been interested in new technologies. And, like most other Americans, they have believed in the regenerative powers of technology." African Americans' embrace of self-service stores resonates with the hopes embodied by other new technologies, such as cars and airplanes, that seemed to promise "new economic opportunities, an escape from racism, the chance to claim a place for themselves in American society."[87] But the radical equality of the checkout line was mitigated by other specialized features of self-service design that offered special tools for discriminatory practices. Racial difference was especially a factor in the application of store surveillance. Furthermore, as self-service stores increased in size during the 1920s and 1930s and added products such as fresh meat that could not be sold through self-service methods, Black customers, especially Black women, came to understand self-service stores as spaces designed for racial discrimination, not equality.

Self-service store designs reflected the priorities of the White inventors who created them. In particular, the surveillance features of self-service stores, which were often intended to be invisible to customers, were not racially neutral since clerks used them strategically in practice to target customers of color. The first Piggly Wiggly design featured a gallery over the shelves where a clerk could patrol customers below. Jitney Jungle designer William McCarty offered an improvement of that design, which he explained was "repulsive to the majority of customers of integrity, and tends to exclude this more desirable class of customers from the store." Instead of paying the salary of an additional security guard, the Jitney Jungle design made it possible for the clerk at the front desk to also serve "as a watchman or detective without being considered as such by the customers."[88] Another popular option for self-service stores was to create a second-floor office space with an observation window offering the owner a view of workers and customers below. In Biel's Self-Service Grocery in Corpus Christi, Texas, the manager's office on the second floor offered a bird's-eye view of the entire selling space.[89]

FIG. 6.6. Biel's Self-Service Grocery, ca. 1934, Corpus Christi, Texas. Store owner Emil Biel reportedly suffered from severe arthritis and may have been reluctant to come downstairs to be photographed with his employees. Looking down on the retail space from the window of his second-floor office in the rear of the store, Biel had a commanding view of the entire store. *Source:* Itinerant Photographer Collection, Harry Ransom Center, University of Texas at Austin.

In Austin, Texas, Piggly Wiggly clerks exploited the surveillance mechanisms inside the store to target unsuspecting customers. "A well-laid trap Tuesday resulted in the arrest of two Mexicans," the *Austin American* newspaper reported in March 1922. "Employees of the Piggly Wiggly store had become suspicious that some of their customers were taking advantage of the help-yourself style of service and were dodging the cashier's stand. A floor walker was stationed at an advantageous point to keep an eye on the string of customers and the arrests resulted."[90] The clerks accused the two customers of stealing a quarter of a pound of butter and a box of cinnamon. The police arrested at least two other Mexican customers as a result of the clerks' surveillance, suggesting that the use of self-service features were routinely used for racial profiling. "Caught in the theft of a can of paprika valued at nine cents," a Mexican woman was charged with a misdemeanor. "Recently another Mexican woman was arrested at the request of the manager of this store for the alleged theft of a small can of condensed milk."[91]

As the small groceteria of the World War I era gave way to the combination store of the 1920s, the incorporation of clerk service counters reintroduced the possibility for differential treatment of customers and undermined the depersonalization of self-service. Charles Johnson reported, "The older counter arrangement still persists in the meat market, where each customer must be given personal service. It is here that Negro informants experience most embarrassment and more discrimination in chain stores."[92] Meat could not be sold through self-service methods, and the integration of meat counters along self-service pathways changed the social dynamic of the store.

Two examples vividly demonstrate that African American customers faced more than verbal incivility and discrimination in routine shopping encounters; they also risked physical brutality. Atlanta Piggly Wiggly customer Ruby Morton sent her twelve-year-old son to buy fifteen cents' worth of shinbones. When he got home with the meat, Mrs. Morton discovered that it was spoiled and sent her nineteen-year-old son back to the store to return it. When he was unsuccessful, the woman went to the store herself. The clerk not only refused to refund the money or replace the spoiled meat, he threatened to "slap the hell out of [her]" if she didn't leave. When Morton persisted, the clerk hit her, and an officer on duty joined the attack, slapping her, wrenching her head and neck and tearing clothes from her body. She was pregnant at the time. The police arrested Morton, and a court fined her ten dollars plus two dollars in court costs on a charge of disorderly conduct.[93]

The meat counter was once again the site of a brutal attack on Black customer Lillian Banks when she attempted to return spoiled meat sold to her daughter by a Piggly Wiggly store manager. She too was fined for disorderly conduct, but in this case the clerk was charged with assault and battery for smashing Banks in the head with a gallon vinegar jar. At the hearing Banks detailed her experience. "The store manager, she said, struck her first with a metal scoop, then burst a vinegar jar in her face, [and] struck her in the stomach with his fist."[94] The manager openly admitted he had attacked Banks but claimed she had provoked him by throwing the spoiled meat in his face. Two other White customers who witnessed the attack denied the manager's claims. One of them reported that he had "leaped over the meat counter and [begun] beating Mrs. Banks unmercifully, finally smashing the vinegar jar in her face." The witness described the manager as husky and detailed how he "forced Mrs. Banks over to a corner of the store continuing to hit and kick her, despite her plaintive cries."[95] Even with the corroborating testimony of White witnesses in support of Mrs. Banks's account, an all-White jury acquitted the clerk.

People of color faced closer scrutiny by clerks, and, as self-service became a more widespread retailing practice, African American women complained about being targeted more than other customers in store surveillance. In a survey conducted in Racine, Wisconsin, in 1970, after self-service had become standard retailing practice in supermarkets, several women reported that they felt Black customers were more closely watched for stealing than other customers. One, Geraldine Moore, reported, "I think that they watch Black people for stealing more in the larger stores like Turnstyle and Zayres." Maggie Hall agreed: "Turnstyle in particular watches Black people for stealing, more so than any other store. However, they all watch us especially."[96]

Though diverse customers perceived that self-service stores equalized the shopping experience, the rhetoric of democracy and equality associated with American self-service must be tempered by the intrinsic tools for social control built into machines for automatic selling. Evaluating the Jim Crow origins of self-service stores and recognizing the importance of southern inventors and their customers in the creation of self-service as a new social practice offers new insights about the history of mass retailing in the United States. Southern self-service stores do not represent a disconnected branch of self-service experimentation that developed in isolation. The most influential self-service store in the United States before 1940 was designed to serve a culture of segregation and White supremacy.

# Super-Sizing Self-Service in the 1930s

The 1930s marked a decisive turning point in the history of the American self-service store. Just as the economic pressures generated by the labor shortages and food price inflation of World War I had sparked the initial round of self-service experimentation in the 1910s, the Great Depression and war in Europe created economic and social pressures that would transform self-service from a specialized retailing method to an industry standard by the end of the decade. In December 1932, a new self-service store opened in Elizabeth, New Jersey, a factory town and shipbuilding center on the Newark Bay. To keep costs to a minimum the owners built the store fixtures on-site out of cheap pine. They stacked market baskets near the door. Like self-service shoppers anywhere, customers picked up a basket and walked unattended around the store, "helping themselves to whatever attracted them." Then, "With baskets loaded, they returned to the cashier's booth, had their purchases checked, paid for them and left."[1] So far the story is unremarkable. What made this store unlike self-service stores that came before it was its immense size—about fifty thousand square feet. The Big Bear Super Market, installed in an abandoned car factory at the edge of town, devoted only about 30 percent of the space to packaged food display. The rest of the space was filled by a variety of counter-service concessions. Nevertheless, the huge square footage allocated to self-service groceries was unprecedented and drove enormous profits for the store.

Big Bear was started by Robert M. Otis and Roy O. Dawson, both of whom had worked for Piggly Wiggly, among other chain retailers. During their first year of operation, Otis and Dawson reported, "This crude make-shift grocery department, with no service to render except mass displays of canned and packaged foods, popularly priced, sold $2,188,403.20 or approximately 50 per cent of the total sales."[2] When A&P had achieved sales of $352 million in a twelve-month period ending in February 1925, it had been a record-shattering benchmark—more than any individual retailer had ever sold in a single year.[3] But the nation's dominant food chain had reached that volume by selling merchandise in thousands of stores. Big Bear had sold millions in only one huge store. When Big Bear opened a new supermarket in Jersey City, on December 8, 1932, there were two thousand customers waiting at the door. The estimated average sale per person was between $1.50 and $2.00. Within the first six weeks the store had generated over half a million dollars in sales.[4] Supermarkets rocked the chain world.

Max M. Zimmerman, founder of the Super Market Institute, enthused that the Big Bear profits dramatically demonstrated "the difference in mass merchandising under one roof" compared to the typical chain strategy of spreading out expenses and increasing sales volume by opening more stores.[5] During the 1930s Zimmerman, a long-time contributing editor to *Printers Ink*, was a widely recognized expert on chain stores. He was one of the first to study the economic impact of supermarkets, reporting that independent supermarkets in Los Angeles had reduced the percentage of food business done by the grocery chains from 42 percent to 25 percent by 1935.[6] Deep price discounts brought Depression-era customers to supermarkets in droves, some stores "doing more business in one week than the average retailer [did] in a year," Zimmerman reported.[7] In Paterson, New Jersey, fifty percent of Big Bear shoppers were men, "many unemployed, who [drove] many miles for their food supplies."[8] By the end of the 1930s, the major corporate chains were converting their stores to self-service operation and closing smaller, underperforming stores.

Max Zimmerman did not simply study supermarkets from afar. He was one of the architects of a new supermarket industry. In May 1937 Zimmerman invited a small group of the most successful supermarket operators to his office to plan the first Super Market Institute.[9] His books on supermarket history have profoundly shaped scholarly understanding of the origins of supermarkets. His obituary noted that his 1955 book, *The Super Market: A Revolution in Distribution*, was "regarded as the definitive history of the supermarket industry."[10] It remains an influential source in scholarship about the origins of American supermarkets. In his historical account, Zimmerman acknowledged the importance of Piggly Wiggly but traced the origins of the supermarket to the largest self-service stores of the late 1920s and early 1930s. He focused on some of the most successful regional self-service chains of early twentieth century, including Ralphs Grocery Company and Alpha Beta Food Markets of Los Angeles, and J. Weingarten, Inc., Henke & Pillot, Inc., and the ABC Stores, Inc., of Houston, which had all opened self-service stores that were unusually large before 1932, ranging from six thousand to twelve thousand square feet.[11] But supermarkets also depended very much on the design principles established by the small groceterias where customers had been learning to serve themselves for two decades.[12]

The self-service retailing revolution had started in small stores and the small-business pioneers of self-service continued to play an important role in supermarket innovations of the 1930s. Efforts to apply self-service retailing methods on the scale of the supermarket and to expand self-service to products that had proven resistant to self-service methods required a new round of store experimentation to ensure that large store spaces worked effectively as orderly machines for automatic selling. Local store spaces continued to serve throughout the 1930s as important sites of experimentation to make the social practice of self-service work in new ways.

Scholars have studied a variety of complex factors that gave rise to supermarkets in the 1930s. Anti-chain taxes on the number of store units in some states encouraged chains to close smaller underperforming stores and open larger stores. Customers' changing shopping habits, diffusion of the automobile, and economic losses of small-business owners during the Great Depression created strong pressures for remaking the retail landscape during the 1930s.[13] Historian Tracey Deutsch also points to the important role of government policy—particularly the regulations and price controls of the National Recovery Administration—in the spread of chain supermarkets.[14] Throughout the 1930s and 1940s, grocery stores were increasingly embedded in government regulations regarding food prices, rationing, wages, and sales taxes that strained the management resources of small-business owners. Large retail firms had deeper cash reserves and management resources to weather the economic downturn, the demands of regulation, and the store improvements necessary for keeping up with the competition. All of these factors provided fertile soil for the success of supermarkets in the 1930s.

Less well understood in this history of supermarket origins are the spatial challenges and opportunities of super-sizing self-service. At first glance, enlarging a self-service store might appear to be a simple matter of increasing the number of aisles in the store and putting a greater variety of goods on display. But applying self-service to the larger physical scale of supermarkets presented a variety of new practical challenges for store design and functionality.

During the interwar years the core principles of self-service store experimentation had included compartmentalizing self-service as a specialized form of retailing, systemizing self-service pathways for the work of customers and clerks, mobilizing merchandise to maximize sales, and creating sensory design strategies for automating salesmanship. These aspects of self-service store design continued to shape experimentation throughout the 1930s as local stores worked to coordinate methods of product display, customer mobility, and efficient checkout to re-create systems for automatic selling in larger stores.

The extent to which supermarkets would be defined by self-service operation was an open question before 1940. If self-service was to be considered a defining feature of supermarket design, how much of the store operation had to be based on self-service methods to be called a supermarket, especially since some food products were not packaged in ways that made self-service retailing practical? In 1939 the Department of Commerce focused on three key variables in evaluating whether a food store should be called a supermarket: "Among questions unsettled are whether a supermarket must include a meat department, whether it must limit customer service to self-service and cash-carry or may offer full service, and what minimum sales-size is required of a food store before it may be classified as a supermarket." [15] These three elements—selling fresh meat, store arrangement for self-service methods, and the question of store size—presented important, interrelated challenges for store design.

Making self-service work in supermarkets required rethinking the physical strategies of automatic salesmanship and integrating products resistant to self-service methods—none more important than the butcher counter. Local store operators, both independents and chains, experimented with new strategies for systematizing the shopping pathway, mobilizing merchandise, and silent salesmanship. Integrating service departments along the self-service pathway and connecting them to a centralized checkout process at the end of the self-service pathway helped to break down the urge to compartmentalize the self-service grocery department as a specialized retail space. Experimentation was driven not simply by the business goals of increasing volume sales and lowering operating expenses. It was also inspired by the need to reestablish social controls for automatic selling that were diluted or disrupted in supersizing self-service. World War I–era groceterias had applied cafeteria design to organize shoppers along orderly shopping pathways. The first warehouse supermarkets, by comparison, seemed to foster a frenzied shopping free-for-all.

The Big Bear self-service grocery department was enormous compared to the original four-aisle Piggly Wiggly store.[16] No phalanx of contiguous shelving guided customers into a singular circuitous pathway. With plenty of space to spread out, customers circulated around multiple island shelving units that filled the cavernous floor space. At first glance it is the differences that seem to stand out. But a floor plan documenting a Big Bear store in Jersey City shows how existing self-service principles of store arrangement, developed in smaller stores of the 1920s, influenced the arrangement of supermarkets. Like stores of the 1920s, the self-service grocery department was physically compartmentalized as a specialized retailing space, separated from the meat, produce, and bakery counters that were operated by independent counter-service concessions on the other side of the store. To enter the self-service grocery space, customers had to walk through the entire length of the concession space—an intentional design strategy for increasing concession sales. There were no entry or exit turnstiles to control access to the self-service space, but basket bins walled it off from the rest of the store. Big Bear customers used the same hand-held market baskets found in smaller stores to collect packaged groceries. Customers might choose different pathways around the thirty-six shelving units arranged in grid formation, but there was only one way out. Everybody had to pass through one of the cashier booths that lined either side of the entry, where they paid for their grocery purchases before exiting the self-service section of the store.

Though the New Jersey Big Bear store plan shown in figure 7.1 exhibits a rigorous geometric order, represented in the grid-patterned layout, the first supermarkets were perceived as socially chaotic. Photographs of crowded store interiors showed aisles filled with people pressed shoulder to shoulder.[17] The orderly pathway of the patented self-service store was obliterated in the mass confusion of the warehouse supermarket. "It was a common sight to see women fighting for their food bargains just as women struggle in a department store during bargain sales," Max Zimmerman observed.[18] It was also a time of widespread unemployment, when officials worried about food riots, like the hungry protesters who had destroyed the Standard Grocery store in downtown Oklahoma City.[19] Since the new warehouse supermarkets had names like Big Bear, Big Tiger, and Big Bull, and their slogans emphasized "smashing prices" or "price wrecking," some analysts referred to them as "wild animal

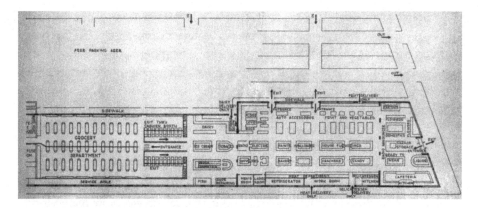

FIG. 7.1. Carl Dipman included a floor plan of the Jersey City Big Bear as an example of the "warehouse type of super-market" in his book on modern food stores. The self-service grocery space to the left featured low prices and was positioned so customers had to "pass the concessions coming and going in an endeavor to make the concession rentals profitable." *Source:* Dipman, *Modern Food Stores,* 21.

stores."[20] Established chain store leaders feared that independent supermarket owners flouted social norms and encouraged disorder. Supermarkets created towering merchandise displays, promoted spectacle sales, gave away thousands of free souvenirs, and sponsored mass cooking demonstrations fostering a carnival atmosphere. Six thousand Miami residents reportedly showed up for a public "super wedding" at Carle's supermarket based on an advertising campaign to promote the store.[21] Zimmerman attributed the chaos to the "restless, bargain-hunting women" self-service grocers had been working to attract for a decade. "[Set free in the supermarket, they] love to follow crowds. They love the bizarre, the dramatic, screeching price cuts, the ballyhoo and even self-service," Zimmerman said, evoking retailers' view of women as irrational consumers exercising their shopping instincts.[22] The first supermarkets on the East Coast, opened in abandoned warehouses at the urban periphery, threatened to undermine the carefully crafted controls of self-service design. "Four walls—crude floors [and] bare ceilings—flimsy fixtures—glaring lights and gaudy signs—merchandise piled anywhere and apparently any old way— that's the inside of a typical 'cheapy' in the food field," an established retailer complained.[23]

One of the most prominent food industry critics of supermarkets in the 1930s was Carl Dipman, editor of *Progressive Grocer* magazine. He had designed a model store for the Commerce Department in 1929 focusing on principles of open display that promoted efficient clerk service. His first book on best principles of modern grocery store operation, published in 1931, did not contain a single chapter on self-service store arrangement and included only one floor plan of a self-service store.[24] Dipman, though an enthusiastic proponent of modernizing grocery stores, initially considered supermarkets to be a step in the wrong direction. "In the early stages of development, many of the super-markets were very strange stores indeed," he wrote in 1939, "and we frequently referred to them as monstrosities." They lacked the organized efficiency of stores with more refined (and expensive) finishes. He described them as "rambling," suggesting that self-service store methods did not automatically ensure systematic selling. Dipman did not care much for the warehouse supermarket, but he did predict a "splendid future" for "the comparatively large food market with a front of from twenty-five to forty feet." In the same 1939 article, he noted that corporate chains had recently joined independent store owners in the trend toward larger self-service stores. "If you wish to call these self-service stores with from $100,000 to $250,000 volume super-markets, then you may safely say we shall have many more super-markets."[25]

By the end of the decade, Dipman had become the foremost proponent of self-service stores. He published the first book on self-service and semi-self-service store arrangement in 1940, offering floor plans and photographs of store interiors that documented a wide variety of self-service stores across the country. A reviewer for the *Journal of Marketing* suggested, "A better title might have been 'A Handbook on the Layout of Self-Service Food Stores.'" The reviewer complained, "No treatment is made of management problems such as pricing, buying, or policy."[26] But the absence of traditional business topics in the book underscores the centrality of store arrangement for operationalizing self-service retailing methods. Dipman asserted that the main challenge store operators faced was the integration of service and self-service features in store arrangement, and he presented examples of store arrangements and design features from chain and independent operations around the country.[27] While his goal was to give local grocers practical advice about how to convert their stores to self-service, Dipman documented the innovation and variety of experimentation that smaller regional stores were already doing during the 1930s. Local grocers played a central role in experimenting with technologies that systematized mass displays and mobilized merchandize into orderly pathways for producing volume sales.

Maximizing supermarket efficiencies required more than an investment in nicer fixtures and finishes; it required rethinking how fixtures were designed to work together. From the earliest patented store designs, volume sales in the self-service store depended on facilitating traffic flow along orderly pathways that led to rapid checkout at the exit. The mobility of shoppers and store products had been a focus of intense design experimentation since the advent of the self-service store. The most practical and affordable solution for the small store had been the market basket. But inventors experimented with modified toy wagons, pulley systems, turntables, monorails for suspending baskets within arm's reach, and conveyor belts for circulating products. Physically attached to shelving or monorails, or facilitated by strategically placed shelf rests, these technologies often defined fixed pathways that supported the primary goal of the self-service store—to ensure that customers would see all of the goods in the store. With their wider aisles and open circulation, supermarkets seemingly gave customers more freedom than ever before to choose their own route through the store. Nevertheless, the new technologies of display and customer mobility produced by inventors in larger store spaces should not be understood as isolated inventions. They were intended to work together as parts of an integrated system of automatic selling designed to shape customer pathways to produce maximum sales.

Larger stores offered the opportunity to arrange more products on the selling floor. "Mass has a magic selling power," Dipman declared. But simply piling up the goods on the floor did not ensure sales in a systematic or predictable way. Dipman inadvertently echoed Clarence Saunders when he wrote, "The objective in a self-service grocery department is to expose *all* the merchandise to consumers on each visit to the store." The challenge was to achieve that goal while allowing customers to take different routes. "To all outward appearances the element of selling has almost disappeared from the modern self-service store," Dipman declared.[28] One early supermarket grocer reported, "The size, the height and the depth of the display, plays a very important part in unconsciously stimulating the consumers to buy."[29] Mass had magic selling power because systematized silent salesmanship was invisible.

In his 1929 model store, Carl Dipman had used tables arranged in the center of the store to create open "island" displays and encourage customers to serve themselves.[30] But flat tables did not raise products to eye level and had limited capacity for holding merchandise, and products stored on the floor under tables were hard for customers to see. For self-service store arrangement Dipman recommended gondola shelving units (fig. 7.2) because the stepped-back shelves raised products to eye level and made displays easy to view. They could be deep to reduce the labor of restocking, and, with their rounded corners and scalability, floating gondola units were the most effective mechanism for arranging self-service pathways in the expansive center floor space of larger stores. The fact that they could be viewed on all sides helped to propel customers around and through the space. Amply sized gondolas made mass displays more visible but contained and organized them so that they would not impede traffic.[31] Displays at the ends of gondolas enticed customers to move forward, rounding the corner to the next aisle. "End displays receive unusual attention from customers for they are in the direct line of circulation."[32] Picturing examples from stores across the United States, Dipman emphasized the versatility of gondolas, which could be scaled to fit large or small spaces. Gondolas might be arranged in rows to form rectilinear paths, or slanted at an angle to direct the eye, and the customer's route, strategically to particular departments in a larger store. Dipman observed the ways that progressive grocers arranged shelving patterns and product displays to pull customers through the store, ensuring that they viewed all the merchandise. Silent salesmanship prevailed in the subtlety of aisle displays that halted the progress of shoppers, at which point they might observe other shoppers and be influenced by their purchases. The low height of gondola shelves also contributed to the overall visibility of the store, making it easier for customers to get the lay of the land and for clerks to surveil the store, discouraging theft.

Beyond establishing self-service pathways, gondolas served multiple functions for automating salesmanship. Scaled to the human body, a properly designed gondola ensured that products could be displayed within easy reach. Dipman emphasized, "To an amazing extent women 'buy through their eyes' in almost every kind of store. But customers who wait on themselves buy through their eyes *entirely*."[33] Thus gondola shelving units could be built so that shelves closest to the floor could be slanted to tilt merchandise up and make labels easier to scan.[34] The ample capacity of gondola shelving also made it possible to put more merchandise directly on the selling floor rather than stockroom storage and thus reduced the labor of restocking.

But the power of mass display would always be limited by the practical limitations of a hand-held basket. One grocer reported, "Early in our Super Market experience, we found out that the average customer will not carry a $5.00 bundle of groceries around the market. It is too much work and too

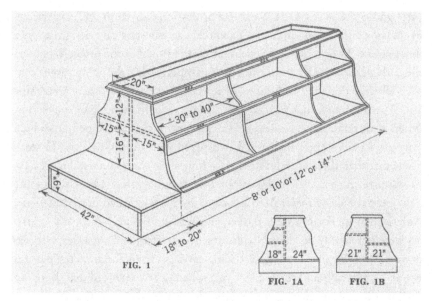

FIG. 7.2. Gondola shelf design recommended by Carl Dipman for organizing the central store space. *Source:* Dipman and O'Brien, *Self-Service and Semi-Self-Service Food Stores*, 75.

tiresome. As a result, many of our customers who came into our market with the intention of buying $5.00 or $10.00 worth of merchandise, after they filled up a basket, got tired and stopped buying." The grocer responded by creating a simple grocery cart using a box set on top of four legs "with ten cent casters for wheels." He found that the shopping cart increased average sales in his store more than $2.00 per customer, especially when families shopped together. "When [the] father comes along, he picks up the tid-bits he likes and sneaks them in [into the cart]—and so do the kids. And we find that these little shoppers['] go-carts are the greatest salesmen ever put into our markets."[35] Self-service grocers experimented with different strategies for putting market baskets on wheels.

Detailed examination of the features inventors included in their early designs shows the interconnections between shopping cart designs and store spaces. As French sociologist Catherine Grandclement puts it, "To configure the shopping cart meant, at least in part, to reconfigure the market." With a focus on the sociology of invention, Grandclement demonstrates that the invention of the shopping cart was a collective process of innovation by multiple actors, not all of whom were grocers. A variety of experimental designs for basket carriers were available by the late 1930s, and experimentation continued throughout the 1940s. Orla Watson, a professional inventor with experience in the air-conditioning industry, patented a telescoping cart design in 1947 that became the dominant supermarket shopping cart of the 1950s. What sets the early versions apart from the postwar supermarket shopping cart is that they all were designed to hold traditional market baskets. There were variations in the frame that formed the carriage—some with basket platforms, others with removeable baskets held in place with clamps. Some frames held only one basket, others included a two-tiered shelf for holding two baskets. Some carts had three wheels rather than four as inventors tinkered with ways to stabilize the vehicle. At least four cart manufacturers advertised in the new journal *Super Market Merchandising* by 1937—United Steel and Wire, American Wire Form, Roll'er Basket, and Folding Basket.[36] But basket carriers were not simply produced by distant manufacturing companies. Grocers played a key role in designing or testing carriages to fit the ways their stores worked, practically and culturally. Grocers had to be convinced that shopping carts could work in their stores, and they were in the best position to observe the difficulty or ease customers had in using them as inventors worked to improve their design.

The invention of shopping carts offers an important example of the role of regional grocery stores in supermarket experimentation. Local store owners' daily interactions with customers and close observation of how they used the store remained a key part of the grassroots experimentation of self-service methods. In 1934 Sylvan Goldman's Standard Food Market chain in Oklahoma City built its largest market to date with a selling space of 50 by 140 feet (7,000 square feet) in a suburban location with a large parking lot. Zimmerman estimated that the average size of a supermarket before 1935 was about 12,000 square feet, so the new Standard store was smaller than most supermarkets of the day.[37] Until 1937, the Standard Food Markets used handheld market baskets, even as the stores got larger and the products diversified. As customers traversed the retail space in his newest store, Goldman instructed his clerks to watch for people with heavy baskets and offer them empty ones to continue their shopping. Clerks took the filled baskets to check stands where the customer could retrieve them when they were ready to pay. Of course, this inefficient use of clerk labor defeated the larger goals of systematized self-service. Goldman worked with his maintenance man and carpenter, Fred Young, to turn a folding chair into a collapsible carriage on wheels. After several months of experimentation Goldman applied for a patent for his basket carrier in May 1937.

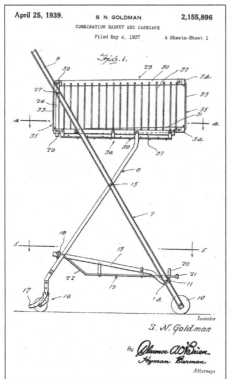
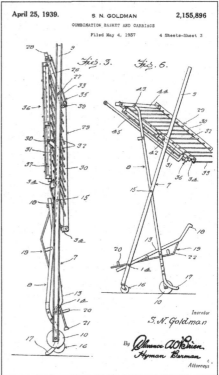

FIG. 7.3. Sylvan Goldman based his first shopping cart design on a folding lawn chair. His patent shows the fully open and folded versions of the invention. *Source:* Goldman, Combination Basket and Carriage patent.

Goldman invented his cart with the medium-sized store in mind, putting an ordinary market basket on a foldable carriage. With floor space at a premium, the collapsible cart "when not in use ... [could] be folded into compact form for convenient placement in an out-of-the-way location in the store."[38] To maximize the storage potential of the invention, Goldman's patent indicated, the wire market basket too was collapsible and could be folded automatically with the carriage so that the whole apparatus could be stored flat. Goldman spent the summer of 1937 working to convince his reluctant Oklahoma customers to use the new basket carriers. At the same time, Goldman displayed his carrier at the first Super Market Institute that year, hoping to promote his shopping cart to other store owners. But initial efforts to sell the carts to other grocery owners met with reluctance as well. Store owners feared that "shoppers' children would regard the carts as playthings and race them up and down the aisles, knocking merchandise off shelves and into customers, causing injuries." Further, "Lawsuits might ensue from cart-related accidents, the storekeepers said, and thus the carriers' possible utility simply did not warrant the risks involved."[39] Indeed, stabilizing the rolling cart had been a key concern of Goldman and Young when in their first trials the carriage folded unpredictably or the basket buckled dangerously or the wheels fell off when the cart navigated a curb. Certainly, grocers who experimented with shopping cart design hoped to maximize sales by making it easier for customers to carry more products. But grocers also designed their basket carrying systems to function effectively along self-service pathways. Goldman's shopping cart reflected the space for new wider aisles in his larger store, the challenges of finding adequate storage space for idle carts, his concerns for ensuring connections between the shopping apparatus and the checkout system, and daily encounters with store customers he observed using the basket carriers in intended and unintended ways.

In hindsight, basket carriers and shopping carts appear to offer straightforward advantages for the self-service system—making it possible for customers to carry (and thus buy) more products and speeding up the flow of goods through the store. But in the developmental stages of inventing the self-service store, there was no standardized vehicle for mobilizing shopping. As stores evolved, there were new practical challenges for owners. Stores had to be large enough to offer wide aisles so that customers could navigate displays without damaging unsold products. Storage of idle shopping carts also required floor space. Carts themselves were more expensive for small retailers to buy than traditional market baskets. Customers resisted using carts or used carts in unintended ways, such as rolling their children around in them rather than using them to hold more products. The extra work of unloading carts at checkout stations slowed down the system, sometimes creating longer lines at the checkout. The turnstile had been the defining mechanism of the first generation of self-service stores, but turnstiles in existing self-service stores impeded the use of shopping carts to transport goods from store to parking lot. Integrating shopping carts required rethinking traffic flow and methods for controlling customers along the self-service pathway.

The most consequential change in self-service store design during the 1930s, however, was the integration of butcher counters. The original goal of the first generation of groceterias had been to eliminate counter service on the selling floor. Points of congestion created by service counters had always been considered antithetical to the production of volume sales that was the core purpose of the self-service store. Nevertheless, self-service grocers enthusiastically embraced the challenge of selling fresh meat during the 1930s, even though it added significant overhead not only to the costs of installing new refrigeration systems but also to the skilled labor required for daily operation of the meat counter. Carcasses did not arrive at the grocery store in ready-made packages like canned beans, and preserving and displaying freshly cut chops and steaks entailed expensive investment in skilled labor and refrigeration technology. The challenge for local store designers was not only how to package meat for self-service operation but also how to integrate counter-service meat departments along the self-service pathway.

## Fresh Meat: The Magnet that Pulled Customers through the Store

While many counter-service grocery stores had begun to incorporate fresh meat into their departmentalized combination stores during the 1920s, selling fresh meat was a different kind of challenge for self-service grocers. Store size was not the issue. Even small counter-service stores sold meat. In 1929 Carl Dipman had included a "model meat department" in his influential eight-hundred-square-foot model store. Dipman's model meat department consisted of an eight-foot-long refrigerated display case at the back of the store, equipped with a slicer, a grinder, and a meat block for cutting meat to order. These were needed, Dipman reasoned: "Such a large percentage of the meat business is now done in grocery stores."[40] By 1939 the trend was even clearer as the Commerce Department reported that almost half of all grocery stores in the United States sold fresh meat.[41] At the same time they also declared, "Self-service is nearly impossible in the meat department."[42] Historian Roger Horowitz notes, "At the end of World War II there were virtually no self-service meat departments [in American grocery stores]."[43] After the war, manufacturers like Armour and DuPont promoted innovations in cellophane-wrapped self-service meat for the supermarket industry. Regional grocery chains experimented with different strategies for packaging self-service meat inside the store or centralizing the process in off-site meat packaging operations.[44] But self-service grocers had made a decisive commitment to selling fresh meat a decade earlier. By 1939 74 percent self-service stores sold fresh meat, regardless of store size.[45] So many self-service store operators had incorporated meat departments that selling fresh meat was one of the three defining features the Commerce Department identified (in addition to sales volume and self-service store format) for evaluating whether a store could be considered a supermarket.[46] That is an astonishing development given the challenges of incorporating clerk-service counters into self-service store designs.

The necessity of cutting meat to order was a major challenge for self-service retailing systems, and the spatial experiments for addressing it recalibrated the overall functioning of self-service store systems. It is important to understand why self-service grocers embraced fresh meat in the 1930s, how they integrated the counter-service requirements of meat and deli retailing along the self-service grocery pathway, and what the significance of those changes was for re-inventing the self-service store itself. In their Big Bear supermarket, Otis and Dawson had physically separated the counter-service meat department on the opposite side of the building from the self-service grocery area. Smaller stores were forced to figure out how to integrate cut-to-order meat counters along the self-service pathway, and in the process they lessened the urge to compartmentalize the self-service space as a specialized spatial system.

Fresh meat counters offered powerful incentives to self-service store owners, not only because they needed to compete with full-service combination stores but also because selling meat offered important advantages to self-service stores in particular. The Commerce Department survey of Louisville grocery stores documented the importance of meat sales in all neighborhoods regardless of the social class of their residents: "While the high-income communities buy choice cuts of meat, which naturally cost more than the cheaper cuts making up the meat ration of the low-income classes, communities of low income are, nevertheless[,] large meat consumers and, despite the fact that they buy less expensive cuts, produce the highest sales ratios for their stores."[47]

The high margin on meat sales and reliable customer demand were powerful incentives for grocers to provide fresh meat in their stores regardless of retailing method. But because customers liked to personally select their own meat cuts, that also ensured regular foot traffic and repeat customers for self-service grocers. As stores increasingly sold the same brand name products, self-service grocers embraced fresh meat counters as a key strategy for distinguishing their stores from the crowd and developing a loyal customer base. The majority of self-service grocers incorporated fresh meat departments inside their stores during the 1930s, especially in places where self-service was already well-established, and the process was not driven by the largest stores alone. There were more self-service combination stores in the West

**TABLE 7.1**  Self-Service Grocery and Combination Stores by Region, 1939

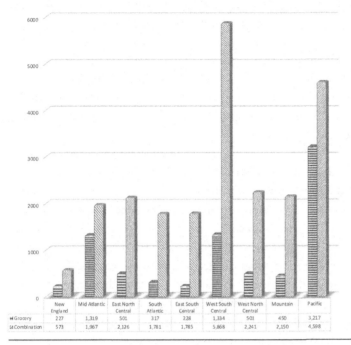

| | New England | Mid Atlantic | East North Central | South Atlantic | East South Central | West South Central | West North Central | Mountain | Pacific |
|---|---|---|---|---|---|---|---|---|---|
| Grocery | 227 | 1,319 | 501 | 317 | 228 | 1,334 | 501 | 450 | 3,217 |
| Combination | 573 | 1,967 | 2,126 | 1,781 | 1,785 | 5,868 | 2,241 | 2,150 | 4,598 |

NOTE: Grocery stores did not sell fresh meat. Combination stores included groceries and fresh meat counters. By 1939, the majority of self-service stores in every region of the country sold fresh meat.
SOURCE: U.S. Department of Commerce, Bureau of the Census, *Sixteenth Census of the United States: 1940, Census of Business: Retail Trade, 1939, Supermarkets and Self-Service Food Stores* (Washington, D.C., 1941).
TABLE: Self-Service Grocery and Combination Stores by Geographic Division.

South Central region, where Texas dominated self-service experimentation and smaller independent owners prevailed, than in the Mid-Atlantic or New England. In the Pacific West, where Southern California supermarkets played such an influential role in the industry, self-service grocery stores without meats continued to occupy a more important place in the retail landscape than in other regions of the country.

In 1938 Max Zimmerman published the results of his supermarket survey in *Harvard Business Review*, estimating that by the time of publication there would be between twenty-five hundred and three thousand supermarkets in the country. Zimmerman reported that supermarkets had "spread into all sections *except* [emphasis mine] in certain parts of the South and the Middle West." California, New York, Michigan, and New Jersey had more supermarkets than most other states.[48] But Zimmerman's regional portrait of the supermarket is misleading. When we consider the sale of fresh meat in self-service stores as a factor in supermarket development, 41 percent of all self-service combination stores were in the South.[49] The South's attraction to self-service unfolded in small independent stores or small local chains, and these grocers were more likely to sell fresh meat than self-service grocers in other parts of the country. By 1939 independent store owners, not chains, dominated experimentation with including fresh meat in self-service stores nationally, except in the Northeast. Self-service stores were newer there, where chain stores were converting to self-service. In the South and West, where self-service stores were older, independent grocers led experimentation.

Meat counters, often leased by independent butchers, were purposefully integrated into the self-service pathway and offered new strategies for speeding up or slowing down the pathway to entice customers to buy more. Zimmerman called the meat department "the magnet which attracts the customer to the store and plays perhaps the decisive part in influencing her purchase of her other groceries and perishables." He noted that most store operators located the meat department at the back of the store "in order to 'pull' the traffic past all the merchandise displays before they reach the meat section."[50] But full-service meat counters where butchers cut steaks and chops to order created new challenges for the smooth operation of the self-service system. The meat counter at the back of the store might clog up the self-service pathway at rush hour as customers lined up to be served by the meat cutters and wrappers.

Dipman thought that the selling power of the store would be stronger if meat departments were at the front door because women made so many shopping decisions based on meal planning and choice of meat often determined other purchases. "Let us consider theoretically how a market would be arranged if there were no other considerations except the housewife's *buying mind*," Carl Dipman mused in his advice about self-service store arrangement. He theorized that when she entered the store the foremost thought on the homemaker's mind was meat! "On her shopping list she may simply have the word 'meat,'" Dipman wrote. She might not make up her mind about what she was going to buy until she had a chance to see the meat display or talk with the butcher. "The meat department, therefore, might well be located up front of the store so the housewife can walk directly to it as soon as she enters." Ideally the produce department would be located nearby because, "having bought the center of her meal (meat or a delicatessen item), the housewife's next pressing problem is likely to be the vegetables and fruit to go with

**TABLE 7.2**     Chain and Independent Self-Service Combination Stores by Region, 1939

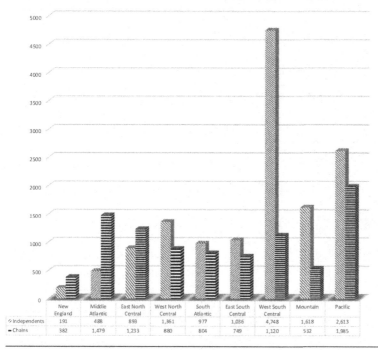

| | New England | Middle Atlantic | East North Central | West North Central | South Atlantic | East South Central | West South Central | Mountain | Pacific |
|---|---|---|---|---|---|---|---|---|---|
| ⊘ Independents | 191 | 488 | 893 | 1,361 | 977 | 1,036 | 4,748 | 1,618 | 2,613 |
| ▬ Chains | 382 | 1,479 | 1,233 | 880 | 804 | 749 | 1,120 | 532 | 1,985 |

SOURCE: U.S. Department of Commerce, Bureau of the Census, *Sixteenth Census of the United States: 1940, Census of Business: Retail Trade, 1939, Supermarkets and Self-Service Food Stores* (Washington, D.C., 1941). TABLE: Chain and Independent Self-Service Combination Stores by Region.

her meal."[51] Arranging the store based on the meal planning strategies of the housewife maximized the sales potential of the store space.

In the real world, the size of the store might dictate a different arrangement, and Dipman acknowledged that small stores often located the meat department at the back of the store. He offered an arrangement of a small combination store (fig. 7.4) only twenty-two feet wide, with space for only three gondolas for display of grocery and baked goods arranged perpendicularly at the center of the store. The meat counter took up considerable space at the back of the store and was integrated along the grocery pathway so that customers circulating around the grocery gondola had to navigate around customers waiting for service at the meat counter. The visual showcase of precut meat mitigated the congestion of cut-to-order meat counters because shoppers no longer had to wait for the butcher to cut and wrap their selections, and the massed display of prepackaged meat increased sales through impulse buys.

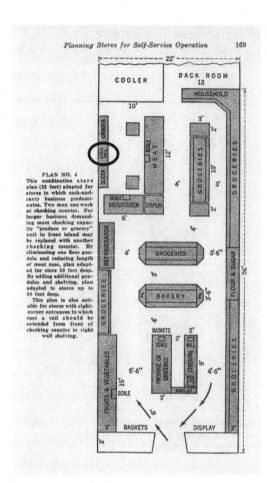

FIG. 7.4. Carl Dipman's plan for a small combination store arrangement. Note the separate cash register in the meat department at the back of the store. *Source:* Dipman, *Self-Service and Semi-Self-Service Food Stores,* 169.

Besides the location of the sales counter, stores had to coordinate the work of butchering and display. Butchering a carcass was the same process whether the meat department was in a traditional counter-service store or a self-service store. What made meat "self-service," however, was precutting, packaging, and displaying chops and steaks or chicken parts for customers to serve themselves with minimal clerk service. The work of converting fresh meat to self-service packaging inside the store was in many ways antithetical to the original goals of self-service store inventors. Self-service stores were expressly designed to reduce labor costs, and so we should not take for granted the fact that so many self-service grocers embraced the labor-intensive requirements of fresh meat retailing. In 1949 a USDA study of food markets that sold self-service meat found that on average each required at least "200 hours of labor from wrappers each week—equivalent to five new workers!" As late as 1966, 75 percent of self-serve meats were still wrapped by hand inside the store, eroding store profits.[52]

Jack W. Dickie's experience offers insights about the risks and rewards for independent store owners, who were among the most avid experimenters with selling self-service meat. Dickie explained how he converted his meat department in Napa, California, to self-service and the reasons why he invested so much effort in the attempt. He started the store conversion by trying to pre-cut all of the meat but found that prepackaging meat with the brown paper used by many butchers was not a useful sales device for self-service since customers liked to see what they were buying. Dickie visited two or three self-service store operations in Southern California to study how they worked and invested in new refrigerator cases and cellophane wrap. But the investment in new display methods did not automatically increase sales. When Dickie reopened his self-service meat market he explained dramatically, "Customer reaction was almost tragic."[53] Dickie estimated that he sold half the meat through self-service that he had sold through traditional counter service. It took six months and a dedicated information campaign and salesmanship effort to regain lost customers.

Dickie warned other grocers that conversion to self-service was also costly. "Self-Service meats require more capital than the conventional type," he wrote. Mass displays of precut meat required more inventory and "more case footage to display your meat." Half-empty refrigerator cases did not have the same psychological impact on customers that full, artfully arranged cases had. Refrigerator cases needed to be able to regulate temperatures for different kinds of meat and be built for display, not just cold storage. Self-service meat also required more labor. "You must have butchers, wrappers, and checkers. These combined obviously require more overhead than just hiring butchers."[54] Maintaining displays could also be labor-intensive. To prevent expensive losses of spoiled meat, Dickie advised, meat display cases needed to be defrosted every twenty-four hours. He said that it was important to stack meat for visual displays carefully to ensure proper air circulation in the case. Despite the expense and labor-intensive challenges of the store conversion, Dickie was nevertheless an enthusiastic promoter of self-service meat. Chief among the advantages he enumerated were the "speed in handling customers" and especially the power of mass displays of meat in promoting impulse buys.

Selling fresh meat was a strategy for keeping the business of small-town customers who might be tempted to drive farther afield to shop for bargains in larger urban stores. Dickie understood his conversion to self-service as key to small-business survival. He cautioned, "The will power to overcome fear or failure in trying something radically new, will have to be possessed by more independent retailers if they are to compete."[55] His concerns were echoed in an article that offered customers in Brownsville, Texas, an overview of the new Piggly Wiggly Meat Markets. "The wide variety of meat products offered by the Piggly Wiggly markets, gives the Valley the advantages of larger city markets and at the same time provides local consumers with the highest quality viands."[56]

While some grocers, like Dickie, experimented with packaging meat for self-service displays, most self-service grocers simply added butcher counters to the store, and that meant integrating a new counter-service department along the self-service pathway. For older self-service stores like Piggly Wiggly, that required a new round of experimentation for configuring store arrangement. Original Piggly Wiggly franchisees had stocked new stores with a variety of processed meat, such as Libby Chicken Loaf and Vienna Sausage, California Sardines, Van Camp Tuna Fish, Wilson Sliced Bacon, and Iowa Pride Picnic Hams.[57] Initially, meat was included on the self-service shelf as long as it was branded and canned (or smoked). But the chain that had originated with a strict adherence to self-service operation was ultimately forced to integrate clerk-service departments. Piggly Wiggly had incorporated fresh produce during the 1920s to compete with the combination store trend, and a few stores had even experimented with including fresh meat departments. During the 1930s the work Piggly Wiggly franchisees did to incorporate fresh meat amounted to a more significant rebranding process for the self-service chain (fig. 7.5). Pigs began to displace the turnstile, forging a new brand identity for the iconic self-service store.

In Greensboro, North Carolina, during the height of the Great Depression, Piggly Wiggly debuted a newly designed meat department that the company asserted was shaped by the stated preferences of female customers across the country. Rather than presenting "great masses of raw meat" in refrigerated display cases, the new meat department worked more like a lunch counter (fig. 7.6). While customers sat at comfortable stools waiting for the meat manager to cut meats to order, the "meat menu" listed the prices of available products and facilitated silent salesmanship by suggesting "plenty of appetizing meat courses" in case shoppers needed meal planning advice. The grand opening advertisement explained an important advantage of the new meat department design: "We don't have to cut up and waste a lot of meat making

FIG. 7.5. Images of pigs were first used by Piggly Wiggly during the 1930s, when the chain began to promote the quality of its meat to set it apart from the competition. Before the 1930s the store symbol was the turnstile. Always attuned to advertising opportunities, perhaps the chain also hoped to capitalize on the popularity of the animated Disney film, *The Three Little Pigs*, released in 1933. *Source: Lubbock (TX) Morning Avalanche*, 4 January 1935.

FIG. 7.6. Ad for a new large "double store" located near the prosperous Fisher Park suburb at the northern edge of downtown Greensboro, a few blocks from the Woolworth on Elm Street where North Carolina A&T students would famously stage a sit-in at the lunch counter in 1960. This meat counter may have been less racially integrated than the first-come, first-served checkout line, perhaps not excluding Black customers from buying meat but requiring that they stand for service. Introducing counter service reintroduced the potential for clerks to differentiate service among customers. *Source: Greensboro (NC) Record*, 22 October 1936.

counter displays and that alone saves you real money."[58] It also streamlined the work of the meat department staff, who were freed from the labor-intensive job of monitoring the refrigerated cases. Dickie had complained about "the customer known as the goffer, or the bottom-of-the-pile shopper," who continually disturbed carefully massed displays. "These things necessitate constant rebuilding," he wrote.[59]

In departmentalized counter-service stores, payments had long been collected at multiple locations throughout the store as customers made purchases at different counters. For example, Dipman included a cash register in the meat department in figure 7.4, separate from the checkout counter at the front of the store. The practice of collecting payments at the meat counter also made sense when meat departments were operated by separate concessions. But Piggly Wiggly advised franchisees, "The selling efficiency of service clerks in the meat, delicatessen and other departments can be increased by making it unnecessary for them to stop and handle money by concentrating the handling of money at the checking stand."[60] Centralizing payment was a key strategy for accountability. The Piggly Wiggly catalog also advised grocers to have checkers periodically check the weight and count of produce and meat sold in service departments: "This method of supervision . . . prevents carelessness and the favoring of friends and relatives." Self-service stores were distinguished by the systematic pathways that led to checkout stations where purchases were totaled and payment was collected at one location near the exit. Increasingly, store operators sought to integrate the meat counter within the self-service pathway by centralizing payment at the checkout counter.

## Checking Out

No part of the self-service pathway has caused more experimentation over the long history of the self-service store than the checkout process at the end of the line. It had been the major focus of Clarence Saunders, who spent a year in Memphis trying to perfect a checking station that worked before he could begin to franchise the first patented store interior. Saunders's patented solution for Piggly Wiggly had configured a checkout counter that coordinated multiple lines of customers but used only one cash register. In small stores during the interwar years, the checkout counter was often designed to serve multiple functions—configured to be operated by a single clerk or perhaps a checker and a wrapper who were also responsible for store surveillance and regulating entry and exit points of the store. As stores got bigger during the 1930s, owners added more checkout stations, but, as Saunders had explained to patent reviewers, simply multiplying checkout lines did not ensure the functionality of the self-service pathway. Adding counters meant higher expenses for clerks to staff them and additional equipment expenses for cash registers and store equipment. Supermarkets required multiple checkout stands to handle a large volume of business, and ensuring fast service often meant staffing checkout counters with multiple clerks. Beyond the concern for speeding up the checkout process, store arrangements of the 1930s show the importance of centralized checkout for controlling cash transactions and coordinating multiple checkout counters with the self-service pathway.

When supermarket store operators met at the first Super Market Institute in 1937, checkout was a subject of considerable conversation. According to Zimmerman, operators agreed that effective functioning and staffing of the checkout counter was a constant problem. In a self-service store, conference

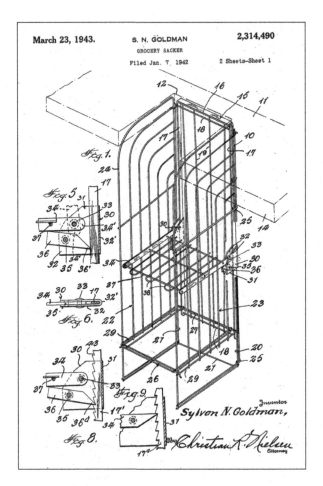

March 23, 1943.   S. N. GOLDMAN   2,314,490

GROCERY SACKER

Filed Jan. 7, 1942    2 Sheets—Sheet 1

*Inventor*
Sylvon N. Goldman,
Christian R. Nielsen
*Attorney*

FIG. 7.7. Sylvan Goldman's Grocery Sacker made it possible for baggers to fill grocery sacks without stooping or lifting items awkwardly. The device was collapsible for storage when not in use. *Source:* Goldman, Grocery Sacker patent.

participants emphasized, "the checking department was the only point of contact with the customer and . . . it was essential to have employees who not only could make adjustments but were [also] able to sense dissatisfaction among the shoppers."[61] In many ways the success of the self-service store was made or broken at the checkout line. Store operators emphasized the importance of training staff but also sought spatial design solutions for improving the checkout. The checkout counter was not simply an independent store fixture. It was a linchpin in the coordination and efficiency of the self-service system.

Because the connection of the checkout counter to the self-service pathway regulated the overall efficiency of the system, new technological developments elsewhere in the store tended ultimately to create new challenges at the checkout counter. The invention of market basket carriers for example, went hand in hand with the reinvention of the checkout station. A key challenge was moving merchandise safely and efficiently from shopping cart to checkout counter without backing up traffic in the store. If checkers were also responsible for weighing produce, this created further bottlenecks in the system. As his customers began using shopping carts, Sylvan Goldman found that moving items from the cart to the checkout counter, and then from the counter to a grocery bag, slowed down the traffic flow through the checkout line. His solution was the "grocery sacker," (fig. 7.7), a device that could be adjusted to position the bag opening at counter level to make the work of the bagger more efficient.

Carl Dipman devoted a full chapter to discuss a variety of configurations for checkout counters in his first book on self-service store arrangement, with floor plans showing how to organize multiple checking stands configured strategically so that customers would "be obliged to exit through a central point."[62] While traditional grocery stores had long used counters for a variety of purposes—weighing bulk goods, wrapping, displaying, acting as equipment stands, providing storage space, and creating barriers to separate customers from shelf merchandise—the only purpose for a counter in a self-service store was wrapping and checking purchases (fig. 7.8). Dipman explained the advantages and disadvantages of L-shaped, U-shaped, and simple rectangular counters depending on the size of the store, with particular attention to effective traffic flows. He pointed out, "Unless checking counters are properly placed the motion will be against the flow of traffic, or perhaps the checker will be obliged to work the register with his left hand, or possibly customers in the store may be obliged to pass one another in narrow lanes."[63]

Because Dipman's central concern was offering grocers advice about how to integrate service and self-service features of store arrangement, he included examples of store designs that did not centralize checkout as the final stop on a self-service pathway. His representation of the floor plan for a typical California supermarket (fig. 7.9) showed a self-service grocery department, compartmentalized in a space controlled by turnstile access, ringed by service departments. Customers paid for their grocery purchases at the U-shaped checkout counters before exiting the self-service space. They paid separately for purchases at the meat, produce, and delicatessen service departments. The

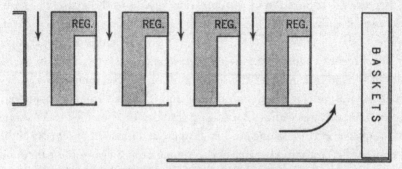

FIG. 16—This is another popular arrangement for large cash-carry self-service stores. The front rail provides a long in-passage past checking counters, thus reducing pilferage. A part or all of the basket space may be used for basket carriers (pushcarts). This arrangement can be easily adjusted for corner entrances.

FIG. 7.8. Carl Dipman's arrangement of L-shaped checkout counters uses arrows to explain the relationship between the counters and traffic flow in the store. *Source:* Dipman and O'Brien, *Self-Service and Semi-Self-Service*, 226.

California Thriftimart was still effectively a self-service "store within a store." As self-service stores began to harness the meat counter to the centralized checkout counter, however, the reasons for spatially compartmentalizing the self-service grocery department blurred. Small and medium-sized stores played an important role in reorganizing self-service pathways because they simply did not have the space to separate self-service and counter-service functions. The centralized checkout process that integrated service departments along the self-service pathway broke down the rigid spatial compartmentalization of self-service store arrangement. Meanwhile, in larger stores, experiments in rationalizing consumer shopping through integrating systems of display, mobility, and checkout harnessed counter-service departments to the self-service pathway and undercut the perception of self-service as a specialized form of retailing.

Herbert Bradley's patent for a checking station for self-service stores (fig. 7.10) shows the mechanical challenges of integrating rolling basket carriers into the checkout process and demonstrates the connectedness of the checkout station to the self-service pathway as a whole. Bradley designed a checkout process that was located at the end of the self-service pathway where checking all items in a shopping basket was the final transaction. He specifically

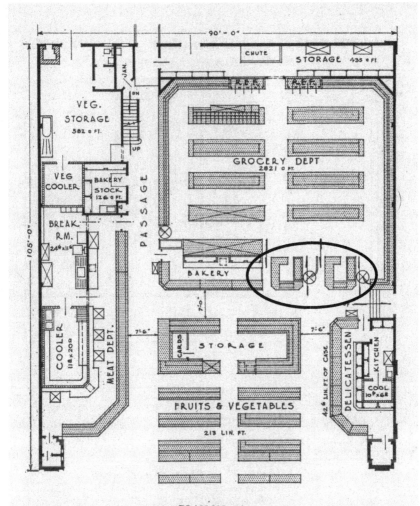

PLAN NO. 14

Floor plan of Thriftimart, Hollywood, Calif. It is the general rule among most large California super-markets to place the meat department on the left front side, fruits and vegetables in the center front, and delicatessen department on right front (sometimes also bakery right front). Note how a storage space is worked into the center of one of the islands.

FIG. 7.9. Floor plan of Thriftimart, Hollywood, California. Turnstiles separated the self-service grocery space from the counter-service produce, meat, and bakery departments. *Source:* Dipman and O'Brien, *Self-Service and Semi-Self-Service Food Stores,* 182.

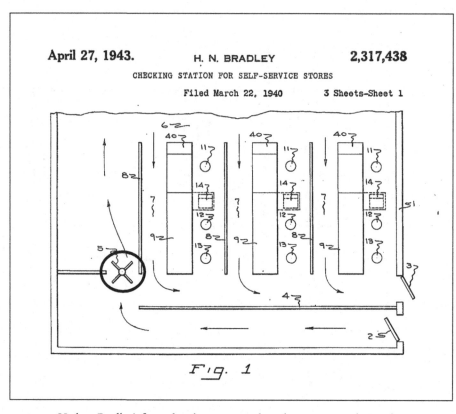

April 27, 1943.   H. N. BRADLEY   2,317,438

CHECKING STATION FOR SELF-SERVICE STORES

Filed March 22, 1940  3 Sheets—Sheet 1

Fig. 1

FIG. 7.10. Herbert Bradley's floor plan shows a turnstile at the entrance to the retail floor at the left of the checking station. This design follows the advice of Dipman: "Large stores should confine exits to fairly narrow lanes adjacent to checking counters and should provide separate inviting entrances." *Source:* Bradley, Checking Station for Self-Service Stories; Dipman and O'Brien, *Self-Service and Semi-Self-Service,* 220.

addressed physical difficulties workers encountered in unloading wheeled basket carriers. When customers wheeled their full carts up to the checkout counter, checkers sometimes reached over the counter to lift the customers' baskets of merchandise from their carriages," placing the full basket onto the counter to unload it. In the process they "often physically injure[d] themselves," Bradley's patent noted. His invention attempted to address the problems by adding an "unloading station at the opposite side of the checking station from the bagging station," eliminating the need for cashiers to lean over to lift heavy baskets from their carriages. But beyond Bradley's concern for workers' welfare, his invention was also intended to address concerns about store overhead and the handling of money. At rush hour, multiple checkout stations had to be opened to keep the customer traffic flowing. "Additional cash registers are not only expensive," Bradley explained, "but also the adding of . . . cash registers requires additions to the number of men [who] must handle money [and thus] increases the bookkeeping." Bradley's checking station arrangement improved traffic flow through the checkout process and reduced "the necessity of resorting to additional cash registers and men handling money."[64] His checking station incorporated conveyor belts and antifriction rollers to convey merchandise more rapidly through the checkout process and coordinate the work of the basket unloader, who systematically removed the items in the carriage according to classification—produce, staples, meats; the checker who tabulated the prices of the items; and the bagger.

Bradley's patent addressed one of the key advantages of the centralized self-service checkout system as a mechanism for controlling access to money. In counter-service stores, multiple cash registers might sit on counters in different departments throughout the store for collecting payments, or in smaller stores clerks might collect payments anywhere on the shop floor and take them to the cash register for recording a sale. The Piggly Wiggly catalog advised franchisees, "Opening the purse but once to pay for all purchases is a fundamental policy of a self-service store."[65] Burroughs Adding Machine Company and the National Cash Register Company (NCR) were among the participants at the first Super Market Institute convention in 1937. NCR subsequently promoted self-service store arrangement as a strategy for controlling cash flow. "Merchants of Chicagoland who have changed their stores from Clerk Service to a Self-Service operation have found the shortage or overage of cash eliminated," an NCR ad stated. This is because only one person operates the cash register and also handles all of the store incoming and outgoing money."[66] J. H. Hutchinson, manager of NCR in Chicago, explained the advantages of self-service store layout in an article for *Food Retailing Magazine*: "At the centralized checkout stand the customer serves as the watchdog," Hutchinson wrote. "She is there watching to see that the proper price is charged and just what is recorded on the cash register." He emphasized that control of cash at the centralized checkout counter was not only an efficient way to process customer purchases but also a method for monitoring workers. "A good system for the control of cash is one that gives the *greatest publicity* to what is happening when money is handled and thus *inspection and supervision are automatic.*"[67] Harnessing the cash register to a checkout counter at the end of the self-service pathway automated the authority of the merchant. Store operators increasingly understood it as the best store layout for processing payments.

Given the importance of centralized checkout design for self-service store design, it seems fitting that the last self-service store patent awarded by the Patent Office (fig. 7.11)—a supermarket patent issued to Garth Close of Lubbock, Texas, in 1969—focused on improvements in the checkout process.[68] Close did not patent a newly configured checkout stand or an improved cash register. He patented a pathway. With the ample square footage of a supermarket space, Close created two checkout stations in different parts of the store. A partitioned pre-checkout area reduced the final wait time in the final checkout at the exit. A customer could check out a full shopping cart at the partitioned checkout station "and then continue on to the remaining aisles to gather more merchandise with an empty shopping cart." The customer was reunited with the pre-checked merchandise from their first cart in the "customer exit zone," where they completed the checkout of the second full grocery cart. [69] In essence Close doubled the sales capacity of the store by reconfiguring the self-service pathway rather than increasing the size of the shopping cart or the square-footage of the store. The centralized checkout process was a defining innovation of the first generation of self-service stores.

Super-sizing self-service fundamentally changed the pathways designed by the first groceterias by connecting service departments to a centralized payment process at the end of the customer's path. Ensuring the systemization of the pathway, mobilizing merchandise using wheeled basket carriers, and using massed displays to activate silent selling power extended the design principles of the groceteria to the supermarket. As the selling power of supermarkets undercut the profitability of chain stores, the major national chains pivoted to self-service store arrangement. Self-service was increasingly embraced as an industry standard rather than seen as a specialized form of retailing.

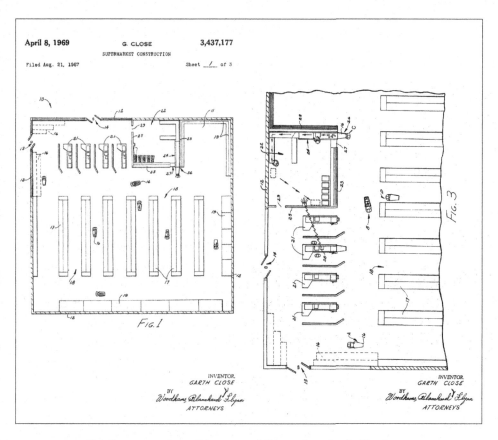

*FIG. 1*

*FIG. 3*

FIG. 7.II. This illustrations shows figure one and figure 3 from Garth Close's supermarket patent. The floor plan in figure 1 shows four checkout lines (upper left) next to a partitioned pre-checkout area customers could use while they shopped to speed the final checkout process. A close-up provided in the patent's third figure showed customers wheeling shopping carts through the store. Customer C is using the partitioned pre-checkout station to check out a full cart of groceries. Another window in the pre-checkout area opens into the exit zone of the store. *Source:* Close, Supermarket Construction patent.

# Conclusion

Achieving Technological Momentum

      In 1952 Harley V. McNamara, president of the National Tea Company of Chicago, addressed the Chicago Federated Advertising Club on "Modern Trends in Food Retailing."[1] He had been in the business for decades and reflected on how much the cost of opening a grocery store had changed. McNamara recalled that in 1920, when National Tea had opened fifty-three new stores in a dramatic expansion of the chain, fixtures and installation costs were about $2,000 per store. Thirty years later, fixtures and installation for the company's new self-service supermarkets cost an average $42,000 per store, not including building construction or inventory. Of course, the investment in inventory to fill larger store spaces and the land required to build supermarkets with their accompanying parking lots made stores more expensive. But it wasn't simply the fact that stores were larger in 1952 than they were in 1920. The material costs of implementing self-service systems for automatic selling were a significant factor in the increased expense of supermarket construction. "In 1920 we built our wood shelving from the floor up—a few boards and a good carpenter would shelve a store for $300," McNamara recalled.[2] Modern supermarkets required refrigerated produce cases, freezers, electrically operated mechanical checkout stands, fleets of chrome shopping carts, and automatic exit doors—all designed to coordinate efficiently as a self-service system.

      McNamara drew stark comparisons between the quaint fixtures of 1920s stores and gleaming, mechanized, modern supermarket installations. His speech constructed a picture of binary opposites contrasting "the corner grocery store of yesterday" with postwar supermarkets. "Today's Super food store," he said, "is a . . . big business. A reasonably scientific business run by experts." The big business of supermarkets, he emphasized, was a world away from the corner grocery store run by "the man and wife out of a job, with a few dollars in the bank, and a good credit rating with the wholesale grocer."[3] This contrast between old-fashioned corner stores and modern supermarkets, between mom-and-pop merchants and retailing professionals, became a trope of postwar narratives of supermarket history. What McNamara did not explain was that during the interwar years National Tea, like most other major chain companies of the 1920s, had not used self-service store arrangement. Instead, following best practices in the industry at the time, the chain had arranged stores for efficient clerk service.

By 1930 National Tea still had not converted stores to self-service, but they had bought the Piggly Wiggly franchise in Chicago. Acquiring Piggly Wiggly stores made it possible to add self-service outlets without converting National Tea stores to self-service. The incorporation of Piggly Wiggly stores into the National Tea chain reflected a larger industry pattern of treating self-service stores as specialized retailing systems. Throughout the 1920s the chains that grew into the largest organizations, with national or extensive regional networks, did not use self-service store arrangement as standard practice in every store. An early supermarket enthusiast in New York declared, "The weakness of the chain set up is that about 65% of its business is service operation." As a result, corporate chains in his community had been unable to meet the price competition of the self-service supermarket.[4] Even many first-generation supermarkets like Big Bear also compartmentalized self-service grocery departments in spaces that operated separately from their counter-service areas. The Great Depression changed the context of risk, and the chain organizations that had treated self-service as a specialized system with limited applicability began to embrace it as an industry standard and convert their stores to self-service. By the mid-1930s the nation's three largest grocery chains—A&P, Kroger, and Safeway—all responded to supermarket competition, anti-chain legislation, and economic crisis by converting existing stores to self-service and opening self-service supermarkets.

Though supermarket promoters claimed self-service as their original invention, technological momentum offers a better explanation for understanding supermarkets as a culmination of a longer-term invention process. While historians of technology debate the degree to which social, economic, and technological forces interact to shape historical change, they agree that technological determinism—the idea that machines drive social change—cannot explain the success or failure of a given invention. Historian, Thomas Hughes, developed the concept of "technological momentum" to explain the complexity of technological change in large-scale systems as both a social and a technological process. Hughes emphasizes that "a technological system can be both a cause and an effect; it can shape or be shaped by society." The process does not automatically ensure that the inventions that work best become profitable, and the social dynamic of technological change varies as the process moves from initial invention to new stages of technology transfer and diffusion. Though it is not an inevitable outcome of the process, successful development of supporting infrastructures of production, information, and consumption can lead to a final stage of technological momentum when the technology becomes standard practice. "As they grow larger and more complex, systems tend to be more shaping of society and less shaped by it," Hughes explains. "Therefore, the momentum of technological systems is a concept that can be located somewhere between the poles of technical determinism and social constructivism."[5] Historian David Nye explains, "'Technological momentum' is not inherent in any technological system when first deployed. It arises as a consequence of early development and successful entrepreneurship, and it emerges at the culmination of a period of growth."[6]

Self-service innovation was a process fueled by economic crises. It originated in the high inflation and labor shortages of the World War I era. It evolved as a form of specialized retailing in the entrepreneurial experimentation of the 1920s. These experiments were crucial for the systems of automatic selling deployed by supermarkets during the economic crisis of the Great Depression. In 1940 the Super Market Institute embraced self-service as an industry standard, a major turning point in the history of American self-service when food retailers and their supporting manufacturers began to embrace self-service as standard practice rather than a specialized form of retailing. Store design shifted from a process of local vernacular experimentation to being driven by corporate financing and policy making. Self-service entered a new stage of development with the broad conversion of diverse retail spaces to self-service after World War II. Supermarkets became the coveted design projects of influential architectural firms. Store managers bought their fixtures from companies that specialized in the manufacture of self-service equipment. But modern supermarket operation was a direct descendant of the principles of automatic selling first developed in the smaller 1920s self-service stores that mobilized merchandise along self-service pathways.

A closer look at what happened to one of the largest independent Piggly Wiggly franchises brings this retail history turning point into sharp focus. Piggly Wiggly had entered California in 1919, and the Los Angeles–based Piggly Wiggly California Company was among the largest franchises in the self-service chain by 1926.[7] The end of Piggly Wiggly in California offers a vivid example of how self-service stores ceased to be a specialized form of retailing in the 1930s.

## Safeway–Piggly Wiggly and the End of an Era

Charles Merrill built the Safeway chain through a series of chain store acquisitions, mostly in western and midwestern states, during the 1920s.[8] With the merger in 1927 of Skaggs and Safeway stores in California, the Skaggs-Safeway company operated nearly one thousand stores in ten western states. The company marketed itself explicitly as an alternative to self-service stores. "Skaggs-Safeway stores are not the so-called 'self-service' type of store," the Santa Cruz, California store manager insisted then. "We believe every housewife appreciates the advantages of personal service—particularly when it costs nothing to have it."[9] Architectural historian Richard Longstreth describes Safeway as the most conservative chain in the Southern California market in terms of store size and design innovation.[10] Certainly from a regional perspective Safeway appears conservative, especially because Southern California was a major center of self-service experimentation. But viewed from a national perspective Safeway adhered to best practices of chain stores.

The Safeway chain employed the visual display principles promoted by Carl Dipman in the 1920s and early 1930s. At first glance the Safeway store in Pocatello, Idaho, pictured in figure 8.1 appears to be a self-service store, with its open displays inviting customers to pick up merchandise. [11] But a customer there would not have been able to collect more than an armload unless she brought her own marketing basket or shopping bag. While such stores were intended to encourage customers to serve themselves and stimulate their "shopping instinct" through visual display, customers in stores like this had a choice about how much work they were willing to do when they came in to shop. They could pick up an item or two as they made their way to the counter at the back of the store to give their shopping list to the clerk who would assemble the rest of the order. The center of the floor is open space to allow customers to gather at rush hour while they waited for clerk service. This store was arranged to improve efficiencies by organizing merchandise for faster work of clerks.

The acquisition of the Piggly Wiggly Western Company stores in California reinforced the message that service was free at Safeway. In 1929 local

FIG. 8.1. Interior of Safeway Store No. 31 in Pocatello, Idaho. With its open shelving and accessible displays, this could be mistaken as a self-service store. Notice the counter at the back left corner of the retail space where customers paid for their purchases or consulted with one of the four clerks who assembled their orders while they waited. *Source: Uno Animo* (Safeway) 4, no. 10 (July 1929): 39. Courtesy David Gwynn.

newspapers reported, "The Safeway Stores company, a holding organization, will become the third largest chain grocery concern in America tomorrow, when it formally acquires 183 Piggly Wiggly stores in the Los Angeles metropolitan district."[12] The organization rebranded as Safeway–Piggly Wiggly. Combined ads presented Safeway and Piggly Wiggly as different options— one service, one self-service—with no difference in prices. Heinz Ketchup cost nineteen cents a bottle whether you bought it from clerks at a Safeway store or served yourself from Piggly Wiggly shelves. And ads featured fresh meat specials in both service and self-service store formats (fig. 8.2). Thus, the appeal was not price but consumer preference for shopping method. "Take advantage of Safeway and Piggly Wiggly Service and Self-Service," declared Safeway-Piggly Wiggly advertisements.[13] The Safeway chain added self-service as an option for customers, not by converting Safeway stores to self-service but by acquiring Piggly Wiggly stores.

During the early 1930s Piggly Wiggly sustained an important and distinctive role as a self-service option in the Safeway chain. Safeway–Piggly Wiggly continued to develop new Piggly Wiggly stores like the one in Stockton, California, opened in 1933—a new deluxe version with a fresh meat department prominently located at the front of the store (fig 8.3). But by 1937 Max Zimmerman reported, "Safeway has closed more than seventy Piggly Wiggly units and more than 250 of its smaller units, replacing them with large departmentalized combination food stores of the super market type."[14] Self-service was no longer compartmentalized as a specialized store format in the chain; all Safeway stores would be self-service supermarkets.

FIG. 8.2. Ad for Safeway–Piggly Wiggly. Safeway became the third-largest grocery chain in the United States when it acquired the Piggly Wiggly franchise in the Los Angeles metropolitan area in 1929. The acquisition of Piggly Wiggly created a self-service option in the consolidated chain without converting Safeway stores to self-service. *Source: Woodland (CA) Daily Democrat*, March 29, 1929.

The opening of Piggly Wiggly de luxe store and market No. 600, Stockton, California, was announced in the December UNO ANIMO. At that time, however, pictures were not available, so we are submitting these views of the store and its attractive departments together with a complete description and highlights of the opening event.

[Above] Store No. 600 is most attractive in appearance. [Left] Grocery department.

## Stockton's New Deluxe
# Piggly Wiggly Store

Friday, October 14, was a red letter day for Stockton housewives as it marked the opening of our beautiful Piggly Wiggly de luxe store No. 600.

The store is located in one of Stockton's finest residential districts. A large corner lot next to the store affords ample parking space for machines, which is a most convenient and pleasing feature. Illumination of the outside of the building and parking space is accomplished by floodlights arranged along the front and side of the store.

The interior of the store is very attractive and pleasing to the eye with its wide aisles and neat rows of merchandise. The shelves and display fixtures are new and modern, giving the customer every convenience in shopping. There are also two checking aisles equipped with up-to-date cash registers.

The meat and produce departments are located at the front of the store and show

up very well from the street through three large plate glass windows. The meat case is of green porcelain and lends an effective background for the display of meats.

B. J. Oliver is manager of this store and Ben DeGanna is manager of the market. Both of these men have been employees of the Piggly Wiggly and Safeway companies for several years and are working hard to make the store a success. E. N. Austin is supervisor of the grocery department, Bob Van Sandt supervises the market and Tony Cademartori supervises the produce department.

The National Biscuit, Jell-Well, Sperry

Flour and American Chicle companies were among those giving free samples of merchandise to the customers on the opening day. The General Foods Company also gave away balloons to the kiddies, the supply of which was exhausted long before the day was over.

The two opening days of Friday and Saturday were a grand success, over 5000 people visiting the store. That the people of Stockton were pleased to have such a beautiful store opened in their city was clearly evident both in patronage and comment and we feel that they have accepted it as a real asset to the community.

Interior views of Stockton's new Piggly Wiggly store showing the produce and meat departments which are located opposite each other in the front part of the store.

FIG. 8.3. Safeway continued to open new Piggly Wiggly stores in California through the mid-1930s. The Stockton, California, store interior visible here documents a new focus on fresh meats, a product not offered in the original patented store interior because it was incompatible with the self-service system. In this case the meat department is located at the front of the store (bottom photograph at right). The meat case was covered in a green porcelain called Vitrolite that Piggly Wiggly's Jackson, Tennessee, factory used to update older store interiors and fixtures during the 1930s. *Source: Uno Animo* (Safeway) 8, no. 4 (February 1933): 30, Courtesy of David Gwynn.

The closure of Piggly Wiggly stores in the Safeway system marks an important turning point, not just in the history of this particular chain but also in the history of the American self-service store. During the 1920s franchisees had created numerous independent Piggly Wiggly companies. As many of them cashed in on their success and sold their organizations to other chains, Piggly Wiggly stores began to act as a specialized self-service option within other chain networks that prioritized clerk-service store arrangement. In Chicago, Piggly Wiggly was absorbed by National Tea by 1930.[15] Kroger bought Piggly Wiggly Stores, Inc., including the Jackson factory, in 1928 and soon announced ambitious plans for international expansion.[16] The company explained, "[Kroger is] preparing to introduce the Piggly Wiggly self-service idea in England. It will be something new in British merchandising methods. Kroger has arranged for the experimental use of Piggly Wiggly equipment in one of the largest chain-store systems in England."[17] The company effectively used its Piggly Wiggly stores to compartmentalize self-service store locations in the chain organization until the late 1930s. While Kroger stores remained committed to clerk-service operation, the company's Piggly Wiggly stores offered customers a self-service option.

Kroger's plans to export Piggly Wiggly stores were cut short as the rapidly changing food retailing landscape of the 1930s transformed the risks of self-service in unanticipated ways. In 1930, when Kroger president William Albers failed to respond to Michael Cullen's proposal to open five enormous self-service stores on a trial basis, Cullen resigned his position as a general sales manager and went on to success with his King Kullen supermarkets in New York.[18] By 1935 Kroger had embraced self-service and opened fifty new supermarkets.[19] As the largest chains began to convert their stores to self-service and build new supermarkets, they increasingly understood self-service as standard operating practice. Piggly Wiggly no longer served a distinctive purpose as a specialized form of retailing. Instead of exporting Piggly Wigglies to England, the Kroger chain sold its controlling stock in the Piggly Wiggly Corporation to financier William R. Lovett of Jacksonville, Florida, in 1939. Piggly Wiggly increasingly became a regional brand, not a national one.[20]

Though the self-service pioneer retreated from the national stage, Piggly Wiggly continued to offer smaller franchisees, especially in the South, an affordable opportunity to convert their businesses to self-service. The Piggly Wiggly factory in Jackson, Tennessee, focused on efforts during the 1930s to update the patented interiors sold in the 1920s. They crafted Art Deco materials to reface original oak store cabinetry and created a tiny self-service store with one aisle in response to the financial challenges of the Great Depression. Piggly Wiggly did not convert stores in the South to supermarkets until after World War II. "The fifties and sixties were 'turnaround' years" for Piggly Wiggly Southern stores, Delma Presley writes, because in part the company decided to sell or close "the smaller 'mom and pop' stores—holdovers from the twenties and thirties" and become "a supermarket chain both in name and in fact."[21] Ironically, the only national self-service chain of the 1920s and early 1930s became a casualty of supermarket self-service. The patented machines for automatic selling originally produced by the Piggly Wiggly factory and marketed as tools for scientific retailing came to be viewed as quaint mom-and-pop relics in the hindsight of supermarket enthusiasts.[22]

## Self-Service Becomes a New Industry Standard

Max Zimmerman observed a sea change among chain store organizations by 1940. "Derisive at first of the Supers and constituting their most belligerent opponents, the large national chains by 1940 were rushing into the field and, as far as the eye could reach, were changing their units as rapidly as possible into Super Markets," he declared.[23] It is not simply that larger stores finally made self-service profitable. Self-service stores already had established a convincing record of selling more food at lower cost than the most efficient counter-service stores of the interwar years. The most important change was the revision of attitudes about self-service store systems that were the foundation of supermarket profits. It is useful at this point to consider historian Philip Scranton's question: "How does the lust for technical novelty overcome the calculus of risks, the conservatism of traditional practice, and the fear of failure?"[24] Scranton emphasizes that technological momentum is best understood as "a concept of local determination (rather than comprehensive determinism)."[25] While the extreme economic dislocations of the Great Depression challenged the inertia of major chain organizations in their dramatic shift toward self-service store conversion, regional variations in the history of self-service store experimentation underscore the need for a contextual approach to evaluate supermarket expansion. Smaller regional firms continued to play a key role in innovations that shaped supermarket methods, and large chains managed store conversions differently depending on regional contexts of store operation.

Significantly, A&P chose the South for its first self-service supermarket, in Paducah, Kentucky, in 1935, and began a slow process of conversion to self-service as unit managers debated the supermarket trend. Unit managers in the eastern divisions of the company, a region where self-service had made few inroads during the 1920s, were more resistant to the chain's supermarket initiative. A Central Division unit manager in Olean, New York, opened a supermarket in 1936 but refused to close four traditional counter-service stores, which undermined pricing strategies and profit margins. And the head of the New England Division complained that his managers had only opened two supermarkets in 1938.[26] The new A&P supermarkets showed impressive profits, and the chain succeeded in closing 4,000 conventional counter-service stores and opening 750 new self-service supermarkets in 1937 and 1938 combined. Volume sales in those new supermarkets cut operating costs in half compared to traditional counter-service A&P stores (fig 8.4).[27]

Store ads often promoted self-service as a customer demand, but there was little research at the time to back up the claims. Myrtle Lohner Hatfield studied what women in Chicago liked and didn't like about self-service shopping for her master's degree from the University of Chicago School of Business in 1936. She chose a focus on the Jewel Food Stores chain because at the time it was "the only grocery chain in Chicago [operating] completely on the self-service plan."[28] Jewel had entered the city in 1932 when it bought Loblaw's Groceterias, a Canadian self-service chain that had started in Toronto in 1919 (inspired by Piggly Wiggly's expansion into Montreal and Toronto) and expanded into the Great Lakes region during the 1920s. In addition to Jewel customers, Hatfield ultimately interviewed almost five hundred other shoppers, choosing store locations with particular care to ensure that that she was able to compare customer attitudes about different practices in counter-service and self-service stores. Sixty percent of her interviewees shopped at the largest chains in the city—Jewel, A&P, National Tea, and Kroger. Forty percent shopped at independent stores.

While the Jewel customers Hatfield interviewed were relatively satisfied with their self-service shopping experience, most of the women she surveyed shopped at both service and self-service stores. Hatfield reported that 73 percent of women who were most committed to self-service "found service convenient for some items; on the other hand, only 48% of the 'service' customers felt a need for some self-service." The vast majority of Jewel customers felt self-service produce was essential because they did not trust the clerk to select the best quality fruits and vegetables. Hatfield was surprised by some of her findings about self-service because they did not fit prevailing assumptions in the business literature. "The rather generally accepted belief [is] that the

FIG. 8.4. "The 'Super Market' in Durham, North Carolina," Jack Delano photographer, May 1940. During the 1940s A&P alerted customers before they entered the store that they would encounter a self-service format, as the national chain converted stores and built new supermarkets. *Source:* FSA/OWI Collection, Library of Congress Prints and Photographs Division.

clerks in a self-service store are of little importance compared to those in a service store," Hatfield wrote. But she found that clerks actually played a more important role in customer satisfaction in the Jewel chain than in any of the other stores she surveyed.[29]

Jewel customers showed the highest store brand loyalty of any of the stores in Hatfield's sample, and their preference for self-service set them apart from other shoppers. Although she described them as "unusually 'self-service-minded,'" Hatfield discovered that only 26 percent of Jewel customers preferred self-service for the "sheer enjoyment of choosing items" by themselves.[30] The majority of women did not choose self-service as their primary shopping method. "When independent stores and National Tea are considered," Hatfield concluded, "it is seen that the majority of women, 73 percent and 61 percent, respectively, preferred service."[31] Customers who chose not to shop at Jewel stores criticized the lack of free delivery (a strong loyalty factor for independent grocers). They also complained about self-service store methods, mentioning difficulty in locating items in the store, the perception that it took too long to buy groceries in Jewel, lack of variety, lack of a meat department, and a feeling that self-service store prices should be lower.[32] Hatfield's research suggested that for a significant proportion of women shoppers, self-service remained a specialized shopping method, generating strong loyalty from early adopters but ongoing resistance from the mainstream.

Hatfield's findings about Jewel customers' level of satisfaction with self-service should also be understood in light of an intensive renovation and marketing campaign the company had launched two years before she began her research. In 1934 Jewel had significantly redesigned its stores based on an extensive survey of Chicago women. A full-page Jewel ad in 1934 in the Chicago Tribune declared: "18,389 Women Planned This Store." "Day after day, for many months," it said, "several of our young women have called on Chicago women in their homes. (We have actual records of 18,389 calls.)" While the ambitious canvass reportedly revealed strong support for self-service, the company said it had rearranged "many things around the stores" for customers' "greater convenience." Jewel assured customers they could shop "in half a jiffy" with the new layout. "No one will bother you or urge you to buy anything." But Jewel also emphasized, "If you *want* assistance—just notice how quickly and politely one of our attendants will come forward to help you."[33] The fact that Jewel was the only self-service chain in Chicago in the mid-1930s and that it had made a considerable investment to generate customer loyalty suggests the challenges supermarkets faced. Jewel would not be able to count on customer demand for self-service as an automatic growth strategy. As chains began to convert stores to self-service in the late 1930s, selling self-service would be a new focus of the food industry.[34]

Embracing self-service as an industry standard, at the fourth annual meeting of the Super Market Institute, in 1940, conference sessions and displays focused on how to use self-service to sell fresh produce, meats, dairy, and frozen foods. Godfrey M. Lebhar, editor in chief of *Chain Store Age*, noted, "New, highly original, and practical methods for expanding self-service into departments until then undreamed of as possibilities for self-service were exhibited by the manufacturers that year."[35] Attendees also planned an aggressive marketing campaign they boldly called "National Self-Service Food Week" to promote self-service when they returned to their communities. Zimmerman reported that more than one thousand supermarkets joined the promotion campaign nationally.[36] The Benner Tea Company was one of them.

Benner Tea Company used the National Self-Service Food Week campaign to advertise its new "mammoth store," a Food City store in Muscatine, Iowa. Declaring that ten years earlier the self-service supermarket had been unheard of, the local chain positioned itself in contrast to "old, traditional methods." Although self-service stores had been around for decades, the company presented self-service as "a new standard of efficiency" that dramatically lowered food costs. The ad (fig. 8.5) featured a woman using a shopping list to fill her double-tiered basket carrier and urged Muscatine residents to join her: "Learn why millions of wise housewives are turning to this new way of food buying."[37] The national self-service marketing campaign succeeded in presenting supermarkets as the inventors of self-service.

The Super Market Institute presented supermarkets as an "industry" built on "advanced research and technology," and self-service operation methods became a subject of intensive study for supermarket chains and their suppliers.[38] "The location of departments has become an exact science," declared the *Architectural Record* in a feature about supermarkets in Paterson, New Jersey, and Los Angeles designed by major architectural firms whose engineering expertise was essential for store design. "In almost all cases the entire width of the store is free of column supports. There are also no interior supports to obstruct the floor plan."[39] National Cash Register offered a design service free to grocers in Chicago, with "trained men" sent out to stores to "measure up, lay out and discuss Self Service" as it applied to each store.[40] As stores converted to self-service, the impetus for innovation shifted from

NATIONAL *Self-Service* FOOD WEEK

## Celebrating the Economies and Savings of SELF-SERVICE

Ten years ago the Self-Service Super-Market was unheard of. Today it is an important step in bringing foods to you at amazingly low prices. Breaking away from the old, traditional methods, self-service stores set a new standard of efficiency that makes it possible for you to cut the cost of food from 10 to 30 per cent.

The Benner Tea Company, always eager to adopt modern methods and bring lower food costs to its customers, has opened this, and many other of these mammoth stores. All are furnished with the latest and best equipment . . . Accurate scales . . . Cash registers that print the price of every item you buy

on a strip of paper, which you can check against your purchases . . . Modern electric refrigeration, which insures the quality and freshness of the meats and dairy products you buy . . . And shelving and displays conveniently arranged so shopping, with easy rolling basket-carriers, is a real pleasure.

Yes—self-service super-markets are a great stride forward . . . They offer a wider variety of carefully selected foods, always fresh, and at EVERYDAY low prices that leave a good share of your grocery budget free to buy things you thought you couldn't afford! Why not pay Food City a visit today? Learn why millions of wise housewives are turning to this new way of food buying.

FIG. 8.5. Members of the Super Market Institute launched a national campaign in 1940 to promote self-service as a supermarket innovation. Supermarket narratives erased more than two decades of self-service innovation that preceded the supermarket. *Muscatine (IA) Journal and News-Tribune*, 18 April 1940.

local experimentation to large companies that employed specialists trained in self-service methods.

In 1946 Carl Dipman dropped the subject of "semi-self-service" stores and simply titled his new book on store arrangement *Self-Service Food Stores*, declaring that "self-service food store operation is no longer on trial." In his manual for converting traditional grocery stores to self-service design he asserted, "It has been amply demonstrated that self-service has its application to most any kind of a store large or small, city or country, service or cash-carry."[41] But the vernacular invention of self-service was over. "Modern food stores have long outlived the crude hammer-and-saw days in favor of finished factory-built equipment—especially so if stores wish to appeal to discriminating trade," Dipman proclaimed.[42] Among the sponsors of his book were Boston Metal Products Company, Burroughs Adding Machine, Frigidaire, Modern Store Equipment Company, and Tyler Fixture Corporation. Some of them had been selling equipment to grocers for years. Now they were all fully committed to designing their machines for self-service store operation.

Self-service stores were no longer considered patentable machines for automatic selling, but the supermarket was built on the foundations pioneered by their small-town inventors—the alchemists of the machine age, whose patented pathways automated salesmanship and turned pennies into gold. Because self-service stores represented a small segment of the grocery trade before 1940, most Americans did experience self-service shopping for the first time in supermarkets. The innovative "basketerias" and "marketerias" of the World War I era disappeared, and Piggly Wiggly became just another supermarket. To understand the complex development of mass consumer capitalism in the twentieth century, it is essential to replace the oversimplified, ahistorical landscape drawn by supermarket enthusiasts with a more complete picture of the grassroots invention and diverse origins of the American self-service store in the economic upheavals of the early twentieth century, two decades before the first supermarket sold millions.

In 1939 moviegoers flocked to see the new technicolor *Wizard of Oz*. Before Frank Baum had published the first Oz story in 1900, he made a living as editor of *The Show Window*, a trade journal focusing on designing store displays. Baum was a founding member of the National Association of Window Trimmers of America and published *The Art of Decorating Dry Goods Windows and Interiors* the same year as his novel *The Wonderful Wizard of Oz*.[43] The film version of Oz, created twenty years after he died, had more in common with the modern self-service store than with the Victorian department store displays Baum had staged. Moviegoers watched Dorothy walk the winding yellow brick road carrying Toto in her woven market basket while the wicked witch spied on her through a crystal ball. When she finally reached her destination, she was admonished to pay no attention to the man behind the curtain. Thus the movie evoked contemporary consumption experience along circuitous self-service pathways designed for surveillance. Dorothy ultimately escaped the dreamworld of Oz through her own power, waking up to her "real life" in rural Kansas. But the American self-service store was as much an invention of the small-town midwestern heartland as it was the creation of the urban capitalist. It belonged as much to Kansas as to the Emerald City.

The American self-service store originated in a national process of invention that embodied important irreducible contradictions in the consumers' republic. It failed in New York City and succeeded in Clovis, New Mexico. It integrated democracy (the freedom to choose) with the paternalistic controls of automated salesmanship and surveillance. The radical equality of the checkout line was created in a culture of segregation. The self-service store was a mechanism for mass retailing that enjoyed its greatest popularity in anti-chain territory. It was a capital-intensive effort to reduce the cost of doing business. The considerable sums invested in experiments to replace workers with automated systems belie assumptions about self-service as an obvious or a cheaper form of retailing.

The chain store owners and independent grocers who invented the self-service store in the early twentieth century reconfigured the way stores had worked for centuries. They changed more than their store layouts. Inventing the self-service store was a social process that fundamentally transformed the meaning and experience of consumption. It all started as a futuristic fantasy: for consumers, the thrill of stepping behind the counter and having unfettered access to the store; for petty capitalists, the dream of inventing a reliable machine for automatic selling. In many ways it is still the capitalist's ultimate fantasy. A new generation of self-service store designers aspires to reshape the twenty-first-century retail landscape. Some of them are redeploying the store entry mechanism used by the original inventors. Now, as we consider whether to scan our palms at turnstiles equipped with biometric technology, the open question is: how much of ourselves will we be willing to surrender to avoid the checkout line?

# Acknowledgments

I set out to write a book about the South, but Piggly Wiggly took me farther afield. I had no idea when I started how long it would take.

I would like to thank the following people for their support along the way:

The two anonymous readers of the University of Georgia Press who were willing to read a work in progress multiple times. Their recommendations improved this book immeasurably.

The exceptional staff of the University of Georgia Press, especially Nathaniel Holly and Rebecca Norton for their guidance and support on the long road from manuscript review to publication. I particularly appreciate that the Press placed such a high priority on the design of the physical book. They never hesitated about including lots of illustrations and worked with me to ensure that all of them were the right size and in the right location to make sense to readers.

Participants in the 2006 Hagley Seminar Series, who inspired a decisive turning point in the project.

The University of North Carolina Greensboro (UNCG) Office of Research and Community Engagement for supporting research, editing, and publication expenses.

The UNCG Faculty First Award Program for precious writing time.

Chuck Bolton, for funding my research in patent case files when he was my department head and for taking the time to read a really rough manuscript and offer valuable comments.

David Gwynn, for generously sharing his knowledge and personal collection of grocery history. Sometimes it seemed like he was mapping a city for Groceteria.com just when I needed that exact store location information.

UNCG Agraphia, founded by Paul Silvia, for incredibly collegial writing support. They were a weekly Zoom lifeline during pandemic writing.

The UNCG Humanities Network and Consortium (HNAC) Writing Group—Jeff Jones, Frances Bottenberg, Adam Rosenfeld, Jonathan Zarecki, Teresa Walch, and Denisa Jashari—for their incisive feedback and unwavering enthusiasm for the project.

Meghan Drury, Book Smart Editing, who helped me turn disconnected chapters into a coherent argument.

Margaret Newlin, whose impeccable undergraduate research provided the foundation for chapter 3.

Sarah Maske, for invaluable research support in the final stages of manuscript production.

Anne Parsons, who helped me find my way out of grief to finish the book and pushed me to the end to write clearly. This book would not have been possible without her.

And finally Lynn and David Holdzkom. They did not get to read this book, but I know they would love how it turned out. I miss them more than I can say.

# Appendix

Store Patent Inventors and Locations

| Patent No. | Inventor | Location | Invention | Patent Date |
|---|---|---|---|---|
| 1,242,872 | Clarence Saunders | Memphis | Self Serving Store | 9 October 1917 |
| 1,305,033 | Robert A. Tribble | Rolling Fork, MS | Vending Apparatus | 27 May 1919 |
| 1,313,794 | Edward L. da Roza | Elk Grove, CA | Self Serving Store | 19 August 1919 |
| 1,321,571 | Edward M. Stiles | Mt. Pleasant, IA | Self Serving Store | 11 November 1919 |
| 1,337,050 | Shiker M. DeBakey | Lake Charles, LA | Home Store | 13 April 1920 |
| 1,345,481 | Frederick W. Davis | Dayton, OH | Self-Serving Store | 6 July 1920 |
| 1,347,936 | James H. Carroll | Atlanta | Store Self-Service | 27 July 1920 |
| 1,348,024 | William B. McCarty | Jackson, MS | Self-Serving Store | 27 July 1920 |
| 1,350,088 | Robert A. Tribble | Cedarbluff, MS | Vending Apparatus | 17 August 1920 |
| 1,350,996 | Henry C. Harvey | Huntington, WV | Self-Serving Store | 24 August 1920 |
| 1,354,957 | Edward L. da Roze | San Francisco | Self Serving Store | 5 October 1920 |
| 1,355,408 | Jason B. Moody | Houston | Self-Serving Vehicle Store | 12 October 1920 |
| 1,357,521 | Clarence Saunders | Memphis | Self Serving Store | 2 November 1920 |

| Patent No. | Inventor | Location | Invention | Patent Date |
|---|---|---|---|---|
| 1,368,924 | Henry Claude Goode | Macon, GA | Self Serving Store | 15 February 1921 |
| 1,372,854 | H. A. Wieman | Dallas | Vehicle Body | 29 March 1921 |
| 1,378,417 | Hoard Lee | Shreveport, LA | Self Serving Store | 17 May 1921 |
| 1,379,463 | Clyde W. Martin | Little Rock, AR | Portable Grocery-Store | 24 May 1921 |
| 1,380,968 | Alva W. B. Johnson | Birmingham, AL | Self Service Store | 7 June 1921 |
| 1,381,202 | Jewel Warren King | Memphis | Store Construction | 14 June 1921 |
| 1,383,980 | William Midgley Campbell | Hot Springs, AR | Store Furniture | 5 July 1921 |
| 1,390,673 | Thomas David Crawford | Hammond, IN | Fixture for Self Serving Stores | 13 September 1921 |
| 1,392,418 | Leslie A. Hill | Dallas | Arrangement and Construction of Self Service Store | 4 October 1921 |
| 1,397,379 | Frank E. Jones | San Diego | Self Serving Store | 15 November 1921 |
| 1,397,824 | Clarence Saunders | Memphis | Self Serving Store | 22 November 1921 |
| 1,408,679 | Clarence R. Ball | Washington, DC | Store Service | 7 March 1922 |
| 1,425,789 | Annie L. Moseley | San Antonio | Portable Automobile Grocery Store | 15 August 1922 |
| 1,437,554 | Clarence Saunders | Memphis | Self Serving Store | 5 December 1922 |
| 1,435,395 | Hasting P. Howard | Memphis | Store | 14 November 1922 |
| 1,446,215 | Alfred J. Schwartz | Detroit | Silent Sales Storeroom for Perishable Goods | 20 February 1923 |
| 1,450,086 | Alva Wright Boswell Johnson | Birmingham, AL | Self Service Store | 27 March 1923 |
| 1,450,803 | Grover C. Greene | Nashville | Self Serving Store | 3 April 1923 |

| Patent No. | Inventor | Location | Invention | Patent Date |
|---|---|---|---|---|
| 1,460,332 | Jesse Tripp Jr. | Los Angeles | Store Furniture | 26 June 1923 |
| 1,461,374 | Lorenzo Norwood Anderson | Hawkinsville, GA | Self Serving Store | 10 July 1923 |
| 1,466,539 | Clyde Martin and Leonard E. Hoffman | Little Rock, AR | Itinerant Vending and Sales Vehicle | 28 August 1923 |
| 1,473,850 | Edward J. Greene | Toledo, OH | Serve-Self Motor Store | 13 November 1923 |
| 1,474,106 | James H. Carroll | Charlotte, NC | Self Service Store for a Bldg. Having Limited Floor Space | 13 November 1923 |
| 1,477,492 | Miller Reese Hutchison | Orange, NJ | Self Service Store | 11 December 1923 |
| 1,494,390 | Robert A. Stevenson | Lancaster, OH | Self Serving Store | 20 May 1924 |
| 1,510,435 | Edwin W. Trapp | San Francisco | Apparatus for Vending Merchandise | 30 September 1924 |
| 1,528,243 | John E. Briggs | Wichita Falls, TX | Fixture for Self Serving Stores | 3 March 1925 |
| 1,534,644 | Hastings P. Howard | Memphis | Store Furniture | 21 April 1925 |
| 1,544,949 | John F. Smiley | Dallas | Self Serving Store | 7 July 1925 |
| 1,592,931 | Albert E. Fritsche | Los Angeles | Store System | 20 July 1926 |
| 1,625,490 | Roger T. Morris | Seattle | Self-Serving Store Equipment | 19 April 1927 |
| 1,633,886 | James R. Duffin | Louisville | Self-Serving Store | 28 June 1927 |
| 1,633,907 | William Rylander | Austin, TX | Storage and Display Apparatus for Merchandise | 28 June 1927 |
| 1,647,889 | Clarence Saunders | Memphis | Store Fixtures | 1 November 1927 |
| 1,664,945 | Alexander C. Robert | Desdemona, TX | Self-Service Store Equipment | 3 April 1928 |

| Patent No. | Inventor | Location | Invention | Patent Date |
|---|---|---|---|---|
| 1,684,637 | John T. Myers and James H. Carroll | West Palm Beach, FL | Self-Service-Store Fixtures for Vending Merchandise | 18 September 1928 |
| 1,688,551 | Tommy C. Nix and Macon D. Miller | Hazel, KY | Self-Service Store | 23 October 1928 |
| 1,703,477 | Thomas L. Conder | Columbia, SC | Store Service | 26 February 1929 |
| 1,704,061 | Clarence Saunders | Memphis | Self Serving Store | 5 March 1929 |
| 1,718,512 | Raymond Wright and Edgar B. Kellogg | Porterville, CA | Self-Serving Store | 25 June 1929 |
| 1,720,260 | Francis J. Bowen Jr. and John G. Bowen | San Antonio | Vending and Serve-Self Store and Vehicle | 9 July 1929 |
| 1,720,917 | Melville M. Moore | New Orleans | Store System | 16 July 1929 |
| 1,724,235 | William Carter Thornton and John McAlpine | Johnson City, TN | Mechanical Store | 13 August 1929 |
| 1,766,409 | Charles E. Stocks | El Paso, TX | Self-Service Haberdashery | 24 June 1930 |
| 1,717,123 | Nelson T. Sharp | Memphis | Self Serving Store | 11 June 1929 |
| 1,750,060 | John F. Smiley | Dallas | Self-Service-Store Equipment | 11 March 1930 |
| 1,751,199 | Joseph N. Grant | Louisville | Self-Serving Store | 18 March 1930 |
| 1,771,659 | Robert A. Stevenson | Lancaster, OH | Customer Control Means for Self-Serving Stores | 29 July 1930 |
| 1,773,540 | Jesse J. Moss | Temple, TX | Store Service Device | 19 August 1930 |
| 1,788,759 | Jason T. Anderson | Harrisburg, OR | Automatic Self-Servicing Device for Mercantile Stores | 13 January 1931 |
| 1,821,541 | James Franklin | Cincinnati | Store | 1 September 1931 |

| Patent No. | Inventor | Location | Invention | Patent Date |
|---|---|---|---|---|
| 1,839,617 | Ross K. Tiffany | Olympia, WA | Store Construction | 5 January 1932 |
| 1,843,280 | Frank E Hall | Boise, ID | Conveyor for Self Serving Stores | 2 February 1932 |
| 1,861,671 | David W. Webb | New York City | Self Service Store | 7 June 1932 |
| 1,873,852 | Charles E. Rorrer and Abert R. Mitterer | Denver | Store | 23 August 1932 |
| 1,882,488 | Warren C. Ellis | Flint, MI | Store | 11 October 1932 |
| 2,005,286 | James H. Carroll | Atlanta | Self-Service Store with Revoluble Shelves | 18 June 1935 |
| 2,096,959 | Leonard F. Clerc | Detroit | Store | 26 October 1937 |
| 2,176,384 | Lloyd W. Varney | Los Angeles | Self-Service Store Construction | 17 October 1939 |
| 2,628,691 | Richard W. Barrett | Cincinnati | Self-Service Store | 17 February 1953 |
| 2,980,211 | Walter H. Richter | Glenview, IL | General Merchandise Self-Service Store | 18 April 1961 |
| 3,437,177 | Garth Close | Lubbock, TX | Supermarket Construction | 8 April 1969 |
| 4,154,027 | William Searcy | Tarpon Springs, FL | Store Arrangement | 15 May 1979 |

# Notes

## Preface. Piggly Wiggly 2.0

1. Bosker, "The Pandemic Shows Us the Genius of Supermarkets"; Severson, "7 Ways the Pandemic Has Changed How We Shop"; Matt Galassini, "Pandemic-Era Shopping Trends Are Blurring the Lines."

2. Berg, "The Rise of 'Dark Stores.'"

3. Cheng, "Why Amazon Go May Soon Change the Way We Shop."

4. Bowles, "Stealing from a Cashierless Store."

5. Wingfield, "Inside Amazon's Store of the Future."

6. Cheng, "Why Amazon Go May Soon Change the Way We Shop"

7. Kang, "Here Comes the Full Amazonification of Whole Foods."

8. Kang, "Here Comes the Full Amazonification of Whole Foods."

## Introduction. *Looking Backward*

1. Bellamy, *Looking Backward*.

2. Bellamy, *Looking Backward*, 92–96, for description of the clerk-less store.

3. For department store history, see Leach, *Land of Desire*; Benson, *Counter Cultures*; Jan Whitaker, *Service and Style*; Abelson, *When Ladies Go A-Thieving*.

4. Quoted in Resseguie, "Alexander Turney Stewart and the Development of the Department Store," 314.

5. Emile Zola, *Au Bonheur des Dames* (Paris: G. Charpentier, 1883), initially serialized in the Parisian literary periodical *Gil Blas*. See also Benson, "Palace of Consumption and Machine for Selling."

6. Nystrom, *The Economics of Retailing*, 42.

7. Parker and Temple, *Unified Kindergarten and First-Grade Teaching*, 133, 135–46. Teacher Isabel Robinson contributed this account of her social studies lesson taught over three months during the winter of 1921 at the University Elementary School at the University of Chicago.

8. Lebhar, *Chain Stores in America*, 27.

9. For example, James R. Beniger argues that self-service stores were instrumental in a larger "control revolution" that laid the foundation for the creation of an information society. Beniger focuses on Piggly Wiggly as the only example of pre-supermarket self-service. Beniger, *The Control Revolution*, 333–36. See also Gordon, *The Rise and Fall of American Growth*, 334, 560.

10. *World's Work*, February 1918, 362.

11. Susan Spellman discusses the important role of independent grocers in the invention of self-service in *Cornering the Market*, 141–45, 168.

12. See Tracey Deutsch's discussion of the difficulties chain stores faced in substituting packaging and manufacturer advertising for clerk service in *Building a Housewife's Paradise*, 70–71.

13. For the history of vending machines and automats, see Epple, "Automatic Trade: Self-Service and the Polycentric Early History of Slot Machines"; and Shuldiner, "Trapped behind the Automat."

14. Media historian Michael Palm and business historian Susan Spellman offer very different approaches for studying the technologies that enabled self-service. Palm traces the origins of self-service to the phone and cash register industries in *Technologies of Consumer Labor*. In contrast, Spellman documents the importance of independent grocers in shaping and cash register technology during the early stages of invention in *Cornering the Market*.

15. Isenstadt, "The Spaces of Shopping," 23.

16. "Five-and-Ten-Cent Grocery Stores"; Isenstadt, "The Spaces of Shopping," 23. Sharon Zukin, *Point of Purchase*, 71, emphasizes that by 1909 Woolworth "stopped building storage shelves behind counters, and moved all items to counter tops where shoppers could reach them without asking a sales clerk for help." In a book about how shopping changed American culture in the twentieth century, Zukin dispenses with the history of self-service in two pages. Susan Strasser provides the best overview of the role of Woolworth in the origins of mass consumption in "Woolworth to Walmart." Strasser includes on page 50 a 1941 photograph of shoppers exploring open table displays at Woolworths in her brief overview of the origins of self-service, which she attributes to chain stores.

17. "Woolworth's to Try Out Self-Service Store Here," *New York Times*, August 16, 1952.

18. Robinson and May, *Self-Service in Variety Stores*, 7. Converting the store to self-service meant eliminating the clerk aisles and creating a centralized checkout process. See especially Robinson and May, *Self-Service in Variety Stores*, 4, 8, 14, for discussion of eliminating clerk aisles in variety stores. Clarence Saunders tried a short-lived experiment with applying self-service to the variety store business. Piggly Wiggly Variety Stores included a soda fountain and candy counter with self-service fixtures arranged behind turnstile entrance and exit, but only a few Piggly Wiggly Variety Stores were ever

built. See *Turnstile*, December 29, 1922. By 1926 Piggly Wiggly Variety Stores had closed. See advertisement for store fixture sales in *Nashville Tennessean*, May 11, 1926.

19. Robinson and May, *Self-Service in Variety Stores*, 1.

20. Chandler, *The Visible Hand*; Tedlow, *New and Improved*.

21. McCrae, "Little Oddities of Life." The first Piggly Wiggly store opened in Memphis on September 11, 1916. The American popular science journal *Scientific American* also published an article about self-service stores. See Vestal, "The Cousin of the Cafeteria."

22. Gerrard also toured Ward's Groceteria, another store in the area that was testing self-service design, before installing his version. Esther Cramer includes two fascinating photographs of the Triangle Groceteria in her book about Gerrard. In addition to the interior photograph that was originally published in *Illustrated World* in January 1916, a longer-angle view of the full store shows that the self-service space was actually a tiny, compartmentalized space installed at the back of the store. To reach the turnstile, customers walked past Ed Rolls's meat market and Riddle's Confectionary, organized on opposite counters in the front half of the store space. Gerrard went on to create the Alpha Beta chain. Cramer, *The Alpha Beta Story*, 28–29.

23. McCrae, "Little Oddities of Life."

24. Saunders, Self-Serving Store patent (1917).

25. Saunders presented a meticulous accounting of store profits and operation costs as part of his rationale for seeking a patent for his self-serving store. See E. W. Bradford to Commissioner of Patents, June 5, 1917, Record Group 241: Records of the Patent and Trademark Office, 1836–1978, Patent Case File 1,242,872, National Archives, Kansas City, Missouri.

26. "Woods to Open Store Saturday, Groceteria Will Be Located at 377 Rose Street, Near Euclid," *Lexington (KY) Herald-Leader*, September 14, 1934.

27. *Lexington (KY) Leader*, September 19, 1930. The advertised opening date, Saturday September 20, 1930, is the same date documented on the photograph by Lexington photographers Lafayette Studios.

28. "Woods to Open Store Saturday, Groceteria Will Be Located at 377 Rose Street, Near Euclid," *Lexington (KY) Herald-Leader*, September 14, 1934.

29. For example, historian Susan Strasser presents self-service as part of the new practices introduced in the early twentieth century made possible by branded products with marked prices. See *Satisfaction Guaranteed*, 26. Strasser argues that self-service solved two key problems. For store owners it cut labor costs, and from the food manufacturers' point of view it eliminated the grocer's ability to make substitutions when a customer asked for a particular brand. *Satisfaction Guaranteed*, 248.

30. For supermarket history, see especially Humphery, *Shelf Life*; Mack, "Speaking of Tomatoes"; Deutsch, "'Wild Animal Stores' to Women's Sphere"; Bowlby, *Carried Away*; Hamilton, *Supermarket USA*; Longstreth, *The Drive-In, the Supermarket, and*

*the Transformation of Commercial Space*. Longstreth is one of the few architectural historians to evaluate the experimental stores that preceded the supermarket. Though self-service is not Longstreth's primary focus, his overview of Los Angeles stores includes examples documenting self-service experimentation before 1940. Southern California was an important region of self-service innovation.

31. Du Gay, "Self-Service: Retail, Shopping and Personhood," 151.

32. Mayo, *The American Grocery Store*, 89, 117. See also Palm, *Technologies of Consumer Labor*. Palm de-emphasizes the role of store owners in the invention of self-service, arguing that although self-service shopping occurred inside stores it was really the control revolution of chain store business practices and mass production innovations that explain the success of self-service. Palm argues, "The first Piggly Wiggly stores were less the origin of self-service than its tipping point" (32).

33. Bowlby, *Carried Away*, 141.

34. For example, Chester Liebs considers the self-service store in his chapter on supermarkets but presents Piggly Wiggly as a representative example of the first self-service stores and does not distinguish self-service stores from combination stores that operated using traditional counter service arrangements. *Main Street to Miracle Mile*, 118–24. More recently, the contributors to Andrews, *Shopping*, evaluate a variety of spaces of modern shopping, including variety stores, shopping malls, farmers' markets, and independent neighborhood grocery stores. While the book is explicitly "not intended as a comprehensive or chronological history of shopping," it is notable that the self-service store is largely invisible in the shopping landscape; self-service is presented primarily as a modern retail practice of open display introduced by variety stores in the early twentieth century. An important exception to the treatment of self-service as a general retail practice is French scholar Frank Cochoy's study *On the Origins of Self-Service*. Cochoy explains that stores designed for open display should be distinguished from self-service arrangement because they were still arranged to promote traditional counter service (133–38). However, Cochoy relies exclusively on evidence from the *Progressive Grocer* magazine, which obscures the complex origins of self-service stores more than two decades before the trade journal began publication in 1922. Cochoy does not contextualize the evolving support for self-service by *Progressive Grocer* editor Carl Dipman.

35. Hughes, "The Evolution of Large Technological Systems," 45.

36. Cowan, "The Consumption Junction," 253.

37. LeFebvre, *The Production of Space*.

38. For example, see Mayo, *The American Grocery Store*, 92, for the idea that a turnstile was cheaper than a store counter.

39. Self-service store experimentation fits longer-term patterns of small-business innovation. Susan Spellman's research on independent grocers of the late nineteenth century documents long-term patterns of small-business innovation in the countryside. In her "Putting Cash Registers on the Map," Spellman maps the geospatial diffusion of

cash registers in 1885, documenting the simultaneous adoption of the new technology by city and country businessmen. Spellman shows that technology innovation was a large-scale process in which rural retailers did not simply adopt urban business methods; they helped to create the new business methods that produced the control revolution.

40. See Tolbert, "The Aristocracy of the Market Basket."

41. Dipman, Mueller, and Head, *Self-Service Food Stores*, 9. Dipman published his first book on self-service store arrangement in 1940. He included semi-self-service stores as a substantial component of that book. See Dipman and O'Brien, *Self-Service and Semi-Self-Service Food Stores*.

## Chapter 1. Machines for Automatic Selling

1. "Edison Plans an Automatic Clerkless Shop," *New York Times*, May 15, 1910.

2. Spellman, *Cornering the Market*, 131.

3. Edison detailed his automatic store invention in two articles, one for popular audiences in the *New York Times* and the other for entrepreneurs who read the magazine for advertisers, *Printer's Ink*. For an example of complaints about the inefficiencies of grocery stores, see McClintock, "Costly Corner Grocery."

4. "Edison Plans an Automatic Clerkless Shop," *New York Times*, May 15, 1910.

5. Turner, *How the Other Half Ate*.

6. "The Piggly Wiggly Stores," *World's Work*, February 1918, 362.

7. Nystrom, *The Economics of Retailing*, 327.

8. Nystrom, *The Economics of Retailing*, 2.

9. For the transformation of the American food industry between 1880 and 1930, see Levenstein, *Revolution at the Table*.

10. Strasser, *Satisfaction Guaranteed*, 204–6.

11. Nye, *Technology Matters*, 49.

12. Epple, "The 'Automat.'" See also Haley, *Turning the Tables*. Haley found at least twenty patents for "waiterless restaurants" between 1880 and 1925 (183). These patents focus on specific tools and technologies to replace waiters rather than the systematized arrangement of restaurant spaces.

13. Epple, "Automatic Trade," 103.

14. Bailey, "When Fixtures Sell Goods."

15. Quoted in Strasser, *Satisfaction Guaranteed*, 248.

16. Biggs, *The Rational Factory*, 2. The rational factory predates the invention of the assembly line.

17. "Edison Plans an Automatic Clerkless Shop," *New York Times*, May 15, 1910.

18. Chaffee and Kerbey, "Self-Service in the Retailing of Food Products," 3.

19. Shuldiner, "Trapped Behind the Automat," 15.

20. Shuldiner, "Trapped Behind the Automat," 36.

21. Shuldiner, "Trapped Behind the Automat," 60

22. Shuldiner, "Trapped Behind the Automat," 34.

23. Mariani, *America Eats Out*, 116–20.

24. Barry, "Cafeteria," 37.

25. Whitney, "Housing and Welfare Work."

26. Haskin, "Quick Lunch Rooms," *Washington Post*, March 29, 1910, quoted in Epple, "The 'Automat,'" 112–14.

27. Jacobs, *Pocketbook Politics*, 15.

28. Hurd, Vending Apparatus patent.

29. "Childs Restaurant Founder Is Dead," *New York Times*, March 18, 1925.

30. Mumford, "Machinery and the Modern Style," 264.

31. Vestal, "The Cousin of the Cafeteria," 193.

32. Weston, Serving Device for Eating-Houses patent.

33. DeWitt, "On Making New Words." The word was sometimes spelled "grocerteria." Self-service stores were also called "basketerias," signaling the centrality of the market basket as an essential tool for self-service shoppers.

34. Steadman, "Basketeria and the Meaning of the Suffix—Teria."

35. For analysis of self-service pioneers in California such as Ralphs Grocery Company, see Longstreth, *The Drive-In, the Supermarket, and the Transformation of Commercial Space*. Ralphs was founded in 1875, and Longstreth argues that the stores they built in the 1920s were among the first true supermarkets in the United States, but the Los Angeles chain first experimented with self-service store arrangement between 1925 and 1928 and so did not participate in the initial stage of self-service invention during World War I (86). See also Davison, "Super City."

36. "'Groceteria' Store Has but One Clerk," *Asheville Gazette-News*, May 22, 1915. See also "Groceteria Is Latest," *Fayetteville (NC) Weekly Observer*, September 8, 1915, for coverage of self-service in California.

37. Epple, "Automatic Trade," 103.

38. "'Wholesale to the Consumer' Store of Lutey Brothers."

39. Cristman's Self Service Grocery advertisement, *Marion (Ohio) Star*, March 8, 1916.

40. Turner, *How the Other Half Ate*, 1.

41. For the politics of World War I era food inflation, see Macleod, "Food Prices, Politics, and Policy in the Progressive Era"; and Jacobs, *Pocketbook Politics*.

42. King, "Can the Cost of Distributing Food Products Be Reduced?"; Patterson, "The Cost of Distributing Groceries."

43. Jacobs, *Pocketbook Politics*, 55.

44. Murphy, "In Piggly Wiggly Stores the Product Has to Sell Itself," 19.

45. "Pantry Food Hoards Feed Mice: Reverses Old Plan of Buying," *Daily Capital Journal*, June 22, 1918.

46. See, for example, "Twelve Patriotic Reasons for Piggly Wiggly Stores," *Oklahoma City Times*, August 2, 1918; and "Piggly Wiggly Store Coming to Ardmore," *Daily Ardmoreite* (Ardmore, OK), June 15, 1918.

47. "Piggly Wiggly Store Coming to Ardmore," *Daily Ardmoreite* (Ardmore, OK), June 15, 1918.

48. Nichols, "How about Waiting on Yourself?," 31.

49. Murphy, "In Piggly Wiggly Stores the Product Has to Sell Itself," 20.

50. "Was Cash and Carry Only a War Baby?," 48.

51. "Was Cash and Carry Only a War Baby?," 70. See also *Business Digest*, 686, for stories about self-service store successes and failures including Larkins, H. G. Hills, and a groceteria in California that closed because of problems with theft.

52. "Cash and Carry Is Permanent, Say Grocers Who Make It Pay," 15.

53. "Cash and Carry Is Permanent, Say Grocers Who Make It Pay," 16–17.

54. "Carl W. Dipman, Food Trade Editor Dies; Helped Develop the Self-Service Grocery," *New York Times*, July 24, 1954.

55. Dipman, "Uncle Sam Builds a Model Store," 19.

56. Dipman, "Uncle Sam Builds a Model Store," 24.

57. Hayward and White, *Chain Stores*; Chaffee and Kerbey, "Self-Service in the Retailing of Food Products."

58. Jones and Tadajewski, "Percival White (1887–1970)."

59. Hayward and White, *Chain Stores*, 331.

60. Chaffee and Kerbey, "Self-Service in the Retailing of Food Products."

61. Chaffee and Kerbey, "Self-Service in the Retailing of Food Products," 4.

62. Chaffee and Kerbey, "Self-Service in the Retailing of Food Products," 4.

63. Stein and Bauer, "Store Buildings and Neighborhood Shopping Centers," 176.

64. Chaffee and Kerbey, "Self-Service in the Retailing of Food Products," 40.

65. 1/a RG2 USA and International Offices: New York Office, Minutes of Representatives Meetings, January–December 1927, p. 9, J. Walter Thompson Collection, Duke University Libraries, Durham, North Carolina.

66. 1/a RG2 USA and International Offices: New York Office, Minutes of Representatives Meetings, January–December 1927, p. 9, J. Walter Thompson Collection, Duke University Libraries, Durham, North Carolina.

67. Dipman, *The Modern Grocery Store*, 56.

68. Dipman, *The Modern Grocery Store*, 21.

69. Dipman, *The Modern Grocery Store*, 19, 18.

70. Dipman, "Uncle Sam Builds a Model Grocery Store," 21.

71. Holsey, "The C.M.A. Stores Face the Chains," 211.

72. The Colored Merchants Association was founded by D. F. Lowe Sr. and A. C. Brown in Montgomery, Alabama, on July 31, 1928. In February 1931, D. F. Lowe & Sons remodeled their grocery store (where the C.M.A. had held their first meeting) using Dipman's model store plan. They reported a steady increase in sales after remodeling. Frank N. Lowe to Albon Holsey, [1931?], Moton Family Papers, Subject File, National Negro Business League, Box 12, Folder 10, Library of Congress. Holsey's selection of Winston-Salem for the first demonstration store coincided with his efforts to expand the C.M.A.

beyond Montgomery. The *Winton-Salem Journal* explained that "Winston-Salem was selected because of its large number of colored grocers and existing Grocers' Association." H. A. Wiseman, "News of Colored People," *Winston-Salem Journal*, May 4, 1929. Black grocers in Winston-Salem had previously formed a Negro Business Men's League, led by William S. Scales. A month-long series of lectures in April at Winston-Salem Teachers College directed at students and local homemakers built organizing momentum by focusing on home economics, advertising, consumer protection agencies, and the modern grocery store. For coverage of the events surrounding the Ellington store conversion, see *Winton-Salem Journal* articles "Movement Started Here to Aid Negro," April 17 1929; "Negro Merchants Organize Here," April 19, 1929; and "Demonstration Is Held by Grocers," April 28, 1929. When Ellington's redesigned store debuted at 7:30 p.m. on May 4, Saturday, 583 persons passed through the store. "Famous Negro Here Monday: Dr. Moton of Tuskegee Institute to Speak Here; Grocers Close Drive," *Journal and Sentinel* (Winston-Salem, NC), May 5. Holsey's article for *Opportunity* included before-and-after photographs of the store interior.

73. Holsey, "The C.M.A. Stores Face the Chains," 213. With the exception of one Piggly Wiggly franchise in Tuskegee, Alabama (see Holsey, "What the Negro Is Doing in Business"), I did not find any examples of self-service stores owned by Black grocers before 1940. Numerous Black grocers transitioned to self-service store operation after 1940. A 1948 film of the Black business district in Durham, North Carolina, the Hayti neighborhood, featured shoppers serving themselves in Smith's Grocery. The film, *Negro Durham Marches On*, by Don Parisher, was commissioned by the Durham Business and Professional Chain, Durham's oldest African American business advocacy organization. North Carolina Collection, Durham County Library, Durham, North Carolina.

74. Dipman, *The Modern Grocery Store*, iv.

75. Dipman, *The Modern Grocery Store*, v.

76. Bowker, "What's in a Patent?" 33.

77. "Miller Hutchison, Inventor, 67, Dead: Devised Acousticon, Klaxon Horn, and the Dictograph—Former Edison Executive," *New York Times*, February 18, 1944.

78. Hutchison, Self-Service Store patent.

79. I was able to identify thirty-nine self-service patent holders in the 1920 and 1930 population census.

80. Moseley, Portable Automobile Grocery Store patent.

81. Carroll, Store Self-Service System patent; Carroll, Self-Service Store for a Bldg. Having Limited Floor Space patent; Myers and Carroll, Self-Service-Store Fixtures for Vending Merchandise; Carroll, Self-Service Store with Revoluble Shelves patent; *Atlanta Constitution*, September 14, 1924, p. 4.

82. The Piggly Wiggly legal team, including E. W. Bradford, pursued their patent infringement case all the way to the Supreme Court, which allowed the circuit court ruling in favor of Jitney Jungle to stand. See Piggly Wiggly Corporation v. Jitney Jungle Corporation.

83. A. W. B. Johnson opened the Garden Cafeteria on the fifth floor of his Steele-Smith department store, describing it as "Birmingham's first and only strictly modern cafeteria." ("It is a war-time plan of café operation which benefits us all.") *Birmingham News,* August 14, 1918. Johnson renamed the cafeteria after a popular H. G. Wells wartime book, *Mr. Britling Sees It Through,* and expanded the restaurant to other southern cities. According to John Mariani, Britling's was the first cafeteria in the South. Mariani argues that cafeterias were especially popular in the South, "where they offered access to a bright, spotlessly clean, modern, mechanized world of abundance, especially at a time when the South was in severe economic distress." See Mariani, *America Eats Out,* 118–19.

84. Hintz, "The Post-Heroic Generation," 734.

85. See, for example, the Piggly Wiggly advertisement "Vision" in *Washington Times,* August 26, 1921.

86. Saunders, Self-Serving Store patent (1917).

87. Crawford, "Piggly Wiggly—How It Has Grown to $5,000,000 a Month in Five Years"; Goudis, "Piggly Wiggly"; Weaver, "Step In and Help Yourself," 557.

88. "The Piggly Wiggly Stores," *World's Work.*

## Chapter 2. Inventing Piggly Wiggly

1. T. A. Hostetler to Bradford & Doolittle, February 21, 1917, Patent Case File 1,242,872, Record Group 241: Records of the Patent and Trademark Office, 1836–1978, Patent Case Files Series, 1836–1993, National Archives, Kansas City, Missouri.

2. Zimmerman, *The Super Market: A Revolution in Distribution,* 21.

3. This error appears in both scholarly and popular accounts. See for example Strasser, "Woolworth to Walmart," 51. *Smithsonian* presented Piggly Wiggly as the first self-service grocery store in a 2017 article by Kat Eschner, "The Bizarre Story of Piggly Wiggly."

4. For a history of the importance of traveling salesmen in the grocery business, see Walter A. Friedman, *Birth of a Salesman*; and Susan Spellman, *Cornering the Market,* especially 81–108.

5. "Man Who Conceived Chain of Piggly Wiggly Stores," *Nashville Tennessean,* March 12, 1922.

6. Freeman, *Clarence Saunders and the Founding of Piggly Wiggly,* 14.

7. *Commercial Appeal,* August 13, 1916.

8. *Commercial Appeal,* August 27, 1916.

9. *Commercial Appeal,* September 3, 1916.

10. For the best documented work on Clarence Saunders, see the work of Mike Freeman, including his well-documented master's thesis and article "Clarence Saunders: The Piggly Wiggly Man." See also his account without citations, *Clarence Saunders and the Founding of Piggly Wiggly.*

11. "'Wholesale to the Consumer' Store of Lutey Brothers."

12. Jacobs, *Pocketbook Politics*, 61.

13. Lutey, "Lutey Brothers Marketeria."

14. According to Oakley's obituary, he opened the first self-service grocery store in Terre Haute in 1917. *Indianapolis News*, July 18, 1967.

15. McCrae, "Little Oddities of Life."

16. *R. L. Polk and Co.'s 1915 Memphis City Directory*, 1183. The first Memphis location opened at 11 South Main Street. For a history of the Thompson's chain, see Jan Whitaker, "Early Chains: John R. Thompson," *Restaurant-ing through History*, June 10, 2010, https://restaurant-ingthroughhistory.com/2010/06/10/early-chains-john-r -thompson; and [Gene Gill], "Historic Memphis Restaurants . . . and some High School Hang-outs," Historic-Memphis, https://historic-memphis.com/memphis-historic /restaurants/restaurants.html.

17. E. W. Bradford to Commissioner of Patents, Record Group 241: Records of the Patent and Trademark Office, 1836–1978, Patent Case File 1,242,872, National Archives, Kansas City, Missouri.

18. See White, "Bradford, Ernest Wilder," 227.

19. Clarence Saunders, Self Serving Store patent (1917).

20. T. A. Hostetler to Bradford & Doolittle, February 21, 1917, Record Group 241: Records of the Patent and Trademark Office, 1836–1978, Patent Case File 1,242,872, National Archives, Kansas City, Missouri.

21. E. W. Bradford to Commissioner of Patents, June 5, 1917, Patent Case File No. 1,242,872.

22. E. W. Bradford to Commissioner of Patents, June 5, 1917, Patent Case File No. 1,242,872.

23. F. W. Holt to Bradford & Doolittle, August 28, 1917, Patent Case File No. 1,242,872.

24. Clarence Saunders, Self Serving Store patent (1917).

25. Clarence Saunders, Self Serving Store patent (1917).

26. "Piggly Wiggly with a Carnation," *Richmond Times-Dispatch*, May 21, 1918, 5.

27. *Commercial Appeal*, September 17, 1916.

28. *Commercial Appeal*, October 1, 1916.

29. John A. Covington affidavit, August 2, 1918, Record Group 241: Records of the Patent and Trademark Office, 1836–1978, Patent Case File 1,357,521, National Archives, Kansas City, Missouri.

30. Hubert T. McGee affidavit, August 2, 1918, Patent Case File 1,357,521.

31. Irl C. Rainwater affidavit, August 1, 1918, Patent Case File 1,357,521.

32. "Piggly Wiggly," *News Scimitar* (Memphis), June 19, 1917.

33. Clarence Saunders, Self Serving Store patent, 1920.

34. Clarence Saunders, Self Serving Store patent, 1920.

35. E. W. Bradford to Patent Commissioner, May 15, 1916, Record Group 241:

Records of the Patent and Trademark Office, 1836–1978, Patent Case File 1,357,521, National Archives, Kansas City, Missouri.

36. F. W. Holt to Bradford & Doolittle, May 24, 1918, Patent Case File 1,357,521.

37. E. W. Bradford to Commissioner of Patents, November 20, 1918. Patent Case File 1,357,521.

38. Clarence Saunders, Tape for Adding Machines patent.

39. Elmo Pullin affidavit, August 1, 1918, Patent Case File 1,357,521.

40. F. W. Holt to Bradford & Doolittle, December 28, 1918, Patent Case File 1,357,521.

41. E. W. Bradford to Board of Examiners-in-Chief on Appeal, Brief for Applicant, April 14, 1919, Patent Case File 1,357,521.

42. E. W. Bradford to Board of Examiners-in-Chief on Appeal, Brief for Applicant, April 14, 1919, Patent Case File 1,357,521.

43. See the final decision of the Examiners-in-Chief to Bradford & Doolittle, May 27, 1919, Patent Case File No. 1,357,521.

44. Saunders, Price-Tagging Means patent.

45. Clarence Saunders, Tape for Adding-Machines patent.

46. Clarence Saunders, Lighting System for Self-Serving Stores patent.

47. *Commercial Appeal*, October 15, 1916.

48. Saunders, *Inside of Things*, 1.

49. *Commercial Appeal*, advertisement for Bowers Stores, August 24, 1917, describes forty-three stores in the chain.

50. The 1917 Memphis City Directory listed only five Piggly Wiggly stores (976).

51. *Commercial Appeal*, September 18, 1917.

52. Saunders, *Eligibility to Piggly Wiggly*.

53. The first Piggly Wiggly store outside of Memphis opened in Houston in April 1917. See "The Piggly Wiggly Opens This Morning at 8 o'Clock in the New City Market," *Houston Post*, April 21, 1917.

54. Murphy, "In Piggly Wiggly Stores the Product Has to Sell Itself."

55. See Esperdy, *Modernizing Main Street*, 148. Esperdy analyzes storefronts applied to "modernized buildings as consumer goods."

56. Board members included lawyers, bankers, auto dealers, and other businessmen, from New York City and D.C. as well as Tennessee. See *Commercial Appeal*, February 1, 1922, for list of board members.

57. Bass, "How 'bout a Hand for the Hog," 310.

58. "The Retail Store as a National Advertiser," *Printers' Ink*, June 6, 1918, 140.

59. "Eligibility to Piggly Wiggly," 3.

60. Clarence Saunders, *Piggly Wiggly Store Investment Requirements*.

61. "A Fixture for Fruit and Vegetables," *Progressive Grocer*, July 1922, 15.

62. Dipman, "Uncle Sam Builds a Model Grocery Store," 25.

63. Levinson, *The Great A&P and the Struggle for Small Business in America*, 63.

64. "Piggly Wiggly Factory Payroll $1100 per Day," *The Turnstile*, August 20, 1922,

Memphis and Shelby County Room, Benjamin Hooks Central Library, Memphis Public Libraries.

65. Saunders, *Piggly Wiggly Contract Requirements*, see "Standard Equipment" section.

66. Saunders, *Piggly Wiggly Contract Requirements, see "Merchandise Classification" and* "Standard Equipment" sections.

67. Saunders, *Merchandise Needed as Memphis Stocks a New Piggly Wiggly*.

68. Business correspondence, December 21, 1921, Marr and Holman to Fletcher Scott, Vice Pres., Piggly Wiggly Corporation, Memphis, folder 3, box 11, Tennessee State Library and Archives, Nashville.

69. Saunders, *Store Buildings and Equipment Instructions, 23.*

70. Rohr, "Making Fixtures for Piggly Wiggly Stores."

71. Saunders, *Store Buildings and Equipment Instructions*, 3.

72. Saunders, *Store Buildings and Equipment Instructions*, 5.

73. Saunders, *Store Buildings and Equipment Instructions*, 4.

74. Saunders, *Store Buildings and Equipment Instructions*, 6.

75. Saunders, *Store Buildings and Equipment Instructions*, 11–12.Sears, Roebuck had been selling mail order house kits since 1908.

76. Rohr, "Making Fixtures for Piggly Wiggly Stores"; *Washington Times*, May 5, 1920.

77. Rohr, "Making Fixtures for Piggly Wiggly Stores," 48.

78. "Piggly Wiggly Factory Payroll $1100 per Day," *The Turnstile*, August 20, 1922, Memphis and Shelby County Room, Benjamin Hooks Central Library, Memphis Public Libraries.

79. Saunders, *Store Buildings and Equipment Instructions*, 25.

80. "Piggly Wiggly—Quebec LTD., Will Open Its First Store in Montreal Soon," *The Turnstile*, July 20, 1922, 1, Memphis and Shelby County Room, Benjamin Hooks Central Library, Memphis Public Libraries.

81. "Piggly Wiggly Comes to New York," *New York Times,* April 17, 1922.

82. "Help Wanted—Male. Salesmen," *New York Times*, April 6, 1922.

83. "Piggly Wiggly Serves by Self-Service," *New York Times*, June 6, 1922.

84. "Piggly-Wiggly Here in Receiver's Hands," *New York Times*.

85. "Piggly Wiggly Stores in East in Financial Trouble," *American Food Journal* December 1922, 40.

86. For the most detailed account of the attempt to corner the market and the legal woes of Saunders, see Freeman, *Clarence Saunders and the Founding of Piggly Wiggly*.

87. This still holds true today. In the many years I have been working on this book, "Where did Piggly Wiggly get its name?" is the most-asked question of professional and popular audiences alike.

88. Saunders, *Fore and Aft of Piggly Wiggly*, 1.

89. *Oklahoma City Times*, March 21, 1919.

90. "Piggly-Wiggly Co. Seek Writ against Hoggly-Woggly Co."

91. A. C. Jones, "An Analysis of Piggly Wiggly Progress," 39.

92. "The Piggly Wiggly Stores and Their Unique Advertising Copy," 33.

93. "Piggly Wiggly Store Coming to Ardmore," *Daily Ardmoreite* (Ardmore, OK), June 15, 1918.

94. See also references to "piggly wiggly aisles" in *St. Joseph (MO) Observer*, June 8, 1918; *Ogden (UT) Standard*, June 12, 1918.

95. "Enjoyed Visit with an Old Friend after Forty-One Years," *Ward County Independent* (Minot, ND), September 8, 1921.

96. "Piggly Wiggly Store Coming to Ardmore."

## Chapter 3. Selling the Store

1. "Introducing Andrew Williams, Manager of the Piggly-Wiggly Dept. of the Sacramento Public Market," *Sacramento Bee*, October 27 1923.

2. Sacramento Public Market advertisement, *Sacramento Bee*, December 28, 1923.

3. "On Chicago's North Shore," *Ladies' Home Journal* (hereafter *LHJ*), September 1930, 184. The franchise department was located in Cincinnati, because the Memphis home office had sold its operation to Kroger in 1928. See *Evening Sun* (Baltimore), February 11, 1929. Kroger acquired the Piggly Wiggly factory and the store outlets owned by Piggly Wiggly, Inc., in that transaction. Kroger sold its stake in Piggly Wiggly in 1939.

4. See, for example, Sewell, "Gender, Imagination, and Experience in the Early-Twentieth-Century American Downtown," 155. Sewell explores the contradictions between the socially experienced and ideologically gendered representations of downtown San Francisco in the early twentieth century. She notes how department store spaces and office spaces that were physically designed to separate men and women actually undercut gender separation in daily experience and consequently opened opportunities for suffragists.

5. Foner, *The Story of American Freedom*, 147; Marchand, *Advertising the American Dream*, 169–70; and McGovern, *Sold American*, 45, 47–48.

6. Foner, *The Story of American Freedom*, 147.

7. Staff meeting minutes, January 26, 1932, p. 2, box 4, folder 8, J. Walter Thompson Collection, Archives and Manuscripts, Duke University Libraries, Durham, North Carolina; J. Walter Thompson Company, staff meeting minutes, 1927–1938, David M. Rubenstein Rare Book and Manuscript Library, Duke University, Durham, North Carolina. See also Representatives Meeting, Tuesday, July 26, 1927, p. 1/26, box 1, folder 1, J. Walter Thompson Collection ("I might just announce a few things, You all know probably . . . that the Chicago office has gotten Piggly Wiggly and they are actually going ahead with that"); *LHJ*, July 1926, 72 (first A&P ad) and October 1927, 154 (first Piggly Wiggly ad; both Piggly Wiggly and A&P advertised monthly in *LHJ* until 1932); Saturday Evening Post October 15, 1927, 143 (first Piggly Wiggly ad) and March 24, 1928, 81 (first A&P ad).

8. These frequently repeated themes are defined by Marchand in *Advertising the American Dream*. He calls them advertising "parables" because they conveyed moral lessons (207). Marchand describes "the democracy of goods" as "one of the most pervasive of all advertising tableaux of the 1920s" (271).

9. For example, Charles McGovern analyzes a Piggly Wiggly ad as broadly representative of a widely shared "vision of women consumers at the height of 1920s prosperity," writing that "women were independent, sure of their skills, and willing participants in the adventure of shopping, but always the junior partners of the male domains of production and publicity." *Sold American*, 48.

10. *The Turnstile*, February 1923.

11. Levinson, *The Great A&P and the Struggle for Small Business in America*, 103.

12. Saunders, *Eligibility to Piggly Wiggly*, 3,; Piggly Wiggly Corporation, "A Word of Explanation,"

13. Saunders, *Piggly Wiggly Contract Requirements Etc.*, 16.

14. "Hundreds Visit New Piggly Wiggly," *News and Observer* (Raleigh, NC), March 18, 1921.

15. Adelman, *A&P*, 58.

16. "Sky-Rocket Growth from Newspaper Advertising," 58.

17. See Isenberg, *Downtown America*, 42–77, for her analysis of postcard representations of Main Street business culture.

18. Esperdy, *Modernizing Main Street*, 25.

19. Lebhar, *Chain Stores in America*, 130.

20. "Piggly Wiggly the Second," *El Paso Herald*, September 13, 1918.

21. "Piggly Wiggly Growing," *The Turnstile*, January 25, 1923, 3, an article reprinted from the small-town newspaper *Raton (NM) Range*.

22. *"Class 'A' Common Stock of Piggly Wiggly Stores, Inc. $55.00 Per Share," The Turnstile*, February 26, 1923.

23. A. C. Jones, "An Analysis of Piggly Wiggly Progress," 38.

24. A. C. Jones, "An Analysis of Piggly Wiggly Progress," 6.

25. A. C. Jones owned 59 Piggly Wiggly stores in Los Angeles in 1926, and by 1929 he was president of Piggly Wiggly Western States Company, with 215 stores, "mostly in California, but extending as far east as Ohio." Jones sold his Piggly Wiggly stores to Safeway in 1929 for $4,450,000. "At the time of the sale it was said to be the highest per store unit price ever paid for a chain of stores." See "Piggly Wiggly Stores to Add 20 New Units: A. C. Jones, of Los Angeles, Comes Here to Help Plan Expansion," *Atlanta Constitution*, October 27, 1929.

26. A. C. Jones, "An Analysis of Piggly Wiggly Progress," 6, 7.

27. Saunders, *Piggly Wiggly Contract Requirements, Etc.* 17.

28. *Carlsbad (NM) Current*, March 24, 1922. The Piggly Wiggly ad indicated that 1,400 customers turned up on opening day. The total population of Carlsbad, New Mexico, was 2,205 according to the census of 1920.

29. *Turnstile* 1, no. 13. June 8, 1919.

30. Allen, *Only Yesterday*, 229–30.

31. Lewis, *Babbitt*, 359.

32. Lestico, *Building the Story of Piggly Wiggly*.

33. "The Retail Store as a National Advertiser," 140–41.

34. "The Piggly Wiggly Stores and Their Unique Advertising Copy," 33.

35. Quoted in "Sky-Rocket Growth from Newspaper Advertising," 58.

36. Lestico, *Building the Story of Piggly Wiggly*.

37. Lestico, *Building the Story of Piggly Wiggly*.

38. Lestico, *Building the Story of Piggly Wiggly*.

39. *Washington Times*, May 5, 1920.

40. *El Paso Herald*, September 13, 1918.

41. "A Piggly Wiggly Store Is Your Very Own!," *Oklahoma City Times*, March 28, 1919.

42. *Colored Directory* (Columbia, Mo.: N.p., 1927), 23, State Historical Society of Missouri, Columbia.

43. "Let's Reason," *Negro Star*, August 25, 1922.

44. Parker, "Race and Class Identities in Early American Department Stores," 18.

45. "Where Little Red Wagon Meets Limousine," *Ogden (UT) Standard-Examiner*, March 31, 1922, 16.

46. "Sky-Rocket Growth from Newspaper Advertising," 57–61.

47. "Where Little Red Wagon Meets Limousine."

48. Adelman, *A&P*, 33.

49. Levinson, *The Great A&P and the Struggle for Small Business in America*, 103.

50. Anderson, *A&P*, 22.

51. Quoted in Adelman, *A&P*, 61–62. See also Levinson, *The Great A&P and the Struggle for Small Business in America*, 100, for an explanation of the roles of division managers. Levinson does not address the division managers' experimentation with self-service in 1927 and 1928.

52. Adelman, *A&P*, 2.

53. Adelman, *A&P*, 62.

54. Lestico, *School of the Chain Store*, book 5, *Dressing the Store*, 89.

55. "Piggly Wiggly Why Shop Around?," *Oakland Tribune*, January 20, 1925.

56. Lohner, "Customer Attitude toward Chicago Grocery-Store Practices," 248.

57. Longstreth, "The Diffusion of the Community Shopping Center Concept during the Interwar Decades." It is notable that several self-service store patent holders were real estate brokers. For example, Joseph N. Grant (patent 1,751,199) and Frank E. Jones (patent 1,397,379).

58. Longstreth, "The Diffusion of the Community Shopping Center Concept during the Interwar Decades," 271–72; Worley, *J. C. Nichols and the Shaping of Kansas City*, 249–53, 258.

59. Quoted in Worley, *J. C. Nichols and the Shaping of Kansas City*, 251.

60. Longstreth, "The Neighborhood Shopping Center in Washington, D.C., 1930–1941," 13–14.

61. Jones, "An Analysis of Piggly Wiggly Progress," 38.

62. Lestico, *The School of the Chain Store*, book 11, *The Chain at Headquarters*, 9.

63. Jones, "An Analysis of Piggly Wiggly Progress," 38.

64. Levinson, *The Great A&P and the Struggle for Small Business in America*, 89.

65. J. Walter Thompson Company (New York office), "Piggly Wiggly Stepping Out in Novel Fashion," *NewsLetter* no. 187 (September 1, 1927), 377.

66. Parkin, *Food Is Love*, 17.

67. Frederick, "Teach Women What Advertising Does," 178.

68. Piggly Wiggly Stores, "She Has Astonished Her Husband . . . and the World," *Saturday Evening Post*, October 15, 1927, 143.

69. She Pays $40 for Her Hats," *LHJ*, December 1930, 119.

70. "Sports . . . Major and Minor. . at Miami Include This Adventure in Shopping," *LHJ*, February 1930, 205. The ad declared that swimming and sunning were "major sports in fashionable Miami" and described Piggly Wiggly as a minor sport "only because it takes so little time!"

71. "Washington. . . City of Etiquette . . . Gives Precedence to This Vogue in Shopping," *LHJ*, April 1930, 154.

72. "In Mile-High Denver Society Lives the Modern Life . . . Even to Marketing," *LHJ*, June 1930, 142.

73. "She Pays $40 for Her Hats," *LHJ*, December 1930, 119.

74. "Into the Scrap-Basket Modern Women Have Cast Another Tradition," *LHJ*, November 1928, 73.

75. "Now She Is Free to Choose for Herself," *LHJ*, June 1928, 183.

76. "All by Herself She Decides Just What She Wants," *LHJ*, October 1928, 204.

77. Day Monroe, "You and Your Food Dealers," *LHJ*, January 1930, 87.

78. APW toilet paper advertisement, *LHJ*, January 1924, 127.

79. "Priceless This Confidence of American Mothers," *LHJ*, May 1928, 71.

80. Daniel Thomas Cook evaluates the ways that department stores in the 1930s began to create separate spaces to appeal directly to children and in the process crafted a new understanding of children as consumers. See Cook, "Spatial Biographies of Children's Consumption." Cook does not consider the history of children's consumption in grocery spaces, and the impact of self-service offers a different perspective on the historical process of consumer practices and the construction of childhood. The 1948 first edition of the Little Golden Books volume *Let's Go Shopping* features siblings whose mother sends them "all by themselves" to the neighborhood grocery store to buy a gift for their father. When the story was reissued ten years later as a Wonder Book, *Let's Go Shopping* featured children contained in a shopping cart seat while their mother shops at a new supermarket. Lenora Combes, *Let's Go Shopping*

(New York: Simon and Schuster, 1948); Guyon Brooke, *Let's Go Shopping* (New York: Wonder Books, 1958).

81. "Piggly Wiggly Mothers . . . Send the Children to Piggly Wiggly," *Santa Ana Register*, January 18, 1929.

82. Parkin, *Food Is Love*, 30.

83. Miller, *A Theory of Shopping*, 9.

84. "They Like to Show Their Friends This Fascinating Way to Shop," *LHJ*, February 1929, 161.

85. "Is She a Better Business Man than Her Husband?," *LHJ*, April 1928, 181.

86. "Here She Is Free to Reach Her Own Decisions," *LHJ*, October 1929, 185.

87. "A Matrimonial Piggly Wiggly," *The Turnstile*, January 25, 1923.

88. Carrier, "Reconciling Personal Commodities and Personal Relations in Industrial Society," 582–83.

89. Chaffee and Kerbey, "Self-Service in the Retailing of Food Products," 3.

## Chapter 4. Navigating the Self-Service Landscape

1. Schlereth, "Country Stores, County Fairs, and Mail-Order Catalogues," 375.

2. Kline, *Consumers in the Country*; Katherine Jellison, *Entitled to Power*.

3. Moreton, "It Came from Bentonville," 58, 72.

4. Chaffee and Kerbey, "Self-Service in the Retailing of Food Products," 4.

5. Hayward and White, *Chain Stores*, 331.

6. Chaffee and Kerbey, "Self-Service in the Retailing of Food Products," 14.

7. U.S. Department of Commerce, *Louisville Grocery Survey*, 17.

8. Hamilton, *Supermarket USA*, 11.

9. Hayward and White, *Chain Stores*, 24.

10. *Management Problems in Retail Grocery Stores*, 20.

11. U.S. Department of Commerce, *Louisville Grocery Survey*, 17.

12. Chaffee and Kerbey, "Self-Service in the Retailing of Food Products," 14.

13. Hayward and White, *Chain Stores*, 24.

14. Gosnell, *Supermarkets and Self-Service Food Stores*, 7.

15. Question 1h. on the short form and long form Retail Schedule, Department of Commerce, Bureau of the Census, Washington, Census of Business: 1930, Appendix D, p. 843, Appendix E, p. 847.

16. Gosnell, *Supermarkets and Self-Service Food Stores*, 2. Census results are supported by store patent data and photographic evidence documenting the popularity of self-service among small, independent proprietors.

17. Gosnell, *Supermarkets and Self-Service Food Stores*, 2.

18. See Miller, *Itinerant Photographer, Corpus Christi, 1934*. The unknown photographer abandoned 560 glass plate negatives at the George Tallmadge studio in

Corpus Christi where he probably rented darkroom facilities to process photographs he made during the month of February 1934. Tallmadge gave the collection to his friend Dr. John F. McGregor, who donated them to the photography collection at the University of Texas at Austin in 1976. According to Miller, "absolutely no information on either photographer or subject came with the glass plates, no list of names or receipt book. Store locations and people in the photographs were carefully identified through the research and "remarkable eye and memory" of long-time Corpus Christi resident Eric Warren (xiii, xiv).

19. Gosnell, *Supermarkets and Self-Service Food Stores*, 1.

20. Gosnell, *Supermarkets and Self-Service Food Stores*, 2. "Independents account for 1,321 of the 6,221 self-service stores of more than $100,000, and chains for the remaining 4,900."

21. Gosnell, *Supermarkets and Self-Service Food Stores*, p. 3.

22. "Piggly Wiggly Stores in East in Financial Trouble," *American Food Journal*, December 1922, 40.

23. Deutsch, "Exploring New Insights into Retail History," 131, 132.

24. Elvins, *Sales and Celebrations*, 17, 18.

25. The East North Central states were Ohio, Indiana, Illinois, Michigan, and Wisconsin. The Mid-Atlantic states were New York, New Jersey, and Pennsylvania. The census measured store size based on sales volume, not square footage. To understand the relationship between sales volume and store size, it can be helpful to consider that Piggly Wiggly stores would likely have been in the group with sales of about $100,000 to $199,999 annually. This estimate is based on A. C. Jones's report that sales per store throughout the Piggly Wiggly chain averaged $2,200 per week. Jones, "Analysis of Piggly Wiggly Progress," 7.

26. Spellman, *Cornering the Market*. See especially pp. 47–80.

27. Data for Dallas based on *Worley's Dallas (Texas) City Directory 1928*.

28. Scroop, "Local and National Identities in the Politics of Consumption," 957.

29. Elvins, *Sales and Celebrations*, 21.

30. Interrante, "You Can't Go to Town in a Bathtub," 158.

31. Veblen, "The Country Town," 418.

32. McKenzie, *The Metropolitan Community*, 6–7.

33. Wilson, *The Cart That Changed the World*, 33.

34. "Piggly Wiggly No. 4," *Tulsa Tribune*, April 6, 1923.

35. "Chain of Grocery Stores Established by Tulsans," *American Saturday Night* (Tulsa), June 15, 1923.

36. Wilson, *The Cart That Changed the World*, 35.

37. Wilson, *The Cart That Changed the World*, 38.

38. Wilson, *The Cart That Changed the World*, 42.

39. Chang, *The Color of the Land*, 130–31.

40. Sun Grocery Company ad, *Okmulgee (OK) Daily Times*, February 4, 1928.

41. "The A and E Grocery's Definition of Self Service," *Okmulgee (OK) Daily Times*, February 10, 1923.

42. "Korn Kribs Feed the World," *Shawnee (OK) News-Star*, March 15, 1922.

43. "Announcing the New Self-Service," *Blackwell (OK) Journal-Tribune*, August 7, 1924.

44. See Wilson, *The Cart That Changed the World*, 59, for a photograph of the downtown Reno Avenue Standard Food Store in 1930.

45. "Mob Wrecks City Store in Food Riot," *Oklahoma News* (Oklahoma City), January 20, 1931.

46. Wilson, *The Cart That Changed the World*, 60–61.

47. Goldman, "The Produce Market on a Self-Service Basis."

48. Goldman, "The Produce Market on a Self-Service Basis," 85.

49. Chaffee and Kerbey, "Self-Service in the Retailing of Food Products," 19.

50. Julius Cytron, Gate Construction for Stores patent. The fact that Cytron was a Piggly Wiggly franchisee offers interesting evidence of independent experimentation by Piggly Wiggly franchisees who made local adjustments in the patented store design. See "Piggly Wiggly Anniversary," *Tulsa Tribune*, November 12, 1922, for a history of Cytron's Piggly Wiggly franchise in Tulsa.

51. Nelson T. Sharp, Self-Serving Store patent.

52. Alexander C. Robert. Self-Service Store Equipment patent.

53. Lorenzo Norwood Anderson. Self Serving Store patent.

54. Chaffee and Kerbey, "Self-Service in the Retailing of Food Products," 6.

55. "Main St., U.S.A."

56. I am indebted to my University of North Carolina Greensboro (UNCG) colleague David Gwynn, digital projects coordinator at UNCG Libraries, for insights and evidence regarding grocery store locations. In 1999 David launched Groceteria.com, a site about the history of American and Canadian urban chains and supermarkets from the 1920s through the present, with an emphasis on the physical structures and locations. David calls it a hobby site because he works on it in his free time, but over the past twenty-three years and counting he has built an incredible repository of chain store and supermarket history. A core element of the site is the location histories of chains David maps using twentieth-century city directories and phone books collected during his travels. To date David has mapped historical store locations in well over three hundred places in Canada and the United States.

57. Adelman, *A&P*, 58.

58. See David Gwynn's map of Winston-Salem grocery chain locations: Groceteria .com, http://www.groceteria.com/place/north-carolina/winston-salem/winston-salem -history.

59. Levinson, *The Great A&P and the Struggle for Small Business*, 90.

60. *Uno Animo* (Safeway), July 1929, 47. Courtesy of David Gwynn.

61. Herman A. Wieman, Shelving patent.

62. Crawford, Fixture for Self Serving Stores patent.

63. Briggs, Fixture for Self Serving Stores patent.

64. Howard, Store Furniture patent.

65. Lu Ann Jones, *Mama Learned Us to Work*, 29.

66. U.S. Department of Commerce, *Louisville Grocery Survey*, 73.

67. For examples of self-service rolling stores, see patents by Moody, Self-Serving Vehicle-Store; Wieman, Vehicle Body; Martin, Portable Grocery-Store; Moseley, Portable Automobile Grocery Store; Edward J. Greene, Serve-Self Motor Store; Bowen, Jr., Vending and Serve-Self Store and Vehicle.

68. Clyde Martin was a newspaper editor, and Leonard Hoffman was a druggist. How they knew each other or came to work on self-service design is unknown. Drug stores were experimenting with self-service at the time, but their patent specifically addresses grocery delivery.

69. Clyde W. Martin and Leonard E. Hoffman, Itinerant Vending and Sales Vehicle patent.

70. "Davis-Gilcrease Install 'M' System of Store Service, Latest Help Yourself Grocery Store Idea Opens Saturday," *Corsicana (TX) Daily Sun*, October 30, 1925.

71. *Vernon (TX) Record*, August 8, 1924.

72. *"M" System Stores brand trademark 218,671 registered September 28, 1926; store fixtures trademark 223,645, registered 2 November 1926; "Massie-Coffee to Re-Open Saturday, New Fixtures and New Methods of Merchandising Announced by Store," *Vernon (TX) Record*, August 5, 1924; "'M' System Store Will Be Opened in Sedalia Tomorrow," *Sedalia (MO) Democrat*, December 7, 1928.

73. "Large New Industry Coming to Atlanta," *Atlanta Constitution*, March 1, 1925.

74. "A New 'M' System Comes to Manhattan," *Morning Chronicle* (Manhattan, Kans.), June 22, 1928.

75. "The World's Most Beautiful Grocery Stores," *Atlanta Constitution*, February 17, 1929.

76. "Large New Industry Coming to Atlanta," *Atlanta Constitution*, March 1, 1925.

77. "Carolinas Welcome New Chain Grocery System," *Asheville Citizen-Times*, February 16, 1926.

78. *"Carolina Chambers of Commerce and Bankers Approve Locally Owned 'M' System Chain Grocery," *Asheville Citizen-Times*, July 24, 1927.

79. "Carolinas Welcome New Chain Grocery System. M System Self-Serving Stores Now Opening Rapidly," *Asheville Citizen-Times*, February 16, 1926.

80. "Carolina Chambers of Commerce and Bankers Approve Locally Owned 'M' System Chain Grocery," *Asheville Citizen-Times*, July 24, 1927.

81. "Evolution in Retail Grocery Methods, *Asheville Citizen-Times*, January 22, 1928.

82. "Carolinas Welcome New Chain Grocery System, M System Self-Serving Stores Now Opening Rapidly," *Asheville Citizen-Times*, February 16, 1926.

83. "The Self-Serving Store of the Hour," *Atlanta Constitution*, July 19, 1925.

84. "Carolina Chambers of Commerce and Bankers Approve Locally Owned 'M' System Chain Grocery," *Asheville Citizen-Times*, July 24, 1927.

85. "The Self-Serving Store of the Hour," *Atlanta Constitution*, July 19, 1925.

86. "New Chain Store Will Be Opened by Thurston Cole," *Bryan (TX) Daily Eagle*, January 24, 1929.

87. "Mrs. A. E. Nelson, owner 'M' System Store," *Atlanta Constitution*, March 24, 1935. The announcement included a picture of Mrs. Nelson.

88. "Evolution in Retail Grocery Methods," *Asheville Citizen-Times*, January 22, 1928.

89. "Locally Owned Stores Can Now Make Money in Grocery Business," *Greenville (SC) News*, March 19, 1930.

90. "'M' System, Piggly Wiggly Celebrate Anniversary," *Amarillo Globe*, October 30, 1931.

91. Scroop, "Local and National Identities in the Politics of Consumption," 954.

92. Scroop, "Local and National Identities in the Politics of Consumption," 948–49.

93. Quoted in Moreton, "It Came from Bentonville," 71.

94. Swann, "Human Nature," *Sermons*, 187.

95. M System ad, *Clovis (NM) News-Journal*, July 4, 1930.

Chapter Five. The Purchase-Inducing Force of the Store

1. Saunders, Arrangement and Construction of Store Fixtures patent.

2. Chaffee and Kerbey, "Self-Service in the Retailing of Food Products," 15.

3. Longstreth, *The Buildings of Main Street*.

4. Esperdy, *Modernizing Main Street*, 7.

5. Esperdy, *Modernizing Main Street*, 27. Emphasis in original.

6. Longstreth, *The Buildings of Main Street*, 19.

7. Beasley, *The Corner Store*, remains an important model for empirical analysis of small-business store interiors. The book was published in conjunction with the exhibition *The Corner Store*, presented at the National Building Museum, Washington, D.C., September 22, 1999–March 6, 2000.

8. Liebs, *Main Street to Miracle Mile*, 120–122.

9. Liebs, *Main Street to Miracle Mile*, 122. See also Richard Longstreth, *The Drive-In, the Supermarket, and the Transformation of Commercial Space*, 87. Emphasizing the impact of the automobile on American commercial architecture, Longstreth evaluates the drive-in market in Los Angeles as a precursor to supermarket building in the city and discusses the self-service innovations of Ralphs Grocery Company, explaining that the company started experimenting with self-service in 1925 and that within four years self-service had become standard for the grocery departments of all Ralphs stores. While Longstreth describes the gondola shelving in the display space, he does not offer details about the evolution of Ralphs self-service store arrangements or how the company coordinated store fixtures to operationalize self-service in the late 1920s.

10. Andrews, *Shopping*.

11. Cowan, "The Consumption Junction," 255.

12. "Uphams Corner Market, 1920–1927" National Register Nomination, prepared 1990, https://web.archive.org/web/20200305233122/http://www.dorchesteratheneum.org/page.php?id=598.

13. Marnell, *Once upon a Store*, 146.

14. *The Turnstile*, August 20, 1922.

15. Marnell, *Once upon a Store*, 149, 150.

16. Marnell, *Once upon a Store*, 33.

17. Marnell, *Once upon a Store*, 150.

18. Marnell, *Once upon a Store*, 154.

19. Marnell, *Once upon a Store*, 152.

20. U.S. Department of Commerce, *Louisville Grocery Survey*, 54–55.

21. Lutey, "Lutey Brothers Marketeria," 52.

22. "Alphabetical Self-Service Grocery."

23. Rogers/Nifty Jiffy advertisement, *Atlanta Constitution*, June 30, 1928. On September 14, 1924, the *Constitution* published a picture of the Nifty Jiffy interior crammed with shoppers on opening day. It was described as the first self-service store system ever organized in Atlanta—home-grown, financed by Atlanta capital and led by Atlanta men. It was said, "A customer can enter a Nifty-Jiffy store and visit any part of it without being required to follow a particular marked or fenced path as in other self-service stores [such as Piggly Wiggly]," *Atlanta Constitution*, September 18, 1926.

24. Smiley, Self Service Store Equipment patent.

25. U.S. Department of Commerce, *Louisville Grocery Survey*, 65.

26. U.S. Department of Commerce, *Louisville Grocery Survey*, 61–62.

27. U.S. Department of Commerce, *Louisville Grocery Survey*, 2.

28. Tedlow, *New and Improved*, 230.

29. Tribble's reasoning was explained by his attorneys, Shepard & Campbell to Commission of Patents, April 11, 1919, Patent Case File No. 1,305,033, Record Group 241: Records of the Patent and Trademark Office, 1836–1978, Patent Case Files Series, 1836–1993, National Archives, Kansas City, Missouri.

30. Tribble, Vending Apparatus patent, 1919.

31. Patterson, "The Cost of Distributing Groceries," 75.

32. Tribble, Vending Apparatus patent, 1919. One of the first cash register inventors called his device "The Incorruptible Cashier." See Spellman, *Cornering the Market*, 51.

33. Rorrer and Mitterer, Self Service Store patent.

34. Carroll, Self-Service Store with Revoluble Shelves patent.

35. Fritsche, Store System patent.

36. Fritsche, Store System patent.

37. Fritsche, Store System patent.

38. DeBakey, Home Store patent.

39. Tribble, Vending Apparatus patent, 1919. For a similar shelf mechanism, see Hill, Arrangement and Construction of Self Service Store Fixtures patent.

40. Smiley, Self Serving Store patent.

41. Carroll, Store Self-Service System. This is not the patent that inspired Nifty Jiffy.

42. Clerc, Store patent.

43. Duffin, Self-Serving Store patent.

44. A *Women's Wear Daily* article about the store described Duffin as a Louisville attorney who invented the store but "had no plans for developing a chain of stores of his own, his idea being to market the rights for use of the patents." See "Shop Without Leaving Your Car," 15.

45. Duffin, Self-Serving Store patent.

46. Rylander, Storage and Display Apparatus for Merchandise patent.

47. Lestico, *Building the Story of Piggly Wiggly*.

48. Dinerstein, *Swinging the Machine*, 184.

49. Saunders, *Eligibility to Piggly Wiggly*.

50. "No Clerks to Persuade You," *LHJ*, December 1928, 111.

51. Beaujot, "The Beauty of Her Hands," 167.

52. Ball, Store Service patent.

53. *Dry Goods Reporter*, February 16, 1901, 30, quoted in Abelson, *When Ladies Go A-Thieving*, 77.

54. Franken and Larrabee, *Packages That Sell*, 241.

55. Harris, "The Self Service Store and Advertising," 37.

56. Thompson, *The Soundscape of Modernity*, 1. Thompson's focus is on the architectural acoustics of elaborate, architect-designed spaces such as theaters, music halls, and churches, but she interprets their choices as indicative of a broader new, modern culture of listening.

57. Thompson, *Soundscape of Modernity*, 2.

58. Laird, "Noise Does Impair Production," 59–60.

59. Thompson, *Soundscape of Modernity*, 155–56.

60. Deutsch, *Building a Housewife's Paradise*, 68–69.

61. Jacobs, *Pocketbook Politics*, 27.

62. Chaffee and Kerbey, "Self-Service in the Retailing of Food Products," 9.

63. Da Roza, Self Serving Store patent (1919).

64. Lestico, *Building the Story of Piggly Wiggly*.

65. Chaffee and Kerbey, "Self-Service in the Retailing of Food Products," 10.

66. Ball, Store Service patent.

67. "Stop Fruit Pinching with This Sign," *Progressive Grocer*, June 1922, 33.

68. Chaffee and Kerbey, "Self-Service in the Retailing of Food Products," 35.

69. Chaffee and Kerbey, "Self-Service in the Retailing of Food Products," 11.

70. Lohner, "Customer Attitude Toward Chicago Grocery-Store Practices," 248, 249.

71. Abelson, *When Ladies Go A-Thieving*, 79.

72. Chaffee and Kerbey, "Self-Service in the Retailing of Food Products," 11, 13.

73. *Chicago Daily Tribune*, May 19, 1921.

74. Alva Wright Boswell Johnson, Self-Service Store patent (1923).

75. Chaffee and Kerbey, "Self-Service in the Retailing of Food Products," 33.

76. William B. McCarty, Self-Serving Store patent.

77. William B. McCarty, Self-Serving Store patent.

78. Chaffee and Kerbey, "Self-Service in the Retailing of Food Products," 21.

79. William B. McCarty, Self-Serving Store patent.

80. Lestico, School of the Chain Store, book 2, 53.

81. Saunders Arrangement and Construction of Store Fixtures patent.

82. *Atlanta Constitution*, August 17, 1924.

83. Harvey, Self-Serving Store patent.

84. "This, Too, She Has Done Without Her Husband's Help," *LHJ*, February 1928, 170.

Chapter 6. Mechanizing Paternalism

1. Holsey, "White Folks First Please," 46.

2. Holsey, "White Folks First Please," 46.

3. Hale, *Making Whiteness*, 137.

4. Ling, *America and the Automobile,* 8. The assembly line was initially invented in 1913 by workers at the Ford Motor Company Highland Park Plant in Detroit. It evolved as a managerial tool for monitoring workers on the line. See also Nye, *America's Assembly Line.*

5. Foucault, *Discipline and Punish,* 201. "Hence the major effect of the Panopticon: to induce in the inmate a state of conscious and permanent visibility that assures the automatic functioning of power." The panopticon "automatizes and disindividualizes power" (202).

6. See for example, Rabinowitz, *Race Relations in the Urban South*; Hunter, *To 'Joy My Freedom*; Hickey, *Hope and Danger in the New South City*; Pruitt, *The Other Great Migration.*

7. Blumenthal's—a Store of True Economy," *Savannah Tribune*, September 13, 1919.

8. Edwards, *The Southern Urban Negro as a Consumer*, 97.

9. Johnson, *Patterns of Negro Segregation,* 63, 64.

10. Edwards, *The Southern Urban Negro as a Consumer*, 97.

11. Johnson, *Patterns of Negro Segregation,* 64.

12. Johnson, *Patterns of Negro Segregation*, xxii.

13. Johnson, *Patterns of Negro Segregation*, 267, 270.

14. Edwards, *The Southern Urban Negro as a Consumer*, 234.

15. Edwards, The Southern Urban Negro as a Consumer, 54–56.

16. See Weems, *Desegregating the Dollar,* 26.

17. "Piggly Wiggly Adds Another Link in the Chain," *News Scimitar* (Memphis), June 17, 1919.

18. "Piggly Wiggly All Over the World: The Piggly Wiggly Sign and What It Means to You," *Negro Star*, July 21, 1922.

19. See, for example, *Voice of the People* (Birmingham, AL), *Emancipator* (Montgomery, AL); and *Colored Directory* (Columbia, MO).

20. *Voice of the People*, May 8, 1920.

21. *Voice of the People*, October 1, 1921.

22. *Emancipator*, July 31, 1920.

23. "Your Back Bone! Let It Be Good and Strong," *Commercial Appeal*, August 2, 1928.

24. "Piggly Wiggly Politics," *New York Age*, August 11, 1928, 4. For the history of entrenched racial repression in Memphis, see Honey, *Southern Labor and Black Civil Rights*.

25. "'Boycott Saunders' Negro Paper Plea," *Commercial Appeal*, August 2, 1928. The *Commercial Appeal* endorsed Horton in an editorial titled "For Governor Horton and White Supremacy."

26. Quoted in McKee and Chisenhall, *Beale Black and Blue*, 56.

27. "Boycott Saunders," *Commercial Appeal*, August 2, 1928.

28. Grocery stores were also central to the "Don't Buy Where You Can't Work" campaigns of the 1930s. See Ware, "The New Negro Alliance." *The New Negro Alliance v. Sanitary Grocery Co.* (393 U.S. 552) in 1938 became a landmark civil rights case when the Supreme Court upheld the right of the New Negro Alliance to picket against the hiring practices of a chain store that had moved into an African American neighborhood in Washington, D.C., but refused to hire Black workers.

29. Quoted in McKee and Chisenhall, *Beale Black and Blue*, 56.

30. Edwards, *The Southern Urban Negro as a Consumer*, 125.

31. Edwards, *The Southern Urban Negro as a Consumer*, 126, 131.

32. Holsey, "The C.M.A. Stores Face the Chains."

33. Holsey, "What the Negro Is Doing in Business," 38. This is the only example I have found of a Black-owned self-service store before 1940.

34. Peña, "The History of Technology, the Resistance of Archives, and the Whiteness of Race," 923, 924.

35. Weems, *Desegregating the Dollar*, 20.

36. Haring, "The Negro as Consumer," 68.

37. Sinclair, "Integrating the Histories of Race and Technology," 2.

38. Hale, "For Colored" and "For White," 169. For the importance of crossroads country stores in the southern economy, see Ayers, *The Promise of the New South*; Clark, *Pills, Petticoats, and Plows*; Atherton, *The Southern Country Store*; Schlereth, "Country Stores, County Fairs, and Mail-Order Catalogues."

39. Of thirty-eight self-service store patents approved between 1917 and 1932, twenty-seven were submitted by grocers from Tennessee, Alabama, Florida, South Carolina, North Carolina, Mississippi, Georgia, Kentucky, Louisiana, and Texas.

40. *Worley's Dallas (Texas) City Directory 1928*.

41. Hale, *Making Whiteness*, 188.

42. Weyeneth, "The Architecture of Racial Segregation," 23–24.

43. Berrey, *The Jim Crow Routine*, 38.

44. Robert A. Tribble, Vending Apparatus patent (1920). Some scholars have begun to analyze the historical experience of queuing as a turning point in shopper experience. See, for example, Bailey, Alexander, and Shaw, "Queuing as a Changing Shopper Experience." Sociologists were the first to evaluate queuing as a social practice. See Mann, "Queue Culture."

45. Abel, *Signs of the Times*, 16.

46. LeFebvre, *The Production of Space*, 116.

47. Low, "Spatializing Culture," 35, 37.

48. Gregson, Crewe, and Brooks, "Shopping, Space, and Practice."

49. Weyeneth, "The Architecture of Racial Segregation," 12.

50. *Commercial Appeal*, September 24, 1916.

51. *Commercial Appeal*, September 7, 1916.

52. "The Piggly Wiggly Will Establish a New Fashion," *Commercial Appeal*, September 3, 1916.

53. *Commercial Appeal*, August 27, 1916.

54. *Atlanta Constitution*, July 31, 1920.

55. Hale, *Making Whiteness*, 87–93.

56. *Commercial Appeal*, June 3, 1917.

57. "Piggly Wiggly," *Memphis News Scimitar*, June 19, 1917.

58. *Commercial Appeal*, September 24, 1916.

59. Howse, *Falling Stars*, 161.

60. Hunter, "The Women Are Asking for BREAD, Why Give Them STONE," 74.

61. Felton, *Country Life in Georgia in the Days of My Youth*, 33.

62. Remus, "Disruptive Shopping"; Domosh, "Creating New York's Nineteenth-Century Retail District."

63. Ownby, *American Dreams in Mississippi*, 87–90, 93.

64. Hal Edmunds interviewed by LuAnn Jones, August 4, 1994, quoted in Jones, "Gender, Race, and Itinerant Commerce in the Rural New South," 308.

65. *Winston-Salem Journal*, May 26, 1929.

66. "Clubbed to Death by Furious Woman," *Evening Star* (Washington, DC), May 25, 1929.

67. *Winston-Salem Journal*, June 14, 1929.

68. Cutchins, *Memories of Old Richmond*, 28.

69. Howse, *Falling Stars*, 6.

70. Howse, *Falling Stars*, 65.

71. Welty, "The Little Store," 639.

72. *Commercial Appeal*, September 7, 1917.

73. "One Man's Idea Built Up a Big Business," *Commercial Appeal*, August 19, 1916.

See Spellman, *Cornering the Market*, 13–21, for the origins of grocery stores as grog shops that sold liquor.

74. One Man's Idea Built Up a Big Business," *Commercial Appeal*.

75. *Commercial Appeal*, September 12, 1916.

76. *Commercial Appeal*, August 29, 1916.

77. Holman, *Save a Nickel on a Quarter*, 12, 14.

78. McCarty, Self-Serving Store patent.

79. Holman, *Save a Nickel on a Quarter*, 22.

80. National Register of Historic Places Registration Form, Belhaven Historic District, Hinds County, Mississippi, 13, 296. Form prepared by David Preziosi, Mississippi Heritage Trust, July 2, 2011.

81. Betty McCarty Edwards quoted in Yancy, "Eudora's Jitney."

82. Holman, *Save a Nickel on a Quarter*, 15. Holman estimated that by 1946, 90 percent of Jitney customers were women.

83. Yancy, "Eudora's Jitney." Welty shopped regularly at Jitney Jungle 14.

84. "Eudora Welty, Pulitzer Prize-Winning Author from Jackson, Shares Her Thoughts on Jitney 14," *Clarion Ledger/Jackson (MS) Daily News*, October 2, 1988.

85. Dipman, "Uncle Sam Builds a Model Grocery Store", 19, 22.

86. Quoted in Deutsch, "Untangling Alliances," 166.

87. Sinclair, "Integrating the Histories of Race and Technology," 10.

88. McCarty, Self-Serving Store patent.

89. See Sybil Miller's evocative analysis of the series of five photographs the itinerant photographer made in Biel's Self-Service Grocery in *Itinerant Photographer, Corpus Christi, 1934*, 46, 48.

90. "Clerk Sets Trap Which Catches Two Mexicans," *Austin (TX) American*, March 29, 1922.

91. "Mexican Woman Jailed on Minor Theft Charge," *Austin (TX) American-Statesman*, March 28, 1922.

92. Johnson, *Patterns of Negro Segregation*, 65.

93. Jim Klash, "Dixie Grocery Denies Refund to Housewife," *People's Voice*, May 16, 1942.

94. "Over 'Bad Meat' Charge," *People's Voice*, December 18, 1943.

95. "Claim Store Clerk Beat Woman for Protesting Rotten Meat," *Plaindealer* (Kansas City, KS), November 5, 1943. The report originated from Atlanta.

96. "Black Shoppers 'Tell It Like It Is' about Shopping in Racine," *Racine Star News*, December 19, 1970.

Chapter 7

1. Zimmerman, *Super Market* (1937), 8. Zimmerman offers one of the most detailed histories of Big Bear and credits Robert Otis, one of the founders of the chain, "for

his generous and timely cooperation in supplying . . . valuable information" during his supermarket research (viii).

2. Zimmerman, *Super Market* (1937), 12.

3. Levinson, *The Great A&P and the Struggle for Small Business in America*, 97.

4. "Big Bear Shopping Center—A Supermarket."

5. Zimmerman, *Super Market* (1937), 12. For chain stores' reliance on multiple units, see Lebhar, *Chain Stores in America*, 7.

6. Phillips, "The Supermarket," 194n18.

7. Zimmerman, *Super Market* (1937), 16.

8. "Markets," 205.

9. Clarence Saunders was not among the small group of supermarket operators Zimmerman invited to his office in May 1937 to plan the first Super Market Institute. See Zimmerman, *The Super Market* (1955), 72–73. In 1932 Saunders had broken ground in Memphis on what he called his "mammoth store," planned to encompass sixty thousand square feet in a two-story building with twenty checkout stands. But the supermarket was never completed. Saunders declared bankruptcy and closed his last Clarence Saunders, Sole Owner store in 1933. From then on he turned his inventive attention to smaller store formats based on vending machine technology. Reviving the ideal of a clerk-less store, Saunders anticipated that his Keedoozle store of the 1930s would need one-fifth of the personnel of a supermarket. When he died in 1953, he was working on a new store called Foodelectric, also based on vending machine technology, in which customers used handheld adding machines for self-checkout. See Freeman, *Clarence Saunders and the Founding of Piggly Wiggly*, 129–57.

10. "Max M. Zimmerman, an Expert on Supermarkets, Is Dead at 82," *New York Times*, May 17, 1972.

11. Zimmerman, *The Super Market* (1955), 21–28.

12. For a contrast to my emphasis on design continuities, see Bowlby, *Carried Away*. In her pioneering work on self-service shopping, Bowlby primarily interprets self-service as an invention of supermarkets in the 1930s and presents Piggly Wiggly as a small self-service store disconnected from supermarket versions of self-service (141).

13. Tedlow, *New and Improved*; Longstreth, *The Drive-In, the Supermarket, and the Transformation of Commercial Space*; Strasser, "Woolworth to Walmart"; Mack, "Speaking of Tomatoes." Robert Gordon emphasizes the role of chain stores and supermarkets in self-service innovation. Gordon, *The Rise and Fall of American Growth*.

14. Deutsch, *Building a Housewife's Paradise*.

15. Gosnell, *Supermarkets and Self-Service Food Stores*, 1.

16. "Big Bear Shopping Center."

17. See, for example Zimmerman, *Super Market* (1937), 9.

18. Zimmerman, "The Supermarket and the Changing Retail Structure."

19. "Mob Wrecks City Store in Food Riot," *Oklahoma News* (Oklahoma City), January 20, 1931.

20. Deutsch, "From 'Wild Animal Stores' to Women's Sphere," 147.

21. "Carle's Market Invites Miami to a Super Wedding."

22. Zimmerman, *Super Market* (1937), 73.

23. Quoted in Zimmerman, *Super Market* (1937), 17.

24. Dipman, *The Modern Grocery Store*, 7. See Dipman, *The Modern Grocery Store*, 56, for the self-service floor plan described as a "type of store popular in the South."

25. Dipman, "Merchandising Trends in the Food Trade," 271, 272.

26. Wales, review of Dipman and O'Brien, *Self-Service and Semi-Self-Service Food Stores*.

27. Dipman and O'Brien, *Self-Service and Semi-Self-Service Food Stores*. O'Brien was associate editor of *Progressive Grocer*.

28. Dipman and O'Brien, *Self-Service and Semi-Self-Service Food Stores*, 70, 35, 229.

29. Zimmerman, *Super Market* (1937), 101.

30. Dipman "Uncle Sam Builds a Model Grocery Store," 25.

31. Dipman and O'Brien, *Self-Service and Semi-Self-Service Food Stores*, 78.

32. Dipman and O'Brien, *Self-Service and Semi-Self-Service Food Stores*, 90.

33. Dipman and O'Brien, *Self-Service and Semi-Self-Service Food Stores*, 35.

34. Dipman and O'Brien, *Self-Service and Semi-Self-Service Food Stores*, 85.

35. Grocer quoted in Zimmerman, *Super Market* (1937), 100.

36. Grandclement, "Wheeling One's Groceries around the Store," 239.

37. Zimmerman, *The Super Market* (1955), 18.

38. Goldman, Combination Basket and Carriage patent.

39. Wilson, *The Cart that Changed the World*, 91.

40. Dipman, "Uncle Sam Builds a Model Grocery Store," 25.

41. Gosnell, *Supermarkets and Self-Service Food Stores*. Data for the supermarket report was tabulated from the 1939 retail census, which included a special schedule for enumerating grocery and self-service stores (see 19–20, tables 10 and 11).

42. Gosnell, *Supermarkets and Self-Service Food Stores*, 2.

43. Horowitz, *Putting Meat on the American Table*, 140.

44. Carey, "A Study of Centralized and Decentralized Prepackaged Meat Operations." After World War II, individual retail stores continued to play an important role in packaging meat along with centralized prepackaging operations of some chain stores and the increasing role of meatpackers and processors in experimenting with self-service meat packaging. While the large supermarkets of the Grand Union chain in New York created meat processing departments inside their stores, a small chain of five grocery stores in Minot, North Dakota, centralized meat processing in a warehouse and distributed self-service packages for display in their rural stores (56–61). Carey noted, "Some chains are still not firmly convinced that self-service meat is particularly applicable to their type of business and therefore continue to merchandise meat by the old time-worn and established service system" (4).

45. Gosnell, *Supermarkets and Self-Service Food Stores* documented 31,183 self-service

stores; 23,089 of them were combination stores that sold meat.

46. Gosnell, *Supermarkets and Self-Service Food Stores*, 1.

47. U.S. Department of Commerce, *Louisville Grocery Survey*, 27.

48. Phillips, "The Supermarket," 194.

49. There were 23,089 self-service combination stores. South Atlantic, East South Central, and West South Central: 9,439 (41 percent); West South Central, Mountain, and Pacific: 8.989 (39 percent); New England, Middle Atlantic, and East North Central: 4,666 (20 percent). Gosnell, *Supermarkets and Self-Service Food Stores*.

50. Zimmerman, *The Super Market* (1955), 221, 222.

51. Dipman, *Self-Service and Semi-Self-Service Food Stores*, 166.

52. Horowitz, *Putting Meat on the American Table*, 141, 142.

53. Dickie, "Self-Service Meats," 16.

54. Dickie, "Self-Service Meats," 18.

55. Dickie, "Self-Service Meats," 18.

56. "Piggly Wiggly Meats Are Guaranteed Fresh and Good," *Brownsville Herald*, Piggly Wiggly Section, January 15, 1931.

57. Saunders, *Merchandise Needed—as Memphis Stocks a New Piggly Wiggly*.

58. "Come—See This New Store," *Greensboro (NC) Record*, October 22, 1936.

59. Dickie, "Self-Service Meats."

60. *Piggly Wiggly Catalog* no. 35 (1935), Hagley Museum and Library, Wilmington, Delaware. See "Suggestions for Self-Service Stores."

61. Zimmerman, *The Super Market* (1955), 85.

62. Dipman and O'Brien, *Self-Service and Semi-Self-Service Food Stores*, 226.

63. Dipman and O'Brien, *Self-Service and Semi-Self-Service Food Stores*, 223.

64. Bradley, Checking Station for Self-Service Stores patent.

65. *Piggly Wiggly Catalog* no. 35. See "Suggestions for Self-Service Stores."

66. National Cash Register Company advertisement, *Food Retailing: Chicagoland's Food Trade Magazine*, June 1947, 13.

67. Hutchinson, "Control of Money in the Food Store," 12. My emphasis.

68. This continues to be an area of concern for contemporary supermarkets, as the recent history of self-service checkout systems demonstrates. See, for example, Maria Halkias, "Supermarkets Consider Replacing Self-Checkout Lanes," *Dallas News*, July 7, 2011; Dan Berthiaume, "Survey Results Show Shopper Frustration with Self-Service Checkouts," *Chain Store Age*, October 15, 2013. http://www.chainstoreage.com/article/survey-results-show-shopper-frustration-self-service-checkouts.

69. Garth Close, Supermarket Construction patent.

Conclusion. Achieving Technological Momentum

1. McNamara's speech is quoted at length in Zimmerman, *The Super Market* (1955), 172–75.

2. Zimmerman, *The Super Market* (1955), 174.

3. Zimmerman, *The Super Market* (1955), 174.

4. Quoted in Zimmerman, *Super Market* (1937), 101.

5. Hughes, "Technological Momentum," 112.

6. Nye, *Technology Matters*, 53.

7. "The 'Piggly Wiggly' Stores and How They Located and Enlarged in Oakland and the Eastbay," *Oakland Tribune*, August 1, 1920. For an overview of Piggly Wiggly in Southern California, see "Piggly Wiggly Expansion Program," *Los Angeles Times*, February 13, 1927. According to the article, Piggly Wiggly started with six stores in Los Angeles 1919. "By April 1, 1927 there will be one hundred and twenty-six stores [in Southern California]."

8. Edwin J. Perkins offers the best history of the origins of the Safeway chain and explains how Charles Merrill, in partnership with Marion B. Skaggs, built Safeway into one of the largest grocery chains in the United States during the 1920s and 1930s. Skaggs handled operational business, and Merrill provided financing and expanded the chain through mergers and acquisitions. Perkins, *Wall Street to Main Street*, 109–26.

9. "Rapid Development of Skaggs-Safeway Store in This City Makes New Location Necessary," *Santa Cruz (CA) Evening News*, February 21, 1927.

10. Longstreth, *The Drive-In, the Supermarket, and the Transformation of Commercial Space*, 104–5.

11. *Uno Animo* (Safeway) 4, no. 10 (July 1929): 39. Published for the employees of Safeway Stores, Inc., and affiliated companies.

12. "183 Piggly Wiggly Stores Acquired by Safeway Firm," *Santa Ana (CA) Register*, February 4, 1929.

13. "Safeway Stores/Piggly Wiggly" ad, *Woodland (CA) Daily Democrat*, March 29, 1929.

14. Zimmerman, *Super Market* (1937), 40.

15. Piggly Wiggly stores remained in the Chicago area through the 1930s. *Chicago Tribune*, March 9, 1930.

16. In his celebratory history of the Kroger organization, George Laycock promotes the idea that Kroger was a self-service pioneer. The photographs of early self-service store interiors featured in the book, however, are actually of Piggly Wiggly stores. George Laycock, *The Kroger Story*, 53. Kroger had a rocky tenure in its takeover of the home company stores. In 1936 Memphis Piggly Wiggly and Kroger clerks went on strike for higher wages, better hours, and the right to join the Retail Clerks Union. Over a hundred clerks picketed seventy-seven stores for six weeks before the strike ended with an open shop agreement that allowed union members to return to work. Women played a significant role in organizing store boycotts and support for the strikers. A meeting of six hundred sympathizers at the Labor Temple, "held primarily for women, was presided over by Mrs. G. C. Frazier, wife of a union machinist and mother of a striking clerk." See *Commercial Appeal*, February 2, 1936. See coverage in the *News Scimitar* (Memphis) and

*Commercial Appeal* in January and February 1936. The strike was settled on February 22, 1936.

17. Eugene M. Lokey, "Piggly Wiggly in England," *New York Times*, August 16, 1931. British cooperative societies were the first to experiment with self-service retailing in Britain in the 1940s. See Shaw, "British Co-Operative Societies as Retail Innovators." See also Du Gay, "Self-Service," for the history of self-service in British retailing just after World War II.

18. Zimmerman, *The Super Market* (1955), 34.

19. Laycock, *The Kroger Story*, 53.

20. "William R. Lovette, Grocery Chain Chief," *New York Times*, March 17, 1978.

21. Presley, *Piggly Wiggly Southern Style*, 30.

22. The Piggly Wiggly factory in Jackson, Tennessee, continued to build store fixtures and offer updated options for franchisees until it closed in 1982. "Piggly Wiggly Fixture Business Closed Out," *Jackson Sun*, June 11, 1982.

23. Zimmerman, *The Super Market* (1955), 89.

24. Scranton, "Determinism and Indeterminacy in the History of Technology," 150.

25. Scranton, "Determinism and Indeterminacy in the History of Technology," 150.

26. Levinson, *The Great A & P*, 169.

27. Levinson, *The Great A & P*, 171.

28. Hatfield, "An Analysis of Some Grocery Store Practices from the Viewpoint of the Woman Buyer," 1.

29. Lohner, "Customer Attitude toward Chicago Grocery-Store Practices," 235.

30. Hatfield, "An Analysis of Some Grocery Store Practices," 52, 49.

31. Hatfield, "An Analysis of Some Grocery Store Practices," 54.

32. Hatfield, "An Analysis of Some Grocery Store Practices," 64

33. "18,389 Women Planned This Store," *Chicago Tribune*, May 20, 1934.

34. See Deutsch, "Making Change at the Grocery Store," for analysis of National Tea Company efforts to update store interiors and services to attract Chicago women as customers.

35. Lebhar, *Chain Stores in America*, 88.

36. Zimmerman, *The Super Market* (1955), 128.

37. "National Self-Service Food Week," *Muscatine (IA) Journal and News-Tribune*, April 18, 1940.

38. Zimmerman, *The Super Market* (1955), 325.

39. "Markets" (*Architectural Record*).

40. National Cash Register Company ad, "Does *Your* Store System Prevent You from Taking a Vacation This Year?," *Food Retailing Magazine* 140, no. 4 (July 1947), 13.

41. Dipman, Mueller, and Head, *Self-Service Food Stores*, 9.

42. Dipman, Mueller, and Head, *Self-Service Food Stores*, 22.

43. Baum, *The Art of Decorating Dry Goods Windows and Interiors*.

# Bibliography

## Primary Sources

PATENTS

Anderson, Jason T. 1931. Automatic Self-Servicing Device for Mercantile Stores. US Patent 1,788,759, filed June 24, 1929, and issued January 13, 1931.

Anderson, Lorenzo Norwood. 1923. Self Serving Store. US Patent 1,461,374, filed February 14, 1921, and issued July 10, 1923.

Ball, Clarence R. 1922. Store Service. US Patent 1,408,679, filed January 30, 1920, and issued March 7, 1922.

Barrett, Richard W. 1953. Self-Service Store. US Patent 2,628,691, filed June 5, 1948, and issued February 17, 1953.

Bowen, Francis J., Jr. 1929. Vending and Serve-Self Store and Vehicle. US Patent 1,720,260, filed March 15, 1928, and issued July 9, 1929.

Bradley, Herbert. N. 1943. Checking Station for Self-Service Stores. US Patent 2,317,438, filed March 22, 1940, and issued April 27, 1943.

Briggs, John E. 1925. Fixture for Self Serving Stores. US Patent 1,528,243, filed June 2, 1923, and issued March 3, 1925.

Brown, James Franklin. 1931. Store. US Patent 1,821,541, filed March 19, 1928, and issued September 1, 1931.

Campbell, William Midgley. 1921. Store Furniture. US Patent 1,383,980, filed August 12, 1920, and issued July 5, 1921.

Carroll, James. 1920. Store Self-Service System. US Patent 1,347,936, filed July 19, 1919, and issued July 27, 1920.

Carroll, James H. 1923. Self Service Store for a Bldg. Having Limited Floor Space. US Patent 1,474,106, filed May 6, 1922, and issued November 13, 1923.

Carroll, James H. 1935. Self-Service Store with Revoluble Shelves. US Patent 2,005,286, filed May 16, 1932, and issued 18 June 18, 1935.

Clerc, Leonard F. 1937. Store. US Patent 2,096,959, filed December 26, 1935, and issued October 26, 1937.

Close, Garth. 1969. Supermarket Construction. US Patent 3,437,177, filed August 21, 1967, and issued April 8, 1969.

Conder, Thomas L. 1929. Store Service. US Patent 1,703,477, filed February 19, 1925, and issued February 26, 1929.

Crawford, Thomas David. 1921. Fixture for Self Serving Stores. US Patent 1,390,673, filed October 5, 1920, and issued September 13, 1921.

Cytron, Julius. 1925. Gate Construction for Stores. US Patent 1,564,534, filed November 13, 1922, and issued December 8, 1925.

Da Roza, Edward L. 1919. Self Serving Store. US Patent 1,313,794, filed 7 November 1918, and issued August 19, 1919.

Da Roza, Edward L. 1920. Self Serving Store. US Patent 1,354,957, filed December 31, 1919, and issued October 5, 1920.

Davis, Frederick W. 1920. Self-Serving Store. US Patent 1,345,481, filed April 12, 1919, and issued July 6, 1920.

DeBakey, Shiker M. 1920. Home Store. US Patent 1,337,050, filed September 6, 1919, and issued April 13, 1920.

Duffin, James R. 1927. Self-Serving Store. US Patent 1,633,886, filed December 4, 1926, and issued June 28, 1927.

Ellis, Warren C. 1932. Store. US Patent 1,882,488, filed August 4, 1931, and issued October 11, 1932.

Fritsche, Albert E. 1926. Store System. US Patent 1,592,931, filed August 18, 1925, and issued July 20, 1926.

Goldman, Sylvan N. 1939. Combination Basket and Carriage. US Patent 2,155,896, filed May 4, 1937, and issued April 25, 1939.

Goldman, Sylvan N. 1943. Grocery Sacker. US Patent 2,314,490, filed January 7, 1942, and issued March 23, 1943.

Goode, Henry Claude. 1921. Self Serving Store. US Patent 1,368,924, filed April 6, 1920, and issued February 15, 1921.

Grant, Joseph N. 1930. Self-Serving Store. US Patent 1,751,199, filed March 12, 1928, and issued March 18, 1930.

Greene, Edward J. 1923. Serve-Self Motor Store. US Patent 1,473,850, filed October 9, 1922, and issued November 13, 1923.

Greene, Grover C., et al. 1923. Self Serving Store. US Patent 1,450,803, filed August 4, 1921, and issued April 3, 1923.

Hall, Frank E. 1932. Conveyor for Self Serving Stores. US Patent 1,843,280, filed July 22, 1930, and issued February 2, 1932.

Harvey, Henry C. 1920. Self-Serving Store. US Patent 1,350,996, filed October 16, 1918, and issued August 24, 1920.

Hill, Leslie A. 1921. Arrangement and Construction of Self Service Store Fixtures. US Patent 1,392,418, filed December 9, 1920, and issued October 4, 1921.

Howard, Hasting P. 1922. Store. US Patent 1,435,395, filed November 30, 1921, and issued November 14, 1922.

Howard, Hasting P. 1925. Store Furniture. US Patent 1,534,644, filed November 30, 1921, and issued April 21, 1925.

Hurd, Judson B. 1903. Vending Apparatus. US Patent 739,417, filed Oct. 4, 1902, and issued September 22, 1903.

Hutchison, Miller Reese. 1923. Gate and Barrier Control Mechanism. US Patent 1,477,493, filed June 15, 1922, and issued December 11, 1923.

Hutchison, Miller Reese. 1923. Monorail System for Stores. US Patent 1,477,495, filed January 23, 1923, and issued December 11, 1923.

Hutchison, Miller Reese. 1923. Self-Service Store. US Patent 1,477,492, filed June 9, 1922, and issued December 11, 1923.

Johnson, Alva W. B. 1921. Self Service Store. US Patent 1,380,968, filed April 8, 1918, and issued June 7, 1921.

Johnson, Alva Wright Boswell. 1923. Self-Service Store. US Patent 1,450,086, filed April 25, 1921, and issued March 27, 1923.

Jones, Frank E. 1921. Self Serving Store. US Patent 1,397,379, filed September 22, 1919, and issued November 15, 1921.

King, Jewel Warren. 1921. Store Construction. US Patent 1,381,202, filed November 13, 1920, and issued June 14, 1921.

Lee, Hoard. 1921. Self Serving Store. US Patent 1,378,417, filed May 11, 1920, and issued May 17, 1921.

Martin, Clyde W. 1921. Portable Grocery-Store. US Patent 1,379,463, filed June 13, 1920, and issued May 24, 1921.

Martin, Clyde W., and Leonard E. Hoffman. 1923. Itinerant Vending and Sales Vehicle. US Patent 1,466,539, filed January 14, 1921, and issued August 28, 1923.

McCarty, William B. 1920. Self-Serving Store. US Patent 1,348,024, filed June 7, 1919, and issued July 27, 1920.

Moody, Jason B. 1920. Self-Serving Vehicle-Store. US Patent 1,355,408, filed February 24, 1920, and issued October 12, 1920.

Moore, Melville M. 1929. Store System. US Patent 1,720,917, filed August 10, 1927, and issued July 16, 1929.

Morris, Roger T. 1927. Self-Serving Store Equipment. US Patent 1,625,490, filed June 29, 1925, and issued April 19, 1927.

Moseley, Annie L. 1922. Portable Automobile Grocery Store. US Patent 1,425,789, filed December 31, 1920, and issued August 15, 1922.

Moss, Jesse J. 1930. Store Service Device. US Patent 1,773,540, filed October 15, 1928, and issued August 19, 1930.

Myers, John T., and James H. Carroll. 1928. Self-Service-Store Fixtures for Vending Merchandise. US Patent 1,684,637, filed March 17, 1926, and issued September 18, 1928.

Nix, Tommy C., and Macon D. Miller. 1928. Self-Service Store. US Patent 1,688,551, filed May 20, 1926, and issued October 23, 1928.

Richter, Walter H. 1961. General Merchandise Self-Service Store. US Patent 2,980,211, filed May 14, 1959, and issued April 18, 1961.

Robert, Alexander C. 1928. Self-Service Store Equipment. US Patent 1,664,945, filed January 12, 1926, and issued April 3, 1928.

Rorrer, Charles E., and Albert R. Mitterer. 1932. Self Service Store. US Patent 1,873,852, filed August 28, 1928, and issued August 23, 1932.

Rylander, William P. 1927. Storage and Display Apparatus for Merchandise. US Patent 1,633,907, filed July 3, 1926, and issued June 28, 1927.

Saunders, Clarence. 1917. Self-Serving Store. US Patent 1,242,872, filed October 21, 1916, and issued October 9, 1917.

Saunders, Clarence. 1919. Price-Tagging Means. US Patent 1,297,405, filed 5 February 1918, and issued March 18, 1919.

Saunders, Clarence. 1920. Self Serving Store. US Patent 1,357,521, filed October 23, 1917, and issued November 2, 1920.

Saunders, Clarence. 1921. Self Serving Store. US Patent 1,397,824, filed June 20, 1917, and issued November 22, 1921.

Saunders, Clarence. 1921. Tape for Adding-Machines. US Patent 1,380,081, filed December 10, 1917, and issued May 31, 1921.

Saunders, Clarence. 1922. Lighting System for Self-Serving Stores. US Patent 1,407,680, filed September 18, 1920, and issued February 21, 1922.

Saunders, Clarence. 1922. Self Serving Store. US Patent 1,437,554, filed November 17, 1917, and issued December 5, 1922.

Saunders, Clarence. 1927. Arrangement and Construction of Store Fixtures. US Patent 1,647,889, filed March 4, 1924, and issued November 1, 1927.

Saunders, Clarence. 1929. Self Serving Store. US Patent 1,704,061, filed November 3, 1921, and issued March 5, 1929.

Schwartz, Alfred J. 1923. Silent Sales Storeroom for Perishable Goods. US Patent 1,446,215, filed November 2, 1922, and issued February 20, 1923.

Searcy, William. 1979. Store Arrangement. US Patent 4,154,027, filed August 22, 1977, and issued May 15, 1979.

Sharp, Nelson T. 1929. Self-Serving Store. US Patent 1,717,123, filed March 2, 1928, and issued June 11, 1929.

Smiley, John F. 1925. Self Serving Store. US Patent 1,544,949, filed November 2, 1921, and issued July 7, 1925.

Smiley, John F. 1930. Self Service Store Equipment. US Patent 1,750,060, filed November 12, 1928, and issued March 11, 1930.

Stevenson, Robert A. 1924. Self Serving Store. US Patent 1,494,390, filed May 29, 1920, and issued May 20, 1924.

Stevenson, Robert A. 1930. Customer Control Means for Self-Service. US Patent 1,771,659, filed January 9, 1928, and issued July 29, 1930.

Stiles, Edward M. 1919. Self Serving Store. US Patent 1,321,571, filed August 22, 1918, and issued November 11, 1919.

Stocks, Charles E. 1930. Self-Service Haberdashery. US Patent 1,766,409, filed September 24, 1927, and issued June 24, 1930.

Thornton, William Carter, and John McAlpine Cameron. 1929. Mechanical Store. US Patent 1,724,235, filed July 22, 1924, and issued August 13, 1929.

Tiffany, Ross K. 1932. Store Construction. US Patent 1,839,617, filed February 1, 1930, and issued January 5, 1932.

Trapp, Edwin W. 1924. Apparatus for Vending Merchandise. US Patent 1,510,435, filed July 23, 1921, and issued September 30, 1924.

Tribble, Robert A. 1919. Vending Apparatus. US Patent 1,305,033, filed March 5, 1919, and issued May 27, 1919.

Tribble, Robert A. 1920. Vending Apparatus. US Patent 1,350,088, filed March 21, 1919, and issued August 17, 1920.

Tripp, Jesse, Jr. 1923. Store Furniture. US Patent 1,460,332, filed November 11, 1920, and issued June 26, 1923.

Varney, Lloyd W. 1939. Self-Service Store Construction. US Patent 2,176,384, filed May 10, 1937, and issued October 17, 1939.

Webb, David W. 1932. Self Service Store. US Patent 1,861,671, filed September 26, 1928, and issued June 7, 1932.

Weston, Albert M. 1916. Serving Device for Eating-Houses. US Patent 1,170,790, filed June 3, 1909 and issued February 8, 1916.

Wieman, Herman A. 1920. Shelving. US Patent 1,344,106, filed March 19, 1920, and issued June 22, 1920.

Wieman, Herman A. 1921. Vehicle Body. US Patent 1,372,854, filed November 1, 1919, and issued March 29, 1921.

Wright, Raymond, and Edgar B. Kellogg. 1929. Self-Serving Store. US Patent 1,718,512, filed July 11, 1928, and issued June 25, 1929.

NEWSPAPERS

*Amarillo Globe*
*American Saturday Night* (Tulsa)
*Asheville (NC) Citizen-Times*
*Asheville (NC) Gazette-News*
*Atlanta Constitution*
*Austin (TX) American*
*Austin (TX) American-Statesman*

*Blackwell (OK) Journal-Tribune*

*Brownsville (TX) Herald*

*Bryan (TX) Daily Eagle*

*Carlsbad (NM) Current*

*Chicago Daily Tribune*

*Chicago Tribune*

*Clarion Ledger/Jackson (MS) Daily News*

*Clovis (NM) News-Journal*

*Commercial Appeal* (Memphis)

*Corsicana (TX) Daily Sun*

*Daily Ardmoreite* (Ardmore, OK)

*Daily Capital Journal* (Salem, OR)

*El Paso Herald*

*Emancipator* (Montgomery, AL)

*Evening Star* (Washington, DC)

*Evening Sun* (Baltimore)

*Fayetteville (NC) Weekly Observer*

*Greensboro (NC) Record*

*Greenville (SC) News*

*Indianapolis News*

*Jackson Sun* (Jackson, TN)

*Journal and Sentinel* (Winston-Salem, NC)

*Lexington (KY) Herald-Leader*

*Lexington (KY) Leader*

*Los Angeles Times*

*Lubbock (TX) Morning Avalanche*

*Marion (OH) Star*

*Morning Chronicle* (Manhattan, KS)

*Muscatine (IA) Journal and News-Tribune*

*Nashville Tennessean*

*Negro Star* (Wichita)

*News and Observer* (Raleigh, NC)

*News Scimitar* (Memphis)

*New York Age*

*New York Times*

*Oakland Tribune*

*Ogden (UT) Standard*

*Ogden (UT) Standard-Examiner*

*Oklahoma City Times*

*Oklahoma News* (Oklahoma City)

*Okmulgee (OK) Daily Times*

*People's Voice* (New York City)
*Plaindealer* (Kansas City, Kan.)
*Racine (WI) Star News*
*Richmond (VA) Times-Dispatch*
*Sacramento Bee*
*St. Joseph (MO) Observer*
*Santa Ana (CA) Register*
*Santa Cruz (CA) Evening News*
*Savannah Tribune*
*Sedalia (MO) Democrat*
*Shawnee (OK) News-Star*
*Tulsa Tribune*
*Vernon (TX) Record*
*Voice of the People* (Birmingham, AL)
*Ward County Independent* (Minot, ND)
*Washington Post*
*Washington Times*
*Winston-Salem Journal*
*Woodland (CA) Daily Democrat*


## TRADE AND CONSUMER MAGAZINES

*Chain Store Age*
*Collier's*
*Food Retailing Magazine*
*Judicious Advertising*
*Ladies' Home Journal* (LHJ)
*Printers Ink*
*Progressive Grocer (PG)*
*Saturday Evening Post*
*Uno Animo*
*World's Work*


## GOVERNMENT RECORDS

Chaffee, F. E., and McFall Kerbey. "Self-Service in the Retailing of Food Products." United States Department of Agriculture. Bulletin 1044. Washington, D.C., April 19, 1922.

Flowers, James N., et al. "Brief for Respondent in Opposition to the Petition for Writ of Certioriari, Piggly Wiggly Corporation, Petitioner v. Jitney Jungle Corporation. No. 269. In the Supreme Court of the United States, October Term 1930.

Gosnell, Fred A. *Supermarkets and Self-Service Food Stores.* Sixteenth Census of the
    United States: 1940. Census of Business: 1939. Retail Trade. Washington, D.C.,
    August 21, 1941.
Piggly Wiggly Corporation v. Jitney Jungle Corporation. 282 U.S. 858 (1930). U.S.
    Supreme Court Records and Briefs.
U.S. Department of Commerce. Bureau of Foreign and Domestic Commerce. *Louisville
    Grocery Survey*, pt. 2, *Costs, Markets, and Methods in Grocery Retailing*. Distribution
    Cost Studies 8. Washington, D.C.: U.S. Government Printing Office, 1931.
Whitney, Anice L. "Housing and Welfare Work: Lunch Rooms for Employees." *Monthly
    Review of the U.S. Bureau of Labor Statistics* 5, no. 6 (December 1917): 207–8.


ARCHIVES AND SPECIAL COLLECTIONS

Carolina Power and Light Photograph Collection, State Archives of North Carolina,
    Raleigh.
Caufield and Shook Collection, CS 091203, 1928, Archives & Special Collections,
    University of Louisville Libraries.
Durwood Barbour Collection of North Carolina Postcards, North Carolina
    Photographic Archives, Wilson Library, University of North Carolina at Chapel Hill.
Hagley Museum and Library (HML), Wilmington, Delaware.
Itinerant Photographer Collection, Harry Ransom Center, University of Texas, Austin.
J. Walter Thompson Collection, Archives and Manuscripts, Duke University Libraries,
    Durham, North Carolina.
Lafayette Studios Photographs, Audio-Visual Archives, University of Kentucky
    Libraries, Lexington.
Library of Congress Prints and Photographs Division, Washington, D.C.
Memphis and Shelby County Room, Benjamin Hooks Central Library, Memphis Public
    Libraries
Moton Family Papers, Library of Congress, Washington, D.C.
North Carolina Collection, Durham County Library, Durham, North Carolina.
Piggly Wiggly Grocery Store Collection, Memphis and Shelby County Room, Benjamin
    Hooks Central Library, Memphis Public Libraries.
Records of the Patent and Trademark Office, 1836–1978, Record Group 241, Patent Case
    Files Series, 1836–1993, National Archives at Kansas City, Missouri.
State Historical Society of Missouri, Columbia, Missouri.
Tennessee State Library and Archives, Nashville.

*A&P Past, Present and Future.* New York: Progressive Grocer Magazine, 1971.

Allen, Frederick Lewis. *Only Yesterday: An Informal History of the Nineteen-Twenties*, New York: Harper & Row, 1931.

"Alphabetical Self-Service Grocery." *Printer's Ink* 103, no. 5 (May 2, 1918), 82.

Bailey, Marshall J. "When Fixtures Sell Goods--II: How New Methods of Store Arrangement and Display Make Buying Easy for the Customer." *System: The Magazine of Business*, June 1913, 579.

Barry, Phillips. "Cafeteria." *American Speech* 3, no. 1 (October 1927), 37.

Baum, Frank L. *The Art of Decorating Dry Goods Windows and Interiors*. Chicago: Show Window Publishing, 1900.

Baum, Frank L. *The Wonderful Wizard of Oz*. Chicago: Geo. M. Hill, 1900.

Bellamy, Edward. *Looking Backward*. New York: Viking Penguin, 1982. First published 1888 by Ticknor.

"Big Bear Shopping Center." *Architectural Record* 76 (September 1934): 204–5.

"Big Bear Shopping Center--A Supermarket . . . Paterson, New Jersey, B. Sumner Gruzen, Architect." *Markets*, September 1934, 205.

Brooke, Guyon. *Let's Go Shopping*. New York: Wonder Books, 1958.

*Business Digest: The Current Business Cyclopedia, January-June 1918*. New York: Cumulative Digest Corporation, 1918.

"Carle's Market Invites Miami to a Super Wedding." *Super Market Merchandising* 4 (1939): 53.

"Cash and Carry Is Permanent, Say Grocers Who Make It Pay." *Progressive Grocer* 1, no. 3 (March 1922): 15–17, 70–80.

Combes, Lenora. *Let's Go Shopping*. New York: Simon and Schuster, 1948.

Crawford, R. P. "Piggly Wiggly--How It Has Grown to $5,000,000 a Month in Five Years." *Forbes Magazine*, October 1921, 431–32, 439.

Cutchins, John A. *Memories of Old Richmond*. Verona, Va.: McClure Press, 1973.

DeWitt, Norman W. "On Making New Words." *Classical Weekly*, January 16, 1922, 91.

Dickie, Jack W. "Self-Service Meats." *Food Retailing*, September 1947, 16–18.

Dipman, Carl W. "Merchandising Trends in the Food Trade: With Special Reference to Super-Markets." *Journal of Marketing* 3, no. 3 (January 1939), 269–73.

Dipman, Carl W. *The Modern Grocery Store*. New York: Butterick Publishing, 1931.

Dipman, Carl W., Robert W. Mueller, and Ralphe E. Head, *Self-Service Food Stores*. New York: Butterick Company, 1946.

Dipman, Carl W., and John E. O'Brien. *Self-Service and Semi-Self-Service Food Stores*. New York: Butterick Company, 1940.

Dipman, Carl. "Uncle Sam Builds a Model Store." *Progressive Grocer* 8 (April 1929): 18–25.

Doyle, Bertram Wilbur. *The Etiquette of Race Relations in the South: A Study in Social Control*. Chicago: University of Chicago Press, 1937.

Edwards, Paul K. *The Southern Urban Negro as a Consumer*. New York: Prentice-Hall, 1932.

Felton, Rebecca Latimer. *Country Life in Georgia in the Days of My Youth*. Atlanta: Index Printing Company, 1919.

"Five-and-Ten-Cent Grocery Stores: New Chain, Started in Philadelphia, Combines Self-Service and Woolworth Ideas." *Business Digest and Investment Weekly* 23, no. 18 (May 1919): 571.

"Fixture for Fruit and Vegetables." *Progressive Grocer* 1, no. 7 (July 1922): 15.

Franken, Richard B., and Carroll B. Larrabee. *Packages That Sell*. New York: Harper & Brothers, 1928.

Frederick, Christine. "Teach Women What Advertising Does." *Printer's Ink*, June 10, 1920, 178.

Goldman, Sylvan. "The Produce Market on a Self-Service Basis: Is It Practical and Profitable?" *Super Market Merchandising* 3 (October 1939): 42–43, 85–86.

Goudis, C. Houston. "Piggly Wiggly." *Mother's Magazine*, October 1918, 945.

Haring, H. A. "The Negro as Consumer: How to Sell to a Race That Now, for the First Time in Its History, Has Money to Spend." *Advertising and Selling* 15 (September 3, 1930): 20–21, 67–68.

Harris, Emerson P. "The Self Service Store and Advertising." *Advertising and Selling*, August 30, 1919, 37.

Hatfield, Myrtle Lohner. "An Analysis of Some Grocery Store Practices from the View-point of the Woman Buyer." Master's thesis, University of Chicago, December 1936.

Hayward, Walter S., and Percival White. *Chain Stores: Their Management and Operation*. New York: McGraw-Hill, 1922.

Holman, William Henry, Jr. *"Save a Nickel on a Quarter": The Story of Jitney-Jungle Stores of America*. New York: Newcomen Society in North America, 1974.

Holsey, Albon L. "The C.M.A. Stores Face the Chains." *Opportunity: A Journal of Negro Life*, July 1929, 210–13.

Holsey, Albon T. "What the Negro Is Doing in Business." *Forbes*, May 1, 1929, 38.

Holsey, Albon L. "White Folks First, Please." *Messenger* 10, no. 2 (February 1928), 46.

Howse, Elizabeth O. *Falling Stars*. N.p: N.p., 1960. Rutherford County Historical Society, Murfreesboro, Tennessee.

Hutchinson, J. H. "Control of Money in the Food Store." *Food Retailing Magazine*, June 1947, 11–13.

Johnson, Charles S. *Patterns of Negro Segregation*. New York: Harper & Brothers, 1943.

Jones, A. C. "An Analysis of Piggly Wiggly Progress." *Chain Store Age* 2 (January 1926), 6–7, 38–39, 44.

King, Clyde Lyndon. "Can the Cost of Distributing Food Products Be Reduced?" *Annals of the American Academy of Political and Social Science* 48 (July 1913): 199–224.

Laird, Donald. "Noise Does Impair Production." *American Machinist* 69 (July 12, 1928): 59–60.

Lestico, Henry Harrs. *Building the Story of Piggly Wiggly*. Los Angeles: H. H. Lestico, 1926.

Lestico, Henry Harrs, and H. R. Barnett. *School of the Chain Store*, book 2, *Individual Store Maintenance, Operation and Storekeeping*. Los Angeles: H. H. Lestico, 1929.

Lestico, Henry Harrs, and H. R. Barnett. *School of the Chain Store*, book 5, *Dressing the Store*. Los Angeles: H. H. Lestico, 1930.

Lestico, Henry Harrs, and H. R. Barnett. *School of the Chain Store*, book 11, *The Chain at Headquarters*. Los Angeles: H. H. Lestico, 1930.

Lewis, Sinclair. *Babbitt*. New York: Harcourt, Brace, 1922.

Lohner, Myrtle M. "Customer Attitude toward Chicago Grocery-Store Practices," *Journal of Business of the University of Chicago* 10, no. 3 (July 1937): 233–50.

"Main St., U.S.A." *Architectural Forum* 70, no. 2 (February 1939): 81.

*Management Problems in Retail Grocery Stores*. Bureau of Business Research Bulletin 13. Cambridge, Mass.: Harvard University Press, 1919.

"Markets." *Architectural Record*, September 1934, 204–6.

Marnell, William H. *Once upon a Store: A Biography of the World's First Supermarket*. New York: Herder and Herder, 1971.

McCrae, Lee. "Little Oddities of Life: The New 'Grocerteria,'" *Illustrated World*, January 1916, 655–56.

McKenzie, Roderick Duncan. *The Metropolitan Community*. New York: McGraw-Hill, 1933.

Mumford, Lewis. "Machinery and the Modern Style." *New Republic*, August 3, 1921, 263–65.

Murphy, John Allen. "In Piggly Wiggly Stores the Product Has to Sell Itself: A Plan of Retailing that Emphasizes the Easy Salability of Advertised Goods." *Printers Ink*, December 20, 1917, 17–20.

*The National Cyclopaedia of American Biography*, vol. 16. New York: James T. White, 1918.

"The Negro as Consumer." *Advertising and Selling*, September 3, 1930, 68.

Nichols, Perry F. "How about Waiting on Yourself?" *American Magazine*, April 1919, 31, 150, 152–53.

Nystrom, Paul H. *The Economics of Retailing*. New York: Ronald Press, 1915.

Parker, Samuel Chester, and Alice Temple. *Unified Kindergarten and First-Grade Teaching*. Boston: Ginn, 1925.

Patterson, E. M. "The Cost of Distributing Groceries." *Annals of the American Academy of Political and Social Science* 50 (November 1913), 74–82.

Phillips, Charles F. "The Supermarket." *Harvard Business Review* 16 (1938): 188–200.

Piggly Wiggly Corporation. *Price List Piggly Wiggly Store Equipment*. Memphis: Piggly Wiggly Home Office, 1918. Memphis and Shelby County Room, Benjamin Hooks Central Library, Memphis Public Libraries

Piggly Wiggly Corporation. *The Turnstile* (periodical). 1919–1923. Memphis and Shelby County Room, Benjamin Hooks Central Library, Memphis Public Libraries.

Piggly Wiggly Corporation. *A Word of Explanation*. Memphis: Piggly Wiggly Home Office, n.d. Memphis and Shelby County Room, Benjamin Hooks Central Library, Memphis Public Libraries.

"Piggly-Wiggly Co. Seek Writ against Hoggly-Woggly Co." *Simmons' Spice Mill*, July 1920, 1102.

"The Piggly Wiggly Stores." *World's Work*, February 1918, 362.

"The Piggly Wiggly Stores and Their Unique Advertising Copy." *Judicious Advertising*, April 1918, 33–38."Piggly Wiggly Stores in East in Financial Trouble." *American Food Journal*, December 1922), 40.

"The Retail Store as a National Advertiser." *Printer's Ink*, June 6, 1918, 140–41.

*R. L. Polk and Co.'s 1915 Memphis City Directory*. Memphis: R. L. Polk, 1915.

*R. L. Polk and Co.'s 1917 Memphis City Directory*. Memphis: R. L. Polk, 1917.

Rohr, W. H. "Making Fixtures for Piggly Wiggly Stores," *Woodworker*, March 1923, 48–50.

"'Shop without Leaving Your Car' Is Idea of New 'Automarket.'" *Women's Wear Daily*, July 21, 1928.

"Sky-Rocket Growth from Newspaper Advertising." *Judicious Advertising*, October 1920, 57–61.

Saunders, Clarence. *Eligibility to Piggly Wiggly*. Memphis: Piggly Wiggly Home Office, 1918. Memphis and Shelby County Room, Benjamin Hooks Central Library, Memphis Public Libraries.

Saunders, Clarence. *Fore and Aft of Piggly Wiggly*. Memphis: Piggly Wiggly Home Office, 1918. Memphis and Shelby County Room, Benjamin Hooks Central Library, Memphis Public Libraries.

Saunders, Clarence. *Inside of Things*. Memphis: Saunders, 1917. Memphis and Shelby County Room, Benjamin Hooks Central Library, Memphis Public Libraries.

Saunders, Clarence. *Merchandise Needed as Memphis Stocks a New Piggly Wiggly*. Memphis: Clarence Saunders, 1918. Memphis and Shelby County Room, Benjamin Hooks Central Library, Memphis Public Libraries.

Saunders, Clarence. *National Standard for Piggly Wiggly Store Conduct and Maintenance*. Memphis: Piggly Wiggly Home Office, 1919. Memphis and Shelby County Room, Benjamin Hooks Central Library, Memphis Public Libraries.

Saunders, Clarence. *Piggly Wiggly Contract Requirements, Etc.* Memphis: Piggly Wiggly Home Office, 1919. Memphis and Shelby County Room, Benjamin Hooks Central Library, Memphis Public Libraries.

Saunders, Clarence. *Piggly Wiggly Store Investment Requirements*. Memphis: Saunders, 1918. Memphis and Shelby County Room, Benjamin Hooks Central Library, Memphis Public Libraries.

Saunders, Clarence. *Piggly Wiggly System*. Memphis: Saunders, 1917. Memphis and Shelby County Room, Benjamin Hooks Central Library, Memphis Public Libraries.

Saunders, Clarence. *Store Buildings and Equipment Instructions*. Memphis: Piggly
Wiggly Home Office, 1919. Memphis and Shelby County Room, Benjamin Hooks
Central Library, Memphis Public Libraries.

Saunders, Clarence. *Whats and What Nots of Piggly Wiggly System*. Memphis: Piggly
Wiggly Home Office, 1918. Memphis and Shelby County Room, Benjamin Hooks
Central Library, Memphis Public Libraries.

Steadman, J. M., Jr. "Basketeria and the Meaning of the Suffix--Teria." *American Speech* 5,
no. 5 (June 1930): 417–18.

Stein, Clarence S., and Catherine Bauer. "Store Buildings and Neighborhood Shopping
Centers." *Architectural Record* 75 (February 1934): 176.

"The Supermarket." *Harvard Business Review* 16 (Winter 1938): 194.

Swann, George Betts. *Sermons*, vol. 4. Louisville: Pentecostal Publishing, 1920.

Veblen, Thorstein. "The Country Town." *Freeman*, July 11 and 18, 1923): 417–20, 440–43.

Vestal, A. G. "The Cousin of the Cafeteria." *Scientific American*, September 7, 1918, 193.f

Wales, Hugh G. Review of Dipman and O'Brien, *Self-Service and Semi-Self-Service Food
Stores*. *Journal of Marketing* 5, no. 2 (October 1940): 179–80.

"Was Cash and Carry Only a War Baby? These Grocers Thought So." *Progressive Grocer*
1, no. 2 (February 1922), 47–48, 68–70.

Weaver, Frank G. "Step In and Help Yourself." *Association Men by the YMCA* 46, no. 12
(August 1921): 557.

White, James T., and Company. "Bradford, Ernest Wilder." In *The National Cyclopaedia
of American Biography*, vol. 16. New York: James T. White, 1918, 227.

"'Wholesale to the Consumer' Store of Lutey Brothers." *Simmons' Spice Mill*, 37, no. 5
(May 1914): 556.

*Worley's Dallas (Texas) City Directory 1928*. Dallas: John F. Worley Directory Co., 1928.

Yancy, Jesse. "Eudora's Jitney." *Mississippi Sideboard*, August 5, 2014. https://jesseyancy
.com/eudoras-jitney.

Zimmerman, M. M. "The Supermarket and the Changing Retail Structure." *Journal of
Marketing* 5, no. 4 (April 1941): 403–4.

Zimmerman, M. M. *The Super Market: A Revolution in Distribution*. New York:
McGraw-Hill, 1955.

Zimmerman, M. M. *Super Market: Spectacular Exponent of Mass Distribution*. New
York: Super Market Publishing, 1937.

## Secondary Sources

Abel, Elizabeth. *Signs of the Times: The Visual Politics of Jim Crow*. Berkeley: University
of California Press, 2010.

Abelson, Elaine S. *When Ladies Go A-Thieving: Middle-Class Shoplifters in the Victorian
Department Store*. New York: Oxford University Press, 1992.

Adelman, M. A. *A&P: A Study in Price-Cost Behavior and Public Policy*. Cambridge, Mass.: Harvard University Press, 1959.

Amsden, Jon. "Historians and the Spatial Imagination." *Radical History Review* 21 (Fall 1979): 11–30.

Anderson, Alvis H. *A&P: The Story of the Great Atlantic and Pacific Tea Company*. Images of America Series. Charleston, S.C.: Arcadia Publishing, 2002.

Andrews, Deborah C., ed. *Shopping: Material Culture Perspectives*. Newark: University of Delaware Press, 2015.

Atherton, Lewis E. *The Southern Country Store, 1800–1860*. Baton Rouge: Louisiana State University Press, 1949.

Ayers, Edward. *Promise of the New South: Life after Reconstruction*. Oxford: Oxford University Press, 2007.

Bailey, Adreian R., Andrew Alexander, and Gareth Shaw. "Queuing as a Changing Shopper Experience: The Case of Grocery Shopping in Britain, 1945–1975." *Enterprise and Society* 20 (2019): 652–83.

Bass, S. Jonathan. "'How 'bout a Hand for the Hog': The Enduring Nature of the Swine as a Cultural Symbol in the South." *Southern Cultures* 1, no. 3 (Spring 1995): 301–20.

Bay, Mia, and Ann Fabian. *Race and Retail: Consumption across the Color Line*. New Brunswick, N.J.: Rutgers University Press, 2015.

Beasley, Ellen. *The Corner Store: An American Tradition, Galveston Style*. Washington, D.C.: National Building Museum, 1999.

Beaujot, Ariel. "'The Beauty of Her Hands': The Glove and the Making of the Middle-Class Body." In *Material Women, 1750–1950: Consuming Desires and Collecting Practices*, edited by Maureen Daly Goggin and Beth Fowkes Tobin, 167–84. Burlington, Vt.: Ashgate, 2009.

Beniger, James R. *The Control Revolution: Technological and Economic Origins of the Information Society*. Cambridge, Mass.: Harvard University Press, 1986.

Benson, Susan Porter. "Palace of Consumption and Machine for Selling: The American Department Store, 1880–1940." *Radical History Review* 21 (Fall 1979): 199–221.

Benson, Susan Porter. *Counter Cultures: Saleswomen, Managers, and Customers in American Department Stores, 1890–1940*. Urbana: University of Illinois Press, 1988.

Berg, Nate. "The Rise of 'Dark Stores'--and How They Could Save Struggling Retail." *Fast Company*, September 11, 2020. https://www.fastcompany.com/90549066/the-rise-of-dark-stores-and-how-they-could-save-struggling-retail.

Berrey, Stephen A. *The Jim Crow Routine: Everyday Performances of Race, Civil Rights, and Segregation in Mississippi*. Chapel Hill: University of North Carolina Press, 2015.

Biggs, Lindy. *The Rational Factory: Architecture, Technology, and Work in America's Age of Mass Production*. Baltimore: Johns Hopkins University Press, 1996.

Bosker, Bianca. "The Pandemic Shows Us the Genius of Supermarkets." *Atlantic*, June 20, 2020. https://www.theatlantic.com/magazine/archive/2020/07/supermarkets-are-a-miracle/612244.

Bowker, Geof. "What's in a Patent?" In *Shaping Technology/Building Society: Studies in Sociotechnical Change*, edited by Wiebe E. Bijker and John Law, 33–74. Cambridge: MIT Press, 1992.

Bowlby Rachel. *Carried Away: The Invention of Modern Shopping.* New York: Columbia University Press, 2001.

Bowles, Nellie. "Stealing from a Cashierless Store (without You, or the Cameras, Knowing It." *New York Times*, September 13, 2018.

Carey, William H., Jr. "A Study of Centralized and Decentralized Prepackaged Meat Operations." Master's thesis, Michigan State College of Agriculture and Applied Science, 1951.

Carrier, James. "Reconciling Personal Commodities and Personal Relations in Industrial Society." *Theory and Society* 19, no. 5 (October 1990): 579–98.

Chandler, Alfred D., Jr. *The Visible Hand: The Managerial Revolution in American Business.* Cambridge, Mass.: Harvard University Press, 1977.

Chang, David A. *The Color of the Land: Race, Nation, and the Politics of Landownership in Oklahoma, 1832–1929.* Chapel Hill: University of North Carolina Press, 2010.

Cheng, Andria. "Why Amazon Go May Soon Change the Way We Shop." *Forbes*, January 13, 2019. https://www.forbes.com/sites/andriacheng/2019/01/13/why-amazon-go-may-soon-change-the-way-we-want-to-shop/?sh=40a69cb16709.

Clark, Thomas D. *Pills, Petticoats, and Plows: The Southern Country Store.* New York: Bobbs-Merrill, 1944.

Cook, Daniel Thomas. "Spatial Biographies of Children's Consumption: Market Places and Spaces of Childhood in the 1930s and Beyond." *Journal of Consumer Culture* 3, no. 2 (2003): 147–69.

Cochoy, Frank. *On the Origins of Self-Service.* Trans. by Jaciara Topley-Lira. New York: Routledge, 2016.

Cowan, Ruth Schwartz. "The Consumption Junction: A Proposal for Research Strategies in the Sociology of Technology." In *The Social Construction of Technological Systems: New Directions in the Sociology and History of Technology*, edited by Wiebe E. Bijker, Thomas P. Hughes, and Trevor Pinch, 253–72. Boston: MIT Press, 2012.

Cramer, Esther R. *The Alpha Beta Story.* La Habra, Calif.: Alpha Beta Acme Markets, 1973.

Davison, Benjamin. "Super City: Los Angeles and the Birth of the Supermarket, 1914–1941." *California History* 93, no. 3 (Fall 2016): 9–27.

Deutsch, Tracey. *Building a Housewife's Paradise: Gender, Politics, and American Grocery Stores in the Twentieth Century.* Chapel Hill: University of North Carolina Press, 2010.

Deutsch, Tracey. "Exploring New Insights into Retail History." *Journal of Historical Research in Marketing* 2, no. 1 (2010): 130–38.

Deutsch, Tracey. "Making Change at the Grocery Store: Government, Grocers, and the Problem of Women's Autonomy in the Creation of Chicago's Supermarkets, 1920–1950." *Enterprise and Society* 5, no. 4 (December 2004): 607–16.

Deutsch, Tracey. "Untangling Alliances: Social Tensions Surrounding Independent Grocery Stores and the Rise of Mass Retailing." In *Food Nations: Selling Taste in Consumer Societies*, edited by Warren Belasco and Philip Scranton, 156–74. New York: Routledge, 2002.

Deutsch, Tracey. "'Wild Animal Stores' to Women's Sphere: Supermarkets and the Politics of Mass Consumption, 1930–1950." *Business and Economic History* 28, no. 1 (Fall 1999): 143–53.

Dinerstein, Joel. *Swinging the Machine: Modernity, Technology, and African American Culture between the World Wars*. Amherst: University of Massachusetts Press, 2003.

Domosh, Mona. "Creating New York's Nineteenth-Century Retail District." In *American Architectural History: A Contemporary Reader*, edited by Keith Eggener, 206–25. New York: Routledge, 2004.

Du Gay, Paul. "Self-Service: Retail, Shopping and Personhood." *Consumption Markets and Culture* 7, no. 2 (June 2004): 149–63.

Elvins, Sarah. *Sales and Celebrations: Retailing and Regional Identity in Western New York State, 1920–1940*. Athens: Ohio University Press, 2004.

Epple, Angelika. "The 'Automat': A History of Technological Transfer and the Process of Global Standardization in Modern Fast Food around 1900." *Food and History* 7 (2010): 97–118.

Epple, Angelika. "Automatic Trade: Self-Service and the Polycentric Early History of Slot Machines." in *Transformations of Retailing in Europe after 1945*, edited by Ralph Jessen and Lydia Langer, 103–14. Burlington, Vt.: Ashgate, 2012.

Eschner, Kat. "The Bizarre Story of Piggly Wiggly, the First Self-Service Grocery Store." *Smithsonian*, September 6, 2017. https://www.smithsonianmag.com/smart-news /bizarre-story-piggly-wiggly-first-self-service-grocery-store-180964708.

Esperdy, Gabrielle. *Modernizing Main Street: Architecture and Consumer Culture in the New Deal*. Chicago: University of Chicago Press, 2008.

Foner, Eric. *The Story of American Freedom*. New York: W. W. Norton, 1999.

Foucault, Michel. *Discipline and Punish: The Birth of the Prison*. New York: Vintage Books, 1995.

Freeman, Mike. *Clarence Saunders and the Founding of Piggly Wiggly: The Rise and Fall of a Memphis Maverick*. Charleston, S.C.: History Press, 2011.

Freeman, Mike. "Clarence Saunders: The Piggly Wiggly Man." *Tennessee Historical Quarterly* 51 (1992): 161–69.

Freeman, Mike. "Clarence Saunders, 'The Piggly Wiggly Man.'" Master's thesis, Memphis State University, 1988.

Friedman, Walter A. *Birth of a Salesman: The Transformation of Selling in America*. Cambridge, Mass.: Harvard University Press, 2004.

Galassini, Matt. "Pandemic-Era Shopping Trends Are Blurring the Lines between E-Commerce and Physical Retail, Finds New Research from 1WorldSync." *PRNewswire*, December 7, 2021. https://www.prnewswire.com/news-releases

/pandemic-era-shopping-trends-are-blurring-the-lines-between-e-commerce-and -physical-retail-finds-new-research-from-1worldsync-301438472.html.

Gordon, Robert L. *The Rise and Fall of American Growth: The U.S. Standard of Living since the Civil War*. Princeton: Princeton University Press, 2017.

Grandclement, Catherine. "Wheeling One's Groceries around the Store: The Invention of the Shopping Cart, 1936–1953." In *Food Chains: From Farmyard to Shopping Cart*, edited by Warren Belasco and Roger Horowitz, 233–51. Philadelphia: University of Pennsylvania Press, 2009.

Gregson, Nicky, Louise Crewe, and Kate Brooks. "Shopping, Space, and Practice." *Environment and Planning D: Society and Space* 20, No. 5 (2002): 597–617.

Gwynn, David. "Groceteria.com: Exploring Supermarket History." https://www. groceteria.com/.

Hale, Grace Elizabeth. "'For Colored' and 'For White': Segregating Consumption in the South." In *Jumpin' Jim Crow: Southern Politics from Civil War to Civil Rights*, edited by Jane Dailey, Glenda Elizabeth Gilmore, and Bryant Simon, 162–82. Princeton: Princeton University Press, 2000.

Hale, Grace Elizabeth. *Making Whiteness: The Culture of Segregation in the South, 1890– 1940*. New York: Pantheon Books, 1998.

Haley, Andrew P. *Turning the Tables: Restaurants and the Rise of the American Middle Class, 1880–1920*. Chapel Hill: University of North Carolina Press, 2011.

Hamilton, Shane. *Supermarket USA: Food and Power in the Cold War Farms Race*. New Haven: Yale University Press, 2018.

Hickey, Georgina. *Hope and Danger in the New South City: Working-Class Women and Urban Development in Atlanta, 1890–1940*. Athens: University of Georgia Press, 2003.

Hintz, Eric S. "The Post-Heroic Generation: American Independent Inventors, 1900– 1950." *Enterprise and Society* 12, no. 4 (December 2011): 732–48.

Honey, Michael K. *Southern Labor and Black Civil Rights: Organizing Memphis Workers*. Urbana: University of Illinois Press, 1993.

Horowitz, Roger. *Putting Meat on the American Table: Taste, Technology, Transformation*. Baltimore: Johns Hopkins Press, 2006.

Hughes, Thomas P. "The Evolution of Large Technological Systems." In *The Social Construction of Technological Systems: New Directions in the Sociology and History of Technology*, edited by Wiebe E. Bijker, Thomas P. Hughes, and Trevor Pinch, 45–76. Boston: MIT Press, 2012.

Hughes, Thomas P. "Technological Momentum." In *Does Technology Drive History?*, edited by Merritt Roe Smith and Leo Marx, 101–14. Cambridge: MIT Press, 1994.

Humphery, Kim. *Shelf Life: Supermarkets and the Changing Cultures of Consumption*. Cambridge: Cambridge University Press, 1998.

Hunter, Tera W. *To 'Joy My Freedom: Southern Black Women's Lives and Labors After the Civil War*. Cambridge, Mass.: Harvard University Press, 1997.

Hunter, Tera W. "'The Women Are Asking for BREAD, Why Give Them STONE': Women, Work, and Protests in Atlanta and Norfolk during World War I." In *Labor in the Modern South*, edited by Glenn T. Eskew, 67–72. Athens: University of Georgia Press, 2001.

Interrante, Joseph. "You Can't Go to Town in a Bathtub: Automobile Movement and the Reorganization of Rural American Space, 1900–1930." *Radical History Review* 21 (Fall 1979): 151–68.

Isenberg, Alison. *Downtown America: A History of the Place and the People Who Made It.* Chicago: University of Chicago Press, 2004.

Isenstadt, Sandy. "The Spaces of Shopping: A Historical Overview." In *Shopping: Material Culture Perspectives*, edited by Deborah C. Andrews, 1–32. Newark: University of Delaware Press, 2015.

Jacobs, Meg. *Pocketbook Politics: Economic Citizenship in Twentieth-Century America.* Princeton: Princeton University Press, 2005.

Jellison, Katherine. *Entitled to Power: Farm Women and Technology, 1913–1963.* Chapel Hill: University of North Carolina Press, 1993.

Jessen, Ralph, and Lydia Langer, eds. *Transformations of Retailing in Europe after 1945.* Farnham, England: Ashgate, 2012.

Jones, D. G. Brian, and Mark Tadajewski. "Percival White (1887–1970): Marketing Engineer." *Marketing Theory* 11, Nno. 4 (December 2011): 474.

Jones, Lu Ann. "Gender, Race, and Itinerant Commerce in the Rural New South." *Journal of Southern History* 66, no. 2 (May 2000): 297–320.

Jones, Lu Ann. *Mama Learned Us to Work: Farm Women in the New South.* Chapel Hill: University of North Carolina Press, 2002.

Kang, Cecilia. "Here Comes the Full Amazonification of Whole Foods." *New York Times*, February 28, 2022.

Kline, Ronald R. *Consumers in the Country: Technology and Social Change in Rural America.* Baltimore: Johns Hopkins University Press, 2000.

Laycock, George. *The Kroger Story: A Century of Innovation.* Cincinnati: Kroger, 1983.

Leach, William. *Land of Desire: Merchants, Power, and the Rise of a New American Culture.* New York: Vintage Books, 1994.

Lebhar, Godfrey M. *Chain Stores in America, 1859–1950.* New York: Chain Store Publishing, 1952.

LeFebvre, Henri. *The Production of Space.* Oxford, England: Blackwell, 1991.

Levenstein, Harvey. *Revolution at the Table: The Transformation of the American Diet.* Berkeley: University of California Press, 2003.

Levinson, Marc. *The Great A&P and the Struggle for Small Business in America.* New York: Hill and Wang, 2011.

Liebs, Chester. *Main Street to Miracle Mile: American Roadside Architecture.* Baltimore: Johns Hopkins University Press, 1995.

Ling, Peter J. *America and the Automobile: Technology, Reform, and Social Change.* Manchester: Manchester University Press, 1990.

Longstreth, Richard. *The Buildings of Main Street: A Guide to American Commercial Architecture.* Walnut Creek, Calif.: Alta Mira Press, 2000.

Longstreth, Richard. "The Diffusion of the Community Shopping Center Concept during the Interwar Decades." *Journal of the Society of Architectural Historians* 56, no. 3 (September 1997): 268–93.

Longstreth, Richard. *The Drive-In, the Supermarket, and the Transformation of Commercial Space in Los Angeles, 1914–1941.* Cambridge, Mass.: MIT Press, 1999.

Longstreth, Richard. "The Neighborhood Shopping Center in Washington, D.C., 1930–1941." *Journal of the Society of Architectural Historians* 51, no. 1 (March 1992): 5–34.

Longstreth, Richard. "Sears Roebuck and the Remaking of the Department Store, 1924–1942." *Journal of the Society of Architectural Historians* 65, no. 2 (2006): 238–79.

Low, Setha. "Spatializing Culture: An Engaged Anthropological Approach to Space and Place" In *The People, Place, and Space Reader*, edited by Jen Jack Gieseking et al., 34–38. New York: Routledge, 2014.

Lutey, Kent. "Lutey Brothers Marketeria: America's First Self-Service Grocers." *Montana: The Magazine of History*, Spring 1978, 51–57.

Mack, Adam. "'Speaking of Tomatoes': Supermarkets, the Senses, and Sexual Fantasy in Modern America." *Journal of Social History* 43, no. 4 (Summer 2010): 815–42.

Macleod, David I. "Food Prices, Politics, and Policy in the Progressive Era." *Journal of the Gilded Age and Progressive Era* 8, no. 3 (July 2009): 365–406.

Mann, Leon. "Queue Culture: The Waiting Line as a Social System." *American Journal of Sociology* 75 (1969): 340–54.

Marchand, Roland. *Advertising the American Dream: Making Way for Modernity, 1920–1940.* Berkeley: University of California Press, 1985.

Mariani, John. *America Eats Out.* New York: William Morrow, 1991.

Massey, Doreen B. *Space, Place, and Gender.* Minneapolis: University of Minnesota Press, 1994.

Mayo, James M. *The American Grocery Store: The Business Evolution of an Architectural Space.* Westport, Conn.: Greenwood Press, 1993.

McGovern, Charles F. *Sold American: Consumption and Citizenship, 1890–1945.* Chapel Hill: University of North Carolina Press, 2006.

McKee, Margaret, and Fred Chisenhall, *Beale Black and Blue: Life and Music on Black America's Main Street.* Baton Rouge: Louisiana State University Press, 1981.

Miller, Daniel. *A Theory of Shopping.* Ithaca, N.Y.: Cornell University Press, 1998.

Miller, Sybil. *Itinerant Photographer, Corpus Christi, 1934.* Albuquerque: University of New Mexico Press, 1987.

Moreton, Bethany E. "It Came from Bentonville: The Agrarian Origins of Wal-Mart Culture." In *Wal-Mart: The Face of Twenty-First-Century Capitalism*, edited by Nelson Lichtenstein, 57–84. New York: New Press, 2006.

Moreton, Bethany. *To Serve God and Wal-Mart: The Making of Christian Free Enterprise*. Cambridge, Mass.: Harvard University Press, 2009.

Nye, David. *America's Assembly Line*. Cambridge, Mass.: MIT Press, 2013.

Nye, David. *Technology Matters: Questions to Live With*. Cambridge, Mass.: MIT Press, 2006.

Ownby, Ted. *American Dreams in Mississippi: Consumers, Poverty, and Culture, 1830–1998*. Chapel Hill: University of North Carolina Press, 1999.

Palm, Michael. *Technologies of Consumer Labor: A History of Self-Service*. New York: Routledge, 2016.

Parker, Traci. "Race and Class Identities in Early American Department Stores." Chap. 1 in *Department Stores and the Black Freedom Movement: Workers, Consumers, and Civil Rights from the 1930s to the 1980s*. Chapel Hill: University of North Carolina Press, 2020.

Parkin, Katherine J. *Food Is Love: Food Advertising and Gender Roles in Modern America*. Philadelphia: University of Pennsylvania Press, 2006.

Peña, Carolyn de la. "The History of Technology, the Resistance of Archives, and the Whiteness of Race." *Technology and Culture* 51, no. 4 (October 2010): 919–37.

Perkins, Edwin J. *Wall Street to Main Street: Charles Merrill and Middle-Class Investors*. Cambridge: Cambridge University Press, 1999.

Presley, Delma E. *Piggly Wiggly Southern Style: The Piggly Wiggly Southern Story, 1919–1984*. N.p.: [Piggly Wiggly Southern], 1984.

Pruitt, Bernadette. *The Other Great Migration: The Movement of Rural African Americans to Houston, 1900–1941*. College Station: Texas A&M University Press, 2013.

Rabinowitz, Howard N. *Race Relations in the Urban South, 1865–1890*. New York: Oxford University Press, 1978.

Remus, Emily. "Disruptive Shopping: Women, Space, and Capitalism." *American Historian*, May 2017, 16–23.

Resseguie, Harry E. "Alexander Turney Stewart and the Development of the Department Store, 1823–1876. *Business History Review* 39, no. 3 (Autumn 1965): 301–22.

Robinson, Lawrence R., and Eleanor G. May. *Self-Service in Variety Stores*. Division of Research, Bulletin 147. Boston: Harvard Business School, 1956.

Schlereth, Thomas. "Country Stores, County Fairs, and Mail-Order Catalogues: Consumption in Rural America." In *Consuming Visions: Accumulation and Display of Goods in America, 1880–1920*, edited by Simon J. Bronner, 339–47. New York: Norton, 1989.

Scranton, Philip. "Determinism and Indeterminacy in the History of Technology." In *Does Technology Drive History?*, edited by Merritt Roe Smith and Leo Marx, 143–68. Cambridge: MIT Press, 1994.

Scroop, Daniel. "Local and National Identities in the Politics of Consumption: The Anti-Chain Store Movement Reconsidered." *History Compass* 6, no. 3 (2008): 947–68.

Severson, Kim. "7 Ways the Pandemic Has Changed How We Shop For Food." *New York Times*, September 8, 2020.

Sewell, Jessica. "Gender, Imagination, and Experience in the Early-Twentieth-Century American Downtown." In *Everyday America: Cultural Landscape Studies after J. B. Jackson*, edited by Paul Erling Groth and Chris Wilson, 237–54. Berkeley: University of California Press, 2003.

Shaw, Gareth. "British Co-Operative Societies as Retail Innovators: Interpreting the Early Stages of the Self-Service Revolution." *Business History* 50, no. 1 (January 2008): 62–78.

Shuldiner, Alec Tristin. "Trapped behind the Automat: Technological Systems and the American Restaurant, 1902–1991." PhD diss., Cornell University, 2001.

Sinclair, Bruce. *Technology and the African-American Experience: Needs and Opportunities for Study.* Cambridge: MIT Press, 2004.

Spellman, Susan. *Cornering the Market: Independent Grocers and Innovation in American Small Business.* New York: Oxford University Press, 2016.

Spellman, Susan. "Putting Cash Registers on the Map." Miami University. https://sites.miamioh.edu/spellmsv/digital-humanities.

Stobart, Jon, Andrew Hann, and Victoria Morgan. *Spaces of Consumption: Leisure and Shopping in the English Town, c. 1680–1830.* New York: Routledge, 2007.

Strasser, Susan. *Satisfaction Guaranteed: The Making of the American Mass Market.* New York: Pantheon Books, 1989.

Strasser, Susan. "Woolworth to Walmart: Mass Merchandising and the Changing Culture of Consumption." In *Wal-Mart: The Face of Twenty-First-Century Capitalism*, edited by Nelson Lichtenstein, 31–56. New York: New Press, 2006.

Tedlow, Richard S. *New and Improved: The Story of Mass Marketing in America.* New York: Basic Books, 1990.

Thomas, Bernice L. *America's 5 & 10 Cent Stores: The Kress Legacy.* New York: John Wiley and Sons, 1997.

Thompson, Emily. *The Soundscape of Modernity: Architectural Acoustics and the Culture of Listening in America, 1900–1933.* Boston: MIT Press, 2004.

Tolbert, Lisa C. "The Aristocracy of the Market Basket: Self-Service Food Shopping in the New South. " In *Food Chains: From Farmyard to Shopping Cart*, edited by Warren Belasco and Roger Horowitz, 179–95. Philadelphia: University of Pennsylvania Press, 2009.

Turner, Katherine Leonard. *How the Other Half Ate: A History of Working-Class Meals at the Turn of the Century.* Berkeley: University of California Press, 2014.

Ware, Gilbert. "The New Negro Alliance: 'Don't Buy Where You Can't Work.'" *Negro History Bulletin* 49, no. 3 (1986): 3–8.

Weems, Robert E. *Desegregating the Dollar: African American Consumerism in the Twentieth Century*. New York: New York University Press, 1998.

Welty, Eudora, "The Little Store." In *Mississippi Writers: Reflections of Childhood and Youth*, vol. 2: *Nonfiction*, edited by Dorothy Abbott, 639–46. Jackson: University Press of Mississippi, 1985.

Weyeneth, Robert R. "The Architecture of Racial Segregation: The Challenges of Preserving the Problematical Past." *Public Historian* 27, no. 4 (Fall 2005): 11–44.

Whitaker, Jan. "Early Chains: John R. Thompson." *Restaurant-ing through History*, June 10, 2010. https://restaurant-ingthroughhistory.com/2010/06/10/early-chains -john-r-thompson.

Whitaker, Jan. *Service and Style: How the American Department Store Fashioned the Middle Class*. New York: St. Martin's Press, 2006.

Wilson, Terry P. *The Cart That Changed the World: The Career of Sylvan N. Goldman*. Norman: University of Oklahoma Press, 1978.

Wingfield, Nick. "Inside Amazon's Store of the Future." *New York Times*, January 22, 2018.

Worley, William S. *J. C. Nichols and the Shaping of Kansas City: Innovation in Planned Residential Communities*. Columbia: University of Missouri Press, 1990.

Zukin, Sharon. *Point of Purchase: How Shopping Changed American Culture*. New York: Routledge, 2004.

# Index

Page numbers in italics indicate illustrations; those with a *t* indicate tables.

Printed in the United States
by Baker & Taylor Publisher Services